THE RISE OF CORPORATE FEMINISM

COLUMBIA STUDIES IN THE HISTORY OF U.S. CAPITALISM

COLUMBIA STUDIES IN THE HISTORY OF U.S. CAPITALISM

Series Editors: Devin Fergus, Louis Hyman, Bethany Moreton, and Julia Ott

Capitalism has served as an engine of growth, a source of inequality, and a catalyst for conflict in American history. While remaking our material world, capitalism's myriad forms have altered—and been shaped by—our most fundamental experiences of race, gender, sexuality, nation, and citizenship. This series takes the full measure of the complexity and significance of capitalism, placing it squarely back at the center of the American experience. By drawing insight and inspiration from a range of disciplines and alloying novel methods of social and cultural analysis with the traditions of labor and business history, our authors take history "from the bottom up" all the way to the top.

THE RISE OF CORPORATE FEMINISM

WOMEN *in the*

AMERICAN OFFICE, 1960–1990

ALLISON ELIAS

Columbia University Press
New York

Columbia University Press
Publishers Since 1893
New York   Chichester, West Sussex
cup.columbia.edu

Library of Congress Cataloging-in-Publication Data
Names: Elias, Allison, author.
Title: The rise of corporate feminism : women in the American office,
1960–1990 / Allison Elias.
Description: New York : Columbia University Press, [2022] | Series:
Columbia studies in the history of U.S. capitalism | Includes
bibliographical references and index.
Identifiers: LCCN 2022008914 | ISBN 9780231180740 (hardback) |
ISBN 9780231180757 (trade paperback) | ISBN 9780231543231 (ebook)
Subjects: LCSH: Women white collar workers—United States—History—
20th century. | Women executives—United States—History—20th century. |
Businesswomen—United States—History—20th century. | Feminism—
United States—History—20th century.
Classification: LCC HD6073.M392 U5236 2022 | DDC 331.4/8165800973—
dc23/eng/20220504
LC record available at https://lccn.loc.gov/2022008914

Cover design: Noah Arlow
Cover art: Alamy

FOR ROB

CONTENTS

THE RISE OF CORPORATE FEMINISM

INTRODUCTION

I n 1971 Gloria Steinem, then a journalist with *New York* magazine, delivered the commencement address to the graduating class at Smith College. She spoke about the ways in which the social construction of gender had disadvantaged women and devalued their work. Graduates from Smith, an all-women's college, faced inequities that men graduating from Yale or Columbia did not. "Why go to law school," asked Steinem of the graduates, "just to get a typing job in the back room of an office?"

According to Steinem, women were given the "shit work" while managers reserved advancement opportunities for men. She noted that educational institutions contributed to this inequality in the workplace. While the staff at Smith College's vocational center asked its graduating women how many words per minute they could type, no one in vocational services at peer institutions like Amherst or Harvard asked men about their typing: "Perhaps a whole generation of us should not learn how to type."[1] The crowd erupted with cheers. The *Boston Globe* reported, "She struck closest to the heart of the graduating class when she talked about typing."[2]

This speech captured a distinct moment in American history. A generation of young, mostly white, college-educated women looked to their futures and saw possibilities that had not been available to their mothers. Once confined to a few female-dominated occupations—teaching, nursing, secretarial work—women could now select from a variety of professional paths in the sciences, business, law, or medicine. In the words of author Ruth Rosen, "the world split open" as the modern women's movement changed the legal, social, and political landscape for women in America.[3] Following passage of Title VII of the Civil Rights Act of 1964, which prohibited discrimination on the basis of race, sex, ethnicity, or religion, women and underrepresented men gained access to a host of new job opportunities.[4] Previously excluded from the white-collar environment, women of color were permitted to move from "field and kitchen to office."[5] Access to and legalization of contraception allowed many young women to delay marriage, control family planning, and pursue professional education. In turn, the proportion of women in the workforce, and in particular those pursuing nontraditional professions, rose quickly in the 1970s and 1980s.[6]

But most of the traditionally female occupations remained female. Through these transformational decades, as activists wore buttons reading "Make Policy Not Coffee," the most common job for women was secretary.[7] Since 1950 women have been more likely to work in a clerical job than in practically any other occupation. This was true before, during, and after feminists threw stenography pads (as well as other materials symbolic of women's oppression) in the Freedom Trash Can at the Miss America pageant in 1968.[8] Even as the rate of workforce participation for American women increased from about 35 percent in 1950 to almost 60 percent in 2010, the most common job for women remained clerical work, and clerical workers remained over 95 percent female.[9]

This book traces the secretary and her changing identity during a period of great transformation—and stability—for women in corporate America. In many instances, revolutionary ideas about equality sparked individual and collective rebellion among secretaries.[10] New beliefs about gender dismantled some long-standing corporate policies and practices such as the explicit sorting of women and men into different jobs. Other structural elements of the corporation, however, particularly those regarding the social and economic value of women's work, retained previous imprints of gender inequity. Ultimately, corporate promotion of equal opportunity settled comfortably alongside occupational segregation by gender. As employers, employees, policy makers, activists, and academics pushed for equality, the lines of progression into management—or eventually into the most exclusive corner offices—still reflected a devaluation of jobs performed by women.

In the 1960s, when the ideas of a second wave of feminism entered public discourse, an underlying contradiction between two gendered identities—secretary and feminist—posed challenges to those seeking to advance women in corporate America.[11] Second-wave feminists insisted that gender was historically and socially constructed; as such, it should not define one's professional opportunities. To destabilize customary thinking, feminists called on women to reject traditional roles. Yet secretarial work depended on conventional displays of femininity. Consider the Katharine Gibbs School, which reigned for most of the twentieth century as the premier institution for secretarial training. It prepared many women, mostly white, to enter the masculine world of business while simultaneously preserving—even enhancing—their feminine poise and grace. Though women became secretaries without access to a Gibbs education, the chain indelibly influenced the logics of the occupation, as other training programs and career literature reinforced its approach and values.

The core issues important to second-wave feminists intersected with the problems facing secretarial workers in the founding in 1973 of a labor organization called 9to5, which called for raises and respect for women office workers. The 9to5 mission was to challenge secretarial workers to organize collectively and push for upgrades to the secretarial job. As a grassroots organization started in Boston, 9to5 eventually became a national organization with chapters in thirteen major cities. Although many secretaries did not categorize unfair treatment as gender-based discrimination or consider themselves feminists, they did begin to notice, question, and resent aspects of their professional life, in part due to 9to5's efforts. Two core elements of gender equity in the office—raising wages for women's work and moving women into men's jobs—remained intertwined in the 1970s, and the publishing industry serves as a case study through which to examine the breadth of corporate feminism in that decade. Pushes to advance women into management existed alongside the unionization of clerical women, and briefly, cross-class alliances in the corporation sought to advance gender equity.

After the 1970s, however, upward mobility for managerial women moved onto the corporate agenda. With the rise of human resources (HR) offices, hiring women into the managerial ranks became an organizational imperative.[12] Representation of women in all-male spaces, and representation of people of color in all-white spaces, began to matter. But promotional paths within the corporation that could provide clerical women with advancement opportunities were not of great concern to HR managers. Throughout the 1980s corporate interest in integrating women into management only increased, which undermined clerical workers' unionization and professionalization efforts in the private sector. When faced with a wave of office automation, the 9to5 of the 1980s launched a national union to aid those complaining of physical and psychological ailments from all-day use of video display terminal workstations. Using the language of protective legislation that had aided unskilled factory workers in the early twentieth century, 9to5 lobbied for government regulation of workstations. Meanwhile, the response of the National Secretaries Association (NSA; renamed Professional Secretaries International in 1981) was to push those with highly routinized jobs out of the secretarial profession. NSA described itself as having "historical roots in support of management" and accordingly, it promoted the professionalization of executive secretaries, who should be "accepted as 'real' members of the management team."[13] And while managers began to do much of their own typing on personal computers, other routinized clerical work was outsourced to women who lived in lower-cost global markets.

Independent and unattached, all clerical workers, whether word processors or executive secretaries, became subject to the promises and perils of the same HR policies that were allowing other women entry into management. Consider the implementation and enforcement of affirmative action policies, which failed a generation of working-class women who lacked the social capital to acquire higher positions. Without job analysis or pay equity audits, corporate attention to affirmative action left intact the strict division between clerical and managerial work, doing little to build bridges across women's and men's job ladders. As more middle-class women of all races attended college, they no longer had to enter corporations as secretaries. New equal employment opportunity (EEO) mandates and changing gender norms gave female college graduates a more extensive array of professional choices than ever before, even if they faced discrimination once on the job. But working-class women without bachelor's degrees, often needing to find work in a particular location to support a family, actually faced the same limited options as before. In sum, affirmative action did less for women who entered corporations on a clerical ladder, which disadvantaged working-class women.

As the agenda of corporate feminism would come to focus on the problems facing white-collar professionals at the top of the organizational hierarchy, what would happen to lower-level office workers who had little internal mobility? Women in the NSA, the association that had founded National Secretaries Week and chosen the red rose as its symbol, argued that executive secretaries were skilled professionals too, with leaders stating that "feminity [sic] and professionalism in a woman are compatible."[14] Others in 9to5 and the labor movement were trying to organize secretaries into a national union. But seniority-based systems of organized labor clashed with merit-based advancement and performance-based pay, which were endemic to the logics of human resource management. Still other career advisors recommended that women avoid or flee the traditional confines of secretarial work, and those with the stigma of the job title should recast their prior clerical experience in the hopes of attaining managerial jobs. These approaches to advancing equity at work would promise vastly different outcomes for the status of the secretary. If feminism were to provide women with the freedom not to be secretaries, then could it also upgrade secretarial work at the same time? Could new ideas of about gender equality spur the unionization and professionalization of secretaries?

In the end, these different approaches to the advancement of clerical women proved to be ideologically incompatible. Professionalization and unionization both struggled to gain ground within a vast occupational category filled with a variety of job descriptions and a lack of credentialing. The flourishing discourse of career advisors, which emphasized that women now had freedom *not* to be a secretary, reflected and even strengthened a "new spirit of capitalism," marked by its focus on individual initiative and autonomy.[15] As more Americans were facing precarious employment, career self-help literature proposed ways to leverage an employee's detachment from a single employer. Professional women utilized this advice to search for self-fulfillment through work and to craft career paths across organizational boundaries. The advice was less relevant to clerical women who had trouble rebranding their work experience and had to prioritize economic need over self-fulfillment.[16] Finding one's professional fit and developing one's personal brand required additional capital that many working-class women and men lacked.

Given the cultural, legal, and political transformations that accompanied the social movements of the 1960s and 1970s, how could the belief in equality of opportunity coexist so comfortably with the endurance of occupational segregation in the United States by the 1990s? Only the American ideal of meritocracy, rooted so deeply in historical ideas like the Puritan work ethic and the Horatio Alger myth, could reconcile two seemingly contradictory phenomena.[17] Embracing gender equality and individual merit, corporate feminism came to mean freedom of choice, particularly freedom of occupational choice. An equality of opportunity ostensibly enjoyed by women and underrepresented men could be reconciled with an inequality of outcomes by attributing professional success to hard work. The veil of merit and choice offered by expanding HR offices strengthened the ideological alignment between feminism and capitalism, obscuring the reality that only some women and men could pursue work that reflected their personal values.[18]

This narrative tends toward contingency rather than inevitability in historical perspective. In literature from social scientists, inevitability typically characterizes broader currents of the political economy whereby the stability of the employment relationship was disintegrating, the strength of internal labor markets was weakening, and the outsourcing of labor was increasing.[19] Yet in historical literature, these trends emerge due to the choices and actions of individual persons or groups of persons.[20] From the standpoint of women, precarious employment status and lack of upward mobility have characterized their experiences at work for many decades, not just of late.[21] But in the postwar period, as managerial ladders for men were starting to weaken, women were gaining access to those ladders.[22] *The Rise of Corporate Feminism* poses the question: Although women never had access to the stable ladders enjoyed by "the organization man," could they have?[23]

This narrative points to contingencies at the occupational and organizational levels when considering the ways that women's jobs remained devalued as internal labor markets continued to weaken. Corporate HR practices, though well intentioned, failed to institute structural changes regarding lines of progression. Managerial and clerical job ladders have remained distinct, but I argue that they could have been bridged as part of a more robust EEO implementation. Many women who had to prioritize earning wages above attending college could have used entry-level clerical work as a springboard into an array of other job functions within the corporation. If such work could have offered upward mobility, similar to a college internship position, perhaps the secretarial job as a port of entry would have become more attractive to college-educated men and women. The actual skills and tasks required for performing clerical work often prepare job incumbents to move into management; yet the occupation's stigma has precluded career clerical workers from enjoying advancement opportunities that are granted to temporary interns. Objectively, there is nothing about being a secretary, other than the gender of the job, that makes it an inherently inferior or an unskilled type of work relative to any other entry-level positions. Social scientists have shown that the value assigned to work in different occupations depends on the characteristics of the occupations' incumbents.[24] Thus predominantly female jobs are devalued socially and economically because the work is viewed as lower in status relative to the work performed in predominantly male jobs.[25] Research demonstrates that a heavily female-dominated occupation like secretarial work results in a ghetto effect for its occupants, whereby they have trouble transitioning out of the job.[26]

To suggest that secretaries could have become managers requires creative and counterfactual thinking. As part of the "opening of the American workplace," what if men had initially entered secretarial work in greater numbers, resulting in a more gender-integrated occupational demography?[27] What if EEO enforcement had mandated that managers should account for internal promotions as part of an organization's goals and timetables? What if HR managers had conducted job analysis, performed pay equity audits, and reconsidered lines of progression when looking to increase the representation of women in managerial positions?[28] What if professional associations like the NSA had successfully recast secretarial work as an occupation requiring a standardized credential, much like teaching or nursing? The invisible and inferior status of secretaries remains so ingrained in our psyche that historical scholarship in the postwar period has completely overlooked the millions of women performing this work.[29] Historians have not properly considered the specific choices of activists, policy makers, and managers that preserved and even bolstered the secondary status of this major occupational category during and after the feminist era.

Despite the mainstreaming of a corporate feminism focused on individual career advancement, occupational segregation by gender has remained entrenched in the current labor market. After a shift toward integration in the 1970s and 1980s, progress began to stall in the 1990s and has remained slow.[30] Until recently, few men have had economic or social incentives to enter female-dominated occupations, while many college-educated women are eager to integrate into higher-paid, traditionally male professions. And regarding female-dominated work, college-educated women avoid clerical paths while still entering credentialed careers like nursing or teaching. The endurance of occupational segregation, which has an acute influence on the economic opportunities for working-class women and women of color, led sociologist Paula England to call the gender revolution "uneven and stalled." We know that in occupations not requiring a college degree, particularly in the male-dominated trades, occupational segregation remains most severe.[31] And women's jobs generally pay less than men's, contributing to a significant portion of the gender pay gap.[32] Any serious effort to analyze gender disparities in labor market outcomes, including the gender pay gap, "cannot simply 'control away' occupations," according to sociologists at the Stanford Center on Poverty and Inequality.[33] Scholars must attend to the historical and social processes that sustain gender segregation (between and within occupations) if we want to mitigate inequity.

Understanding that the resulting ideology of corporate feminism came to justify occupational segregation requires us to uncover some uncomfortable truths about the operation of social movements in a broader political economy. On the one hand, feminism, like any other social movement in the United States, is at the mercy of larger capitalist forces.[34] The for-profit logics of corporations tend to refashion more progressive impulses of equity and justice into organizational mechanisms that bolster productivity and profitability. Other scholars have documented the limitations of EEO law and merit-based employment policies, which often fail to address systemic inequalities based on class, race, and gender. Sociologists have identified a "paradox of meritocracy" whereby an organizational culture promoting egalitarian ideals can give rise to managers who demonstrate greater biases against lower-status employees.[35] In this book, the feminist principle of equality of opportunity, as well as the corporate mechanisms designed to increase the representation of women in management, hardened the low-status of the American secretary and overlooked imprints of inequity that were less obvious.

On the other hand, capitalist forces do not completely obscure dissenting voices; less powerful persons manage to enter the historical record, often by way of collective action. While equality of opportunity became a dominant paradigm of feminism that was adopted by the corporation, the women's movement has always been composed of various strains of thought and an array of agenda items.[36] Important revisionist histories about gender and work have found activism in less visible places and among populations of women that initially were not considered core to the American feminist project. Scholars have shown that women in the labor movement fought continuously throughout the twentieth century for economic justice and gender equity in their unions and at their workplaces.[37] Others have looked to female lobbyists and policy makers to show that activists in the 1940s and 1950s sustained political activity on behalf of women's rights.[38] Still others have uncovered the grassroots activism of Black and Latina women who fought for adequate income and dignity through the welfare rights movement.[39]

As a social and intellectual history of the intersection of a social movement and an occupation, this book traces ideas about secretaries, secretarial work, and feminism but also is grounded in evidence of women's lived experiences. As one of the largest categories of women workers, clerical workers are diverse, both in their demography and in their credentials. Employer autonomy over job titles and changing technological trends have resulted in contested boundaries of the clerical category across space and over time. Are receptionists secretaries? It depends whom you ask. A professional organization like the NSA would have said no. A government body like the Bureau of Labor Statistics would say yes. This book traces the descriptive and prescriptive debates among different stakeholders about the appropriate boundaries for the occupation. At times I rely on the voices and experiences of clerical workers, while at other moments I use conventional ideas about secretarial work to trace the stability and change in the occupation. Given the prevalence of stereotypes about secretaries, the descriptive and prescriptive come together such that preconceptions and expectations about the nature of the job ultimately limit the professional possibilities of those doing the work.

Of course, some women proudly owned the labels of feminist *and* secretary, fighting individually and collectively to improve the pay and standing of the job.[40] Those secretaries who became activists for the occupation were more likely to identify with a clerical group like 9to5, a trade union, or even a professional association than with mainstream feminist organizations like the National Organization for Women (NOW).[41] Historian Dorothy Sue Cobble has shown how feminism and unionism overlap, as those in female-dominated work have contributed to a rising tide of women union members as well as a more flexible approach to union agendas and structures.[42] From the 1960s to the 1980s, the increasing rates of women in unions relative to the declining rates of overall private-sector membership demonstrated that the feminist movement had pushed women to unionize. Not just secretaries but also home health workers, waitresses, domestics, and flight attendants used the trade union model to fight for childcare, maternity leave, and equitable pay.[43] White women and people of color from the service and clerical sectors have kept trade unions afloat since the 1970s, particularly in the public sector; and major unions have adopted clericals' organizing strategies like the worker-center model.[44]

The Rise of Corporate Feminism intentionally turns to the private sector to explore how capitalism fueled certain elements of feminism while quelling others. Merit-based policies and beliefs are more pronounced in the private sector, and the changing nature of capitalism (away from long-term employment relationships and strong internal labor markets) has more severe consequences for private-sector relative to public-sector employees. As for other content, I engage with the issues and concerns that appeared most often in the historical archives, as well as those that had the most relevance to the professional image and lived experience of the secretary. Thus some gender and work issues appear more often than others.[45]

To properly represent the multiple experiences of women in the past and incorporate new moments and sites of activism, scholars have shifted away from using the terminology of feminist waves (first-wave feminism, second-wave feminism).[46] Revisionist histories demonstrate that important streams of activism were occurring across time (not just during the wave periods). Looking between the waves has uncovered different understandings of gender equity and new contributors to women's progress.

While finding activism beyond mainstream periods and channels has allowed for the flourishing of gender history, I seek to temper this revisionist approach.

This book rehabilitates—cautiously—the conventional wave metaphor of feminist activism. With abandonment of feminist waves, historians unintentionally portray all past actors and ideas as possessing similar agency in their influence on the broader society. In reality, some feminist actions and ideas have had more influence, depending on the status of the actors and the nature of their messages. *The Rise of Corporate Feminism* demonstrates that feminist tropes most aligned with the current state of American capitalism gained greater currency and prominence. What used to be called the second wave successfully normalized new distinctions between sex and gender, convincing many Americans that gender was a historical and social construction, and that one's gender should not limit one's life choices. As government and business entities clung to and subsumed certain ideas of feminism that bolstered equal opportunity, individual advancement, and meritocracy, other strains of feminism regarding pay equity, occupational segregation, and unionization lost clout in the private sector. This fresh, even if unwelcomed, perspective argues that not all ideas, actions, and events in the past have survived the forces of capitalism: a broader political and economic context inevitably has shaped the way we interpret the problems facing corporate women and our search for possible solutions.

—— ക്ക ——

Across America, women in the 1960s to 1990s experienced discrimination on account of their gender but nevertheless remained detached from the feminist movement. This is not to say that feminist currents did not influence their lives, just that many women did not assume a feminist identity. Scholars have shown that although Americans tended to agree with most of the core ideals, particularly equal pay for equal work, they accumulated a negative view of the feminist label.[47] When eight clerks protested gender-based inequities in pay and promotions at Citizens National Bank in Minnesota, eventually creating a union and going on strike, one of the women admitted that she thought a feminist was "somebody who was out of control, and just totally strange, kinky if you would." Another said, "I didn't know what a feminist was until I looked it up in the dictionary."[48]

In this small conservative town of Willmar, Minnesota, and despite the women's avowed distance from feminism, the first organization to support them on the picket line was the National Organization for Women (NOW).[49] NOW promoted dignity for those performing women's jobs by taking issue with stereotypical portrayals of women office workers. In New York the organization confronted the Olivetti Corporation about the highly sexualized "Olivetti girl" who was used in print advertisements to sell typewriters.[50] In Indiana it protested Canada Dry's marketing language—"A Good Club Soda Is Like a Good Woman: It Won't Quit on You"—alluding to high turnover rates of secretaries.[51] Although mainstream feminist organizations were intending to advocate on behalf of all women, not all women wanted to assume a feminist identity.

The news media is partly responsible for creating prototypes and framing the movement in ways that overlooked feminism's diversity of thought and participation. For instance, traditional images of women, usually white, in traditional roles were starkly juxtaposed against women's liberationists in the mass media.[52] The tendency to "cognitively reduce" a multitude of feminist agendas meant that even slight differences in thought were cast as full-blown opposition.[53] Although most feminists intended to help women in traditional roles as well as those moving into nontraditional spaces, feminism became a binary "catfight" on television, given the media's tendency to portray extreme dichotomies.[54] Many activists fought against cognitive reduction by trying to shun hierarchical leadership structures whereby some women became figureheads and spokeswomen for the movement's masses. Feminist Carol Hanisch said her consciousness-raising group decided, "Everybody talks to the press or nobody talks to the press . . . but it didn't work out that way." Hanisch insisted that the feminist movement "must learn how to fight against the media's desire to make leaders and some women's desire to be spokesmen," but in reality a few leaders claimed the most visibility. In particular, the platforms of Betty Friedan and Gloria Steinem became representative of feminist ideology to the broader public.[55] The first chapter examines the places where dominant messages of the feminist movement intersected with broader understandings of secretarial work.

1

FEMINIST OR SECRETARY?

In March 1970 in Chicago, feminist leader and bestselling author Betty Friedan spoke at the third annual conference of the National Organization for Women, an organization that she had cofounded in 1966. She explained her vision for a nationwide day of action to bolster the "revolution against sexual oppression." Friedan argued that NOW was the best organization to lead this effort, which would bring greater public awareness to the laws and norms that prevented women from attaining full equality with men. She continued to sell her idea to NOW members: "I propose that the women who are doing menial chores in the offices as secretaries put the covers on their typewriters and close their notebooks and the telephone operators unplug their switchboards, the waitresses stop waiting, cleaning women stop cleaning and everyone who is doing a job for which a man would be paid more stop."[1] Friedan convinced other NOW leaders to endorse the idea of a coordinated protest. NOW—just over three years old and with more than three thousand members—declared that the event would "signal the start of a major political effort for the liberation of the women of the United States of America."[2]

On the fiftieth anniversary of women's suffrage, Friedan's vision became the historic Women's Strike for Equality. On Fifth Avenue in New York City, an estimated fifty thousand women gathered on August 26, 1970. In cities across the nation, women came together to bring attention to the systemic political, legal, and economic discrimination that disadvantaged women at home and at work. Signs told women to stop doing tradition-ally female work: "don't cook dinner—starve a rat today," and "don't iron while the strike is hot."[3] In Syracuse, women threw bras, hair curlers, and lipstick into large public trash cans to protest the objectification of women.[4] Women in Boston chained themselves to large paper typewriters to dem-onstrate that their options were limited to dead-end and low-paid jobs.[5]

The strike catapulted what became known as "the second feminist wave" into the national discourse.[6] Within several months, NOW's mem-bership increased by 50 percent.[7] The strike proved, according to the *New York Times*, that "anyone who thought [the] intentions [of feminism were] frivolous was mistaken." From the mainstream media's point of view, as well as her own, Betty Friedan was the mother of this new feminist move-ment. As founding president of NOW and bestselling author of *The Femi-nine Mystique*, Friedan cast herself as the voice of all women, feminist and nonfeminist, at one point telling a U.S. Senate committee, "I am here speaking for the silent majority, the truly silent majority." Because she presented her views as the best path to advance women's status, Friedan received as much condemnation as praise. She employed a leadership style that at best radiated confidence but at worst projected arrogance. Yet regarding the Women's Strike in 1970, even her critics acknowledged that she deserved credit for its success: radical feminist Susan Brownmiller, who often found fault with Friedan, admitted that "without the name of Betty Friedan, the strike would never have happened."[8]

Friedan and NOW fought to increase the social and economic value of female-dominated labor, arguing that the work performed by housewives and secretaries was underappreciated. She wanted to advance a type of feminism that would simultaneously allow women access to unchartered territory while also bringing attention to the devaluation of women's paid and unpaid labor. She didn't want to belittle women themselves but instead to call attention to their belittled work. Yet in the age of televised news and daily newspapers, the most outrageous events and the most sensa-tional language were also the most indelible.[9] The media cast Friedan as domineering and aggressive and presented the new feminist movement as a complete rejection of feminine ideas, behaviors, and norms. News coverage captured and conveyed the most striking aspects of the move-ment, narrowing the movement's vision for those removed from the fem-inist front lines.[10]

This popular image of Friedan's brand of feminism, as well as more radical emergent strains, proved to have unintended, negative consequences for those engaged in female-dominated labor. Laypeople had difficulty reconciling calls to appreciate women in their current roles with calls to reject those sex-stereotyped roles and seek new ones. Eventually the inability to reconcile the two identities—of secretary and feminist—would pose challenges to advancing women's rights at work.

The first section of this chapter profiles the Katharine Gibbs School, which reigned for most of the twentieth century as the premier institution for secretarial training. Much of the leading prescriptive literature about performing well in clerical occupations, and in particular about mastering the position of executive secretary, echoed the mission and values of Gibbs. Generally these how-to books emphasized that perfecting the secretarial role meant not just acquiring certain skills but also adhering to feminine norms while remaining ambitious and diligent. The second section details the feminist perspective on the secretarial role and argues that the values of equality and independence at the core of second-wave feminism wildly diverged from the popular meaning and performance of secretarial work.

Many women—aspiring executive secretaries, seasoned pink-collar workers, and instructors in clerical training programs—did not view secretaries as oppressed in the 1940s, 1950s, and early 1960s. To succeed as a secretary in these decades was to epitomize the modern woman, a woman with the ability to be feminine yet smart, docile yet ambitious. Private secretaries had to balance submission with initiative. Secretarial work could lead to professional opportunities for upward mobility and personal opportunities for self-improvement, and it was an esteemed job for a woman until the 1960s. This chapter argues that it acquired negative connotations only when larger numbers of women begin to have opportunities for other types of work.

Institutions such as the Katharine Gibbs School, which sociologist Rosabeth Moss Kanter described as Harvard Business School for the typing pool, as well as advice books and prescriptive literature for aspiring secretaries, exemplified the view that to be a secretary was a skilled professional calling. Secretaries needed to master certain tangible skills while also embodying intangible feminine values and normative personal attributes such as empathy and diligence.[11] Until another wave of automation began to change the nature of clerical work in the 1970s (see chapter 4), success as a clerical was based in a separate-spheres approach. White women were seen as uniquely positioned by their moral, religious, and submissive nature to master the tasks and values of secretarial work. Secretarial work was a respectable calling, distinct from men's office work and unquestionably subordinate to the boss, yet not necessarily any less essential to corporate functioning and organizational success.

Since the early twentieth century, when clerical jobs were feminized, certain tangible skills positioned a woman to succeed in secretarial work.[12] In 1911 sisters Katharine Gibbs, who functioned as manager, and Mary Gibbs, who taught lessons, founded the Katharine Gibbs School in Providence, Rhode Island. For decades the school epitomized this view that secretaries were professionals who had acquired a distinct body of knowledge and a certain degree of polish and poise. Part boot camp, part finishing school, the Gibbs School included classes in shorthand, stenography, and bookkeeping. By 1929 the school had expanded into New York City and Boston, with about a thousand young women enrolled.[13] In New York, "Gibblets," a nickname for students from the Gibbs School, lived in the famed Barbizon Hotel alongside fashion models and Seven Sisters graduates.[14]

While other institutions taught clerical skills to high school students, the Gibbs School positioned itself as a refined boutique relative to other secretarial programs, such as public school courses or other private training programs with higher enrollments.[15] Initially Katharine Gibbs advertised the school as "especially adapted to meet the needs of those to whom attendance at a large commercial school would be distasteful." To establish the school as elite among competitors, she marketed her program in bulletins for selective colleges (Radcliffe, Smith, and Barnard) as well as in magazines that appealed to the wealthy, such as *Harper's Bazaar*. Some women entered after attending boarding school for a two-year program, while others began the second year of the Gibbs program following college graduation.[16] To encourage privileged daughters to enroll in a job-training program, Gibbs had to emphasize the importance of economic self-sufficiency while also selling the program as appropriate for genteel young women. She noted in the school's catalog that inherited money could be "the most uncertain of all forms of protection," revealing that she conceived of her program as a backup plan for elite young women if something in their family situation went awry.[17] These daughters might not have to work for long or at all, but they would have the security of skills to sustain themselves if necessary. This focus on economic independence likely came from Gibbs's own life experience: her husband had fallen off a yacht and drowned off the coast of Rhode Island. Following his death, she began work as an office manager to support herself and her two boys.[18] Gibbs eventually sold her jewels and used the proceeds to begin the school.[19]

The Gibbs School was founded on a duality, if not a paradox: it trained women to enter the unrefined world of wage work while enhancing their feminine poise and grace. It provided women with tools for economic independence but did not intend to overturn the male breadwinner ideal. The curriculum carefully preserved and even enhanced the intangible qualities of femininity that would make a young white woman attractive to marry. The liminal state of the Gibbs School, between the public world of work and the private sphere of marriage and femininity, was not a contradiction in its day: success in paid secretarial work required a mastery of feminine values. A school catalog from 1927 stated, "Practical training for a vocation should emphasize, not minimize, the cultivation of gentle manners and social poise."[20]

By the 1940s Gibbs students were known for wearing hats and white gloves, which were required until the mid-1960s. They also always wore stockings and shoes with heels when out of the classroom. They were fined twenty-five cents for chewing gum in class.[21] Coffee was served out of a silver-plated urn, not just a stained, glass pot.[22] Instructors addressed students as "Miss or Mrs., never by their first name."[23] The Gibbs School was the "Emily Post of the business world."[24] A secretarial instructor who became director of business communications at Gibbs, Lucy Graves Mayo, told *Business Week* in 1961, "The Gibbs girl is at all times an understatement—nobody likes a pushy female."[25]

While it catered to the most gracious young women and schooled them in femininity, the program also provided a rigorous curriculum that professionalized women's office work. In her school, Katharine Gibbs challenged the widespread beliefs that women lacked intellectual potential and that working women were dull and unintelligent. She acknowledged the discrimination that working women faced: "A woman's career is blocked by lack of openings; by prejudice; by the fact that business is outside of a woman's natural sphere; and finally, that she seldom is granted a just reward by way of salary, recognition, or responsibility." Katharine Gibbs offered substantive training and a substantial curriculum that included courses in personnel administration, business writing, and advertising, taught by lecturers from prestigious universities, including one faculty member who was an academic dean at the Massachusetts Institute for Technology (MIT).[26] A Gibbs School promotional pamphlet in 1959, "The Private Secretary," explained its program as covering three broad areas: personal (e.g., grooming, grace, poise); educational (e.g., fundamentals in economics and math as well as expertise in grammar, writing, editing); and technical (e.g., typing, filing, shorthand).[27]

The training was challenging: executives cited "technical excellence" as a key attribute of successful secretaries.[28] When one unfortunate student made a mistake at the beginning of a typing test, she was expelled for putting in a new paper and starting over. "You weren't allowed to start over," said the fearful student who sat beside her and witnessed the incident.[29] Grading was strict: one typing error in an assignment would automatically mean a failing grade for that assignment. Many women claimed that the Gibbs School was more difficult than college.[30] Sarah Pileggi, who arrived at Gibbs in 1960 with a Stanford University degree in history, disclosed that she "hated every minute" of Gibbs in large part because students "had to spend four hours a day practicing [drills] to get through the next day's classes." Another graduated described it as "dreadful." Still another noted that although the program was "grueling," the training was relevant: she "never encountered a situation [at work] that was more difficult than Katie Gibbs."[31]

Because of its demanding curriculum, as well as the refined pedigree of its students, employers competed for Gibbs graduates to fill clerical openings. By the 1960s employers openly advertised that they wanted "Katie Gibbs girls." In fact, the school claimed that its graduates were more likely than college graduates to have job offers following graduation. School administrators touted seven job openings for each graduate.[32] According to Gibbs records, by 1960, 20,000 private business and secretarial schools were training 90,000 clerical workers. The Gibbs systems graduated about 1,500 to 1,700 students a year and received between 10,000 and 12,000 employment requests, an astonishing number.[33]

Often, college graduates attended Gibbs because they had trouble getting job offers with their undergraduate degrees. Stories abounded of women like Katherine Davis, a twenty-two-year-old graduate of Colorado Women's College in Denver, who had majored in European history. She had spent about $17,000 on her four-year education. "But no job offers awaited her. So now she's shelling out nearly another $5,000 for a year of postgraduate study at the Katharine Gibbs school."[34]

Women who did not have access to Gibbs training looked for other ways to gain credentials. Membership in a professional organization such as the National Secretaries Association (NSA) could supplement their development. Founded in 1942, the NSA aligned with the beliefs and mission of the Gibbs School: it sought to professionalize the job of secretary.[35] According to an NSA official, "We in the NSA recognize the fact that secretaryship *is* a profession. . . . It is our responsibility as secretaries to convenience management that this is true."[36] A department within the NSA, the Institute for Certifying Secretaries, first began issuing formal certifications for secretaries in 1950. The standardized test for the Certified Professional Secretary (CPS) designation was rigorous. It lasted two days and had six parts: behavioral science in business, business law, economics and management, accounting, secretarial skills and decision making, and office procedures and administration.[37] The NSA Credo, developed in the 1960s, underscored the professional nature of the work, holding that secretaries should maintain high standards for their work and improve themselves through continuing education.[38] NSA literature declared that secretarial work was a "meaningful" job, and a secretary functioned as a "confidante" who was entrusted with much responsibility. By 1970 the NSA had over 38,000 members around the world.[39]

Those affiliated with secretarial instruction or secretarial associations published prescriptive literature to enhance the professional development of aspiring and current secretaries. These advice manuals reinforced the Gibbs School message that secretarial work did not depend only on mastering tasks like shorthand, typing, letter writing, bookkeeping, and filing. Most books endorsed a type of femininity based in the nineteenth-century separate-spheres tradition, at the same time as they encouraged women to shed their submissiveness and compete on the free market as individual actors in the world of private enterprise.[40]

Great secretaries had "certain attributes that [enabled them] to stand out among others," wrote Marie Lauria, instructor of secretarial practice at Fordham University and former executive secretary, in her book *How To Be a Good Secretary.* The qualities that distinguished excellent from mediocre secretaries—likability, empathy, listening, adaptability, loyalty, submissiveness, neatness, and diligence—were overwhelmingly feminine characteristics. According to Lauria, adherence to traditional gender norms constituted mastery of secretarial work. Even her suggestion of having "self-confidence" did not mean that secretaries should attempt to acquire greater power or status. Nor should they pose a challenge to the status quo by defying orders from the boss. Self-confidence, in Lauria's account, meant "emotional stability" to maintain poise on the job.[41]

Lauria warned against impatience with colleagues or clients: "Wait until the other person is ready to hear what you have to say" before speaking, and especially with your boss be "constantly on guard not to offend him," avoid a "disagreeable attitude," and demonstrate a *"pleasing personality."* If a colleague or client were to approach you with a problem, request, or concern, always comply. Never tell someone, "I can't speak right now," or "I'm busy, come back later" lest you be considered "emotionally immature" or even "disagreeable and hard to get along with." To remember these rules of the job, Lauria had an acronym: be CALM, which stood for cheerful, amiable, likable, and magnetic.[42]

Embracing one's biological and social role as a woman made for excellence on the job. A former recipient of the International Secretary of the Year award from National Secretaries Association, Alicia Cogan, stated that in good secretaries, "first and foremost there must be that quality of womanliness which makes a woman 'the heart of the home.' It can be defined as a desire to serve. . . . It is the boss who is ever the leader, while she is the follower who serves."[43] Patricia Flynn, executive secretary to the president of the National Broadcasting Company and author of *So You Want to Be an Executive Secretary,* agreed. According to Flynn, an executive secretary had many functions, but her "most important role . . . is that of a woman." She lamented: "I have seen a lot of girls on their way to the top who seem to drop a little bit of their femininity on each step. When they reach the top, they no longer quite resemble women," and consequently colleagues would describe them in harsh and unattractive terms.[44]

The maintenance of femininity required recognition that the "boss is KING," according to Lucy Graves Mayo, a seasoned Gibbs School instructor and author of *You Can Be an Executive Secretary.*[45] In contrast, the secretary was to be "the shock absorber of the office," even if receiving undeserved criticism, according to a Gibbs School pamphlet.[46] Other advice literature confirmed that, as a secretary, "you are hired to do work for someone else, not to do work as you would have it done," according to the *Private Secretary's Manual,* a guide that claimed to be used by over 100,000 secretaries.[47] The secretary was to follow the directions of the boss, no questions asked. According to Flynn: "Do whatever you are asked to do cheerfully . . . don't start out by making rules about what you will or won't do in any office."[48] Lauria maintained, "Carry out *his* wishes, not yours." She added that to be a "perfect helpmate" to the boss, "it becomes a distinct advantage if you adjust your own personality to that of your executive and *adapt* yourself to his individual and particular methods."[49] Flynn agreed. She explained that the boss's feelings are more important than the secretary's: "Your boss will have bad days and bad moods. You will have them too, but as an executive secretary you don't have license to practice them in the office. Your boss has."[50]

The secretary was to be the invisible force behind a flawless and knowledgeable executive. Lauria maintained, "Relieve him of as much work and worry as you possibly can" so that he could be available to do the most important tasks. An excellent secretary knew how to make the boss appear more skilled and informed than he actually was. Build up his executive image, and respect his weaknesses or mistakes. Never undermine his authority, even to the extent that you should accept his errors as your own. For example, if he thinks you typed the wrong word but indeed your shorthand notes show that he used that word in dictation, recognize that it "is a mistake to try to exonerate yourself," wrote Lauria. Only a " 'novice' secretary who lacked proper training in diplomacy" would point to the boss's error. Instead the secretary should reply, "I'm sorry, Mr. Brown, that I made the error. I probably did not hear you correctly."[51]

While much of the advice in prescriptive literature emphasized mastery of feminine traits, some messaging simultaneously pushed secretaries toward more masculine qualities of rationality, autonomy, and initiative.

Helen Whitcomb, the former managing editor of *Today's Secretary*, a trade magazine published by the Gregg Publishing Division of McGraw-Hill, authored (either individually or with her husband) several advice books for secretaries. Whitcomb encouraged secretaries to avoid emotional displays when receiving negative feedback: "The girl who interprets criticism of her work as a direct insult had better close up her typewriter and take up a career of knitting." Great secretaries had to control their emotions, embrace reason, and overcome the feminine tendency to pout or cry in the office environment.[52] Lauria agreed that secretaries needed emotional toughness: "Don't be the kind of secretary who falls to pieces every time you are asked to perform an important rush assignment. This is no time to become hysterical or confused."[53]

In addition to resilience, another masculine quality, autonomy, was required for secretarial success. Although usually the boss was always right, occasionally a secretary should exercise independent thought. According to Lauria, secretaries should use judgment as to when to act independently as "self-starters," exercising initiative only in service of the boss or the larger organization.[54] Whitcomb agreed: "The girl who stands out head and shoulders above the drones is the one who shows that she can assume responsibility—that she can think for herself and that she possesses the initiative to work out problems on her own."[55] A great secretary had to have intuition to know when to demonstrate initiative versus follow orders, given contradictory advice. The *Private Secretary's Manual*, for instance, contained a chapter, "Personal Qualifications for Success," that captured the tension between self-reliance and submission within a few pages. The manual proclaimed on page 220 that secretaries needed the "ability to carry things through to a conclusion without instruction," but then, just two pages later, they were instructed to follow directions because "training has put too much emphasis on initiative and not enough on the less spectacular quality of obedience." The conflicting messages of independence and dependence continued throughout the manual.[56]

The idea of taking initiative could translate into a requirement that secretaries should be workhorses and do as many tasks as possible each day. The *Private Secretary's Manual* advised the secretary to "be a pioneer in assuming responsibility in your office," which translated into the expectation that a secretary should relieve the boss of his chores before he has to ask.[57] Lauria advised secretaries to be "continually on the lookout for new and better ways of aiding your executive," but "be careful not to convey the slightest impression that you are trying to step into his shoes.[58] Knowing when to follow orders and when to lead the way required the discretion of an astute secretary who was familiar with the office environment. "If you see a job around the office that you feel capable of doing, ask if you can try it. This will develop initiative," according to Flynn in *So You Want to Be an Executive Secretary.*[59]

While messaging toggled between independence and dependence, unquestionably, for all executive secretaries, an attractive appearance was crucial. Articles, pamphlets, and books told secretaries how to dress and groom themselves. According to a national survey conducted by typewriter company Remington Rand in 1951, bosses had several "pet peeves" regarding appearance. Several hundred respondents cited problems such as "too much make-up," "hair untidy," wears "bobby socks" instead of hosiery, or "slip always shows" under skirts. In contrast, a "super-secretary" knew how to dress appropriately, saving "glamour for evenings" but not appearing "over-casual," wearing high-quality dresses and suits that were simple and tailored.[60] *Life* magazine reported on the "don'ts" of office dress and appearance, according to a small, prestigious secretarial school in Beverly Hills: avoid perfume and low-cut dresses. Plaid skirts along with bright colors were inappropriate for the office.[61] Gibbs instructor and author Lucy Graves Mayo recommended certain grooming rituals, such as manicuring hands, shaving legs, and washing hair. As for hair styles, she strongly discouraged "pony tails (immature), exaggerated bouffants ('ridiculously artificial'), overlong 'boudoir' styles (unkempt or too informal), and any other styling that distracts."[62]

Many advice books equated inappropriate appearance with character flaws in potential applicants. A secretary who had held several senior secretarial positions commented, "One just does *not* get a job in the head office—no matter how efficient and capable and faithful—*unless she looks the part.*"[63] In a chapter entitled "What Mr. Employer Considers," Helen and John Whitcomb claimed that first and foremost, "he will discard the applications of any girls who don't measure up in appearance." Posture, clothes, and appearance, according to the Whitcombs, were "important clues to [a woman's] self-confidence, self-discipline, and respect for the opinions of others.[64] Maintaining a slim figure was imperative. Mayo issued a warning: "Don't let a figure problem develop. . . . A bad figure fault can eliminate you from consideration for the really important job."[65]

In a 1961 publication from the National Secretaries Association, one vignette concerned the issue of an overweight secretary. Management hired her pending a six-month prohibitory period, which would allow her time to lose weight or face termination. Although some may find this management action to be unfair, the NSA maintained, "generally speaking, an obese person is inclined to be untidy in his work." According to the NSA, "Before a girl can hope to become an efficient secretary, she must first become efficient in the management of herself."[66] The NSA award for International Secretary of the Year emphasized appearance as late as 1979. A three-judge panel scored the candidates based not only on writing composition but also "on the basis of appearance, poise, and ability to answer a question presented by three judges."[67] Sample résumés in several advice manuals instructed women to include height, weight, and even age on their resumes, reiterating the importance of body shape and appearance to the executive secretary position.[68] Another advice book suggested that subtracting a few years from one's real age for the purpose of the résumé may help with landing a job.[69]

The Whitcombs explained the reason for this emphasis on physical looks: a secretary's appearance in turn reflected on her employer's status: "In the same way that men take great pride in owning sleek new cars, they feel that a Cadillac-caliber secretary also adds to their prestige."[70] According to Mayo, "it is impossible to disassociate personality *from* personal appearance. A secretary's appearance contributes to the 'tone' of her executive's office. It reflects *his* prestige. It goes further and reflects the prestige of the organization she represents. It sometimes even elicits from office visitors (male) the friendly, often envious, question—'Where did you find *her*?'—spoken, of course, with the right inflection."[71] Flynn also supported the connection between attractiveness and status: "No man wants to be embarrassed by the appearance of his secretary. It's a reflection on his taste."[72]

It might have come as a relief for aspiring secretaries to read that they did not have to be the most naturally beautiful woman to excel, but only should make the most of their assets. Most employers could not require that their secretary be a "beauty-contest winner."[73] Flynn wrote that natural beauty was not required: women could work to improve their figures, color their hair, wear contacts, and even undergo plastic surgery for "that nose which seems out of proportion" or "that sagging chin." Given so many remedies, Flynn determined that no longer did a woman have "to accept whatever nature handed out."[74] Mayo confirmed that the responsibility for being attractive rested with the secretary herself; in fact, each woman had "a fighting chance to succeed in *looking impressive*."[75]

Just as they should attempt to maximize their appearance, secretaries also should exert effort when mastering their job tasks. "Secretaries are made, not born" began the foreword to the *Private Secretary's Manual*, imprinting the notion that hard work and determination, more than natural ability, accounted for the success of some women and the failure of others.[76] Advice literature noted that the best secretaries were always striving to improve themselves, as delineated in *Your Future as a Secretary*: "Like being a great pianist or an expert golfer or a skilled physician, the secretary must maintain the high standards aimed at while in school and preparing for this career. You must stay in practice. If you have determined to become a secretary, you will want to be the very best secretary you can be."[77] Thus becoming an accomplished secretary, similar to mastery of other professions, required ambition and determination. Gordon Gibbs told *Business Week* that the key to success at Gibbs was selecting women for admittance, claiming that those chosen were not necessarily the brightest and richest but the most motivated to succeed.[78]

The Gibbs brand espoused a version of the Puritan work ethic and a belief in Benjamin Franklin's self-improvement framework, suggesting that, armed with a Gibbs education, almost any woman could acquire the necessary skills to become an executive secretary. In this way, Gibbs viewed itself as offering upward mobility to graduates, enabling those with perseverance to achieve the status of an executive secretary role. Marion Beck, a Gibbs School vice president, emphasized the importance of hard work: becoming a great secretary meant embracing the saying, "I'll try."[79] In this way, secretarial success reflected meritocratic values: those who tried the hardest became the best secretaries.

Other advice literature suggested that secretaries apply self-improvement principles to their personality traits, calling on those with nonnormative dispositions to adjust their tendencies accordingly. Lauria offered a survey so readers could take inventory of their own temperaments and then adjust accordingly. She listed several statements and instructed readers to become aware of their "most serious faults." In reviewing a list of qualities, such as "I speak quietly and calmly" and "I am adaptable, intuitive, and levelheaded," readers could determine misalignments between their own personalities and the ideal qualities of secretaries and then "seize this opportunity to develop and cultivate [those ideal qualities] immediately." The desire to improve marked a great secretary: "A mere accumulation of relevant skills is not sufficient; there must also be intellectual and personal growth" to become successful.[80] Women should view secretarial work as a professional challenge that would result in a better version of themselves.[81]

The advice literature affirmed that upward mobility was possible for ambitious clerical women with career aspirations. For those seeking executive secretarial work, or even managerial roles, experts claimed that secretarial work offered opportunities to the "deserving secretary [who] wants to take a giant step on the Up road," according to the Whitcombs in *Strictly for Secretaries*.[82] To be sure, some jobs were dead end, but no secretary should ever feel trapped. What distinguishes "just 'another girl in the office'" from an executive secretary "lies in your willingness to prepare yourself for a career at the top," according to Flynn. In this way, hard work paid off in allowing for upward mobility. In support of meritocracy, Flynn maintained that "*what* you know" mattered more than "*who* you know" when trying to ascend to the executive floor. She claimed that anyone who had developed the requisite skills and disposition could start in a lower-level job like "running an old fashioned mimeography machine" and then move into a role as executive secretary. She referenced two friends who had made these sorts of career leaps and noted that they "look back with amusement on their humble start."[83]

Other advice books agreed that any secretary could forge a path upward if she was diligent, strategic, and ready to grow and develop. Lauria stated, "Better opportunities are the result of conscientious, hard work, and a readiness to perform as efficiently as possible in all phases of modern office routine."[84] According to author and experienced secretary Nell Braly Noyes, "Your future as a secretary is elastic. You have a wide range of fields from which to choose. Work is available in every area. Salaries vary from good to excellent. Advancement depends upon YOU. Our opportunities for success are unlimited." Noyes encouraged her readers to stay motivated by affirming the meritocratic ideal. Once she received a first small raise or promotion, a savvy secretary should take inventory of her professional goals. Noyes wrote: "Stop—look at yourself. Decide where you want to go next. Are you perfectly content to remain secretary to the same employer for the rest of your working days, or do you prefer to use the knowledge and acquired professional or business know-how to go on to an executive assistant's position or a court reporter's job or to launch out into business for yourself?"[85] The emphasis on individual agency imbued much of the advice literature, depicting girls at the office as limited only by their own ambitions. Lower-level clericals who wanted promotions to the executive secretarial ranks should seek formal and informal training and development opportunities. The *Private Secretary's Manual* encouraged motivated secretaries to inquire about their employer's training policies because "occasionally firms pay tuition" for satisfactory completion of approved courses.[86] But informal training could also benefit the ambitious secretary: "Anything you can do that rates in the improve-your-mind-or-personality category will also increase your value as a secretary." The Whitcombs recommended perusing books and newspapers, watching informative television shows, observing top secretaries, and even learning the history of the firm so that "you understand its workings and how you fit into the picture."[87] For curious secretaries with a learning mindset, the Gibbs School offered informative lectures to the public intermittently throughout the year on topics such as etiquette, health, and interviewing.[88]

Not only did the literature claim that those in routine clerical work could achieve status as an executive secretary, but it also touted the possibility for upward mobility from secretarial work into an array of managerial and executive roles. According to *Strictly for Secretaries*, "opportunity knocks enthusiastically for the girl with secretarial know-how," meaning that experience as a secretary proved valuable when transitioning to other careers. Many female professionals, including "department store buyers, magazine editors, copywriters, personnel experts, public relations executives, television directors, real estate brokers," had begun their careers in secretarial work. "Many women in top jobs today started as secretaries and learned the business while taking dictation and pounding typewriters." The Whitcombs wrote, for example, of a young woman who found a secretarial job in an advertising agency, learned the business, and then was promoted to a copywriter position.[89]

Other experts reaffirmed this path from support staff to autonomous professional. Even Gibbs School administrators began by the 1960s to market the degree as the first step on a career ladder into management or supervisory roles. In *You Can Be an Executive Secretary*, Marion Beck, a Gibbs School vice president, declared, "Secretarial training has led to fascinating careers for many women whose eagerness to learn on the job and to improve has remained constant." Former secretaries had moved into an array of fields as "authors, vice-presidents, researchers, administrative assistants, personnel directors, fashion editors, club leaders—even engineers." Mayo did temper the rags-to-riches depiction, shifting some of the responsibility away from individuals and toward organizations. She warned women who wanted "a serious career" to enter into "a large company with a broad 'mind' about women in high places." Nevertheless, she explained that many female managers and executives had started their careers as secretaries. Regarding the "lady boss," she told secretaries to "give her the benefit of the doubt" and "give her the respect that is due her" because "she probably once sat behind a desk like yours."[90]

In some key respects, messaging about secretarial work epitomized, and even sought to professionalize, the very feminine ideals that second-wave feminism would subvert in the late 1960s. Yet in other ways, the logics of secretarial work actually bolstered select second-wave values: women who were engaging in paid work did have potential to master a profession and achieve upward mobility. Some elements of the secretarial occupation—those emphasizing ambition, self-reliance, development, and competence—aligned with new ideas that women were capable of professional growth.

And since almost all secretaries were women, this occupation would have been a logical headliner for second-wave feminism. The second-wave feminist movement sought to bring awareness to the social and economic devaluation of women's labor, whether that labor was unpaid domestic work for loved ones in the home or paid support work to assist professional men in the labor force. If housewives were suffering, trapped in their suburban homes, then women in the typing pool and even the exalted private secretaries were trapped in workplace versions of the housewives' comfortable "concentration camps."[91] As the next section shows, critiques of the system that segregated office work along gendered lines were construed as critiques of the women themselves who were working in secretarial jobs.

⸙

"The women's movement has made women embarrassed to be secretaries," one longtime secretary told sociologist Rosabeth Moss Kanter in the 1970s.[92]

Some of the tension between feminist and secretary reprised conflicts evident in a first momentous protest of the movement. At the Miss America pageant in 1968, those undermining conventional gender norms were interpreted as casting reproach on the women who were fulfilling traditional roles. Carol Hanisch, a member of New York Radical Women and organizer of the protest, admitted that some of the actions were counterproductive, positioning women against one another as feminist protesters criticized the pageant and its contestants. Some of the protesters' activities and signs, "Miss America Sells It" and "Miss America Is a Big Falsie" among them, relayed messages that were "antiwoman" and against sisterhood, Hanisch later reflected: "Miss America and all beautiful women came off as our enemy instead of as our sisters who suffer with us." Although most of the protesters did not want such signs to be used, a few decided to use them anyway. One of the actions, crowning a live sheep, gave the impression that protesters saw pageant contestants as animals. Hanisch explained that the use of the sheep was supposed to represent that "we [women] are viewed as auction-block, docile animals."[93]

The myth that bras were burned in the Freedom Trash Can at the Miss America protest seized the popular imagination. But even if the public took no notice, protestors also were tossing into the trash stenography pads—emblems of the oppression of secretarial work. Feminists who were part of what Martha Weinman Lear famously coined the "second wave" in the New York Times Magazine in 1968 had several ideological problems with the myth and reality of secretarial work.[94] Whether most secretaries adhered to prescriptive literature or conformed to cultural depictions was irrelevant to new feminists, who were trying to overturn traditional gender norms. The role of secretary in so many ways epitomized what feminists were fighting against. The main issue with secretarial work, from the feminist perspective, was the idea that it represented the entrenchment of male patriarchy. Feminists perceived the individual relationships between women and men, whether at home or at work, as representative of larger problems regarding gender and power. The organizational charts of nearly every firm in every industry had developed over decades such that women existed in lower-paid clerical support roles, on separate ladders from men, who were advancing into higher-paid managerial positions. Feminists had major issues with the construction of economic, political, and social institutions whereby women, based on their sex alone, occupied positions of lower status and had limited opportunities. More than one feminist aligned secretarial work with prostitution, according to historian Julie Berebitsky.[95]

In Lear's famous article, NOW members were shown picketing with signs such as "WOMEN CAN THINK as well as TYPE," suggesting that typing was distinct from thinking: in other words, clerical work did not require strong analytical skills. According to Lear, NOW was protesting laws and ideas that "exclude [women] from jobs that [utilized] intelligence in any significant way."[96] Writing about the popular image of clerical work in the *New York Times*, journalist Judy Klemesrud explained that a secretary represented a number of uncomplimentary female stereotypes: a "gum-chewing sex kitten; husband hunter; miniskirted ding-a-ling; slow-witted pencil pusher; office 'go-fer'; reliable old shoe."[97] In other words, a secretary could be viewed as sexually alluring, maternal, or dull; or she might be all of these at different moments. Second-wave feminist ideology aimed to debunk gender stereotyping. It contended that ideas about working women as sexy, motherly, or slow represented notions that furthered essentialist thinking. The feminist agenda sought to uncover the historical and social meanings prescribed to sex identity, showing that gendered generalizations about secretaries were at best inaccurate and at worst harmful to women's status.[98]

Regarding the notion of secretary as "sex kitten," feminists remained split about whether greater sexual freedom would advance or degrade women's status. These opposing viewpoints—sex as oppression versus sex as liberation—existed in tension. In particular—and especially relevant here—there were competing views in the growing body of working women's literature aimed at professional development and career success. On the one hand, women, like men, should be socially permitted to pursue sexual desires and be viewed as serious professionals at work, according to famed journalist and founding editor of *Cosmopolitan* Helen Gurley Brown.[99] On the other hand, sexual relations at work could undermine a woman's professional status, according to founding editor of *Ms.* magazine and cofounder of National Women's Political Caucus, Letty Cottin Pogrebin. Although Brown too considered herself a "devout feminist," Pogrebin represented a more mainstream, liberal voice in the movement.[100] She warned against using the office to find romance, counseling women, "Don't sex around in your bread-and-butter bailiwick," which could undermine professional respect from colleagues.[101]

Pogrebin's directives actually echoed the line of the Gibbs School on sex, as both the Gibbs School and the new feminists sought to bring professional respect to women at work. In a chapter of *You Can Be an Executive Secretary* entitled "Lady, Behave," Gibbs instructor Lucy Graves Mayo warned aspiring executive secretaries: "no coyness, no teasing, no *conscious* flirting, no 'little me' helplessness." And if by chance "romance does develop between you and one of your *un*married co-workers, make nothing of it on the company premises." As for romance with married men, "terribly messy," according to Mayo, resulting in "lost job" and "dubious reputation." Another section, "How to Tie Up a Wolf," coached women on avoiding attention from an "Office Wolf," or man who forwards sexual innuendos: "If you encourage (or seem to) Old Wolf's attentions, you will surely get them."[102]

Yet many women tolerated the "office woods" specifically because they hoped to find a suitable husband at work.[103] A Gallup Poll in 1952 found that working as a secretary was rated as the top job for finding a husband (with more than twice the number of votes as nurse, the second-best occupation for finding a husband).[104] A *New York Times* article in 1961 declared that secretaries demanded a "company well-stocked with eligible men," according to anecdotes from employment agencies and personnel managers.[105]

Taking a job to find a husband ran contrary to feminist notions of autonomy and equality. Liberal feminists wanted legal equality between the sexes so that women could have greater choice about whether they wanted to marry (instead of having to marry, and stay married, for economic sustenance). Many radical feminists rejected the institution of marriage as oppressive to women and discerned no plausible way to separate it from patriarchy. Writer Sheila Cronan was one among many outspoken voices who believed that "marriage is a form of slavery."[106] Writer Ti-Grace Atkinson perceived married women as "hostages."[107]

Liberal and radical feminist ideology also challenged another popular secretarial trope: the office wife. Working as an office wife meant supporting and caring for men, as well as complying with traditional gender roles that maintained occupational segregation. Wife and secretary complemented each other, with the secretarial office wife meeting the boss's basic needs at work, much as a wife did for her husband at home. According to the *Private Secretary's Manual* in 1963, secretaries were called office wives "not because they attempt to usurp the rights and privileges of their executives' wives, but because they are usually as thoughtful, kind, and helpful in the office as the most ideal wife could be in the home." A great secretary might take initiative and go get a "well-balanced meal" for her boss, postponing her own lunch to suit the lunch plans and meeting schedule of her boss.[108] Attending to the boss's personal needs constituted part of the job. The *Complete Secretary's Handbook* (1951) contained a subsection on "How to Do Your Employer's Personal Work Effectively." It instructed secretaries about how to keep a record of birthdays and wedding anniversaries, including what presents were given each year and the approximate cost of the gift, so that the boss would not repeat the same gift. If the boss had a family member who passed away, the *Handbook* instructed the secretary as to how to record the cards and flowers received and then send an acknowledgment note to the gift giver. It also gave instructions on managing the boss's personal funds, including his bank account, bills, and personal stocks and other investments.[109] In a chapter of *Strictly for Secretaries* entitled "The Care and Pleasing of Bosses," the Whitcombs described how a secretary should prepare the office before the boss arrived: "She opens the windows to give the room a brief airing, adjusts the blinds, and regulates the heat. Then she dusts his desk and get it in order—sharpens pencils, fills his pens, flips his calendar to the right page, winds his clock, waters plants, checks for matches, and sees to it that he has a sufficient supply of note pad, paper, and other equipment he might need."[110] Such preparation allowed the boss to maximize his time at the office, much as a wife cared for the physical space in the home.

The career trajectory of the secretary depended on the career trajectory of her boss: "the clever secretary . . . grows with her chief," much as a wife's social status improved with the promotion of her husband.[111] For example, Mary Lepis, who worked as executive secretary to Roger Birk, the chairman, president, and CEO of Merrill Lynch, claimed she did not "feel powerful," though the *Los Angeles Times* begged to differ: "Mary Lepis controls access to her boss and, since her boss is everybody's boss, she is certainly among the most powerful people at Merrill Lynch."[112] While much of the literature stressed that the secretary's career success depended on the boss, in reality the boss's career success also could depend on the support of a great secretary. "I think a great portion of the success of any executive depends to a large extent on his secretary," said a retired Texas pipeline executive. Even the U.S. president recognized the crucial role of secretaries to the smooth functioning of larger institutions. President Gerald Ford acknowledged, in commemoration of National Secretaries Week: "There is one service that can never be overestimated—and that is the work of the secretary."[113] An executive's wife played a similar role. Sociologist William H. Whyte acknowledged that a wife was pivotal to her husband's career success: "The corporation now concedes, one of the principal members of its community remains officially almost unnoticed; to wit, the Wife."[114]

While the lot of secretaries and bosses was deeply entwined, with each affecting the other's job performance, the boss ultimately had unilateral power to sever the relationship. Other than quitting her job, the secretary could not extricate herself from her boss, nor could she pursue an independent career plan without her boss's blessing. Her job description was to serve. One manual told secretaries, "To a certain degree, your satisfaction depends on the boss's being satisfied. It is like a wide circle and you are the beginning and the end of the line that draws the circle. It is up to you."[115] The boss could be eccentric or whimsical, but the secretary was expected to remain loyal and prioritize his needs. Advice literature told women to "be loyal" to their supervisor and avoid what was called job hopping. In fact, loyalty in an executive secretary was construed as more important than ability, given the secretary's access to confidential information.[116]

The office, therefore, replicated the inequalities of marriage, as many feminists viewed both institutions as reflecting a devaluation of women's work. In "The Politics of Housework," radical feminist Pat Mainardi described the popular perception that household chores were trivial, which she saw as proof that men's work earned more social and economic value than did women's work. Similarly, Mainardi explained, the work performed by managers or bosses earned much higher wages than did the work performed by secretaries.[117] The segregation of men into managerial work and women into clerical work also reflected an understanding that men were more capable of analytical, higher-level thinking, and women were naturally suited to take care of others. Built on decades of separate-spheres ideology, the relationship between bosses and secretaries sustained the family-wage ideal.[118] Such ideas allowed employers to maintain much lower pay scales for clerical workers and keep women relegated to office support jobs.

Undermining separate-spheres ideology, feminists argued that men and women had similar capabilities for reasoning, analysis, and decision making, rejecting biological and social rationales for separate spheres. The secretarial job function of "office wife" bothered feminists who wanted women to reject sex stereotypes, free themselves from dependence on men, and instead pursue their own interests and passions. In *The Feminine Mystique*, Betty Friedan famously wrote that the American suburban housewife lived in a "comfortable concentration camp"; these women had become "dependent, passive; childlike; they have given up their adult frame of reference to live at the lower human level of food and things."[119] In Friedan's perspective, housewife was not a profession that could lead to self-fulfillment. Secretaries, much like wives, were ignoring calls to become independent and establish their own distinct identities.

While feminists rarely intended to blame women for entering female-dominated careers such as secretarial work, teaching, or nursing, they did try to expose and rectify the processes that underlay these desires and choices. Growing up in a "male chauvinist society," according to one feminist, meant that a "young woman with an inclination toward medicine . . . may feel she has made a free choice" when she pursues nursing. Young women came of age seeing that women in health care were nurses, not doctors.[120] Like nursing, secretarial work was chosen by women who grew up in an era of strict gender norms and limited career choices. Showing women that social forces, not biological truths, had pushed them toward certain types of jobs, beliefs, and behaviors was part of the feminist mission.

In fact, secretarial manuals acknowledged that many young girls chose secretarial work to suit the realities of occupational segregation. Mayo warned that "sometimes career choice is a compromise between idealism and realism," meaning that a woman may have to settle for secretarial work in her field of interest. "You might, for instance, choose to be a lawyer's or a doctor's or a scientist's secretary because you once hoped to be a lawyer or a doctor or a scientist."[121] Another manual echoed sentiments about secretarial work as a compromise between individual interests and social norms. "Common sense told [a] young woman that a seat on the stock exchange was probably not in the picture for her, but becoming an executive secretary to someone important in the field surely could be."[122] Among its major successes, second-wave feminism revealed how sex-role stereotyping limited women's opportunities.

And nothing could be more stereotypical than a woman working as a secretary. To fight against sex stereotyping, women needed to actively reject traditional prescriptions for themselves. Gloria Steinem told students at Smith College to refuse to learn how to type so that they could avoid secretarial work.[123] Betty Friedan urged secretaries to cover their typewriters and join the feminist movement. Some feminists even saw secretaries as suffering from "false consciousness," complicit in the "sexual oppression" that Friedan and others wanted to end.[124] That secretaries cared for their male bosses constituted a matter of political significance, demonstrating the ideology of male chauvinism at work in employment relationships.[125]

In the view of onlookers, however, feminists were urging women to revolt against traditional gender norms, and the movement became synonymous with its most sensational acts: discarding bras into a Freedom Trash Can outside the Miss America Pageant in 1968, for example, which was falsely reported as "bra burning."[126] Calls for women to reject housework, throw away cosmetics, and refuse to have sex with their husbands ultimately marginalized a large portion of nonactivist women who either did not want to shed traditional gender roles completely or engaged with traditional gender roles as their best option for earning a living. In short, a critique of the sexism that produced the secretarial class was construed as a critique of secretaries themselves.

That second-wave feminism marginalized many women is not a new story—depending, of course, on how one defines *second wave*. In addition to marginalizing women who conformed to traditional gender roles, elements of second-wave feminism also isolated other feminist activists based on their difference from key actors. Feminist theorists in the 1980s and 1990s demonstrated that if liberal feminism, which NOW represented, was at the core of the second wave, then the priorities of many women based on color and class were being overlooked. Feminist scholar bell hooks, for example, charged Friedan with "narcissism, insensitivity, sentimentality, and self-indulgence" because Friedan's notion of sisterhood overlooked the diversity of female experience.[127] An entire body of theory emerged to reflect the priorities of women of color, revealing that intersecting identities of race and sex led to different experiences and therefore different feminist agendas. Identity as a woman might not be the most significant factor for many women of color, who were fighting against multiple systems of oppression.[128]

Where Friedan saw oppression based on gender, as experienced by white housewives or white secretaries, Black feminists saw privilege. Black women saw clerical work as an opportunity for higher-paid, higher-status work, especially since employers often relegated Black women to lower paid and less genteel work. Historian Jacqueline Jones explained that white standards of beauty relegated any Black women who were performing clerical jobs to back office positions without public contact.[129] Several court cases in the 1960s and 1970s concerned qualified Black women in the South who were placed in lower-paying production jobs after applying for clerical positions in textile mills.[130] In other words, access to clerical work was a civil right that Black women *sought*. Even in the public sector, white women enjoyed access to jobs from which Black women were excluded. A New York City official claimed that when hiring a secretary to work in the Department of Commerce and Industrial Development, white applicants were preferred "because it is in an office where important officials are greeted."[131] As the government began collecting more demographic data on the workforce in the 1960s, proof of the absence of Black women in the clerical work category became apparent, as historian Katherine Turk reveals in Equal Employment Opportunity Commission records.[132]

Given this history of exclusion, access to secretarial work could elevate the status of Black women and their families. In 1930 less than 5 percent of clerical workers were Black women. Those who were employed worked the lowest-paying pink-collar jobs, where they had no direct contact with the public.[133] Activist Dorothy Height remembered that young Black women working in the federal government never moved out of the typing pool: "Whenever there was a top [secretarial] job available, they [federal officials] would come and look them over and usually select a white girl."[134] Still, office work was a status symbol in the 1930s Black community in Chicago. Era Bell Thompson, who worked as a clerk before becoming a journalist and editor, recalled that on the bus or streetcar after work, "the blacks who had clerical jobs put their pencils behind their ears, to show that they were clerks."[135]

Many newspapers, both mainstream and historically Black, reported on the achievements of Black women who were breaking the race barrier to gain a professional foothold in an office. The *Boston Globe* and the *New York Herald Tribune* ran articles in 1951 commending Mrs. Ruth Williams as the "first Negro ever named to the post of Governor's secretary," citing her husband and daughter as "proud and pleased" about her professional standing.[136] In the Illinois Labor Department, "Miss Etta Mae Porter Cracks the Color Line" as an "attractive young secretary in the state labor director's office," to be the first African American employed in the office. She claimed that "everyone is so very nice I haven't had time to even stop and think 'I'm a Negro.'"[137] The *Chicago Defender* also celebrated Dorothy R. Bishop's status as "the first Negro member of the Lake Shore chapter of the National Secretaries Association," the largest NSA chapter in the country. Bishop announced during her initiation that she would "continue to do everything I can to maintain the respect and prestige of secretaries and of the Lake Shore chapter."[138] More first Black secretaries were reported in Tennessee and Florida. Mrs. Leon Cox became the first African American, male or female, to work on staff for a southern congressman. She became the secretary for Representative Fulton (D-Tenn.).[139] In 1963 the Florida regional office of the Veterans Administration hired two Black secretaries, both honors graduates of the Gibbs School.[140] Even in the private sector, the president of 20th Century Fox hired a Black personal secretary in 1962.[141] For most in the Black community, office work symbolized not dependence and submissiveness but upward mobility and even racial uplift for the entire Black community.

In addition to racial differences, class distinctions could also distance some white women from liberal and radical strains of feminism. Although the liberal agenda sought to increase women's economic opportunities and political rights, some white, working-class women prioritized their roles as wives and mothers. Even many women who held paid jobs outside the home had less interest in gaining status and identity from career advancement. They viewed the concerns of middle-class, college-educated feminists who wanted access to men's professional jobs as remote from their own problems of economic security. Other working-class women used labor unions and voluntary associations (such as the Women's Trade Union League and the Coalition for Labor Union Women) to advance gender equity on the job. Research by historians Annelise Orleck, Dorothy Sue Cobble, and Lane Windham provides alternative visions of feminism by finding collective activism among working women and their allies who lobbied for economic justice.[142] These scholarly contributions prove that our understanding of feminist activism has often neglected working-class women.

Whatever the reasons, in the late 1960s the feminist and the secretary were opposite and elementally incompatible identities in the popular imagination. Reconciling the messaging at the heart of both roles was difficult for a number of women, including many nonwhite and working-class women who had different economic priorities and realities, as well as women with different views of traditional gender roles and those with more optimistic ideas of the professional status of secretarial work and the possibility of upward mobility through clerical occupations.

During the historic Women's Strike for Equality in 1970, NOW chose the Katharine Gibbs School as one of its few stops on the historical march through Manhattan. Sixty members of NOW pushed their way into the lobby of the Gibbs School on Park Avenue to confront Gibbs president Alan L. Baker.[143] According to a Gibbs insider, the women charged the Gibbs School with perpetuating occupational segregation because no men were enrolled, to which Baker replied that no men had applied. Then they questioned Baker about the dress code of white gloves, to which Baker replied, "We don't expect our girls to wear white gloves and hats anymore." NOW immediately reminded Baker that the students should be referred to as women, not girls.[144]

That NOW chose the Gibbs School as one of its few stops was deliberate, since historically the school trained the most coveted and competent secretaries. In the mind of the second-wave feminist, what paid job could be more closely associated with the performance of femininity than the job of secretary? Success as a secretary depended on more than objective skills; it depended on mastering intangible feminine values as well as attributes of service and loyalty.

Feminist ideas influenced even the corporate marketing of word processors. The text for a magazine advertisement for Redactron in 1971 read, "The dead-end secretary is dead for two big reasons—one is the change in you—unlike previous generations you want challenging work."[145] Secretarial work became increasingly dead-end, relative to new career prospects for women that promised higher salaries and greater status into the 1970s and 1980s.

Increasingly, to be liberated was not only to acknowledge the social construction of gender, but also to reject traits, behaviors, and tasks that had defined femininity for decades—and secretarial work epitomized so many of those traits. In 1972, second-wave feminists who were part of the National Women's Political Caucus adopted the slogan, "Make policy, not coffee!" Caucus members were rejecting expectations that in political campaign work, women should make the coffee for male volunteers, staff, and candidates.[146] Yet the message clearly posited traditionally female work (making coffee) as inferior and oppositional to traditionally male work (making policy). The two identities—feminist and secretary—were difficult to reconcile in the popular mind, particularly given the media's distortions of feminism and its creation of a catfight sideshow.[147]

Secretaries had several options to consider if they wanted to reconcile their "dead-end jobs" with the larger cultural milieu of feminism and their new opportunities for professional jobs. One potential response was to continue the professionalization project that institutions such as the Gibbs chain and the National Secretaries Association had begun decades earlier. Women could argue that secretarial work was valuable and professional, on par with other career choices. Dagmar Miller, executive secretary to several prominent newspaper editors, penned a retort in the *Washington Post* to perceived attacks from the women's movement. She outlined the ways in which feminist ideas belittled secretaries, including her hostility to the oft-repeated warning to young girls to not learn how to type lest they be stuck in a dead-end job like hers. She criticized Betty Friedan's comment to *McCall's* magazine that a young woman was "too intelligent to be a secretary for long." As a graduate of Duke University and the Gibbs School, Miller disclosed that she proudly wore her Phi Beta Kappa key to her secretarial job: "I might upgrade my whole profession. You know, sort of 'you can be a secretary and smart, too.'" Yet she joked that her efforts were futile: "I only succeeded in downgrading the image of PBK!"[148]

Another proposed response from secretaries was to embrace the new feminist ideas and become assertive to bosses and fight for access to higher wages and promotions. The feminist movement propelled some clerical women into rebellion at their offices, as they pushed to overturn long-standing norms about wearing skirts or unstated expectations that women should make the coffee. These revolts could be individual acts of resistance or take the form of collection action.

In these ways and others, secretaries of the 1970s—even those who did not identify as members of an overtly feminist organization—began to question the job duties and office policies rooted in traditional gender norms. A grassroots movement for office workers' rights arose in cities across the nation. One such organization, 9to5, began in Boston in 1972, two years after the Women's Strike for Equality. The Boston-area clerical workers who started this labor organization sought to bring awareness to their workplace problems, which included low pay, lack of promotions, and mistreatment from superiors. They wanted to convince other workers that their individual economic problems were part of a systemic pattern of sex-based workplace discrimination. To appeal to the majority of clericals, however, these activists would have to navigate carefully their complicated relationship with second-wave feminism.

2

AT THE INTERSECTION OF SEX EQUALITY
AND ECONOMIC JUSTICE

I n 1972 eight waitresses at Cronin's Restaurant in Cambridge, Massachusetts, decided that they wanted respect for their work and dignity as food servers. Instead of joining the Hotel Employees and Restaurant Employees Union (HERE), they formed their own entity: the Harvard Square Waitresses Organizing Committee (HSWOC).[1] Fighting for more than higher wages, they believed that creating their own organization better represented their demands for respect and dignity as women workers. The Harvard Square waitresses, who did not refer to themselves as feminists, waged a labor and legal battle for months, supported by over twenty other local organizations, including Women for Action against Sexism, Students for a Democratic Society, and the Cambridge Ministers.[2]

Previous scholars have shown that throughout U.S. history, working women questioned, challenged, and protested institutionalized sexism in their workplaces, which often intersected with matters of economic justice.[3] Yet less attention has been given to why and how women formed their own grassroots organizations instead of joining existing associations. Similar to Annelise Orleck's industrial feminists or Dorothy Sue Cobble's labor feminists, women workers in the 1970s found voice by protesting workplace issues at the intersection of sex and class bias. Yet unlike industrial feminists (such as Rose Schneiderman) or labor feminists (such as Myra Wolfgang), some working women of the 1970s were wary of joining long-standing trade unions and instead launched their own groups. In the process, they gained leadership experience: they crafted an agenda to address their own concerns and developed networks to cultivate support for other women office workers.

This chapter addresses the how and why of forming a grassroots organization for women office workers. How did women found such organizations, and why were current institutions inadequate to remedy their concerns? Karen Nussbaum became inspired to cofound 9to5 after participating regularly in picket duty for the Harvard Square waitresses. A former University of Chicago student, Nussbaum paid her bills by working as a secretary at the Harvard Graduate School of Education while she pursued social justice advocacy. She started to "realize the potential that existed in confronting the employer with the power of women's rights." When forming 9to5 in 1972, Nussbaum remembers, "We never used the term *feminist*." She continued, "I wanted to work with women in their own lives—not as part of a women's movement organization, but with women as workers."[4] Nussbaum and the other nine clerical workers who started the new labor organization sought to bring awareness to the workplace problems of Boston-area clericals, which included low pay, lack of promotions, and mistreatment from superiors. 9to5 leaders wanted to convince other workers that their individual economic problems were part of a systemic pattern of sex-based workplace discrimination. To appeal to the majority of clericals, however, they would have to navigate, carefully, their relationship with feminism. 9to5 founders had to contend with clericals' notions about the new feminist movement, ideas that evidenced and even fueled racial and class disparities among women office workers.

Although Nussbaum did not enlist any mainstream feminist groups in the creation of 9to5, the development of the new organization relied on conceptual underpinnings of second-wave feminism. The feminist insistence that sex was not destiny and that biology should not determine social roles inspired many clerical women to question their job duties, pay, career paths, and even corporate policies that mandated skirts.[5] The societal influence of feminism was beginning to soften the once stark distinction between appropriate male and female roles.

But as we will see, as a labor organization that was arising from a new feminist ideology, 9to5 faced an inherent challenge from the start. The women's movement cast suspicion on women who performed traditional gender roles as it worked to disrupt sex stereotyping. Given the occupational history, that for most of the twentieth century clerical work was performed by women in service to men, to be a feminist secretary almost seemed like an oxymoron. There definitely were some. Secretary and feminist Kathi Roche published a critique entitled "The Secretary: Capitalism's House Nigger" in 1975. Although secretaries, mostly white women, were not slaves in terms of legal, social, or political standing, her intended point was that secretaries performed valuable work even though they were stigmatized servants who had no chance of assuming higher status.[6] Despite the seemingly stark distinction between the two roles, many secretaries, though they did not categorize their problems as sex-based discrimination, did start to notice, resent, and question specific gendered aspects of their jobs.

❦

Nussbaum came of age during a period of collective social protest, when a number of causes were mobilizing students: the anti–Vietnam War movement, the civil rights and Black power movements, Cesar Chavez's farmworkers' movement, and a burgeoning feminist movement. Progressive activists engaged in these issues shared certain values and ideals. These included the importance of free speech and freedom of assembly, a distrust of existing authority figures, a greater appreciation for individual rights, and an aspiration to create and maintain a pluralistic society.[7] Nussbaum, born in 1950, was raised in a Jewish family that encouraged activism for social justice and civil rights.[8] She grew up in the affluent, white, Highland Park suburb of Chicago.[9] As a young adult Nussbaum felt strongly that she should act to remedy social problems, and her early career aspiration was to become a social worker. She describes herself as "coming of age when the whole world was blowing apart," believing that "social justice was something that you should fight for." In high school she started an organization that invited progressive speakers from the community to the school. She participated in peace demonstrations in Chicago as her brother resisted the draft.[10] Although she lost, Nussbaum ran for class president in high school, largely because "no girl had ever been president" and she "hated the guy who was running."[11]

When Nussbaum entered the University of Chicago in 1968, she was eager to find new opportunities for activism.[12] She joined the Black Panther Support Committee, a radical sect of the civil rights movement, traveling to New Haven, Connecticut, to protest the imprisonment of Bobby Seale (a Black Panther accused of aiding in the torture and murder of another Black Panther). Yet when she attended a Students for a Democratic Society (SDS) meeting for the first time, the sexist culture repulsed her: "Boys would argue with boys for hours and [they] were giving incredibly long speeches to each other and girls would stand around in circles and listen to them." Male control over the organization's platform was just "what it was like in those days." Rather than take part in SDS, she devoted time to other organizations that gave her and other women more decision-making power.[13]

In 1970 Nussbaum took a leave of absence from the University of Chicago to travel to Cuba along with about seven hundred other American students. She participated in Venceremos Brigade, an effort to support the Cuban Revolution and defy the U.S. government's blockade of Cuba.[14] The revolutionary spirit in Cuba energized Nussbaum, and she became further convinced of the possibility for political and social change.[15] After her trip to Cuba, she did not return to the University of Chicago.[16] She moved to Boston instead, feeling that "academic advancement was not the most interesting thing happening" in the early 1970s, and she wanted to be "totally engaged in trying to fix things that need[ed] fixing."[17] Nussbaum took a clerk-typist job at Harvard University to support herself but then spent time working for the People's Coalition for Peace and Justice, an antiwar organization, where she gained leadership experience giving speeches, running meetings, and raising money.[18] Furthermore, Nussbaum and her three female roommates acted on their own accord; for example, they advanced the antiwar cause by making leaflets and handing them out on street corners.[19]

In the early 1970s Nussbaum began to turn her attention specifically to women's issues. She was less engaged in the National Organization for Women platform; rather, she took part in what she called "a more radical movement." She and other Harvard staff women barricaded themselves inside a university building to protest the absence of a community women's center and the lack of affordable childcare in Cambridge. After a few weeks their efforts resulted in the formation of the Cambridge Women's

Center in 1972.[20] In addition, Nussbaum and her roommates initiated and participated in women-only groups that sought to educate and empower other women in their communities. They held courses in their living room on topics ranging from auto mechanics to political theory to emergency medicine. She says that her group, Female Revolutionary Education, was not really extraordinary; such female groups "were happening everywhere and we weren't particularly the biggest or the best or the most interesting thing."[21] In fact, several women's liberation organizations emerged in Boston in the late 1960s: Bread and Roses, an early socialist-feminist group of educated women and female graduate students; Cell 16, which encouraged women to abstain from intercourse with men; and the Boston Women's Health Book Collective, which in 1973 published the first commercial book on women's health, *Our Bodies, Ourselves.*[22]

With the waitresses' strike at Cronin's Restaurant in 1972 and the formation of the Harvard Square waitresses committee, Nussbaum made a conceptual connection between women's issues and labor issues. While on picket duty, she began to realize that the larger second-wave movement was changing working women's expectations of fair workplace practices, and it was encouraging them to speak up. She believed that great potential existed in "combining the desire for women to be first class citizens in the workplace . . . with women's rights."[23] She stated in 2003, "The women's movement had as its targets cultural values or public services, or legal rights. But there wasn't really a demand [for women's equality] as workers—there was demand about opportunity for better jobs, but not quite in this way, about how you would use the power of an institution on the job, to demand change for women and in which women could become more powerful." She believed that "the women's movement was bubbling among working-class women" as seen in the ways women like the Cronin waitresses were protesting for better wages, improved working conditions, and greater respect. Nussbaum perceived the mainstream second-wave movement as organized by professional women to meet the needs of professional women. However, she saw a gap in the feminist platform concerning the needs of those in low-paying, female-dominated jobs.[24]

Still, the onset of second-wave feminism was essential to the work she would accomplish (even though in contemporary interviews, when Nussbaum reflects on the founding of 9to5, she has emphasized that she did not identify with the mainstream feminist movement).[25] A new feminism was changing baseline attitudes about gender norms and affecting the attitudes of clericals toward their jobs. For instance, before she started 9to5, Nussbaum noticed that another woman in her office was reading Robin Morgan's *Sisterhood Is Powerful*, an anthology of historic and revolutionary feminist essays published in 1970. Nussbaum claims that she had never read the book herself, but she was struck by the fact that this colleague, a woman who did not participate in formal activism, was reading this feminist manifesto: "I began to realize that the ideas of women's liberation had seeped down almost everywhere, and though the women in the office would have rejected being part of a women's organization, or identifying with the media's image of women's liberation, they were questioning what was happening to them."[26] She realized that the feminist movement was shifting women's expectations of what they deserved at work.

Nussbaum formed her own group that could respond to the needs of working-class women such as the Cronin waitresses or Harvard typists.[27] Her experience in other advocacy efforts equipped her with the necessary skills to form a flexible organization that would empower its members and adapt to the changing problems they were facing.[28] Like radical feminists Mary King and Casey Hayden, who split from the civil rights movement and the New Left, Nussbaum also pursued her own agenda while utilizing strategies and values from previous movements. She and her friend Ellen Cassedy saw themselves as diverging from existing options to construct a grassroots organization for clerical workers.[29]

A student with Nussbaum at the University of Chicago, Cassedy also moved to Boston and worked as a Harvard clerical. She had grown up in Baltimore and Long Island with parents who were civil rights advocates. Similar to Nussbaum, Cassedy was a white woman from a liberal, middle-class family, and she too had pursued activism at an early age. When she was thirteen years old, she raised her own travel money to attend the March on Washington in 1963, and as a teenager, she participated in demonstrations for fair housing and against the war in Vietnam. She left Chicago to finish her undergraduate degree at the University of California, Berkeley, where she supported the nascent women's studies program and joined consciousness-raising groups. After graduating with a degree in U.S. women's history, Cassedy moved to Boston, becoming active in anti-war work and helping to organize a multi-issue, single-day community conference called the Women's Assembly. For income, she took a job alongside Nussbaum as a clerical worker at Harvard, giving the two friends common work experiences that fueled their activism. As 9to5 took shape, Cassedy would work more in the background, and Nussbaum would become the public face of the budding organization.[30]

Together Nussbaum and Cassedy gathered eight other like-minded women to start the Harvard Office Workers Group.[31] In 1972 they met on Wednesdays at noon to discuss the disrespect they encountered from Harvard students and professors, as well as the financial strain they endured as low-paid office workers.[32] According to Nussbaum, the inchoate Harvard Office Workers Group lacked a long-term plan and "didn't really know how to move things ahead."[33] In its first year of existence, the group protested a wage freeze at Harvard that limited staff pay raises to 5 percent. Despite obtaining 250 signatures on their petition and meeting with the head of personnel, the women did not succeed in getting the freeze rescinded. They did, however, get the university to agree to publish Harvard's wage policies in the *Harvard Gazette*, which promoted greater transparency about salary structures.[34] Nussbaum remembers that in the first year of the Harvard Office Workers Group, members realized that they were part of something bigger: a movement of women who felt stuck in sex-segregated jobs. Another group of clericals, Women Office Workers at Harvard, had constructed a memo, "Re: Alterations in the Job of Secretary," which requested an end to unjust and disrespectful practices. Although management granted a pay raise, Harvard administrators ignored other complaints about professional respect and promotional opportunities.[35]

Nussbaum recalled of this time that "there were isolated little bubbles of insurgency everywhere" among Harvard's staff.[36] Indeed, in the 1970s secretaries constituted just one of several groups of Harvard employees who were collectively fighting for higher salaries and greater respect.[37] The unionized workers in the Harvard Printing Office and Typing and Copy Center went on strike for over ten weeks, concerning wage rates, in 1974.[38] Dining hall employees struck in 1976.[39] A secretary in the Physics Department started the Harvard Employee Organizing Committee in the spring of 1974 to affiliate the three thousand nonmedical Harvard office workers with District 65 of the Distributive Workers of America.[40] Employees in the medical school and hospital started the Harvard Union of

Clerical and Technical Workers (HUCTW), which campaigned for nearly fifteen years before winning recognition from Harvard administrators in the late 1980s under the leadership of organizer Kristine Rondeau.[41] The Harvard Business School Staff Association of nearly a hundred members published a newsletter and negotiated specific grievances with administrators and faculty (such as requesting the "privilege of eating in the Faculty Club"), while in general seeking "recognition . . . as a legitimate and professional constituency of HBS."[42] In 1974 staff members of the Harvard Divinity School petitioned for a greater voice in their school budget, winning paid tuition for Harvard courses, written salary reviews, open communication between administrators and staff, and representatives on the budget committee.[43]

Harvard's female faculty also took part in efforts to advance equity. Women constituted less than 2 percent of tenured faculty at Harvard in the early 1970s, and they received unequal pay relative to male colleagues.[44] Female faculty across the campus formed Women Employed at Harvard (WEH) in 1972 to lobby the university administration to take affirmative action more seriously.[45] The *Harvard Crimson* reported that one of WEH's greatest successes was its diversity in membership and its attempt to advocate for women at all levels within the university. WEH recruited "salary and wage" (S&W) employees, as Harvard called the nonexempt workers, to join their efforts, and soon around a hundred women became involved in the cause.[46] The organization sought to "include everyone and exclude no one" by making its founding principles broad enough to encompass the concerns of Harvard women at various occupational levels.[47]

While protests by faculty and staff were spreading across campus, Nussbaum and Cassedy set their sights on the world beyond Harvard Yard. They wanted to build a citywide organization that engaged women office workers across the community. They recruited other friends in Boston who worked as clericals, such as Marilyn Albert, who worked at a hospital, and Penny Kurland, who worked in an insurance company, and formed a consciousness-raising group for women's workplace concerns. The ten founding members, according to Nussbaum, "told each other our stories about how we got to be where we were . . . and then we talked about what kind of an organization we wanted to create. And out of that, we built 9to5." She recalled, "There was no organizational form for working women to express themselves in the women's movement but the ideas of women's equality [were] everywhere." In the early days of 9to5, according to Nussbaum, the approach was "practical organizing that met people where they were with the kinds of issues that they had."[48] The immediate needs of office workers would dictate the form and function of the organization.

When it came to setting an agenda for 9to5, perhaps the clearest symbol of disrespect was the matter of making and serving coffee. The fact that men in the office always assumed that women should make coffee in the morning, rarely offering to take a turn or say thank you, encapsulated the anger and dissatisfaction of some office workers about their jobs. One columnist for the *Chicago Tribune* claimed that the issue of secretaries making coffee had acquired the same symbolic importance as the proliferation of reports about bra burning outside the Miss America Pageant in 1968.[49] The National Secretaries Association noted that with the advent of feminism had emerged a "great commotion about the so-called go-fer issue that largely centered on going for coffee."[50]

Nussbaum and Cassedy used the making and serving of coffee to publicize early gatherings of the Harvard Office Workers Group. Around the campus, they hung posters with a simple graphic—an upended coffee cup—as well as a meeting time and place. Nussbaum said that the image of the overturned coffee cup "resonated with people, that there were these unspoken issues, but everyone kind of knew" the larger significance of the picture.[51] During the first few meetings of the Harvard Office Workers Group, Nussbaum noted, "[The women] talked endlessly about the issue of who got the coffee. I know it sounds ridiculous, but women did not want to feel they were office wives. They were real workers with real jobs, and making coffee symbolized the lower-class status of women as workers.[52]" Refusing to make coffee was a form of resistance for those in the growing office workers' movement.[53] Many women wanted to shed long-standing expectations that they assume the unassigned, domestic chores in the office as the proxy wife. They were realizing through feminist messaging that men did not share in these necessary but unrewarded tasks.[54]

The ten women who started 9to5 spent their first year discussing the similar problems they faced as office workers while also planning the future strategy and structure of their organization.[55] They published a newsletter for and about Boston-area office workers, initially distributing it through other activist networks like the antiwar movement and at local feminist meetings, including a multi-issue women's conference that Cassedy organized.[56] While using these channels helped to enlighten other progressives, they wanted to get their newsletters directly into the hands of office workers who were likely not involved in these activist circles. The founding 9to5 members decided to distribute the leaflets in the mornings before work at different subway stations as well as outside the biggest insurance companies in Boston.[57] Within several months they had disseminated five thousand copies, which prompted some interested readers to contact 9to5 and request subscriptions to the newsletter.[58]

9to5 founders made a conscious effort to present themselves as fellow clericals, not as elites or radical activists. When handing out newsletters, they dressed in office attire instead of jeans (since blue jeans could signify more progressive politics).[59] Cassedy remembers, "We were very very careful to make sure that whoever spoke for the organization . . . had to look representative of our base."[60] Early 9to5 members also took care to avoid theoretical phrases or polarizing language.[61] Reader response letters quickly showed a distaste for topics beyond the office, such as the antiwar movement or the United Farm Workers' lettuce boycott. In the fifth issue, a clerical reader wrote that she enjoyed the newsletter but admonished its creator to "stop writing about Vietnam and lettuce."[62]

Staying focused on the specific problems of clericals and not on other progressive causes could ensure that the organization would appeal to as many office workers as possible. Women from a wide variety of class and educational backgrounds composed the clerical workforce of the 1960s and 1970s.[63] Because sex segregation had long characterized the labor force, women had limited options, and secretarial work was one of the most common. This meant that the clerical job category included those with some high school education as well as those with graduate degrees. Cassedy recalled that as 9to5 was gaining momentum, its leaders strove "to make sure that our public face was inviting to the whole range, from those people who were there to express themselves [to] those people who were just getting by, and so on."[64] Because clericals' wages hovered around the poverty line, many relied on their next paychecks for food and rent.[65] Many of these women did not have much time for activism, particularly if they were working to support children. And as a large occupational category (the largest for women workers), not all shared the same social and political viewpoints.

Given the breadth of women engaged in this work, the 9to5 founders began to fill the newsletters with vignettes from other office workers, making sure content was relatable and universal. Founding members crafted articles about common workplace issues, such as ridiculous errands that bosses demanded and failed attempts to petition management for pay increases.[66] The newsletter used anecdotes to reveal a variety of frustrations: boredom at work, lack of control over job duties, and exclusion from decision making. Disrespect was essential to most of the complaints. Clericals felt belittled by bosses who called them anything but their names. One woman wrote into the newsletter saying: "I am not a 'puss,' or a 'chick,' a 'broad,' or a 'dear': I am a WOMAN and I have a name, a full name of my own. I can easily remember the names of all twelve men I work with, and they can remember each other's names—why can they not remember mine?"[67] Wrote a Boston woman in the first newsletter, "It's not so much the work you do (though there are some jobs that are just plain deadly), but how you're treated that determines how you feel about your job."[68] Other articles spoke about not feeling fully human at work: "I am not a person, but a machine, much like the ones in my office, who gets the routine work done for them so they can run around making important decisions."[69]

Newsletter creators wanted women to realize that they were not alone in feeling angry or frustrated about workplace problems. The first issue, in the winter of 1972–1973, declared, "Most of us are unaware of the forceful current of shared feelings about our work, our status, and our lives."[70] A two-page spread in the fourth issue displayed a map of the United States to illustrate nationwide pockets of resistance, delineating a network of discontented women. The map demonstrated that in San Francisco, workers at Equitable Insurance Company were unionizing, and in cities such as Chicago, New York, Detroit, and Hartford, working women were producing their own newsletters to speak out about issues important to them.[71]

Yet a newsletter had obvious limitations because, according to founding members, its distribution "could only raise issues." 9to5 decided to move toward activism in late 1973.[72] Its first official meeting, attended by about fifty women, took place in November 1973, and general meetings followed every other Monday.[73] To move beyond discussion and toward direct action, Cassedy attended the recently founded Midwest Academy on behalf of the fledgling 9to5 organization. Begun in 1973 by leaders from the civil rights and antiwar movements, the Midwest Academy taught other activists how to increase public awareness for a specific cause, move toward direct action, and gain allies.[74] In addition, the academy emphasized the importance of empowering activists themselves, encouraging women to see themselves as capable leaders. Academy cofounder Heather Booth had participated in the Industrial Areas Foundation (IAF), a program started by Saul Alinsky, one of the leading community-organizing strategists in the United States. As the only woman at the IAF, Booth, a feminist, realized that this seemingly progressive association perpetuated traditional gender roles, discouraging women from becoming organizers.[75] She eventually helped to start the Midwest Academy, which had three guiding principles: organizing to win concrete improvements; encouraging people to lead and empower themselves; and holding those in power more accountable for their subjugation of others. Booth and the other founders of the academy wanted women to direct their own movements for workplace change.[76]

Through Cassedy's training in the Midwest Academy, 9to5 gained strategic focus, programmatic direction, and greater visibility. Cassedy noted that Booth praised the 9to5 newsletters but then quickly asked, "What are your activities?"[77] Cassedy's involvement in the academy helped move 9to5 toward engagement and outreach. In addition to Monday meetings, the young organization began to offer courses on certain Wednesdays to educate office workers about labor organizing and leadership skills. On Tuesdays and Thursdays, 9to5 facilitated a workshop at the Boston YWCA that offered free legal advice and counseling to women for their workplace problems.[78]

Also as a result of the Midwest Academy training, 9to5 leaders adopted distinctive organizing strategies, distinguishing the group from traditional industrial unions. Unions counted on a majority vote to attain representation from the National Labor Relations Board (NLRB); consequently, industrial labor leaders cared largely about membership numbers to demonstrate the strength of union support.[79] Although 9to5 leaders also cared about quantity of members, they perceived organizing as a relationship-building process. 9to5 could act as a vehicle to develop women into committed members, teaching them leadership skills and fostering networks of like-minded women. From the Midwest Academy, Cassedy passed along to 9to5 the strategy of the recruitment lunch, a one-on-one lunch meeting of a current and a prospective member. When publishing assistant and future 9to5 leader Debbie Schneider initially wanted to join, she was told, "You can't just join, you have to have a recruitment lunch."[80] Nussbaum explained that a 9to5 member might meet several times with a prospective member, giving her responsibility within the 9to5 organization or a task in her workplace before she officially joined. She described 9to5's organization strategy as trying to identify "people who did things . . . leaders and activists." She wanted to develop an organization that would foster "personal engagement" among workers.[81]

Cassedy explained that her attendance in the Midwest Academy was "the big turning point for us . . . a real eye-opener for all of us, because we had trouble seeing beyond telling our stories to each other, and getting people to come and all gather in the same room." 9to5 learned that it needed to have targets, or common enemies, usually identified as male bosses, supervisors, or even human resource managers. However, its targets could shift: federal and state governments became the opponent in the late 1970s in campaigns to enforce equal employment opportunity and affirmative action policy (see chapter 4). Cassedy also learned from the academy that to have the most impact, 9to5 needed practical solutions that would appeal to a broad audience, including those clericals who were not politically active.[82]

To gauge the attitudes of clerical workers and advance an agenda for a broad base, 9to5 leaders started to gather data and issue reports on Boston-area office work. The first 9to5 report, the "Statistical Study of Boston Area Employment," detailed pay inequity and occupational segregation in offices around the city.[83] The report, released in November 1973 at a public meeting with the Boston Chamber of Commerce, used government data to bolster 9to5's complaints about pay and promotions. Boston men were receiving more than twice the annual median wage received by Boston's working women: $8,290 to $4,031.[84] Although men and women on average had 12.3 years of education, Boston's women remained clustered in the lowest-paid clerical occupations. 9to5 leaders perceived the needs of the city's clerical workforce, 74 percent of whom were women, to be especially acute because of the rising cost of living. Of the fifteen largest cities in the United States, Boston ranked highest in standard of living, but thirteenth in salaries paid to office workers. Additionally, the report claimed that various Boston area employers were violating federal and state equal employment laws, which held that men and women should receive equal pay for equal work, as stated in the Equal Pay Act of 1963. According to the study, in the preceding seventeen months, 618 female employees had been underpaid by $466,500 relative to the salaries that men were earning for the same work.[85]

Next, to determine the most pressing problems of office workers, 9to5 distributed a "9to5 Job Survey" to clericals throughout Boston in early 1974.[86] The first page of this anonymous survey gathered quantitative data about the respondents' income, benefits (health insurance, pensions, sick leave), and overtime pay, as well as qualitative data about their employers' job descriptions, job training, and the presence or absence of union campaigns. The back side of the survey invited insight from respondents about gender and workplace justice. Respondents had an opportunity to select one or more "key issues or problem areas" from among the following: salaries, promotions, job training, health benefits, sex discrimination, pension, overtime, sick leave, union, vacation, racial discrimination, coffee breaks, maternity leave, day care, job description, and other. A "Comments" space allowed for additional qualitative feedback.[87]

The extent to which respondents criticized their jobs, and how they labeled their problems, varied widely from employee to employee.[88] To gain a significant following, the 9to5 organization, founded at the intersection of second-wave feminism and the trade union movement, needed to recruit a broad base of clerical workers who also perceived their problems as emerging at this intersection. 9to5's innovative mission and agenda meant that the new organization would need to make the gender and labor connection more overt for many clericals who had not considered the overlapping nature of these issues. Some clerical comments revealed an awareness of either sex discrimination or economic injustice, yet few individual responses acknowledged their linkage.

Regarding sex discrimination, the survey comments offer a window into the fluidity of the concept during the 1970s. Whereas throughout most of the twentieth century, women had advocated for workplace protections by emphasizing their difference from men, now mainstream notions of fair treatment were shifting toward equality.[89] In *Equality on Trial* (2016), historian Katherine Turk has traced the contestation over the legal definition of sex discrimination during this period. Analysis of the 9to5 survey responses bolsters this lack of consensus about which workplace concerns were considered sex-based grievances.

Examination of whether respondents marked "sex discrimination" reveals that only a few interpreted their problems as clerical workers to fall into this category. Just two comments revealed a perception that occupational segregation was a form of sex discrimination; one mentioned that "sex discrimination goes hand in hand with secretarial work," and another pointed to the lack of women in managerial positions and few promotional opportunities: "Once a secretary at Gillette, always a secretary!"[90] Significantly, and in the minority, these women perceived separate job ladders for men and women at work as unfair treatment based on sex.

Most clericals in the sample did not mark sex discrimination, per se, as an issue of concern, although the problems they described in their qualitative comments likely resulted from the entrenchment of traditional gender roles.[91] A secretary at Boston College wrote, in gender-neutral language, "a lot of talent gets bypassed," while a service representative at New England Telephone stated that she was "treated like a child" without mentioning why. Neither woman checked sex discrimination as a job concern despite the fact that facing few promotional opportunities and lacking respectful treatment from superiors likely reflected institutionalized bias against women. Another clerical who worked at the Massachusetts Teachers Association perceived this lack of respect as endemic to secretarial work, describing "a general lack of respect for myself and the women who work with me . . . and our services are taken for granted." Still other women acknowledged the reality of occupational segregation while hinting that men and women could have different preferences for working in certain jobs or industries. At a large engineering firm in Cambridge, Massachusetts, an accounts clerk wrote that sex discrimination "could be" a problem because almost all the firm's five hundred female employees were secretaries or clerical workers. She clarified, however, that occupational segregation was not the same as sex discrimination, explaining that the absence of women in engineering, drafting, or computer services sections "may be a function of low numbers of women engineers or draftsmen that feel like working for the Bridge Co. rather than active sex discrimination." A secretary for the Boston Red Sox Association attributed the dearth of female professionals in her office to the fact that she worked in a traditionally male space that had mostly male customers: "The nature of the industry makes it discriminatory towards females. Its [*sic*] a male-oriented field and . . . the industry's biggest followers are male and therefore most activities are geared to the male."

While few respondents in the sample marked sex discrimination as an issue of concern, most did check salary: it was the most common problem identified by respondents, who reported their earnings as between $5,000 and $8,000 per year. Of the many women who described economic injustice at work, few connected low pay to sex discrimination. A clerk at Boston University openly rejected sex discrimination as a problem, writing "[there] is no outward sex discrimination [in the office]" while simultaneously complaining that women in her office "are treated like idiots" and "are given low wages and no respect . . . and need a union <u>desperately</u>. Please help." A clerk for the Ritz Carlton Hotel Corporation chose raises and promotions as two problems she faced on the job, explaining that she risked falling below the poverty line if she became ill or lost her job. However, omitting to check sex discrimination as a workplace issue reveals that she did not associate her precarious financial situation with unfair treatment based on sex.[92]

Clericals commented that employer manipulation of job titles posed economic problems. While some women were performing professional work above their current job titles, others held professional titles but received clerical pay. Numerous women reported that their competence was rewarded with the allocation of more responsibility but not more pay. A secretary for residential housing at Hampshire College received a nominal promotion, meaning her manager gave her more duties without more compensation. At an industrial accident office for the Commonwealth of Massachusetts, a senior stenographer described the same problem: "When you are known to be a capable employee, extra responsibilities are put on you. Although this makes my job more meaningful, the pay does not compensate for the additional pressure." A faculty secretary at Harvard Business School wrote a similar comment on her survey. She explained, "If you are capable, you are handed more responsibilities which you do because it makes your job more meaningful. Your superior assumes additional assignments knowing that you can handle the added workload—[I would] like to be paid for this."

As a group not squarely in the camp of feminism or labor, 9to5 presented a new opportunity and an alternative option for those interested in mobilizing to change office politics. Distributing the survey in Boston allowed the newly formed organization to gather information about clericals' concerns, publicize their platform, and recruit new members. The majority of clerical workers, however, would remain uninterested in forging a formal commitment to 9to5, even as the organization gained a national presence.[93] The following comment captures the disconnect between some women office workers and the second-wave feminist movement. Stated one clerical worker about women's liberation and women professionals: "Well, you know, you're not dealing with my type of woman. You're dealing with these educated, attractive, successful, you know, when she speaks I don't even understand what she's saying, all I know is my reality is I've got so much dollars coming in. I've got a house, a husband who's a bum, and who won't work, a kid who's got another problem."[94] Many hard-pressed working women did not perceive the feminist movement and its rhetoric as speaking to their needs. As the highlighted responses to the 9to5 survey demonstrate, many clericals perceived injustice at work, describing real-life examples of the disadvantages they encountered based on their sex. Yet they were reluctant to see themselves as part of the second-wave movement, viewing feminism as elevating the needs and concerns of more privileged women.

Topping the list of priorities for most clerical workers was an increase in pay.[95] According to an insurance clerical from Travelers, "pay is the thing" that most women she knew cared about most.[96] When 9to5 members came to distribute newsletters and surveys at Travelers, she joined the organization while most of her coworkers declined membership. They told her that they did not think membership in 9to5 would help them secure higher pay. And they worried that engagement with 9to5 could strain relationships with their supervisors, believing that a more hostile atmosphere would not lead to higher wages or improved working conditions.[97]

Whether clericals believed that membership in 9to5 could help them obtain higher pay seemed to be a crucial factor for engagement and membership. A temporary worker in Chicago was attracted to join Women Employed (WE) in Chicago, a sister organization to Boston's 9to5, because she thought it could bring economic benefits: "It was very action-oriented and not involved in all this other philosophical business of whether you should wear a bra or not, or shave your legs or not. I quite frankly couldn't care less about that." This temporary clerical, like many rank-and-file office workers, categorized "philosophical" discussion of gender roles as feminism, which she saw as unimportant relative to bread-and-butter issues like pay. She described her attraction to WE: the group was talking about "lack of benefits" for temporary workers, which was "interesting" to her and relevant to her most pressing problems.[98]

While some working women "frankly couldn't care less" about prominent strains of the feminist discourse, others more pointedly rejected the movement. One Boston insurance worker who had recently joined 9to5 described the difficulties of recruiting her coworkers and friends. She claimed that they teased her for being in a women's group and wanted nothing to do with the feminist label: "They're afraid of being stigmatized as a women's libber, and getting harassed like I constantly do."[99] 9to5 had a challenge ahead: as an organization inspired by the second-wave feminist movement, it needed to remain distinct from ideology that was unappealing to its target constituency.

Over the next decade 9to5 would expand its platform and gain visibility. Nussbaum recognized that membership growth, especially recruiting a diverse array of workers, would prove crucial to the organization's success and longevity.[100] By 1977, 9to5 had grown beyond Boston and had a national presence with a central governing body overseeing thirteen active city chapters. With fifty people on the national paid staff, it had a membership of ten thousand and an annual budget of $700,000.[101] Still, 9to5 leaders recorded that the organization needed to "recruit more members from [the] heart of the workforce," meaning non-college-educated women who were not active in or sympathetic to other left-leaning movements.[102] Would 9to5 be able to appeal to workers of varying political persuasions beyond progressives?[103]

Yet 9to5's influence reached beyond its membership. Even for those women who were not engaged with its activities, the organization shaped how nonmembers viewed their jobs. For instance, the 9to5 survey process—posing questions and eliciting responses—forced all clericals to reexamine long-standing policies at their own workplaces.[104] One 9to5 member noticed that after distribution of the surveys at her workplace, even nonmember women were more aware of the negative aspects of their jobs, as well as more likely to challenge their supervisors.[105] Maybe the language of the survey helped women to identify specific complaints, according to one 9to5 member: "A lot of people feel like they don't have any real clear-cut complaints until they start putting things down on paper."[106]

Based on the responses to the Boston survey in 1973, 9to5 drafted an Office Workers' Bill of Rights by 1974, to summarize and standardize clerical workers' frustrations, as well as to delineate a platform for action.[107] This Bill of Rights listed unfair and illegal employment practices that 9to5 prioritized: demand for respect on the job, comprehensive written job descriptions, compensation for overtime work, and regular salary reviews and cost-of-living increases.[108] The women creating and advancing the 9to5 platform lobbied for "rights and respect." Often they did not distinguish between tangible gains (such as pay, benefits, and promotions) and intangible respect issues because they saw them as interrelated and possibly inseparable. Whereas established labor and feminist organizations had preexisting structures and programs, 9to5 offered a new model that clerical workers were building for themselves. Founding member and 9to5 leader Janet Selcer recalled, "We were making it all up. We were really making it up. It is one of my fondest memories."[109]

⸏⸏⸏

By the mid-1970s, 9to5 had left behind its beginnings as a lunchtime discussion group.[110] However, its position within the existing second-wave feminist movement was somewhat unclear, particularly as the social and legal definitions of employment discrimination were evolving and little consensus existed about what comprised unfair or illegal treatment based on sex.[111] Was societal sorting of men and women into different lines of work—and the fact that most clerical workers were women—an example of sex-based discrimination? Many were frustrated and dissatisfied with their jobs yet reluctant to label their own experiences as discrimination based on sex, or even as relevant to the second-wave platform.

Whatever the case, the onset of feminism forced a response from secretaries. This response varied: the strain of pink-collar activism that emerged among younger and more radical women was far from universal among all secretaries. With roots in leftist politics, Nussbaum and

Cassedy began an office workers' movement, drawing on other efforts: the civil rights movement, the antiwar movement, and second-wave feminism. They aimed to create a decentralized organization where clerical workers themselves set an agenda based on shared notions of equity and fairness. Yet 9to5 founders would face the challenge of trying to unify one-third of working women, all women working in clerical jobs, under a coherent headline that appealed widely across political and demographic differences.

A group of workers in the publishing industry would become one of the first segments of clerical workers to shape the 9to5 agenda, pushing to change corporate practices regarding internal job postings, written job descriptions, and paid job training.

3

THE PROGRESSIONAL AND PROFESSIONAL PATHS INTERTWINED

A mong the responses to the Boston 9to5 survey in 1973 were those from women who viewed themselves as capable of performing well in higher-level positions. Emphasizing unfair promotional practices, some working women revealed that they felt overqualified for their current jobs, and they noticed that men either enjoyed higher-status positions or were able to rise into them more quickly and easily. A woman who worked at MIT Press saw her problems both as economic (she wanted a higher salary) and as rooted in sex bias. She wrote, "My main gripe is that inspite [*sic*] of my experience and college training in editorial work, I have to start at the bottom. I'm fighting but it's pretty hopeless." Because she cared about her title as well as her pay, she was angered that she had to start—and stay—in a clerical position while men with the same or lesser qualifications began their careers at higher levels. Another woman who was an associate editor at Houghton Mifflin wrote about her inability to attain a promotion as she watched men ascend. She claimed that sex discrimination was "very obvious." When she asked for a promotion, since she already was "doing the work of that category, the male response [was], 'Oh, you have to stay at the stage you're in now for at least two years. That's the usual time.'"[1] She cared about the promotion to a new job title because she was not receiving the commensurate salary for the work she was performing.

How could secretaries, like the two women just mentioned, gain equitable access to career advancement? Perhaps the feminist movement could help to elevate the secretarial job, increasing its professional status, such that working in a secretarial position could serve as training ground to become the boss. Secretarial schools began to meet the needs of women who wanted to climb the corporate ladder. Director of the Washington School for Secretaries Miryam Drucker reported that her program had adopted two tracks for secretaries: "Those who want to be secretaries and those who want an entrée to management positions." She maintained to the *Washington Post* that formal clerical training provided women on both paths with the potential to assume power and have satisfying jobs.[2] Lynn Salvage, a graduate of Harvard Business School (HBS) and bank executive, took the lead at the Katharine Gibbs School in 1979. She intended to move "away from that finishing school sort of thing" and to rethink the secretary-boss relationship.[3] According to Salvage, Gibbs School graduates should no longer be called secretaries because they were now a part of the management team. She created two paths at Gibbs, for two types of secretaries: progressional, for those who viewed secretarial work as the first step on their career ladder, and professional, for those who planned to make a permanent (or semipermanent) career of being a secretary.[4]

Those women who had ambitions of upward mobility in their careers utilized 9to5 as a professional organization that could help them move out of the pink-collar ghetto. Some of the earliest 9to5 campaigns targeted the needs of women in what Gibbs called progressional careers, or those who saw themselves as management material. Evincing faith in the possibilities of meritocracy, early 9to5 campaigns sought to bridge clerical and managerial job ladders—what sociologists would eventually identify as a major barrier to women's corporate advancement—by pushing for internal job postings, written job descriptions, and paid job training.[5] If the selection of managers were to become more equitable, reasoned early 9to5 activists, then secretaries could have access to men's positions. Clerical workers could learn about managerial openings through mandatory internal postings. Forcing employers to have precise, written job descriptions could set boundaries on regarding appropriate work for those with a clerical job title. Paid training for development into management could allow clericals to start in an entry-level position but still have the chance to advance. This strain of secretary—who used 9to5 as a type of professional association—believed that greater standardization and transparency of personnel processes could result in sex equality.

Grassroots organizing of female employees was augmented by top-down transformations already occurring in corporations. The passage and application of equal employment opportunity (EEO) laws and directives promised to guarantee rights to individuals regardless of race, sex, and religion at work.[6] Congress had passed legislation in 1963 and 1964—the Equal Pay Act and Title VII of the Civil Rights Act—to prohibit sex-based discrimination in the pay, hiring, and promotional practices of the private sector.[7] Then, building on executive orders from previous administrations, President Lyndon B. Johnson had issued Executive Order 11246 in 1965 and Executive Order 11375 in 1967 to address past injustices that had left people of color and women at a disadvantage in the private-sector labor market.[8] Attempting to move beyond a ban on discrimination, Johnson posited that "freedom [was] not enough," urging employers with federal contracts valued at $50,000 or more and fifty or more employees to take "affirmative action" to try to remedy past and current inequities.[9]

Secretarial efforts to change personnel practices thus were aided by Title VII and affirmative action, policies that pushed employers toward a systemic review of job titles, a regular habit of job postings, a written record of job descriptions, and a larger investment in job training. The open-ended language of these government policies meant that employers, and particularly the growing cadre of human resources managers, would define the scope and mandate of EEO policy in organizational life.[10]

In this chapter we see an emergent division, which will be described more in later chapters, between those women who could use changing corporate policy to their benefit and those who were unaided by EEO law. The potential to utilize new employment regulations, as this chapter argues, would ultimately divide workplace feminism. But in the 1970s those women who could avail themselves of EEO law worked alongside those who could not to advance gender equity.

The publishing industry serves as a good case study to examine a lost moment in the history of workplace feminism, as corporate compliance with EEO law bolstered certain elements of feminism but not others. Relative to other private-sector fields, such as financial services, the publishing industry is a terrific example of a pool of clerical workers who had the education and desire to move to editorial and managerial positions. Publishing was therefore the industry most likely to bridge clerical and managerial ladders, if that bridging was to happen anywhere. And although many women worked in publishing throughout the twentieth century, the industry may be, historically, one of the least meritocratic of all. For most of the twentieth century, publishing attracted, or rather permitted, only upper-class, Ivy League–educated young white men who entered on the prompting of a family member or friend who held a position of status in the firm. College-educated women from wealthy families constituted much of the workforce, although they largely remained in clerical positions until the 1970s. Thus, upon passage of EEO laws, elite book publishers in New York and Boston had a lot of work to do to incorporate women and underrepresented men into supervisory positions.

Focusing on publishing, the first part of this chapter considers how working women, including lower-level clericals, supervisors, and professional editors, used a variety of strategies to fight for gender equity within their individual firms. Feminism in the 1970s was more holistic in its approach; activists promoted an array of tactics to seek both individual and collective change concurrently for female employees from top to bottom. Clerical and editorial women collaborated to pursue legal action against employers for their seemingly arbitrary personnel practices. The advancement of women into management and the unionization of clerical women were, briefly, two facets of the same battle to overturn patriarchy.

The second part demonstrates how the rise of HR management subsumed some concerns from the feminist agenda, remedying issues regarding women in management while leaving behind other concerns regarding economic justice. Employers committed to recruiting women into positions where they had been underrepresented historically, and this corporate-sponsored push to pull women into management satisfied regulators. Other working women's concerns, however, such as low pay and pay inequity for female-dominated work, fell outside the HR agenda. College-educated clerical workers welcomed changing personnel practices because they offered increasingly meritocratic options, allowing them access to men's jobs with higher pay and higher status. Yet to fill management positions, employers did little to bridge clerical and managerial job ladders, instead turning to external labor markets to meet EEO guidelines.

The resulting bifurcation in the 9to5 platform, separating raises from respect—in other words, pay from promotion—meant that feminist campaigns to fight for unionization and professional mobility would become almost incompatible ideologically. This chapter's focus on the publishing industry elucidates a moment of possibility for a more united feminist agenda before the eventual divergence of raises and respect.

⧳

In the nineteenth century those engaged in the production of books had seen themselves more as creators of literature than as sellers of consumer products. Relative to other major U.S. industries such as railroads, steel, oil, automobiles, or banks, the founders and owners of publishing firms saw themselves as "business men of letters," according to a historian.[11] Although by the 1970s all publishing houses had to care about profits, as they were usually part of larger corporate entities, publishers felt responsible to advance the public good by accepting some manuscripts with mass appeal to pay for the books of poetry that would earn much less. A leading editor in chief stated, "I don't think we ever turn something of real quality down because it is going to lose money. We know that half of our books are not going to make money."[12] Similar to those in the arts and academia, leading publishers saw their work as cultural production and knowledge advancement.[13] Even when conscious of profits, editors saw themselves not as "responsible to the educated public . . . or to the cultural tradition of America."[14]

Recruiting and selecting personnel relied on nepotism as much as meritocracy. Obtaining a job in publishing required a certain pedigree. Both women and men, clericals and editors, usually gained access to their jobs by knowing someone in the industry.[15] Simon & Schuster was known to hire its secretaries from the Seven Sisters schools, recruiting those from respected families who also had a degree in English.[16] Salaries were not high, which did not concern sons and daughters of wealthy parents: they entered publishing as a respectable industry with a reputable purpose. In fact, publishing executives claimed they could have made two or three times more as executives in other industries, but they chose publishing for its esteem and status. Historian John Tebbel states that most everyone knew that "no one who wanted to get rich should enter publishing."[17] Given the reliance on networks, few people of color—men or women—worked in publishing: according to a publishing employee, "there aren't too many black faces around."[18]

College-educated men and women had different ports of entry into a publishing house, with men entering into higher-paid jobs with greater opportunities for mobility. After college, men started in sales at a salary of about $8,000 plus expenses for travel. A woman started as a secretary or editorial assistant at under $7,000 a year.[19] These white college-educated women—many with liberal arts degrees from top-ranked universities—held clerical jobs under the supervision of male editors who had similar credentials.[20] In the words of sociologist Rosabeth Moss Kanter, men and women entered the 1970s organization in different "opportunity structures." Kanter contends that organizations in the 1970s had a "separate workplace" for men and for women, such that "ability in one workplace is not always transferable to others; what leads to success in one may even be dysfunctional for mobility into another."[21] Employment scholar Paul Osterman has confirmed this lack of transferability in an article on sex discrimination in publishing. Indeed, men and women remained in separate internal labor markets, with women assigned to shorter job ladders, with less potential for upward mobility.[22] In book publishing, because of these separate job ladders, movement from secretary to sales manager was practically impossible.[23] Although secretaries worked on editorial tasks, the job of acquisitions editor required sales experience, meaning that only men had the necessary qualifications. And publishers rarely hired women as sales representatives, believing that they should not be traveling alone, carrying heavy books, or trying to locate buildings in unfamiliar locations.[24] In addition, professors reported feeling "insulted" if women called on them, and thus firms were reluctant to send women to college campuses.[25] The few women who tried sales said that "sometimes people think you are a little loose because you are a salesperson."[26]

Yet women composed the majority of the publishing workforce. In many houses, 75–80 percent of employees were college-educated white women earning low clerical salaries.[27] Women who did move out of the secretarial job category might work in nonmanagerial jobs that were a step above secretary status, in noncore departments such as copyrights and permissions, subsidiary rights, billing, art, marketing, and publicity. Women had to fight hard—but also have extremely good fortune—to move into any sort of editorial or managerial position. It took one woman at Harper & Row eighteen years to become a trade editor. Another woman at Simon & Schuster worked ten years as a secretary before gaining a promotion to assistant advertising manager. After five more years, she earned a position as an in-house editor. Unfortunately, a year later, "she was fired because the publisher didn't like her personality," according to editor Ethel Strainchamps, who published a book of collected vignettes on women in the industry.[28]

Another point of gender inequity was that not all editors were equal: women who did ascend into editorial positions were mostly concentrated in lower-paid, lower-status departments, such as children's publishing or mass-market paperbacks, relative to the male-dominated world of college textbook publishing. In fact, at one publishing house in the 1970s, all the editors in the children's book department were women.[29] And among editorial job titles, women were more likely to be manuscript editors or copy editors while men were more likely to be acquisition editors.[30] Acquisition editors made important decisions about the flow of money in and out of the firm; manuscript editors or copy editors oversaw the detailed work of going through a manuscript line-by-line and correcting errors.[31]

So why did privileged women take these jobs as secretaries if the odds of making editor were clearly stacked against them? As mentioned, work in a publishing house signaled status and was viewed as having cultural value. According to one Harper & Row employee, women from established families would rather be in an atmosphere that elevated knowledge and learning instead of "folding sweaters at Filene's" until they got married. And many female publishing employees believed that even if they had to begin as secretaries, excellent job performance would afford them access to promotions. The presence of a few women working as editors and managers confirmed this belief in meritocracy. According to one woman, "Publishing's world of ideas offered a sphere of influence where I believed I could negotiate on the strength of my brain. I considered being female irrelevant to success" in the industry.[32]

Some employers reinforced this myth—that the secretarial job was the first step on an upwardly mobile career path—to entice women to take such low-paying jobs. An Allyn & Bacon employee said that when she was hired as a secretary, personnel implied that eventually becoming an editor would be possible: she would have to stay in the secretarial position for at least one year before advancing into editorial work.[33] Despite promises of mobility, in reality, very few women moved from the clerical to editorial ranks. Doing a good job did not guarantee any sort of promotion, and women realized that men with sales experience moved into the acquisition editor roles. Rather, the publishing industry stayed afloat by employing low-paid, highly educated female secretaries who could apply their language skills to assist with substantive work.

Given the short job ladders for clericals, a horizontal move from one publishing house to another could be one way for women to try for a promotion or a raise.[34] Newly hired clericals might receive higher starting salaries relative to more senior clericals who had begun at lower pay and subsequently rarely received raises over the years.[35] And internal promotions were rare, according to one woman who claimed that if clericals wanted to move up, they would have to leave to work at another company and then try to come back to a higher position.[36] Simon & Schuster editor in chief Michael Korda confirmed that constant motion could be an effective career strategy for women. In a column for *Glamour* magazine, he advised women that "horizontal movement can be as valuable as vertical movement": they could "make each move *look* like a promotion by treating it in a positive manner," meaning that women could try to rebrand themselves in a new environment.[37] While Korda coached women on how to advance their own careers, he also recognized that the publishing industry relied on a large army of entry-level employees who had little chance of mobility. He authored the books *Male Chauvinism: How It Works* and *Power: How to Get It, How to Use It*, about the injustices of sex discrimination in the workplace. A publishing employee once overheard him lamenting such inequities: "Please don't send me any more bright girls. I only want to see girls who smoke pot and don't want to go anywhere!"[38]

This was the organizational structure of major publishing houses as women graduated from college in the 1970s and assumed secretarial positions, with some hoping that the job could lead upward. The influences of feminism and EEO regulations on the secretarial occupation were unclear. Would social change and legal equality mean that secretarial experience would gain recognition as relevant for promotions? Or was the movement from secretary to editor so exceptional that women's entry-level work would remain disconnected from traditionally male jobs? Women coming of age in the 1970s could find evidence for and against the secretarial job as a stepping stone.

In support of secretaries as promotable was the fact that almost every female manager in publishing had begun as a secretary, and a few had become editors. Profiling the women who had climbed to the top, *Publishers Weekly* ran a story in 1974 about the status of women in the industry. In this widely circulated article, "Women in Publishing: Where Do They Feel They're Going?," journalist Ann Geracimos acknowledged that the industry still had a long way to go to achieve gender equity. Yet she interviewed several exceptional women who had all started as secretaries but had since moved up to editorial, managerial, and even executive positions. The profiles served as anecdotal evidence that career advancement based on hard work and talent was possible. Geracimos reported that the editor in chief of Pocket Books, a division of Simon & Schuster, began as Nelson Doubleday's private secretary. Of three women who received promotions in the early 1970s at Holt, Rinehart, and Winston, all had begun as secretaries. One became an assistant trade editor, another an assistant juvenile editor, and a third a publicity assistant.[39]

Most professional women who had made the jump from secretary to editor did not necessarily *recommend* secretarial work as a clear and direct path to the top. But the implication was that secretarial work—although stigmatized—did not have to be a barrier to advancement. One of the most senior women in the industry, Helen Meyer, president of Dell Publishing and the only woman on the board of the Association of American Publishers, presented an ambivalent message. Meyer boasted of "having done everything she could to learn when first starting out (including operating a switchboard)." While advocating for young women to work hard and apply themselves, she warned readers to not work too hard when presented with secretarial tasks "lest you get stuck where you excel best and not rotated to new positions." Although Meyer had worked the switchboard, she had "refused to learn shorthand," and young women should do the same if they aspired to the executive suite. Similarly, an associate editor at Harper & Row Junior Books, Elizabeth Gordon, cautioned young women against taking secretarial positions if they wanted to advance.[40]

Others promoted the work as a training ground for moving up. Joan Manley became publisher of Time-Life Books in 1970—the first woman in Time Inc.'s history to assume that title and to be named a vice president. Manley had learned shorthand at night during her college years at University of California at Berkeley, during a time when the "idea of starting as a secretary was not so repellent then as it is to some young women today."[41] For those who wanted to be eligible for higher-paid executive positions, Manley thought they should reconsider the secretarial job as an opportunity to learn about being the boss. She advised, "Working for a smart man as a secretary is the best way to learn fast," attributing a lot of her progress to the mentorship of two men who were her bosses while she was a secretary at Doubleday. Yet not all secretarial jobs would lead upward. Her advice to young women: "If you find out you are working for a dumb boss, quit."[42] William Targ, senior editor at G. P. Putnam's Sons, also asserted that secretarial work could be a stepping stone to more advanced positions. Writing a lengthy response to the *Publishers Weekly* article on women in the industry, he championed secretarial work as a growth opportunity for anyone with "eyes and ears open" to digest all of the various matters crossing their bosses' desks. Targ questioned the backlash against secretaries: "Someone from outer space reading the article might construe the secretary's job as something demeaning, subhuman."[43]

The *Publishers Weekly* profile of women in publishing in 1974 demonstrated an emerging awareness among well-educated women of the changing, and increasingly negative, perceptions of secretarial work given new professional opportunities. And there was greater recognition of the ways that gender—as well as race—could hinder such opportunities. Even more uncommon than white women working as editors was the presence of women of color in the upper ranks. Editor Toni Morrison felt her pioneering status as a Black woman actually exerted unfair pressure on other women of color in publishing. "Some people think I'm some kind of Amazon, so in the future they may expect other Black women editors to be Amazons. But for years they have hired dumb whites, so why not include dumb blacks?"[44] She did not want all Black women to have to demonstrate extraordinary talent to have a chance to succeed in the industry.

Like Morrison, Genevieve Young was a woman of color in the white-dominated world of publishing. A Chinese American, Young graduated from Wellesley College and began her publishing career at Harper & Brothers as a stenographer, learning typing and shorthand on the job. She managed to advance with horizontal moves to several other publishing houses. By 1970 Young worked as an executive editor at J. B. Lippincott, where she eventually earned a vice president title. Then she became a senior editor at Little, Brown, followed by editor in chief of Literary Guild of America, and then vice president and editorial director of Bantam Books.[45] She told *Publishers Weekly* that gender, more than race, had been salient in her career: "I'm one of only two female Chinese executive editors in the world—the other is Beverly Loo at McGraw-Hill—but the only minority I was ever conscious of being was female, and that came late."[46]

White women also acknowledged the ways that gender identity challenged their advancement at work. While some did not want a broad social movement to overshadow their individual career achievements, others saw their own success as embodying larger societal change. Sherry Arden, vice president and director of publicity for William Morrow, captured the idea that her individual advancement represented collective progress for all women. "When I was made a vice-president, secretaries came to my office crying. They felt they were sharing in what I was doing and that they had a chance at this point." Yet Ester Margolis, the youngest vice president that Bantam had ever had, did not emphasize her gender identity. She felt "hurt by all the women who came up to congratulate me: I took it as a sort of put-down. I certainly understood but I felt I deserved [the promotion] for my work, not because I was a woman."[47]

Whatever Margolis's opinions, this very discussion—whether pioneering career women saw themselves as exemplary of larger social movements—in and of itself demonstrated the far-reaching influence of feminism in the office.

In the early 1970s Harper & Row (Harper) was one of the most highly regarded publishing houses in the United States. Founded in the early nineteenth century, the firm was an established leader in the industry: according to employees, work experience at Harper could be a "stepping stone" to jobs in other publishing houses. Yet the propriety characteristic of publishing houses did not prevent management overreach: the "brass knuckles were concealed under the velvet glove" at Harper, according to one woman.[48]

Harper's reputation made it all the more astonishing that in 1974, in New York City, dissatisfied professional women joined with clerical and production workers to stage a highly publicized and historic strike. A coalition developed between working-class and middle-class women and, for a moment, traditional union demands merged, albeit uneasily, with professional women's quest for upward mobility.

Strike events can be traced back to 1970, when the in-house union, the Association of Harper & Row Employees, secured a three-year contract. Although the association had existed since the 1940s, it was largely ceremonial and only recently had become empowered as a bargaining agent on behalf of workers.[49] Formal labor activity in the industry was rare, and the founding of this union at Harper represented the first successful unionization drive in publishing since the Great Depression.[50] Formed to acquire cost-of-living pay increases each year, the in-house union initially had little interest in issues explicitly regarding gender.[51] Yet in 1973, as the contract was set to expire, the union expanded its agenda to include sex discrimination, largely because Harper college-educated women were dissatisfied with promotional opportunities.[52]

Also around 1970, Harper executives had formed a women's committee of editorial and managerial female employees. The committee organized events, like a company-sponsored talent show, to increase employee morale.[53] And more substantively, executives tasked the women's committee with overseeing the work of external consultants who had been hired to gather information about pay, promotional practices, and employee satisfaction. Yet after the committee evaluated the consultants' data and suggested changes to corporate policy, the executive board failed to act. Dissatisfied with the board's inaction, women on the committee decided to fight for change outside of management-sanctioned channels.[54]

Committee members, who were college-educated women, began a collaboration with the clerical and production workers who were leading the Harper union.[55] One associate editor called the resulting body a "vertical union" because employees of any rank, editorial and clerical, could and did join.[56] Only those considered "hire-and-fire" supervisory personnel were banned, which meant that most female employees, since they did not typically have such responsibilities, could join.[57]

When members of the women's committee joined in 1973, the union platform in contract renewal negotiations broadened to represent concerns of both professional and wage-earning women. Priority demands from the women's committee included job descriptions and job postings, while the union forwarded traditional labor grievances, demanding 20 percent across-the-board raises and better medical benefits.[58] Harper executives claimed the company was facing financial trouble and could not afford to give raises.[59] With pressure to increase profits, executives refused to incorporate employee demands, particularly those about pay, into a new contract. In turn, the majority of employees working at headquarters went on strike during the summer of 1974. Of the 320 male and female workers, from mailroom runners to associate editors, 200 picketed in midtown Manhattan for seventeen days.[60]

This strike gained support from many employees in almost all ranks within the Harper hierarchy. But some refused to join, claiming that the union—with its broadened agenda—represented the needs of other Harper employees more than their own. A credit analyst remembered that many of the clericals who worked at the manufacturing plant in Scranton, Pennsylvania, described feeling detached from the editorial and managerial women in the New York office. What resulted with the broadened agenda were pockets of discontented clericals who were furious about company policies but unresponsive to the union drive and subsequent strike.[61] In the royalties department, for example, supervisors mandated—illegally— that clericals work overtime or face termination. Although the clericals complained about the mandatory overtime policy, they refused to take part in the union. One union member grew frustrated with her nonunionized colleague's continuous complaining: "I'll say you bitch all the time why don't you grieve [make a grievance through union channels]. And she'll say why bother and I say you bother me every time you bitch." One union organizer called the clericals from royalties "martyrs," believing that they enjoyed moaning about their work conditions.[62]

Upwardly mobile professionals also felt uneasy turning to the union, citing discomfort with the traditional tactics of organized labor. Although a Harper associate editor took her turn on the picket line, she confessed that she felt it was "embarrassing for people of [my] level to walk out," explaining that traditionally professional employees did not join unions or go on strike. One woman said she would never want to participate in a strike because "I'm not an exhibitionist. I find it difficult to put myself on display like that," implying that public protest was both unfeminine and unprofessional. Yet she claimed that because management continued to propose "insulting offers" to women, she overcame her resistance and took shifts on the picket line.[63]

Because a strike in the publishing industry had not occurred for over half a century, the public took notice as employees protested. Media attention and celebrity interest in the strike gave employees additional leverage over their bosses. The *New York Times* "Going Out Guide" in June 1974 announced a fundraising event for the union, calling it "entertainment of a different sort." Writers, politicians, and activists, including Bella Abzug, Noam Chomsky, Benjamin Spock, and Studs Terkel, were to participate in the upcoming event to raise money for those on strike. Protesters announced that they would be auctioning items such as a lunch with a sympathetic Harper executive and the picket signs carried by workers. A flat admission fee to the star-studded event allowed sympathizers "to mingle and bid with the literary and political celebrities."[64]

Given the publicity, as well as the employees from a dozen other New York publishing houses joining the strike in solidarity, Harper executives wanted to negotiate as quickly as possible.[65] Eventually, management gave in to the demands of their employees, who had affiliated with District 65 of the Distributive Workers of America.[66] Although mostly editorial and managerial women served on the negotiation committee, the resulting agreement tried to incorporate the demands of professional, clerical, and production employees.[67] The three-year contract guaranteed substantial, across-the-board, incremental pay increases.[68] Each union member could choose whether to get raises based on a fixed annual sum or raises that were contingent on performance, which was not a traditional term in a union contract.[69] The inclusion of this pay-for-performance option demonstrated that many college-educated publishing employees assumed that with the right policies in place, women could earn equitable rewards for their talents. In addition, the three-year contract guaranteed mandatory internal job postings, which pleased those women who wanted notices about supervisory opportunities and open positions in other departments. Professional women cared deeply for these changes to personnel policy that guaranteed merit-based pay and greater transparency in hiring and promotions. An associate editor thought that the most important result of the strike was that Harper agreed to pay $12,000 for an outside consultant to conduct an extensive job survey on job titles and job descriptions in the company.[70] Ostensibly, she believed that the consultant's examination would reveal that women were performing work that was misaligned with their job titles, and thus Harper executives would be forced to rectify the situation.

The Harper campaign demonstrates an uneasy alliance of women across job function and class status—an alliance that would dissolve with the coming of HR management, which subsumed the concerns of professional women but did not remedy those of clerical women. The campaign exemplifies a moment of vertical feminism in the workplace, whereby women of varying ranks collectively gathered to support sex equality, even though that meant different things to different women.[71] One contemporary unionist noted that although the "leaders of the Harper & Row union are radical-minded, militant, feminist, young women," they deserved credit for appealing to a broader constituency, organizing and sustaining a strike that "kept out 80 percent of the workers."[72]

In this moment—before standardized HR policies seemed to assure ambitious young women that they would be judged on talent, ability, and performance—professional women, as well as those aspiring to professional status, turned to traditional union tactics. And their alliance with wage-earning women resulted in a unique coalition—working-class and professional—that would not flourish in many workplaces beyond the 1970s. For a fleeting moment, concerns about professional mobility became packaged with conventional labor demands in advocacy efforts for women at work.

Propelled by the events at Harper, activist employees at Macmillan, also in New York, forged similar, cross-class alliances. They used several tactics to fight unfair employment practices in the early 1970s, forming a women's group, pushing for unionization, and taking legal action. Unlike the Harper women's committee, the Macmillan women's group formed without management authorization in 1973. At first it existed underground and met during closed sessions that were open only to professional women. Some editors and assistant editors belonged to the group, but it was mostly female managers who organized and led it. Eventually the group would open to all women, and while some clerical women joined, they rarely held leadership positions, reinforcing the perception that the group was more representative of professional interests. One Macmillan employee said the women's group had a reputation for being "too elitist" and having too few clerical workers in it.[73] Nevertheless, female managers used this network to connect with women in other departments and to obtain specific evidence of unequal pay between men and women in the same positions. The women's group discussed the need for internal job postings, which managerial women believed would enable them to seek promotions more easily within the company.[74]

What began as an information-gathering group soon shifted toward action, however, as the women decided to file a class-action suit against Macmillan based on pay inequity.[75] Turning to the government for remedy, they filed charges of sex discrimination with the Equal Employment Opportunity Commission in May 1974. Their complaints included that men and women received different pay for comparable work, and that, once hired, men and women worked in different positions on different job ladders.[76] In addition, the women's group approached the state government with complaints about occupational segregation: 94 percent of women at Macmillan worked in the three lowest clerical positions, and 76 percent of men worked in the top three managerial and editorial positions.[77] The president of Macmillan responded that such statistical imbalances occurred because women chose clerical positions: "It is the nature of the beast that women want to be secretaries."[78] However, New York State attorney general Louis J. Lefkowitz had a different perspective. In response to the conflict at Harper, he had begun investigating publishing houses in the New York City—including Macmillan, McGraw Hill, and Harcourt Brace. The Macmillan women's group requested that he examine their organization closely, submitting a detailed complaint—signed by forty-four female employees at Macmillan—to the New York State Division of Human Rights. This complaint charged that the company engaged in discrimination based on sex as well as on race: of the 370 professional or managerial employees, only 18 identified as Black, Hispanic, or Asian American.[79]

Faced with an active women's group that was taking legal action, the president of Macmillan, Robert A. Barton, was forced to respond. Initially he claimed that Macmillan was not subject to affirmative action guidelines because it did not have government contracts, which was found to be untrue. But eventually he hired an affirmative action officer to create a broader "employee relations plan."[80] The new officer was tasked with formulating goals and timetables for hiring and promoting women and underrepresented men; she would also listen to worker grievances and try to forward solutions. And last, because of low pay and dissatisfaction among hourly employees—both men and women—Macmillan executives issued an 8 percent across-the-board raise for the eight lowest-level positions, hoping to prevent unionization. One employee described the raise as "unheard of," because usually at Macmillan pay increases were infrequent and minimal.[81]

Despite these actions, employees—both hourly and managerial—remained dissatisfied. Most hourly employees wanted more than a one-time pay raise and still found unionization to be an attractive option.[82] Local 153 of the Office and Professional Employees International Union (OPEIU) continued its campaign to organize hourly Macmillan employees.[83] Of the roughly 1,200 employees at Macmillan, about 800 were deemed nonsupervisory and therefore eligible for union membership.[84] An assistant vice president noted that likely the number was higher than 800 since Macmillan classified some women as holding management positions for government reporting purposes.[85] Due to job title inflation (discussed further in chapter 4), Local 153 enjoyed support from a number of female "managers" who were ineligible for union membership. In fact, one member of the women's group, an editor named Donna Mobley, actually quit her Macmillan job to become a union organizer.[86]

Yet other women's group members—both clerical and managerial—felt ambivalent about, or even hostile toward, unionization. Recalled a female executive at Macmillan, "Some people hated the word union. They would have rather have gone with the newspaper guild [than Local 153] because it sounded more [genteel] and it sounded more professional."[87] Several did not think that the union chosen was a strong one and preferred the Harper & Row union, District 65, instead of Local 153.[88] Other women did not prioritize pay as much as other gender-based inequities. One female manager at Macmillan explained that her concerns had little "to do with the lack of money, but [they] had to do with the authoritarian character and lack of dignity . . . the atmosphere of the company." Another woman added,

"The thing is that publishing people have not gone into publishing for money, they have gone into it because they loved the idea of making books."[89]

Nevertheless, by October 1974 about half of the eligible employees supported the union, triggering Local 153 to file a petition with the NLRB to start conducting union elections.[90] A week later, Macmillan executives announced the firing of two hundred employees due to poor profits and dismal economic conditions. On October 14 and 15, employees waited to see if they would be called into the conference room, with the *New York Times* reporting that some "slipped out for a quick drink or took tranquilizers" to manage the anxiety. One employee described the atmosphere as hysterical, with all employees operating in a panicked state.[91]

The board chairman of Macmillan told the *New York Times* that the firings were part of "an over-all corporate belt-tightening program" so that Macmillan could "concentrate our resources and efforts on protecting and developing those parts of our business in which we have been most successful."[92] But sales and revenues actually had increased from 1973 to 1974, causing many Macmillan employees to believe that the dismissals were related to the union drive, and perhaps to the women's group too.[93] In fact, executives had fired the leading supporters of Local 153, as well as vocal participants from the women's group. The cochair of the women's group, the director of marketing for children's books, remembered her disbelief and dismay: "At four o'clock that afternoon [October 15, 1974], after 13 years of service, I was given one hour to get out, as was my staff of five." Although Macmillan had not fired each and every member of either the women's group or Local 153, most employees believed that executives were issuing a warning to those who remained.[94]

Yet the firings generated stronger resistance, as more managerial women protested the actions of Macmillan executives.[95] Two female children's books editors resigned in opposition, claiming that the firings disparately and permanently damaged their department (which had been one of Macmillan's most profitable).[96] Those in the women's group—both former and current Macmillan employees—again contacted the state attorney general. Although Lefkowitz already had begun pursuing sex and racial discrimination charges against Macmillan, they wanted to ensure that he would investigate the legality of the dismissals too. Union activists turned to the NLRB on October 15, filing an unfair labor practice charge. Eventually the board agreed with the union, determining that the terminations were unlawful since they were found to be related to upcoming union elections.[97]

Macmillan employees quickly organized a strike, set to begin on October 17, 1974, just days after the firings and only a few months after the Harper strike. In front of their Manhattan office building, Macmillan former and current employees picketed, joined by sympathetic colleagues from other publishing companies, as well as Macmillan authors.[98] Although the number of reported strikers varied depending on the source, anywhere from twenty-five to a hundred picketers each day were reportedly singing the popular union song "Solidarity Forever" and shouting, "Don't scab for Macmillan" to those entering the building.[99] About thirty employees remained on strike for eight weeks while awaiting a decision from the NLRB on the validity of the firings and the union's legitimacy.[100] Among those who were not on the picket line, hundreds of Macmillan employees called in "sick" for almost a week, staying home to protest the firings.[101] And also in support of the strike, the Teamsters Union purposefully slowed its shipping speed at Macmillan's New Jersey warehouse. In addition, the New York Central Labor Council announced its support of Local 153, calling for the reinstatement of the dismissed workers.[102] The strike managed to damage Macmillan's operations. Those still going to the office admitted that little real work was being accomplished, largely because morale "is terrible."[103] Macmillan stock plummeted and remained depressed for years in the 1970s.[104]

After determining that the dismissals had been unlawful, the government ordered Macmillan to alter its hiring and promotion policies. In 1976 the State Division of Human Rights ruled that there was probable cause to believe that Macmillan had engaged in discriminatory employment practices. As a result, Macmillan negotiated a settlement with the Human Rights Commission to avoid going to court. The company agreed to equalize pay and benefits between men and women, to provide written job descriptions, to post available jobs internally, and to work toward better representation of women in the editorial and managerial ranks. Furthermore, in 1985, eleven years after the women's group initially filed a class action complaint with the EEOC and with the state attorney general, Macmillan signed a consent decree. The company agreed to change hiring and promotion practices in order to advance women, as well as to provide women with career counseling and tuition-refund programs. And the decree provided almost $2 million in back pay to female employees. Lawyers' fees took $700,000 out of the award. Although the women who had initially forwarded the case received larger sums, the majority of women who had worked at Macmillan in the early to mid-1970s received checks for a few thousand dollars.[105]

After these two historic strikes in New York City in 1974, two union drives succeeded in Boston publishing houses. At Beacon Press in 1979, unionized employees achieved, on average, an 8 percent salary increase, as well as greater coverage for paid job training.[106] And in a contract ratified in January 1982, Beacon employees gained an 8.5 percent across-the-board raise—more than standard raises in nonunionized houses—as well as access to merit-based increases.[107] With the support of Beacon employees, Allyn & Bacon employees went on strike in 1980 after management attempted to undermine a union organizing drive. The strike resulted in a contract securing compensatory time off as well as 5 percent across-the-board raises for employees (plus the potential for 7.5 percent more based on performance).[108]

The activism that took place in publishing houses in Boston and New York demonstrates a broader vision of feminism at work that included the concerns of both managerial and clerical women. Employees fought for upward mobility by seeking to change the organizational policies and structures that hindered the advancement of those in female-dominated jobs. Managerial women, like their clerical colleagues, relied on collective action to fight for access to equal opportunity in an industry that historically had privileged men over women. Yet this platform—which united working women across occupational lines—would fracture by the 1980s, as HR departments began to subsume the concerns of professional women.

━━━ ✖ ━━━

Although unions remained rare in the publishing industry, collective action to advance women took place through nonunion channels in a key professional association known as Women in Publishing, or WIP. When Nussbaum and Cassedy founded 9to5 in 1973, WIP was its first industry-based subcommittee.[109] Fifty to a hundred women from across Boston's publishing houses attended weekly meetings of WIP, with stated goals to collect information about women working in publishing firms, to aid women in solving their workplace problems at these companies, and to investigate affirmative action practices in publishing and bring about greater compliance.[110]

In addition to WIP, 9to5 had other industry-based subcommittees in the 1970s (for banking, insurance, and universities). These other subcommittees advanced claims about the economic and social value of clerical work, pushing for higher wages and public recognition. The college-educated women who developed the WIP platform primarily focused on career development, seeing themselves as worthy of exclusively male managerial positions. According to the minutes of a 9to5 meeting, WIP tended to "attract people that are better off," which usually meant white women with advanced degrees who were qualified for editorial and managerial work.[111] Yet, because of their gender, women, regardless of credentials, had been assigned secretarial jobs out of college.

With aspirations of moving to editorial and managerial positions, WIP members set their sights on working with company executives to institute job postings, refine job titles and job descriptions, and expand training opportunities. While advocating for professional advancement to elevate themselves out of clerical work, WIP members simultaneously supported clerical unions for other women. They helped with union campaigns for those at Allyn & Bacon as well as at Beacon. In fact, one WIP founder had union experience prior to helping to start her own organization. Boston editor Anita McClellan, who had risen through the ranks from secretary to department head, tried to help the United Electrical Workers (UE) organize her publishing house. While McClellan had managerial status and could not be a union member, she supported unionization for publishing workers. Yet she became frustrated with UE's lack of knowledge about the industry and about the women they wanted to represent. McClellan reported that the UE's male organizers did not seem to understand the "white-collar prejudice against joining a union."[112] As one associate editor at Houghton Mifflin claimed, women in publishing saw themselves as "intellectuals . . . it's like being an associate professor and people like us don't unionize."[113] McClellan eventually cut ties with the union, annoyed that UE did not understand why having all-male union organizers and leaders could pose a problem when trying to organize publishing clericals.[114]

Initially most WIP members wanted to work "behind the scenes," building the new organization not through public protest but by doing "telephoning, typing, and recordkeeping," according to McClellan. Many women told her that they felt reluctant to defy their bosses openly, with lingering hopes that they might get promoted, and thus they did not want to be viewed as "sexually frustrated 'bra burners,'" which would ruin "good girls' prospects and relationship with management."[115] Thus from the beginning, WIP did push for institutional change, but members wanted to avoid being labeled as radicals.

Reluctant to take part in public demonstrations, WIP founders and members began with the more discreet task of data collection. They wanted to have statistical proof of industry-wide patterns of gender discrimination.[116] Members distributed questionnaires to employees in at least thirty Boston publishing houses; they mined company rosters, annual reports, and other public information for more statistics. After several months of compiling and analyzing information on the workforce, WIP created and released its first public report in March 1975. Revealing this type of industry-wide data was quite revolutionary, at a time before written job descriptions and standard salary ranges existed in most firms, let alone were made public. Statistics showed that between 60 and 70 percent of employees in Boston's publishing industry were women; however, only 5 to 10 percent of women employees had management-level positions. WIP gathered evidence to confirm that almost every woman had begun her career in clerical work, starting at about $6,000 per year, and most reported extreme difficulty moving upward into the editorial positions. Men, in contrast, rarely started in clerical work and constituted the overwhelming majority of managers and executives in the industry.[117]

WIP's data collection efforts began to connect personnel practices with unequal career outcomes, particularly women's lower pay. Survey responses showed that "promotions" often gave women new titles and additional job responsibilities without adequate, commensurate increases in salary. Now, WIP had proof that enhanced job titles often did not promise raises. The average woman who earned a promotion received a merit increase of only 3.5 percent annually (after accounting for cost-of-living increases), according to WIP data. WIP compared male and female employees' salaries, controlling for education and job experience. It found that there was a gap of over $3,000 per year in starting salaries (which represented a significant difference relative to total salary) for college-educated male and female workers.[118]

A few months after compiling this initial report, WIP produced a second report in the summer of 1975 that further exposed gender inequity in Boston area houses. It detailed the various employment policies and practices of firms, including Addison-Wesley; Allyn & Bacon; Atlantic Monthly; Cahners; Educators Publishing Service; Ginn & Co.; D. C. Heath; Houghton Mifflin; Little, Brown; and Prindle, Weber & Schmidt. This benchmark report allowed employees to evaluate their own benefits and working conditions relative to others in the area. It included data about paid sick days per year, pension plans, job postings, salary reviews, in-house training, educational assistance, and overtime policies. The report offered a rough listing of salary ranges and job titles for each company but noted that comparisons could be difficult because of "lack of knowledge about scope of job included under a particular job title."[119] To bring more attention to this survey, WIP issued a public announcement of "dubious distinction awards," including most petty rules, worst company to grow old in, and the company with no maternity benefits.[120]

Armed with proof that personnel practices engendered inequality, WIP members filed legal claims against their employers, forwarding charges to the Office of Federal Contract Compliance (OFCC) against Ginn, Heath, and Addison-Wesley for failing to inform employees about affirmative action programs and failing to post job openings internally.[121] In addition, WIP approached Massachusetts attorney general Francis X. Bellotti to take legal action against the houses it saw as the worst offenders in hiring, promotion, and pay practices.[122] With WIP data reports in hand, Attorney General Bellotti began investigations at Addison-Wesley, Allyn & Bacon, and Houghton Mifflin as WIP proceeded to file charges with the Massachusetts Commission Against Discrimination (MCAD) as well as with the EEOC. Members claimed that the three firms failed to hire and equitably place women and underrepresented men in managerial and executive positions.[123]

WIP maintained that these companies had unlawful practices because they did not post job openings, failed to transfer and promote women, allocated pay unequally to men and women doing the same work, and did not take positive actions to overcome past discrimination.[124] Executives at Allyn & Bacon and Houghton Mifflin argued that they were complying with the law, pointing to tangible copies of their affirmative action plans as well as to specific women who held positions as supervisors and department heads.[125] According to the Ginn personnel director, these flimsy charges were "procedural" in nature and lacked substantive merit.[126] Inequalities in career outcomes should not be blamed on employers.

Tensions continued to rise at Houghton Mifflin in particular, where pay inequality and occupational segregation angered clerical and managerial women alike. Five women filed charges of sex and wage discrimination with MCAD in December 1974 and with the EEOC in February 1975, citing low pay and lack of promotions. Yet neither backlogged agency acted expeditiously on the claims. Thus, the "Houghton Mifflin Five," as they were known in the media, filed a class action suit in November 1975, seeking $2 million in back pay. Combined, these five women had over thirty-two years of experience with Houghton; all had college degrees and previous work experience too. Their case revealed that men entering the firm with lesser qualifications were receiving promotions ahead of them.[147] In addition, Houghton management was not posting jobs for supervisory or managerial positions, which women claimed kept them from knowing about promotional opportunities. WIP urged that all jobs should be posted internally, even those in sales and consulting (male-dominated positions), believing that internal job posting would allow women to move out of clerical work.[148] When WIP met with Houghton personnel officers, the company claimed it would "move towards" more universal job posting. However, WIP reported after the meeting: "Clear timetables for this are lacking."[149]

The legal case against Houghton eventually settled to the plaintiffs' satisfaction, with women at Houghton receiving a $750,000 back-pay award. Also the judge mandated that Houghton move toward more equitable employment practices, which forced it to address WIP's list of concerns. Houghton executives set goals for female representation in higher-level editorial positions, discussed posting all job openings internally, and created a Joint Monitoring Committee to supervise fulfillment of settlement terms. The committee would comprise the Houghton EEO officer, three members selected by the Houghton Mifflin Five, and three additional members (of any rank) chosen by a popular vote of all employees.[130]

WIP stayed vigilant to keep Houghton executives accountable for implementation of settlement terms. It claimed credit for two women becoming vice presidents, a number of clerical women being promoted to editorial and managerial positions, and an adjustment of pay scales to increase clerical compensation.[131]

Beyond its efforts at Houghton, which was reputed to have particularly egregious pay and promotional practices, WIP worked to alter personnel procedures across the Boston publishing industry. It identified certain issues of concern—misappropriated job titles, vague job descriptions, and lack of job postings and job training—that systematically disadvantaged women in their pursuit of promotions. Among these issues, WIP prioritized the issue of internal job posting. Not just at Houghton, but across the industry, women complained that often the most coveted managerial and editorial jobs were the ones that personnel did not post. In New York, women at Harper demanded that openings for supervisory positions appear on the office bulletin boards. Women were convinced that "such matters [meaning promotion to management jobs] were settled behind the scenes," and patronage, not merit, prevailed.[132] Women claimed that they learned of an open position only after a man was hired for the job.

According to the EEOC, lack of transparency about open positions was not just unfair but also illegal. Publications from the American Management Association (AMA) instructed personnel managers on how to comply with government mandates when hiring and selecting. A report in 1974, coauthored by the EEOC, outlined specific guidelines for recruitment, hiring, and selection processes. The EEOC declared that "word-of-mouth recruiting" had become inadequate as a mechanism for filling open jobs.[133]

Employment scholar Jennie Farley echoed this mandate in her prescriptive book for personnel managers. No longer could managers rely on "word-of-mouth recruiting" or "walk-in" as the primary mechanisms to construct an applicant pool. Instead, she claimed that employers now had a legal responsibility to publicize all vacancies and build a demographically diverse pool of applicants. Furthermore, job advertisements should include language such as "equality opportunity employer, M/F" to emphasize that women were welcome to apply. Because managers had "baggage from the past," meaning stereotypical ideas of women's job preferences, posting all available jobs would allow women to decide for themselves if they would want to apply for a job that required travel or relocation.

Farley hoped that with mandatory internal job posting, a woman at the nonexempt level, meaning nonsupervisory, who had been unaware of the opening or "hadn't thought of herself as a potential candidate because of long-ingrained custom" would now consider applying to an exempt, supervisory position.[134] Job postings were viewed as influencing both the supply and demand sides of discrimination: more female candidates would apply to jobs where they were underrepresented historically, and personnel managers would begin to consider a wider range of applicants for each position.

WIP founding member Anita McClellan provided an example of the nepotistic hiring traditions in publishing that had long disadvantaged women (along with many men of color as well as men without the proper pedigree). When selecting summer interns, most senior editors did not publicly post the jobs at all. Rather, an executive personally invited a "Harvard freshman, son of one of the editors or of an editor's friend—always an Adams House man" to read manuscripts each summer. After a summer of training and development, he would receive a junior editor position after college graduation. Angered at this convention, McClellan, a department head who had started as a secretary, flouted the traditional selection process for summer interns. Anonymously she posted an advertisement in the *Harvard Crimson* to notify the entire Harvard community of the coveted summer internship. Hundreds of students immediately began calling the personnel manager to inquire about the internship, which enraged senior editors who felt that they were entitled to make the selection single-handedly without any intervention.[135]

On the whole, the recruitment, hiring, and selection processes in the publishing industry were misaligned with new EEOC guidelines, and WIP stood ready to advocate for change. Because the industry had the best educated, and potentially lowest paid, clerical workers in New York and in Boston, many women saw existing personnel practices as the biggest hindrance to their upward mobility. In an informal poll of female publishing employees, WIP found that 65 percent rated job postings as the *most important* workplace issue they faced. Given that most women prioritized it, yet most publishing houses were not transparent about open positions, WIP began a grassroots campaign in October 1975, while simultaneously waging the legal battle of the Houghton Mifflin Five, to push employers to post all jobs internally.[136]

Tackling this concern had two benefits: women would gain greater access to managerial and editorial jobs, and WIP could attain victory given EEOC mandates about posting. WIP told *Publishers Weekly* that institutionalization of internal job posting represented "a major tool for equal employment opportunity and a weapon against the 'male grapevine' system of promotion."[137] In addition, WIP cited posting as a "clear issue . . . [with] visible proof of victory," which would boost support for the organization. In addition, WIP argued that postings would benefit the corporate bottom line, claiming that internal hires were cheaper than external recruits.[138] Personnel costs would remain lower if companies promoted from within rather than paying agency fees for hiring outside employees, and then expending time and money training them.[139]

WIP perceived affirmative action guidelines as a mandate that all open positions should be posted for two weeks internally before being released to the external applicant pool. Postings should detail the "general purpose of the position," contain a "description of duties involved," list required qualifications, the salary range, and promotional possibilities or limitations. WIP hoped that with job postings would come more standardized job descriptions. Companies would be forced to be more specific about duties and responsibilities for each job, as well as the positioning of the job on company career ladders.[140]

When approaching their own personnel departments about their concerns, WIP members developed a couple of tactics to push for companywide postings. First, they showed that employees prioritized the posting issue, submitting petitions and poll results to management. This evidence drove several corporate management teams to meet with WIP and to consider their recommendations.[141] Second, WIP continued to pursue legal action against companies that failed to post, claiming that they were violating federal affirmative action guidelines.[142] Although the EEOC was issuing orders to try to enforce job postings, the federal government was not investigating each and every private-sector firm. Employees had to initiate complaints against specific employers to bring about adherence to the law.[143]

With the Houghton Mifflin Five case ongoing in the background, employers were receptive to this particular demand from WIP. In less than a year, the job posting campaign had achieved significant success in Boston. WIP's chairwoman Nancy Farrell stated to *Publishers Weekly*, "Our

campaign succeeded through WIP's industry-wide pressure for fair treatment of women."[144] When WIP had started its campaign in October 1975,
only two Boston-area houses posted all jobs, and six did not post any jobs.
By June 1976 four houses had moved to complete postings and five had
partial postings, meaning they posed some but not all managerial jobs.
Both Educators Publishing Service and Allyn & Bacon had transformed
their corporate policies from having no postings at all to instituting full
postings within the year.[145] Three other houses—Cahners Publishing,
Houghton Mifflin, and D. C. Heath—changed their policies to have partial postings. By the fall of 1976 two Boston publishing houses, Atlantic
Monthly and Addison-Wesley, still were not posting any jobs. When WIP
inquired, Addison-Wesley argued that it always tried to promote from
within; furthermore, it claimed that the federal government approved its
employment practices when the company was audited. Atlantic Monthly
maintained that it already had explained why it did not internally post
jobs (although WIP responded that no adequate explanation had been
provided).[146]

The swift win on job posting revealed that amid a changing policy landscape (as detailed in chapter 4), employers wanted to avoid legal entanglements and appease their employees—so long as those demands did not
cast too heavy a burden. And, significantly, job postings were a relatively
easy way for employers to demonstrate EEO compliance, since instituting postings required little financial investment.[147]

But would this move toward greater transparency promise internal
clerical women the opportunity to move into male-dominated managerial and editorial positions? Potentially, it might have. Internal postings
of all positions might have allowed for more clerical applicants, and perhaps employers would have given preference to internal over external
candidates to offer more opportunities for upward mobility. Turnover
among female employees was lower in firms that adhered to affirmative
action mandates like job posting, likely because women perceived greater
potential for promotions. While employers could meet affirmative action
guidelines by recruiting externally for job categories with few women, they
also could have addressed underrepresentation by moving incumbent
female employees upward.[148] And to be sure, job posting did not promise
that a woman or underrepresented man would inquire about the opening, forward her application, or be selected by a hiring manager.

Aside from pushing for the institutionalization of internal job postings, WIP wanted to address the way that job titles were sustaining gender inequity in the office. A female college graduate who expressed a desire to become an editor often would be hired with a title of "editorial assistant," while a similarly situated young man would be hired as a "junior editor." In reality, an editorial assistant and a junior editor had dissimilar career prospects.[149] With the word "editorial" in their job title, women may have believed that they were on a promotional path to become an assistant editor or even an editor. An "editorial assistant," however, was a job title on the clerical job track and thus not traditionally considered when promoting new hires to the position of "assistant editor," which was on the editor track. Furthermore, some firms manipulated job titles to avoid paying overtime. Many had a verbal policy that any employee who had the word "editorial" in her title was exempt from wage and hours laws. Thus publishing houses could squeeze longer hours from editorial assistants without having to pay them time and a half for overtime. In reality, these editorial assistants might really have been performing clerical work, in which case they should have been considered nonexempt employees.[150]

Creative use of job titles allowed employers to maintain occupational segregation and pay inequity while complying with affirmative action guidelines. To keep their government contracts, firms were required to set goals and timetables for the hiring and promotion of women and underrepresented men into job categories where they were underutilized relative to their representation in the broader population. For reporting purposes, firms were to classify all employees into one of seven very broad categories, two of which were "clerical" and "managerial." Because so many women were already performing jobs classified as clerical, firms used job titles such as editorial assistant so that they could categorize a greater number of women as managerial when reporting affirmative action data.[151] Male and female employees rarely had the same titles, even if they were performing the same job tasks. And a proliferation of job titles made discrimination more difficult to prove. The seven editors in the Trade Department at Holt, Rinehart, and Winston held six different titles, allowing Holt to pay them six different salaries.[152] This trend was not unique to the publishing industry. One insurance firm reportedly had 5,000 workers with 2,500 different job titles.[153]

Along with job posting and job titles, the issue of job descriptions was a third area of concern for WIP. If written job descriptions existed at all, employers rarely adhered to them. Without written job descriptions at the point of hire, a matriculating employee could begin a position with a verbal understanding of job duties that could change once she was employed. While in some firms editorial assistants performed clerical duties only and did not receive any editorial work, at other firms women were hired with the title of "secretary" but performed the tasks of an editor (without the pay or title). Even for positions with the same job title, the tasks could vary greatly within a single organization. An associate editor at Harper disclosed that all women with the job title of "editorial assistant" had different responsibilities depending on supervisor and department.[154] Women at E. P. Dutton who had the same job titles as men received lower pay; also, they were expected to "perform functions that men in similar positions would not be asked to do—a little female cleaning up every now and then," according to one woman who worked there. Another woman at Farrar, Straus and Giroux maintained that supervisors would ask a woman to do tasks she was not hired to do and frame it as an opportunity for "'learning the ropes' although it is understood that the ropes lead to nowhere."[155]

The allocation of job titles and the lack of written job descriptions demonstrated how difficult it could be for women to prove discrimination.[156] And knowledge of pay scales was paramount to demonstrate women's disadvantages. When describing the problem of sex discrimination in publishing, advertising director Hilda Lindley said, "There ought to be a survey house to house to see who is employed in what job and how much they earn."[157]

So WIP embarked on gathering salary data. Although the National Labor Relations Act of 1935 forbade employers from penalizing or firing unionized employees who discussed pay, among nonunion employees pay was anything but transparent. White-collar employees rarely shared their salaries with one another, and many publishing women admitted that they were unsure of the formal salary range for their positions. At Bantam Books the personnel manager admitted that no standard pay scale existed. Because secretarial positions could vary widely, the personnel office adjusted salaries to each individual job, usually somewhat related to status of the supervisor.[158] At Allyn & Bacon the company outright denied workers access to this information. At other houses salary ranges existed for some positions but not for others. Most female employees maintained that they reached a ceiling after a few years of service, and they had to fight to receive paid job training for new positions that would promise higher ranges. When WIP investigated by distributing surveys, responses indicated that employees at eleven of the eighteen houses thought their salaries were inadequate, and many were expected to do overtime work without pay. And using salary information from all eighteen houses, WIP's wage surveys concluded that women in Boston earned $1,000 to $5,000 less annually than the national average for publishing employees.[159] On average, publishing salaries in Boston were several thousand dollars lower than earnings for women in teaching.[160]

WIP's compensation report, *Publishing Salaries in the Boston Area: A Comparison Report* (1977), promoted the idea that salary ranges should be assigned to jobs, not people.[161] WIP suggested that women use the report to "check to be sure that they are classified at the right level. It is not unheard of for an employee to be performing the duties of a higher-level position with the title, and pay, of a lower-level position."[162] WIP cofounder Anita McClellan confirmed that members took advantage of the "small database to use in negotiating pay increases and performance reviews."[163]

Several women noted on their surveys that answering questions about equal pay in their firms was difficult, if not impossible. Stated one assistant to the editor at Atlantic Monthly about the issue of pay equality: "Hard to say—all assistants to editors [the company title for secretaries] are women and only one of the editors is a woman."[164] When asked about pay equality at her firm, a secretary in the Ginn marketing department stated, "Don't know—there are no male secretaries." An associate editor at Houghton Mifflin revealed, "Technically yes [there was equal pay for equal work] under the new salary scale but the men have had a traditional advantage in getting the higher paying positions." Another Houghton editor stated, "They've equalized salaries for people in job categories, but men are the ones who move up into new job categories with the higher salaries."[165] In ten of eighteen houses, survey respondents thought that men, relative to women employees, had more favorable salary ranges for the same jobs.[166] The tendency to assign women to lower-status jobs on less prestigious job ladders was preventing female publishing workers from attaining full economic citizenship.

With women pushing for equitable treatment, publishing firms turned to the advice of professional consultants to help review and standardize job titles and job descriptions. Some women viewed these consultants with skepticism: they were perceived as arms of management who did not have their best interest in mind. Other women, usually those who saw themselves as having career potential, welcomed them as allies in the fight to calm the chaos of unruly personnel practices. They believed that more transparent personnel practices—and greater standardization within and between publishing houses—could grant them opportunities for deserved promotions. Recall that after the Harper strike ended, one associate editor had declared that the most promising result of the activism was not the commitment to across-the-board raises, but rather that Harper agreed to pay $12,000 for an outside consultant to conduct an extensive survey about job titles and job descriptions.[167] Given that its members wanted promotions, WIP supported the use of consultants, indicating a belief that more standardized personnel policies would make for meritocratic outcomes. WIP's collaboration with management went even further: it offered its own consulting services to personnel managers. For a fee, it could provide expertise to publishing firms as they revised their procedures.[168]

At Houghton Mifflin executives hired Hay Associates Consulting, a leader in the industry for surveying employees and issuing recommendations about personnel practices. Houghton executives believed that the Hay survey and analysis would improve employee relations and make the office more productive.[169] Consultants conducted extensive interviews to determine the tasks and duties each employee actually performed, regardless of job title. The consultants also inquired about employee satisfaction at Houghton to help executives determine how to quell interest in unions.[170]

When Hay Associates arrived at Houghton, some employees seemed eager to participate in Hay's activities while others doubted that the study would lead to greater equity. Those who were skeptical referred to mandated participation in interviews as being "Hayed." One employee wrote that the surveys were "an expensive lot of baloney" and that "the only people who will profit from all this interviewing and conferring and grading is Hay Associates. The money that HM is handing over to Hay might be better apportioned out in all our paychecks."[171]

While some employees reported significant improvements following the Hay survey, the legal battles waged by the Houghton Mifflin Five actually forced Houghton executives to make substantive changes. By 1978 more Houghton female employees were reporting that they were "generally happy" at the company, which was promoting more women, issuing written job descriptions, and improving salary scales for clerical jobs. And, according to some women, Houghton personnel officers had become very approachable, and were willing to meet with employees to hear whatever was on their minds.[172] By 1979 Houghton had written personnel policies to cover job training, salary ranges, performance reviews, and overtime pay. Written policy also detailed the existence of a permanent Houghton grievance committee, where a panel of "professional" and "nonprofessional" employees would help to resolve intrafirm conflicts.[173]

Like Houghton Mifflin, Beacon Press enlisted consultants to review personnel procedures after WIP-supported union activity. The consultants' reviews revealed widespread employee dissatisfaction.[174] Wells Drorbaugh, director of Beacon Press, hired Olney Association Inc. Management Consultants to review recommendations from in-house attorneys and personnel officers. Olney recommended that in order to comply with EEO policy, Beacon needed to institute a host of new personnel practices: written job descriptions, job postings, salary reviews, in-house job training, tuition reimbursement, and grievance procedures. He warned against hiring people with similar education and experience into positions with different job titles and different salary levels. To encourage employee retention, Olney recommended implementation of cost-of-living adjustments within Beacon's "budgetary limitations." Beacon executives worked with Olney to attach a "price tag" to each of the recommendations, investigating costs before committing to any changes based solely on "philosophical reasons."[175]

After some discussion, Beacon executives began to institute the consultant's recommendations. In 1976 Drorbaugh made some adjustments for exempt employees: he standardized job titles and job descriptions, as well as instituted mandatory job postings. Other changes followed for clerical employees, who had fewer benefits than nonexempt employees. Now, all employees were eligible for life insurance, severance pay, and at least three weeks of vacation time. Beacon began following federal and state laws that required time-and-a-half pay for overtime work. It had never offered maternity leave before, but now the company provided both exempt and nonexempt employees with eight weeks of paid leave for mothers and two weeks of paid leave for fathers.[176]

In sum, faced with EEO mandates and grassroots pressure from WIP, executives decided to move toward standardization of personnel procedures such as job postings, job titles, and job descriptions. The publishing industry was moving away from its history of nepotistic hiring practices and toward a merit-based personnel system that, in theory, would reward talent, performance, and ability.

The resulting systems, however, did not completely end institutionalized gender bias, even in EEO-compliant workplaces. As sociologist Ronnie Steinberg has shown, widely used job evaluations systems, such as the Hay Guide Chart-Profile Method, which was created in the 1940s and 1950s, perpetuated wage inequities between men and women. Steinberg has argued that the Hay system "is one example of an institutional practice that sustains the status quo," labeling the lower pay allocated to nonsupervisory, female-dominated positions as equitable. In the Hay system "all nonmanagerial, nonprofessional work is treated as less complex, less responsible, and less onerous." These evaluation systems actually elevated the content and duties associated with tasks in male-dominated jobs while devaluing the content and duties associated with tasks in female-dominated jobs.[177]

Corporate policies regarding job training likewise tended to institutionalize bias against the content and duties of female-dominated clerical and secretarial work. WIP succeeded in pushing companies toward mandatory job posting, written job descriptions, and standardized job titles, but its efforts to guarantee paid job training for clerical women who wanted to advance to editorial or managerial positions failed. WIP advocated for training and education in areas beyond one's current job duties, which would provide opportunities for upward mobility. For WIP, the question was not just whether publishing firms paid for training, but also which employees were eligible for what types of training. Would publishing houses pay for clerical employees to take classes about editorial work? Or would they only pay for courses related to an employee's present position?[178] This issue of which courses would be considered related to one's job was a proxy for whether executives saw promotional promise in their clerical employees.

Women complained that employers had little interest in training and developing those in clerical positions. A woman who worked at W. W. Norton stated that the "once-a-secretary-always-a-secretary" syndrome pervaded her organization. When hiring for an upper-level publicity position, colleagues would respect an experienced female recruited from the outside more so than a secretary who had risen internally, through the ranks. The secretary "would forever be treated as the 'girl' who had, by accident or indiscretion, been given a man's job." At Harper an employee stated that "if an editor's job were to open up at Harper's, management would in all probability recruit male talent from the outside."[179] A paperback publicist said her publishing house "does not try to develop its personnel or give individual opportunities for advancement . . . no promotions from within."[180]

So starting in December 1976, immediately following the successful campaign for mandatory job postings, WIP began to gather information about training and educational opportunities for employees in different job categories, including clerical, editorial, production, art, design, marketing, business administration, copy writing, and management. It investigated adult education programs at local community colleges; publishing-related classes at Northeastern University, Radcliffe College, Boston University, and Simmons College; as well as courses offered by the professional associations Bookbuilders and the Word Guild. By January 1977 WIP had begun to construct an industry-wide report about in-house training and external educational courses.[181] For ten major publishing houses in Boston, WIP composed a chart that compared training and development information about orientation programs, trainee positions, on-the-job training, in-house courses, and educational assistance. This chart revealed that only a few companies covered tuition for job-related courses, and almost none of them covered tuition for career-related courses (meaning education that would help an employee advance to a higher level). Although most had informal on-the-job training, only a few of the companies had in-house courses.[182] Furthermore, WIP created a survey to measure employee satisfaction with current training practices. Survey returns showed that over half of employees believed that the tuition reimbursement program at their company needed improvement. Over-whelmingly, respondents claimed that their company did not provide training for advancement into a different job category, and most employ-ees were unsure if internal career paths existed for upward mobility.[183]

Survey returns also demonstrated that most training policies, and spe-cifically, which courses an employer would cover financially, did not help clericals to advance to higher levels. Which courses were eligible for employer reimbursement was often decided on a case-by-case basis. An Allyn & Bacon secretary wrote about tuition reimbursement that there were "no written guidelines for what one can/cannot take; seems to be a personality thing—I was denied 2 courses because they 'did not fit my job category.'" She believed that the company should pay for courses that allowed employees to seek promotional positions, not just for those designed for their current jobs. Another employee complained that the company paid only for courses that "directly relate to your job." Thus "if an editor (assistant or associate) wants to take a management course, they will not be reimbursed because only a senior editor could conceivably take such a course."[184]

Another woman contested the current Houghton policy, which reim-bursed 100 percent for job-related clerical courses and only 50 percent for publishing-related courses. She stated, "We believe that, in order to gain skills and training needed to change job categories, women often need to take courses beyond the immediate scope of their jobs." She recommended that Houghton Mifflin expand tuition reimbursement to cover fully any publishing-related courses for any employees.[185] Houghton responded that clericals could attend internal trainings that were already occurring, or even suggest new topics for internal training seminars. But the company refused to expand tuition reimbursement for external education.[186]

After gathering data and surveying employees in Boston, WIP issued formal recommendations regarding training and development in June 1977. "Job Training Proposals" advised employers on WIP's pre-ferred practices for training and development. During the orientation of new employees, WIP wanted employers to delineate career paths by providing organizational charts indicating opportunities for mobility within the corporate hierarchy. Also, WIP requested that companies develop written education policies to make training reimbursement trans-parent to all prospective and current employees.

Regarding in-house training, WIP demanded that all employees have access to programs for advancement beyond their present positions. Typically, publishing houses started women in secretarial training programs and men in higher-level editorial and managerial training.[187] Yet WIP believed that all employees should be given the opportunity to observe those in other jobs and even rotate among different departments and job functions.[188] One female manager told *Publishers Weekly* that companies take a male college graduate and "put him in various departments for several months" so he can figure out where he fits best, yet women did not have the same opportunities for rotations and cross-functional trainings.[189] To encourage an environment of growth and development, WIP wanted experienced employees to receive time and credit for teaching others so that informal training did not become a burdensome, unpaid responsibility.[190]

In addition to internal opportunities, WIP issued several recommendations regarding external education. First, it wanted firms to stay abreast of training opportunities in the larger community and to inform employees of events that may be of interest. WIP also requested that publishing houses pay for employees to attend industry-sponsored seminars, workshops, and conventions. Furthermore, companies should provide full financial support for courses intended to prepare employees for advancement, not just for those aimed to improve performance in their current jobs. Publishing houses should collaborate with local colleges and universities to develop specific courses applicable to the learning needs of employees.[191] And for employees who could not afford the full prepayment of tuition, WIP recommended that publishing houses provide low-interest loans to ease the economic burden of paying upfront for external courses.

Citing high turnover among clericals and many women interested in upward mobility, WIP invited personnel managers to a meeting to hear the results of employee surveys and WIP's recommendations for paid job training. WIP reminded managers that they were losing talented female employees by failing to provide clear career paths for advancement. Although women relinquished some benefits by changing companies, "the employer suffers the greater loss—an employee who 'knows the ropes' and who [had wanted] to contribute" has left.[192] The group estimated that some houses had turnover rates of 30 percent annually. And, by WIP estimates, retraining new employees could cost thousands of dollars per year.[193]

Despite WIP's arguments for enhanced training opportunities, most companies did not endorse recommendations to expand reimbursement so generously. Employers rarely provided full tuition coverage for clerical employees to advance to new levels in the company on different job ladders.[194] And EEO policy did not mandate that employers had to take on the economic burden of providing job training for employees to further their careers beyond their present positions. In fact, employment scholar Jennie Farley wrote, "Of the three personnel functions discussed—recruiting, selecting, and training—the third may be the least changed by the new legislation." Farley further explained that the law was vague as to the responsibility of corporations to assist "members of affected groups to become qualified for advancement." After speaking with different affirmative action officers, Farley concluded that a woman's supervisor had a lot of influence over whether she would grow and advance.[195]

The fact that a supervisor had so much power and authority over an employee's career advancement had ambivalent effects. On the one hand, a merit-based system should reward the employees who showed the most talent and promise, grooming them for advancement. On the other hand, conventional gender norms could result in bias against training and developing women, especially for nontraditional positions. Among personnel, the idea remained that training a young man was an investment opportunity, but training a woman was a waste of money because she would not remain in the workforce, according to Farley.[196] "Women, very simply, are not actively encouraged to develop," declared a woman about the culture at Doubleday.[197]

A survey of Harper employees showed that "three-quarters of the men, but less than half of the women, were offered jobs described as growth positions that could lead to greater responsibilities."[198] Whereas supervisors groomed men for advancement from the start, a female associate editor at Harper told *Publishers Weekly* that it took three years before supervisors believed she was serious about her career.[199] Women had to exercise more initiative and aggressiveness if they wanted to move up, according to a vice president, while men automatically benefited from a "little lift along the way." And unlike salary discrimination, which was more tangible in its inequity, "there is something about job advancement that is much less visible. There is a tendency, I'd say, especially among men of about 40 years of age who still have not had their consciousness raised, to look at the young men coming up and not the women."[200]

When addressing gender imbalances in certain job categories, the EEOC remained quite removed from the issue of internal promotions versus external hiring. In fact, the EEOC's guidelines seemed to condone preferences for external hiring. It issued detailed instructions to personnel about mining the external labor market for suitable women or underrepresented men if internal candidates were not qualified for an open position.[201] A seasoned external hire could potentially save the firm money on training. Internal training could be costly if a firm helped an employee to develop transferable skills but then another company were to "poach" her.[202]

By the end of the 1970s, in an effort to comply with affirmative action regulations, employers were becoming more supportive of college-educated women who were seeking professional mobility. They institutionalized women's demands for equality by establishing more transparent and standardized personnel procedures. In the publishing industry, WIP, while not successful in achieving all its agenda items, did shift personnel managers from a reliance on nepotism to a belief in merit. Transparent and standardized personnel practices would allow women, in theory, to attain any position that was open to men. In moving toward EEO compliance, personnel departments championed a belief in the equality of men and women, mandating that ability and performance should guide hiring and promotional decisions.

The creation of more meritocratic paths for hiring and promotion aligned with one branch of workplace feminism—the branch that benefited women with the education and social capital that qualified them, absent sex discrimination in hiring, for professional positions. This alignment of HR, EEO compliance, and feminism drew on ideas about ambition and women's ability to succeed in a meritocratic competition. But the needs of those confined to clerical and secretarial work, while part of the shared project in the publishing strikes described earlier, would become a separate branch of workplace feminism. Their demands did not so effortlessly or easily align with the motives of HR departments or with the standards for EEO compliance. Cast aside was a type of feminism that valued traditionally female contributions in the workplace and hoped to remedy occupational segregation and pay inequity. These issues, which were beyond the scope of EEO mandates, were relegated to the radical margins, and beyond corporate purview.

Thus, with elements of feminism and capitalism aligned, the rise of a merit-based system of personnel policy unwittingly fractured the feminist agenda at work.[203] Arguably, corporate interpretation of sex equality bolstered a "survival of the fittest" approach. Merit-based personnel policy solidified traditional notions of talent, skill, and ability that devalued feminine attributes. Traditionally male jobs retained higher pay and higher status relative to traditionally female jobs. Pay inequity between different jobs was not unfair in a world where women had "choice" over their occupations and careers, as we will see in chapter 7. The boundaries between unfair and illegal shifted and sharpened, such that occupational segregation would become an artifact of a woman's preferences, indicative of her lack of ambition, and not a legally actionable offense.

Meanwhile, as the 1980s progressed, the demands of a changing capitalism—corporate priorities for leanness, stock value, and agility—also forced publishing executives to abandon nepotistic policies and instead move toward meritocracy. The industry scrambled to maximize sales of paperbacks, and editors lost cultural power as publishing houses struggled to stay afloat financially.[204] Many trade houses introduced editorial "financial accountability" or "performance standards" for meeting sales targets.[205] To ensure profitability, promotions needed to be reserved for the most productive and most talented employees. These broad economic changes aligned with EEOC suggestions that personnel managers use the performance ratings of an individual employee to determine salary increases or promotions.[206] The educated women who forwarded the WIP platform pushed for these types of personnel practices, hoping that reliance on merit would allow for opportunities to ascend. The belief in merit was triumphant despite the persistence of inequitable outcomes, and this belief in merit helped to usher in a new order of HR management, such that labor and management no longer held adversarial positions.

In addition, changing ideas about the employment relationship—from industrial relations to human resource management—altered the conception of merit at work.[207] Theory and practice shifted away from rewards for seniority and toward assessment based on performance, which seemed to give women equal opportunity. Some employees, however, could perform their way to promotions. By the 1980s clerical workers did not expect to have access to opportunities to train for management positions. The perception of having management potential did not align with the notion of consummate performance in clerical work. The HR transformation overhauled the hiring and promotional decision process, implementing standardized procedures to encourage evaluation of candidates based on their individual talents. But it did less to alter the perceptions of what constituted relevant experience or the questions of which standards should be used to determine hiring and promotions.

These changing personnel practices of the 1970s reflected the successes and failures of a larger feminist movement: emergent HR departments supported opportunities for upward mobility through job postings and select job training but did not intervene to adjust the depressed market rate or devalued status of women's work. While women won opportunities to work in male-dominated managerial jobs, they failed to elevate the economic and social value of female-dominated office jobs. And women seeking managerial jobs avoided clerical work because of its disconnect from promotional ladders of greater status. Equal opportunity to compete with men, not economic justice for women's work, came to define our understanding of gender equality in the modern corporation. By the 1980s most 9to5 leaders had abandoned the possibility of collaborating with management to build bridges from female-dominated to male-dominated ladders, and instead they supported unionization. The 9to5 of the 1980s had relinquished the possibility of a progressional secretary who was connected to management opportunities.

EEO laws aligned feminism and capitalism in a way that benefited professional women but disadvantaged working-class women. The concerns of this new corporate feminism did not address occupational segregation, which would continue to perpetuate economic inequalities based on gender, race, and class. These themes are incipient in the publishing house material described in this chapter. We turn in the next chapter to examine just how clerical workers tried to use affirmative action policy for their own benefit—and how their hopes of embedding economic justice in EEO laws were unrealized.

4

OVERUTILIZED AND UNDERENFORCED

Title VII and affirmative action guidelines certainly "opened the workplace," in the words of historian Nancy MacLean, to women and underrepresented men by allowing them to have greater access to managerial positions that previously had been reserved for white men.[1] But to what extent did these laws revolutionize opportunities for those women, mostly white women, already working in clerical jobs? In this chapter we will see that as new government agencies began enforcing open-ended state policies, employers and regulators implemented laws to bolster a model of formal equality between men and women. This approach did not address the most pressing needs of those in sex-segregated office jobs—needs that included greater focus on pay inequity, job analysis, and lines of promotion.

The terms of implementation were not predetermined but depended on the choices, resources, and personalities of corporate, labor, and regulatory leaders, as sociologist Frank Dobbin has shown.[2] 9to5, as one party in the fray, seized on this opportunity to influence affirmative action's interpretation. In the fall of 1975 the 9to5 executive board voted to make affirmative action enforcement its primary issue, above other key concerns such as maternity benefits or cost-of-living raises.[3] Affirmative action "will aid in our campaign for improved working conditions," declared a 9to5 leader. The organization emphasized that affirmative action should be "more than reports. It [should be] hiring, promoting, and training women and minorities within the company."[4] 9to5 called for changes to a range of workplace practices—job postings, career counseling, salary reviews, promotions, raises, and even pay equity—under the umbrella term of affirmative action.[5] The realization of affirmative action, from 9to5's perspective, would provide bridge opportunities for clerical workers to transition into management. According to the organization, "a principle of affirmative action is that job opportunities are expanded for women and minorities within the company" and companies should provide "clear career paths for all of their employees." In other words, affirmative action should mandate "promotion from within" for clerical women.[6]

This is not how the policy and its effects unfolded. The implementation and enforcement of affirmative action policy, which left intact the strict division between clerical and managerial work, would fail a generation of working-class women who lacked the social capital necessary to acquire higher-paid positions.[7] This development was incipient in the publishing industry struggles of the 1970s, described in the previous chapter. While affirmative action helped some publishing women to achieve internal job posting and more standardized job descriptions, it did little to bridge women's and men's job ladders within organizations such that those on the clerical ladder could move into management.

The career paths for clerical and managerial work remained distinct as policy makers focused on correcting underutilization, meaning instances in which certain job categories contained "fewer minorities or women than would reasonably be expected by their availability."[8] Addressing underutilization proved successful in many cases, forcing employers to become aware of—and try to improve—strict labor market segmentation at the point of hiring. For instance, affirmative action opened clerical work to many women of color who had long been excluded from white-collar environments. At the start of the 1960s, 4 percent of Black women worked in the clerical labor force. Yet with new antidiscrimination policies, rising demand for clerical labor, and increasing pressure from civil rights groups, 18 percent of Black women worked in clerical jobs by 1980.[9]

And affirmative action succeeded in permitting college-educated women to move into professional fields: the percentage of women who worked as doctors, lawyers, professors, and managers doubled from 1970 to 1990.[10] Largely due to the entry of women into traditionally male jobs, occupational segregation began to decline in the 1970s and 1980s.[11] The underutilization approach had numerous advantages, as it compelled employers to recognize bias against women and underrepresented men at the point of hiring.

Affirmative action did much less, however, to tackle what historian Dorothy Sue Cobble has called "the sex of class." Women today constitute the majority of the working class, remaining segregated in the lowest-paid, female-dominated jobs. According to Cobble, "market and public policy solutions have had only limited success" in addressing the economic needs of women in the workforce.[12] Women remain overrepresented in minimum-wage clerical and service positions that offer little opportunity for advancement. In fact, the percentage of women working as secretaries had actually increased, from 98 percent in 1970 to 99 percent in 1990.[13] Many support and caregiving occupations have remained more than 95 percent female.[14] From 1970 to 1990 the percentage of women in the skilled trades rose by only 1 to 2 percent, as female pioneers who entered these jobs and subverted traditional gender norms faced overt resistance and harassment from some blue-collar men.[15]

This failure of workplace feminism has rarely been part of the story. Although historians have examined the legal and social implications of affirmative action, their narratives have not focused on affirmative action in the context of occupational segregation.[16] Historian Nancy MacLean has examined the workplace as a site of struggle for the civil rights movement, showing that full citizenship depended on access to jobs and economic opportunities.[17] Yet her book is a story of progress, whereas this chapter points out the lost potential of EEO law. Dennis Deslippe details the contested meanings of affirmative action policy, but he does not engage with private-sector occupational segregation.[18] Katherine Turk does address occupational segregation, highlighting benefits and limitations of EEO law. She notes that secretaries at the *New York Times* were disenchanted with affirmative action, complaining that it did not mandate training for them to take on new, professional positions. However, her narrative focuses on Title VII of the Civil Rights Act of 1964 much more so than the executive orders that became affirmative action.[19]

Ultimately, the continued ghettoization of sex-segregated office work, and affirmative action's failure to integrate clerical and managerial ladders, meant that women with college degrees, professional networks, and financial resources avoided clerical work. College-educated women could have access to managerial and professional work, so long as they avoided experience in an array of female-dominated clerical positions.[20] This chapter shows how affirmative action did little to improve internal mobility for clericals. The first part examines how affirmative action was implemented, focusing on underutilization. Next, it turns to enforcement of affirmative action, showing that 9to5 had to pressure the government to audit, monitor, and regulate private businesses.

Initially, affirmative action was designed and issued to remedy discrimination based on race but not sex or gender. In 1965 President Lyndon Johnson's Executive Order (E.O.) 11246, which established affirmative action, addressed discrimination on the basis of race, color, religion, or national origin. A newly created Department of Labor (DOL) agency, the Office of Federal Contract Compliance (OFCC), was created to oversee implementation and enforcement of affirmative action. It issued Order No. 4 in 1970, requiring federal contractors to submit "goals and timetables" to remedy the absence of racial minorities in certain job categories. Employers were to make a "good faith effort" to meet numerical targets; otherwise, they could face the possibility of investigation or sanctions (such as disqualification from the federal contract bidding process, cancelation of contracts, or possible legal action in court). The OFCC diffused this regulatory burden for compliance: each federal agency retained responsibility for monitoring its own contracts.[21]

Because E.O. 11246 did not include sex or gender, feminists lobbied the DOL to change the order, and in 1967 President Johnson issued E.O. 11375, which amended 11246 to include sex as a protected category. Yet enforcement of the sex provision remained tenuous. Secretary of Labor James Hodgson told feminists that "employment problems of women are different" since not all women were actively looking for full-time work.[22] Although 9to5 had not yet officially formed in 1970, other women's groups challenged the DOL's distinction between race and sex. Higher education was the first site of struggle: the National Organization for Women (NOW) and the Women's Equity and Action League (WEAL) filed complaints against over one hundred colleges and universities. They petitioned to increase the proportion of women in graduate programs and to hire and promote more female faculty.[23]

President Richard Nixon responded to feminist pressure by establishing the President's Task Force on Women's Rights and Responsibilities in 1970. The task force's report, *A Matter of Simple Justice*, focused not just on sex-based educational barriers but also on economic inequality. It called for full enforcement of affirmative action guidelines, stating that such regulation could have far-reaching effects for women at all economic levels. The report suggested that affirmative action could improve the plight of lower-income women by providing female workers with training programs to increase earnings.[24]

Yet training for lower-income women would remain elusive, as the sex provision of affirmative action took shape. In the midst of protests from NOW and WEAL, along with the recommendations of the task force, the DOL issued Revised Order No. 4 in December 1971. The heart of this order was a mandate to correct the *underutilization of women* in previously restricted job categories such as "official, managers, professionals, technicians, craftsmen, and sales workers (except in certain retail occupations)." Secretary Hodgson gave employers 120 days to comply, which meant that "search consultants [were] thrashing about trying to decipher what consequences for them were buried in its turgid, bureaucratic prose."[25]

The Revised Order forced employers to adopt the goals and timetables approach for sex-based affirmative action.[26] According to historian Hugh Davis Graham, Revised Order No. 4 was "an ambiguous abstraction . . . pregnant with possibilities for mischief as well as for beneficence."[27] Employers were to conduct audits of their workforce and surrounding communities, set numerical targets, and work to establish statistical parity between the percentages of women and underrepresented men in the local population and those in certain job categories at their firms.

This numerical analysis might have seemed like an objective exercise, but actually subjective judgments guided each step of the process. Employers retained much interpretative discretion when managing their own data, largely because they were classifying their employees by job title, not by salary. When performing audits and constructing targets, employers delineated the boundaries of their own categories, using titles to label employees as managerial when in reality they had low salaries and worked in positions with very little supervisory authority. Recall from chapter 3 that in the publishing industry, Houghton Mifflin relabeled many clericals, giving women loftier job titles, such as editorial assistant, so that it could shift more of its female workforce into underutilized categories for affirmative action reporting purposes. Most of these women were really doing the duties and receiving the pay of secretaries.[28]

Also in the banking industry, engaging in "title inflation" bestowed managerial titles on women while providing little or no change in responsibility or salary. This practice permitted employers to reclassify their female employees for the purpose of affirmative action reporting. In compliance reviews of the nation's largest banks, some employers reported a 50 percent increase in numbers of managerial women and a corresponding 50 percent decrease in clerical women within one year! According to one vigilant regulator, such "games make for lots of paper work, but no progress; they are simply means of preserving the status quo, and thus ought to serve as grounds for a finding of noncompliance," although usually no government action was taken.[29] In sum, manipulation of job titles could hide the severity of occupational segregation and obscure disadvantages that women faced. Most compliance efforts used titles instead of salaries to categorize employees, such that affirmative action reports could create the illusion of statistical equity.[30]

Further dilution of affirmative action occurred as employers—not regulators—determined the boundaries of the potential labor pool to set goals for underutilized positions. Although many employers determined labor supply by including all women who were "available, interested, and qualified," delineating these terms allowed for an incredible degree of discretion. When determining "availability," some used national data while others relied on local data, which could expand or contract the number of women in the population who were considered available for the target position. When determining level of interest, some included only those who completed the application process for the position, while others assumed that any woman looking for employment would be interested if given the opportunity to apply. When determining qualifications, some included all women who had potential to perform the job if given training, while others included only those who currently possessed the necessary skills or worked in an identical job elsewhere.[31]

Thus, even though Revised Order No. 4 instructed employers to consider both internal and external candidates in labor supply, employers often restricted the quantity of women considered eligible by classifying only external candidates in identical jobs in the local area as potential candidates.[32] As 9to5 was gaining momentum in cities across the nation, it realized that pushing for serious consideration of internal employees could promise upward mobility for many seasoned office workers who had reached the top of clerical job ladders. Although women were underutilized in managerial and supervisory positions, often they composed the majority of the white-collar workforce in banks, insurance companies, and publishing houses. 9to5 claimed that clerical labor should be considered relevant experience for management, which would position experienced female office workers with opportunities for promotion. Karen Nussbaum believed "there should be no such thing as a dead-end job for *anyone*."[33] With affirmative action, "so-called dead end jobs such as many clericals now feel they have would be opened up for promotion to positions of increased responsibility."[34] Furthermore, 9to5 maintained that the clustering of women in low-paying clerical positions did not reflect women's preference for clerical work. Rather, it revealed long-standing gender bias in job ladders and organizational structures.[35]

9to5 wanted employers to redesign "historical flows" into the job categories where women were underutilized, such that experience on the clerical ladder would qualify an internal candidate for a management position. However, government mandates did not force employers to reconsider promotional paths when remedying underutilization. This approach left some systemic gender bias untouched because it preserved historical flows that advanced those in traditionally male, entry-level jobs into managerial positions. Women on clerical ladders therefore still were not considered qualified for positions on managerial ladders. The OFCC even instructed employers to look for employees in traditional feeder jobs when filling target positions. Consent decrees signed by AT&T (1973) and General Electric (GE; 1978) both utilized this approach of historical flows, which in essence announced to employers that their organizational structures—with distinct clerical and managerial ladders—were lawful. While personnel experts noted that historical flows could "perpetuate past discrimination," reliance on such flows was "inexpensive and relatively easy to implement," making the strategy an appealing way for employers to comply with affirmative action. Employers would have to do more extensive job analysis if they wanted to determine which employees outside of a historical flow might have content knowledge (or the potential to acquire content knowledge) relevant to a target position.[36]

An array of professional consultants arose to help corporations comply with Revised Order No. 4. While several female consultants suggested to employers that they should reconsider historical flows, the government push for expediency thwarted such advice. When the DOL issued the directive in December 1972, it required federal contractors to have goals and timetables within 120 days. Given this short timeline for compliance, as well as the financial cost of job analysis, some companies did "the minimum [they could] get by on," according to affirmative action expert Susan Davis. Davis served as vice president for a Chicago-based consultancy, the Urban Research Corporation, that led a two-day conference, "Equal Opportunity for Women: Corporate Affirmative Action Programs," in February 1972 for six hundred executives, activists, and policy makers.[37] According to Davis, companies needed to reexamine how they categorized female-dominated work such as secretarial labor: "Often these job classifications merit higher salary and status. In fact, many jobs done by women are heavy in work load and responsibility, but light in pay and promotional opportunity."[38] Cited in major media outlets nationwide for her knowledge about affirmative action for women, Davis recognized that adherence to traditional job categories and ladders often misrepresented the managerial potential of clerical workers.

An expert on women and work, Barbara Boyle, established a prominent consultancy after leading the creation of International Business Machines (IBM) Corporation's affirmative action program. Boyle and Sharon Kirkman, who had created American Express's program, joined forces and founded Boyle/Kirkman Associates in 1972. *Time* magazine described their work for clients such as Pillsbury and Avon as "therapy for sexists" that could last up to two years and cost up to $50,000.[39]

Referencing "a business case for equal opportunity," Boyle argued that fully integrating women into management would benefit an organization's productivity and profitability. In a *Harvard Business Review* article, she argued that affirmative action compliance benefited the bottom line because women, constituting 40 percent of the work force, were "an almost untapped resource of talent and skills." She urged employers to reconsider the way they identified and tracked women in their organizations. For all female employees, managers should maintain a file that included "prior experience, interests, next two possible positions, long-range potential, and person development plans." Boyle continued that managers often overlooked internal candidates when looking for women to promote. Conducting job analysis and restructuring individual jobs would show personnel directors that they had a "wealth of resources in women filling such positions as administrative assistant and manager of the word-processing center." These women should be "candidates for other positions in their organizations which previously were beyond their reach."[40]

While women such as Davis, Boyle, and Kirkman consulted with corporate executives, 9to5 pushed for grassroots change. It lobbied employers to alter hiring, training, and promotional procedures so that internal employees could become more upwardly mobile. 9to5 focused on several personnel processes across different industries. As explained in chapter 3, Women in Publishing, a subcommittee of 9to5, prioritized internal job posting, reasoning that if clericals could receive notice of management openings, they would have greater opportunity for promotions. And forcing employers to revisit clerical job descriptions would demonstrate that many women were performing skilled work that should qualify them for managerial positions. Chapter 3 detailed how these campaigns for procedural changes were successful in some workplaces. Workers won internal postings and written job descriptions from large publishing houses in Boston.[41]

Yet attention to these formal processes had limitations. Line managers and personnel directors had to adopt a new mindset, which included recognition that clericals made significant contributions to core business functions. They had to perceive clericals, who were nontraditional candidates, as suited for management. Also they had to write more detailed and accurate job descriptions so that clericals could receive public credit for their experience and expertise.

Bias against clerical potential for management became clear when a 9to5 subcommittee investigated the policies of eleven Boston insurance firms regarding internal job postings, written job descriptions, employee training, and promotions. Most companies did not offer their clerical workers training that would enable them to compete for higher-status positions. Women moved into lower-status training programs. 9to5 recorded that at Travelers Insurance, "jobs [were] filled from the outside," and at John Hancock, "promotions [occur] from outside, not [from] within." Training for promotions was available for those working in functions like sales, management, or underwriting, but not for clerical work. And internal postings were common for "lower level positions" or "lower level clerical positions" but not for managerial openings.[42] 9to5's data revealed that information about higher-paid position openings remained elusive for clerical women even within their own companies. Although women constituted 87 percent of the clerical workers in Boston's insurance industry, many companies preferred to hire externally for professional positions, rather than to promote clerical workers internally.[43] While 9to5 considered many insurance companies' practices to be unfair, most of their practices were not illegal. Companies did not have to promote clericals to managerial positions as long as they recruited external female candidates to fill underutilized positions. And the external path seemed to be the less expensive and less cumbersome way to meet affirmative action guidelines.

Indeed, across industries, personnel practices to redress underutilization often favored external applicants, particularly new college graduates, over current employees, as evidenced by public remarks of corporate executives. At a national conference on women and work, an executive vice president for Mobil noted that the company recruited at colleges to fill new openings for professional positions.[44] Similarly, at the Polaroid Corporation, personnel officers recruited talented women and underrepresented men from college campuses. The company disclosed that it strategically advertised in certain publications such as *Black Collegian, Collegiate Women's Careers,* and special issues (targeted toward women and underrepresented men) of *MBA* and *New Engineer* to reach new graduates.[45] General Motors reported that because of its attempt to bring women into underutilized positions, it now included "three 'all-girl' colleges on its 100-member recruiting list."[46] A Chicago insurance company reported that it was "more aggressively keyed to finding competent women" by going to women-only colleges to recruit.[47] The Honeywell Information Systems Affirmative Action Plan declared that recruiters should solicit applicants at local employment agencies for racial minorities. But as for the advancement of current employees into management, Honeywell pointed to its public commitment to post EEO laws in the corporate lobby and in the company newspaper.[48]

Other records confirm that little if any corporate attention was dedicated to the mobility of women in clerical positions because overrepresentation did not trigger compliance reviews. For instance, Honeywell reported in 1974 that it had no EEO problems in the clerical category because underutilization of women was not a problem there.[49] The Cabot Corporation reported similar findings. Only areas with too few women or underrepresented men were marked by Cabot executives as problematic and in need of remedy. In other words, implementation of affirmative action policies focused on areas with too few women, not areas with too many, even though, plausibly, areas with too many could be interpreted as evidence of gender inequity in need of corporate action. Cabot's EEO coordinator claimed to have a "general policy of promoting from within" although the company had no formal training programs to advance clerical women into management.[50] A female human resource officer from the Norton Simon conglomerate explained on a conference panel how she fulfilled government mandates in companies such as Max Factor, Canada Dry, Hunt's Tomato Paste, and Avis Rent-a-Car. Each of her nine companies had to report EEO statistics quarterly to show that they were working toward more equitable distributions of women and underrepresented men in certain categories. No numerical goals, however, had to be established regarding female-dominated jobs.[51]

If managers usually looked externally for young college women to fill managerial positions, then "women already on the staff [became] culturally conditioned not to want the responsibilities of higher positions, or they [were] afraid to ask for them," according to Mary Ralston, a banking personnel director who wrote a book on training women for supervisory positions. Ralston noted, "Hesitancy seems to fade with the encouragement offered by an effective affirmative action program," which she defined as a program that developed clerical women internally for advancement into management.[52] A voice of reassurance from supervisors could help the women see themselves as management material. Leading consultant Barbara Boyle identified a talented receptionist on her own staff and encouraged her to seek a promotion. The receptionist told Boyle, "I never saw a need to go back to school and complete credits necessary for my degree. But now I'm convinced management is sincere to the commitment to equal opportunity, so I'm really working hard to qualify for advancement."[53]

A *Harvard Business Review* article in 1976 questioned if the most common compliance practices of employers, which arose to meet affirmative action mandates, really addressed the root causes of statistical disparities. The two business school professors, Neil Churchill and John Shank, explained that when setting goals, most employers created a "balance sheet," which was akin to a snapshot of demographic data. This report would classify job categories as "professional, sales, clerical, laborers," for instance, and then show percentages of women and underrepresented men in each category. The balance sheet approach had several problems, according to the authors. First, the categories were too broad. One company had a category of "officials and managers," in which it included "positions from the corporate president to the hostesses in the dining room, whose annual salaries [ranged] from $6,000 to over $200,000." Second, the balance sheet approach did not capture the process by which employers did or did not advance women and underrepresented men from certain job categories into others, meaning that it did not reexamine the configuration of internal promotional ladders. Churchill and Shank wrote, "Such reporting encourages companies to pirate minority and female executives from each other in order to beef up their 'head count' in any category. This sort of gamesmanship does little to advance the course of equal employment opportunity."[54]

The conventional balance sheet approach was a snapshot only: it did not measure "rate of progression," meaning how effectively firms could train current women and underrepresented men for promotions. The professors wrote, "A measurement system that does not monitor this rate of development is seriously deficient" because it failed to account for the opportunities available to internal employees.[55]

Instead of the balance sheet, Churchill and Shank recommended that federal guidelines require a flow approach, which could "be real teeth in the law." Firms should capture and submit data over time that would show the number of people in each job category at a certain moment, and then look to a subsequent period to show how many remained in that category as well as how many were promoted to a new position. This approach would push companies not only to measure the "current management mix" but also to account for "current promotion rates" to reflect the development of women and underrepresented men.[56] In sum, academics and activists alike were recognizing that the current manner in which employers were implementing affirmative action had limitations for internal mobility. Even as affirmative action seemed to advance hiring practices based on merit, it also solidified occupational segregation as external to EEO concerns and beyond the purview of the HR agenda.

Career advancement was becoming a matter that each employee needed to manage for herself—and to a large extent, so too was the enforcement process against sex discrimination, which was not the outcome that 9to5 wanted. In addition to advocating for mobility from clerical to managerial ladders, 9to5 wanted systemic affirmative action reviews of all firms with federal contracts. Yet the government allocated relatively few resources to compliance, such that oversight was limited. In the 1970s reviews were infrequent and somewhat random. Between 1973 and 1981 eleven thousand establishments were reviewed, or about 10 percent of all federal contractors.[57] And if reviews were conducted, often they were mismanaged. In Boston, 9to5 communicated with other women's and civil rights groups to try to coordinate efforts. In a letter sent to activist organizations such as WEAL, NOW, the National Association for the Advancement of Colored People, the League of Women Voters, Casa Del Sol Adult Learning Center, and the Chinese American Civic Association, 9to5 announced that it was hosting a luncheon "to discuss what action can be taken" to ensure "stronger enforcement" of affirmative action.[58]

Dialogue among activist groups was necessary given that the government was not conducting systematic reviews: the burden of enforcement shifted to individual workers and their advocates. This was especially apparent in the banking industry, where gender and racial segregation characterized the labor force. In a survey of six major commercial banks in 1970, only 6.3 percent of those promoted to the managerial position of officer were white women, and 3.4 percent were men of color. Zero were women of color.[59] Although not well represented in the managerial ranks, women composed the majority of the U.S. banking labor force; two-thirds in 1970. They worked almost exclusively in clerical jobs as clerks, typists, receptionists, tellers, and data processors. Clerical salaries were low, with those in banking earning about $7,942 in 1970, which was below the average relative to clericals in other industries. Clerical turnover was high, with about 30 percent leaving their jobs each year in the 1970s; in highly routinized data-processing jobs, turnover rates climbed to 50 percent per year.[60]

With men and women on separate job ladders, generations of clerical women watched as their male colleagues, who had been hired initially with similar educational experience, enjoyed promotions to management. To attend to these long-standing gender inequities, female bank employees and feminist activists forwarded legal claims and engaged in collective protest throughout the 1970s. In 1971 WEAL filed a class-action law suit against twenty-seven Dallas banks, alleging that they engaged in illegal personnel practices that included firing pregnant women, promoting women less often than men, and paying women less than men for the same work. The Treasury Department investigated and ordered bank managers to promote nearly forty women to officer positions—a partial victory.[61] According to the former chairman of the EEOC, in 1972 banking was "one of the three worst industries with regard to employment discrimination (along with construction unions and electric and gas utilities)."[62] Despite the passage of Title VII and the issuance of affirmative action orders, the bank industry hesitated to comply without pressure from activists and investigations by regulators.[63]

The mostly white leaders of Boston 9to5 used their campaign for affirmative action enforcement to bring greater visibility to the "double discrimination faced by Third World women office workers," according to one member. By "Third World women," she meant those who "who suffer discrimination because of their race and their sex."[64] The number of women of color working in Massachusetts banks and insurance companies was low: four out of every 100 workers, according to 9to5.[65] Nevertheless, 9to5 leader Janet Selcer highlighted the challenges faced by such women during a Massachusetts legislature public hearing regarding affirmative action.[66] She indicated that her friend, a Black woman she referred to as "Mrs. W. K.," was reluctant to testify for herself due to "intimidation." Selcer cited examples of discrimination that Mrs. W. K. faced at her bank: when she sought to enter a switchboard operator training program, she was told that it was "oversubscribed" at four people. When she sought to be transferred to a different branch closer to her home, she was told she did not have the requisite skills even though, subsequently, she was asked to train the white woman who got the position.[67]

To help publicize these issues and demand change in the banking industry, 9to5 found an ally in Carol Greenwald, appointed Massachusetts banking commissioner in 1975 by Democratic governor Michael Dukakis.[68] Greenwald took her duty to oversee the industry seriously. She investigated banking employment practices, working tirelessly to ameliorate ongoing gender and race discrimination. She claimed that the U.S. Department of the Treasury, which was charged with monitoring affirmative action compliance in the banking industry, rarely conducted reviews or forced meaningful action. In fact, in 1974 only thirty-five people nationwide were charged with enforcing affirmative action in the banking industry. And only 2 percent of all banks were reviewed that year.[69] The General Accounting Office (GAO) reported in 1976, "Treasury had not only failed to enforce the law, but had undermined the credibility of all affirmative action efforts by its record of nonenforcement."[70] A New York–based research organization, the Council of Economic Priorities (CEP), issued a report on the banking industry in 1972, concluding that "existing laws regarding fair employment are adequate, but enforcement by the Treasury Department is not. The department has never denied Federal funds to any major bank for noncompliance," even though CEP found extensive employment discrimination at many institutions.[71] If state and corporate inertia were to persist, the CEP report found that women and underrepresented men would continue to be "overwhelmingly concentrated in low-level, poorly paid jobs."[72]

And inertia did persist, triggering 9to5 to file formal charges of sex discrimination against New England Merchants National Bank of Boston in 1976. 9to5 had charged the bank with denying women access to managerial training programs, forcing women to train men to be their supervisors, and denying women equal pay for comparable work. Treasury officials began to investigate Merchants soon after 9to5 submitted the charges, finding that the bank was not in compliance and was refusing to conciliate. However, no government action was taken against Merchants because Treasury claimed that it had lost its own work records when it moved regional offices. Due to this negligence, the initial stages of the investigation began a second time in 1978, when the Office of Federal

Contracts Compliance Programs (OFCCP), the new name for the OFCC, gained enforcement authority from the Treasury Department. Four years later the investigation was still in its initial stages. Greenwald perceived the federal government's delaying tactics as undercutting "the credibility of 9to5 as an effective organization."[73] 9to5 expressed outrage at the handling of the investigation, declaring that "this case [has been] mismanaged to the point where it is unclear whether the Dep. Of Labor or Merchants is conducting the investigation."[74]

When complaining to the OFCCP about the investigation, 9to5 pointed to three events that it perceived as inequitable. First, when Treasury found that Merchants was not in compliance in 1977, it nonetheless continued to grant numerous extensions to Merchants, claiming that the bank was still deciding whether or not it wanted to conciliate. Yet 9to5 maintained that Merchants was not moving toward conciliation; thus a finding of noncompliance should have been just cause to begin enforcement proceedings. Second, when the OFCCP took over the case in 1978, Leonard Biermann, a regional officer, permitted Merchants to submit entirely new data. 9to5 had evidence that Merchants submitted these revised records to Biermann. The new records claimed that employees had received promotions and raises, although, according to 9to5, the employees themselves were not aware of receiving these benefits. Third, Biermann claimed that he lost the records of the Treasury interviews with Merchants employees; still, he did not conduct new interviews, which meant that the new investigation omitted bank workers' perspectives.[75] Employees had lost the opportunity to formally contradict Merchants managers' statements.

While 9to5 was outraged over the mishandling of the Merchants investigation, these and other types of dubious practices occurred routinely, according to Greenwald. Yet Treasury rarely took systematic action against banks who manipulated data. According to Greenwald, this "implicitly condoned" the practice of manipulating or even falsifying facts. And Treasury reportedly looked the other way if banks did not have the required affirmative action data on file. The GAO reported that from 1971 to 1975, Treasury had not once sanctioned a bank for noncompliance. It had never removed any federal deposits, which should have been the penalty implemented as a "potent sanction."[76] It did not even review the world's largest bank, the Bank of America, until after a fair employment law suit had been filed in court.[77]

If employees themselves were going to have to be responsible for enforcement by way of forwarding complaints, then they needed as much information as possible about their own firms' practices in the context of their legal rights. Many clericals reported that they had never seen their own companies' affirmative action plans, and they were unsure if such plans even existed.[78] According to a contracts compliance program specialist in Treasury, information on compliance reviews was not "a matter of public record."[79] Others thought such information should be publicly available. To gather and distribute this type of data to the public, Greenwald, along with labor and civil rights advocates, conducted surveys in 1976 and 1978 on workforce demographics and pay equity in banking.[80] As Greenwald, 9to5, and their allies sought to publicize their findings on the industry's practices, banking leaders attempted to silence them.[81] The industry claimed that Greenwald's report contained personal information about the managers of many firms; in turn, the Massachusetts Savings Bank Association was able to obtain a court order to limit the report from public distribution. Only the banking commissioner and the attorney general would have access to view it.[82]

Greenwald, 9to5, and their allies believed that the banking industry was trying to hide evidence of its noncompliance and that labor regulators were pawns of the banking industry.[83] Greenwald claimed that initially the OFCCP regional director seemed interested in her survey, maintaining that it could help him find discriminatory patterns in the industry. Yet after the court order muzzling the data, the director recanted, stating that the report would be "of minimal importance to us . . . [and] would not help us target a bank for an affirmative action compliance review."[84] What could account for the OFCCP's change of heart? Greenwald believed that the Massachusetts Savings Bank Association exerted "improper influence" on the Department of Labor and the OFCCP, leading the OFCCP regional director to decide that he should disregard the findings on bank employment patterns.[85]

Since regulators were proving unreliable, Greenwald and 9to5 continued to push for their data to be publicly accessible. To overcome the court order, Greenwald omitted specific names from the report and used the Freedom of Information Act to release the survey in January 1979.[86] The survey results confirmed inequitable pay and discriminatory employment practices in banking.[87] In response to the report, the director of the

OFCCP assured 9to5 that his agency was committed to regulating banks and that it had thirteen reviews scheduled in the New England region for 1979.[88] This data, along with the industry's attempt to silence the findings, further propelled 9to5's vigilance on both the banking sector and its regulators.

This pattern of lax enforcement, whereby employees had to lobby for state action, held true in the insurance industry as well, where women were relegated to the lowest-paid office jobs. Women constituted 87 percent of the clerical workers in Boston insurance industries.[89] Yet at these same insurance firms, 58 percent of full-time file clerks made less than $6,200 per year, a salary considered to be around or below the poverty line.[90] Many full-time clericals were eligible for food stamps and other government subsidies.[91] Yearly raises often did not keep up with the costs of living. Furthermore, women had no ladder into "underutilized" positions—clericals were rarely promoted.[92]

The Department of Health, Education, and Welfare was responsible for monitoring the insurance industry and, within HEW, the Social Security Administration (SSA) was assigned to conduct reviews.[93] Although all insurance companies with federal contracts were required by executive order to have an affirmative action plan, only if the SSA decided to review the company did regulators actually review the plan. Thus unless the SSA requested to see the plan, no one really knew if the company had one or if it was effective or substantial. The SSA reviewed companies depending on the time and staff available or if given a reason to investigate.[94] Sometimes companies resisted the review process, arguing that personnel information was private, even if eventually they submitted the necessary information.[95] Such disputes cost the SSA and HEW time and money, and these agencies had scarce human and financial resources.[96]

9to5 believed that the SSA should have comprehensive data about as many insurance companies as possible. It sent its 1974 report to the SSA, presenting its findings about low salaries and occupational segregation in the Boston insurance workforce.[97] According to 9to5, women constituted almost 60 percent of the Boston insurance labor force, but nearly 90 percent of these female employees held low-wage clerical positions. 9to5 wrote, "No one could accuse the Insurance Industry in Boston of not *hiring* women. . . . But where are these many women employed *within* the companies?" Only 2 percent of women in insurance earned over $10,000, while

51 percent of men earned above that amount. 9to5 blamed weak affirmative action enforcement for the continued clustering of women in low-paying jobs. From 9to5's perspective, federal guidelines should have required that firms work to remedy overutilization and not just focus on the positions in which too few women were employed.[98]

The SSA agreed to take the 9to5 report into account when selecting firms to review. Furthermore, it sent two compliance officers to Boston in early 1975 to meet with 9to5 insurance committee members, advising them on how to initiate complaints. The SSA officers disclosed that "the best way to get action" was to file a charge with the SSA, the OFCCP, or both, and then lobby the SSA to launch the review. Although 9to5 reported that it had a "good" meeting with the SSA, it remained dissatisfied with the investigation model.[99] The SSA was primarily responding to complaints that had been forwarded by charging parties instead of initiating preemptive reviews of all insurance companies.

In lieu of a systemic review, which was not forthcoming, 9to5 issued a complaint against the affirmative action plan at one specific insurance firm, Marsh & McLennan. Boston's 9to5 chapter and two of its sister organizations, Chicago's Women Employed and San Francisco's Women Organized for Employment, launched a tri-city campaign against what was then the largest insurance brokerage firm in the world. These organizations insisted that Marsh "begin obeying the equal opportunity laws," and they argued that the goals and timetables set by personnel managers were inadequate to remedy the existing discrimination. Working women's organizations claimed that Marsh was not in compliance because women were clustered in the lowest-paying clerical positions. Only 4.4 percent of the 1,101 officials, managers, and supervisors in all Marsh's offices worldwide were women. However, 82 percent of the women employed by Marsh were in low-paying clerical jobs. And of the almost 6,000 total employees, only 214 were Black women (and 181 of those were clericals). In its 1974 affirmative action plan, Marsh declared that it would try to fill 19 percent of all positions that paid $10,400 per year with women. This was precisely the attention to underutilization that did little to remedy the plight of Marsh's current clerical employees. Clericals' advocates were outraged, hoping for more attention to clerical pay and internal mobility. "That means 81% of those jobs will remain in the male domain. The [Affirmative Action] Guide goes on to say that this 19% 'goal' need not even be accomplished in one year!"[100] Although 9to5 perceived the Marsh plan as not far-reaching enough, it did in fact fulfill DOL requirements. The plan reported current underutilization areas and set goals for improvement. And it left matters of ghettoization behind.

There was clearly a disconnect between what 9to5 saw as fair, even as legal, and what businesses were required to do to avoid penalty. 9to5 viewed Marsh as engaging in illegal employment practices because its affirmative action plan sought to fill 19 percent of higher-paying jobs with women over a period of several years. Women Employed Chicago wanted more direct attention to occupational segregation and improved clerical ladders for upward mobility instead. It wrote, "[Marsh's] discriminatory employment practices are clearly illegal. We may not be able to change their basic philosophy about women, but we can force them to obey the laws." From the perspective of the clerical coalition, the law required that Marsh develop "meaningful goals and timetables for training and promoting women and minorities," unlike its current affirmative action plan, which could be met through external hires. The clerical groups also recommended regular salary reviews and raising the salary range for clericals, as well as establishing written job descriptions, internal job posting, and on-the-job training. In addition, career "ladders should be instituted with bridge positions allowing clericals to move into professional positions."[101]

When the clerical coalition met with a Marsh vice president of personnel, they received only partially satisfactory answers. Even though the 1976 Affirmative Action Guide would not be available to employees, the vice president claimed that Marsh was committed to affirmative action. When asked about written job descriptions, he claimed the practice to be too "rigid." Although Marsh would begin a job posting system on January 1, 1976, it would post only nonmanagement positions. Clericals would continue to lack knowledge of open managerial positions; the Marsh vice president signaled that clericals were not qualified to apply for them anyway.[102]

Following the Marsh campaign, the 9to5 insurance committee devised a three-month plan to improve affirmative action enforcement at the state and federal levels. One goal of the campaign was to lobby officials at the Massachusetts Commission Against Discrimination and at the OFCCP, placing pressure on the agencies to review reported offenders. To engage more insurance clericals in the cause, 9to5 decided to produce and distribute an insurance newsletter, which would encourage women to evaluate their own company's affirmative action practices.[103] 9to5 initiated task forces at particular Boston companies so that it could assist employees in constructing "criteria for what *we* [the employees] view as an acceptable a.a. plan." To pressure companies to more fully commit to affirmative action, 9to5 planned to publicize companies with strong plans versus those with weak ones.[104]

9to5 empowered employees by disseminating information about affirmative action directly to them. In a worksheet, "How to Evaluate Your Company," it recommended changes in personnel practices to remedy the sex-segregated nature of clerical work. For instance, to gain access to promotional opportunities, employees should urge their managers to implement job posting. According to 9to5, affirmative action mandated that "*all* jobs should be conspicuously posted," preferably internally, for two weeks. To address clericals who were told that their experience was not relevant for internal openings, employees should make sure that the company was using "fair requirements" when choosing applicants to hire for management. In other words, employers should reconsider the skills of clerical women. "The company should look at *related* job experience, and periodically survey to find qualified women in the company." Furthermore, employees could suggest that "training programs" become part of the company's affirmative action plan. A way to "bridge clerical and other jobs should be provided, in order to eliminate dead-end positions."[105]

Some Boston insurance companies, when pushed to implement affirmative action, started to alter their policies on internal job postings and written job descriptions. Frank B. Hall and Massachusetts Mutual began internal postings in 1976.[106] The OFCCP began to negotiate with Prudential in 1976, pushing the company to institute more equitable hiring and promotion policies. Employees from Liberty Mutual, Blue Cross, and Aetna gathered to read and discuss their affirmative action plans, and to make suggestions for improvements. At Aetna, several women met with company managers and secured job postings.[107] 9to5 filed charges against Travelers for failing to institute internal postings, provide accurate job descriptions, and offer training for promotions.[108] Once 9to5 filed complaints with the SSA, Travelers started posting some opportunities on the lunch room bulletin board.[109]

By early 1977 change was occurring in a piecemeal fashion. However, many Boston-area insurance companies still were not following clericals' ideas about affirmative action compliance. 9to5 detailed the practices of eleven firms, accounting for their current policies on job posting, written job descriptions, employee training, and promotions. Most companies offered training for promotions to those working in sales, management, or underwriting but not in clerical work. And postings were common for "lower level positions" or "lower level clerical positions" but not for managerial openings.[110] This data revealed that finding and ascending to higher-paid positions remained elusive for most clerical women, even within their own companies. Many companies preferred to hire externally for professional positions rather than to train or promote an internal clerical worker.

∽∾∽

A highly publicized series of events at Citizens National Bank in Willmar, Minnesota, captured the economic injustice that clerical women routinely encountered and the inadequacy of federal law to remedy these women's grievances. No men worked in teller or clerical positions at the bank, and only one woman worked in the male-dominated officer class. In 1976 bank executives hired a young, inexperienced man for a management position without considering any internal clerical employees as candidates. Women claimed that they had the requisite skills for the job. The male president responded, "We're not all equal, you know," contending that clerical experience did not qualify the women for management positions. The female bank employees filed a sex discrimination complaint with the EEOC, and eight women started their own union. After trying to negotiate a contract with management, Willmar Bank Employees Association, Local 1, known in the press as the Willmar 8, went on strike, picketing for two years during extremely cold Minnesota winters.[111]

Although the strike captured considerable national attention and helped to publicize gender inequality, the Willmar employees gained only negligible back pay as compensation.[112] After months passed without action by the EEOC, the National Organization for Women offered to help monitor the claim. Eventually the EEOC negotiated a conciliatory agreement in which the bank would provide $11,750 in back pay (only about

$1,000 to each of eleven complainants). While bank management promised to obey the law moving forward, the women forfeited their right to sue the bank in the future or to be immediately reinstated in their past positions. After receiving this lackluster package from the EEOC, the Willmar 8 also experienced mediocre results from union efforts. Although the NLRB acknowledged that the bank had engaged in a number of unfair labor practices, it issued minimal penalties. In fact, it denied the women the right to be reinstated to their previous jobs following the end of the strike.[113] The women's disappointment with the outcome reinforced the disparity between clericals' understanding of what equal employment law could do and the manner in which the state and employers were implementing it.

Despite the shortcomings of state and union remedies on behalf of women workers, Willmar epitomized what personnel managers did not want to happen in their respective workplaces: negative publicity, costly legal entanglements, and white-collar unionization. Although only thirty of the country's fifteen thousand banks were unionized in 1981, bank managers remained anxious about the threat of white-collar unionization. The American Bankers Association (ABA) warned members that banks across the country could become targets for union organizers in the aftermath of Willmar. At the ABA's annual conference in 1981, over three hundred personnel directors viewed a forthcoming PBS documentary, "Willmar 8," which cast management at Citizens National Bank as incompetent when addressing workplace conflict and as negligent when complying with EEO mandates.[114] Many banking personnel directors responded by distancing the happenings at the Willmar bank from their own practices. The HR director at Pittsburgh's Equibank claimed that Willmar did not represent "the whole industry and its problems," calling the working conditions "unusual."[115] Even other Minnesota bankers turned their backs on the Willmar president, who was soliciting support from other bank presidents for his own legal defense fund. Another small-town Minnesota banker claimed that "Leo [Pirsch, the Citizens National Bank president] wouldn't have had a labor problem if he'd treated his people the way I treat mine." He compared Pirsch to Bert Lance, the Office of Management and Budget director who had to resign from his post in the Jimmy Carter administration because of financial scandal.[116]

Though the women did not get the pay and promotions they had hoped for, the bank strike exposed the ways that economic justice and workplace fairness could be beyond the purview of the law. It emphasized that as many personnel managers, feminist activists, federal policy makers, and professional women turned to the promise of a rights-conscious framework, many working-class women had concerns that could not be remedied with the dominant interpretation and implementation of EEO policy.[117] The events in this small, midwestern town brought awareness to the issue of low pay and dead-end jobs that beset female banking clericals. The Willmar women were far from adopting a feminist agenda that called for an end to patriarchy in the abstract. Instead, they maintained that they were working to supplement their husbands' incomes, contributing to the greater good of the nuclear family.

As the Willmar 8 dramatized, women who did not consider themselves feminists could demonstrate great resilience when fighting for matters such as fair pay and fair treatment. In fact, one of the strikers claimed she did not know what the term "feminist" meant when she became a part of the Willmar 8. As she began to hear the word in association with her actions, she had to look it up in the dictionary.[118] A Willmar resident expressed her surprise that white-collar women went on strike: "Sure, every once in a while those railroad guys go on strike for a couple of days. But a bunch of women? Never. Some people haven't gotten over it yet."[119]

Even so, the events in Willmar did not spark a massive wave of bank strikes throughout the 1980s, given the difficulty of organizing clericals, which will be explored in chapter 6. As the directives of affirmative action narrowed, such that underutilization became the litmus test for compliance, clerical women realized that state regulations promised little in the way of raises or promotions. Activists came to realize that despite petitioning for investigations into specific firms, occupational segregation could exist comfortably alongside remedies for underutilization. Affirmative action compliance in the office would focus on the top and come to ensure that qualified, educated women and underrepresented men could advance into managerial positions where they had not previously been permitted.

By the 1990s the development and implementation of EEO law had solidified the long-standing distinction between clerical and managerial ladders. In 1989 the secretary of labor created the Glass Ceiling Initiative, followed by the Glass Ceiling Commission, to investigate barriers to women reaching top management positions.[120] Women represented just 6.6 percent, and underrepresented men only 2.6 percent, of executives, according to a government report in 1991.[121] Cornell University's Center for Advanced Human Resource Studies (CAHRS) recommended that companies examine their flows (internal ladders) and sources (external search networks) to diversify the demographic composition of executives. Yet by 1991 the well-intentioned recommendations from CAHRS assumed that internal flow started at "entry management," which meant that the search for high-potential employees did not include women in clerical positions.[122] According to 90 percent of the HR managers surveyed by Catalyst, the nonprofit advocacy organization for women in business, hiring managers tended to nudge women toward traditionally female occupations. Once in those occupations, women had very limited opportunities for advancement into top management.[123]

Despite its limitations, affirmative action facilitated some building blocks of more inclusive workplaces: hiring managers started to focus on racial and gender diversity in candidate pools, and they adhered to more standardized personnel processes in an attempt to advance equality. Activist organizations such as 9to5 had influenced personnel procedures in various industries—insurance, banking, publishing—during the 1970s. It helped to win internal job postings, written job descriptions, and paid job training in workplaces across the nation as employers moved toward compliance with EEO laws. Yet to what extent did these practices offer mobility to female office workers, if the distinction between managerial and clerical ladders was not targeted as an affirmative action violation? Internal postings mattered little if clerical work still was not considered relevant experience for a management position. Written descriptions mattered little if all clerical descriptions included "ad hoc" language. Paid training mattered little if employers interpreted "job related" so narrowly as to exclude training for higher-paid, higher-status positions. The implementation and enforcement of affirmative action in most companies did not effectively address the separation of clerical and managerial ladders, which meant that women who entered clerical work remained confined to clerical positions.

Upward mobility out of clerical work had few organizational remedies, and women remained concentrated in the occupational category, with women of color facing more intense discrimination. From 1964 to 1979 the density of women in clerical occupations actually increased, and women of color, as they entered the office, were relegated to the most precarious jobs.[124] According to Boston 9to5's "Minority Women Office Workers: A Status Report" (1976), women of color "were channeled into traditional low-paid and low-status office jobs (filers, messengers, phone operators, mail clerks) and into the new job of key punching. Higher status, higher paid jobs like secretary and bookkeeper [were] still reserved mainly for whites."[125] A national 9to5 report, *Hidden Assets: Women and Minorities in the Banking Industry* (1980), reaffirmed the Boston findings. The representation of clerical workers in banking was high (66.8 percent of all bank workers, of which 90 percent were women) and the pay was low.[126] 9to5 activists perceived this sort of segregation by race and sex as evidence that affirmative action was not working.

As the 1970s became the 1980s, federal support for affirmative action languished even more. The Ronald Reagan administration attempted to rescind Executive Order 11246. Although this was unsuccessful, President Reagan reduced the OFCCP's budget, which essentially stalled affirmative action enforcement. The appointment of Clarence Thomas, a fervent opponent of affirmative action, as head of the EEOC also weakened implementation.[127]

The next chapter will demonstrate a changing agenda of clerical advocates into the 1980s, as they left behind battles over the boundaries of affirmative action to fight for greater regulation of the automated office. Concomitant with the legal transformation wrought by EEO laws, technology and automation fundamentally changed—and even severed—the relationship between secretary and boss, forcing 9to5 and its advocates to readjust their platforms.

5

THE DECLINE OF THE OFFICE
WIFE AND THE RISE OF THE
"AUTOMATED HAREM"

I n the bestseller *Working: People Talk About What They Do All Day and How They Feel About What They Do*, author Studs Terkel interviewed over a hundred American men and women across the nation. Asking about their working lives, Terkel wanted to hear "about a search for daily meaning as well as daily bread . . . in short for a sort of life rather than a Monday through Friday sort of dying."[1] One of Terkel's interviewees, Sharon Atkins, described the disillusionment she felt in her job after college. As an English literature major, she had hoped to enter the publishing industry after graduating, but she could not find a job as a copy editor. Instead, she found work as a receptionist for a large midwestern business. Atkins had hoped she would never have to become "the dumb broad at the front desk who took telephone messages." She felt trapped at her telephone: "The machine dictates. This crummy little machine with buttons on it—you've got to be there to answer it. You can walk away from it and pretend you don't hear it, but it pulls you. . . . You're [*sic*] job doesn't mean anything. Because *you're* a little machine. A monkey could do what I do."[2] Atkins was not alone in feeling as if technology had resulted in monotonous working conditions.[3]

Throughout U.S. history, the introduction of new workplace technology has ambivalently influenced Americans' quality of life. White-collar work was not immune from the positive and negative effects of technological change, as telephones, typewriters, and adding machines became more advanced throughout the twentieth century.[4] In 1960 only about four thousand computers were in use in American offices—mostly utilized by specialists for technical tasks.[5] Throughout the 1970s and 1980s, personal computers became smaller, cheaper, and more commonplace. Research consultancy SRI International estimated that in 1982, 2.5 million electronic workstations were in operation across the nation, and that the number would continue to grow exponentially over the years.[6]

Just what would the rise of the personal computer mean for the nature and status of clerical work? A National Research Council report, *Computer Chips and Paper Clips*, predicted that, by 1995, demand for some clerical workers—telephone operators, data-entry operations, and stenographers—would shrink drastically.[7] Meanwhile, more clericals would sit at computer workstations all day using what were called video display terminals (VDTs). Women using VDTs were reporting physical ailments such as undue stress, joint pain, vision problems, and even miscarriages. In response, 9to5 moved away from concerns about the interpretation and enforcement of affirmative action, realizing that implementation of the broad EEO agenda was unlikely to address the priorities of career clericals. Instead, the organization shifted its agenda toward improving the health and safety of women in the automated office. As office workers complained of maladies triggered from consistent use of VDTs, 9to5 waged a campaign for government attention to the occupational hazards that could result from this new type of office work.[8]

9to5 approached automation with the concerns of a labor organization, advocating for protective legislation to buffer women workers from their machines. It tried to leverage women's biological difference from men— and their capacity to have children—to push for government regulation of office work. These 9to5 tactics mirrored those of an earlier generation of women who had fought for better conditions in factories, using the argument that mothers needed state protection from the demands of industrial work.[9] This turn toward protective legislation in the 1980s, as well as 9to5's focus on unionization (which will be addressed in the next chapter), deepened a growing division in the corporation between advocacy efforts for clerical women and those for professional women. Whereas in the 1970s the subcommittee on publishing had embraced low pay for clerical work alongside promotional opportunities for college-educated women (chapter 3), by the 1980s the primary focus of 9to5 shifted toward the issues facing those who would spend their careers in clerical jobs.

For their part, employers also took notice of new automation hazards. They realized that productivity was likely to decline and turnover was likely to increase if office workers were uncomfortable or even injured. Employers ultimately moved toward making workstations more user friendly, investing in the improvement of workstation design, and pre-empting the need for extensive regulation of VDTs by the government. This attention to the concerns of employees would undercut 9to5's ongoing efforts to unionize the automated office, as we will see in the next chapter. We now turn to employee perceptions of the changing workplace, and how 9to5 advocated for the problems facing those confined to computer workstations.

Word processing was called the "buzz word" of a national business equipment exhibit in 1971.[10] A word processor looked like a typewriter but had an attached monitor. In the 1970s each machine could cost thousands of dollars, at least $2,500, but they had advantages over the traditional typewriter.[11] Users could type, rearrange, and edit text; then when the text was mistake-free, they could print it on clean paper.[12] Word processors took off: in 1977 companies spent $80 million on word-processing machines, and by 1982 the number had increased to $300 million. By 1980 between 5 and 10 million word processors, increasingly called video display terminals, were in use.[13]

One woman summarized the prevailing attitude among clericals when she said, "There's something about the electronic office that really gives me the willies."[14] In 1983 the *Los Angeles Times* wrote of "genuine fears" from clerical women who worried, "I'm going to be replaced by a machine!"[15] They were not irrational fears: clerical occupations requiring the entering and processing of data declined most heavily in the 1970s with the growing prevalence of word processors. Jobs involving tabulating, bookkeeping, calculating, and keypunching became less common, as did demand for telephone operators and stenographers.[16]

And perhaps not every manager needed a personal secretary. Consultants at IBM researched "office monogamy," or the one-to-one relationship between boss and secretary, to determine the best way to reorganize clerical chores.[17] *Administrative Magazine* recommended complete elimination of the "executive secretary" position.[18] The executive secretary was a "Jill of all Trades," or a skilled generalist who arguably enjoyed a fair amount of variety, autonomy, and responsibility in her job relative to a data entry clerk, for instance.[19] Having varied tasks—ranging from support services to domestic chores—could be a curse or a blessing, depending on the nature of one's particular boss. Elizabeth Anderson, a thirty-year veteran of secretarial work, told author and activist Barbara Garson about the unspoken mutuality that characterized her relationship with her boss: "You typed his personal letters and he let you make personal phone calls; you typed his kid's term paper, he let you leave early on a school holiday."[20]

Now, according to the *New York Times*, "the whole office is talking about it: The Boss and The Secretary are getting a very businesslike divorce" thanks to the "brave new world" of the word processor.[21] Word processing could singlehandedly transform the boss-secretary relationship. Before word processing, executive secretaries spent about 20 percent of their work time typing and proofing documents.[22] But with the word processor, IBM consultants recommended that typing be centralized in a single department called the "Administrative Support Center." Managers who needed typing assistance would complete a request form and then place their typing assignment in the queue. Word processors (the term not just for the machine, but also for the women doing the typing) completed work in the order in which it was received.[23]

—❦—

Without question, the spread of the word processors meant a change in the boss-secretary relationship. But the effects of that change for women's status in the workplace were unclear. Maybe office automation could empower women who had once been under the thumb of a male boss.[24] Sociologist Mary Murphree wrote that word processing ended the "feudal relationship that existed between the boss and secretary."[25] Wilma Gormley, an automation consultant, told the *New York Times* of the change that most secretaries would "look forward to it because they are no longer the chattel of one man."[26] The shift from typewriter to word processors might give women more opportunity for higher-level thought.[27] The *Los Angeles Times* proclaimed that with the introduction of the word processor, "morale actually improves in many cases because the clerical staff is relieved of repetitious typing," no longer having to redraft entire documents on new sheets of paper.[28]

And perhaps the shift toward a centralized word-processing department could undercut male power by way of bureaucratic hurdles. Some companies ordered managers to refrain from speaking directly with their former secretaries who had been transferred into the word-processing center. While some bosses accepted the "trauma" of losing their secretaries, others clung vehemently to their former positions of authority in an attempt to preserve their "ego," in the words of a former executive secretary. She explained that some men continued to approach the word-processing departments to ask their former secretaries to do personal errands. In fact, at Proctor & Gamble, so many managers flouted the rules that the company instituted formal assertiveness training for women so that they could "deal better with the managers hanging around their desks expecting them to do this or find that." The training sessions involved role plays so that the secretaries-turned-word-processors could practice phrases such as, "The work will get done in order. You won't get it any faster by standing there."[29]

Typing in the word-processing center, as opposed to working as an executive secretary, could provide women with some increased discretion and autonomy. For instance, women who had positive relationships with a former boss might still consider prioritizing his typing assignment. Otherwise, they could resort to following the larger queue if they did not want to do him any favors. And those who disliked their former bosses appreciated that sitting in the word-processing center gave them physical separation. One woman explained her form of rebellion: she stopped baking him a cake on his birthday. According to one of her colleagues, "He wasn't the kind of man you'd bake a cake for unless he was your boss." Women in the office delighted that "when it came to his birthday he kept coming out of the office looking, but there was no cake." While he had always bragged to other managers about her delicious cakes, she no longer felt compelled to bake for him.[30]

Some media outlets, too, equated technological advancement with social progress. Automation could become a tool of women's liberation, according to the trade publication *Business Automation*.[31] Some office equipment advertisements depicted the word-processing machine as freeing women from routine work.[32] The *New York Times* heralded word processing as the "answer to Women's Lib advocates' prayers."[33] The *Chicago Tribune* likewise aligned office automation with women's advancement: "Women's Liberation has hit the technology field in the guise of a new theory called 'word processing.'"[34] The thinking was that if word processing could increase the speed and efficiency of typing work, then clerical women could focus on more skilled job tasks. Some executive secretaries (those not moved into the word-processing center) considered their jobs upgraded following automation, given that typing constituted less of their total workload. Select middle management tasks such as database research and graphics production shifted to the agendas of those remaining in executive secretary positions.[35]

Professional associations and secretarial training programs certainly had a stake in defending the reputation of the executive secretary. They used technological change to further segment the vastness of the clerical workforce, distinguishing the more refined role of the executive secretary from the routinized work of the word processor.[36] Automation would promise "more thinking time and less time on typing, collating and copying," according to Lynn Salvage, president of Katharine Gibbs Schools.[37] She told the *New York Times* that executive secretaries could emerge from under their boss's shadow to "become the technological manager of the office of the future."[38] Fran Riley, a public relations professional from the National Secretaries Association, "sounded pretty piqued over the use of the title 'secretary' to describe those using word-processing machines." According to the NSA's official definition, a secretary was an assistant who had the "ability to assume responsibility without direct supervision, who displays initiative, exercises judgement, and makes decisions."[39] Those performing routinized tasks on a machine were usually not part of the NSA's definition, although if their job were enlarged, they could qualify for membership and take the certified professional secretary (CPS) exam.[40] Riley insisted that not all word processors should assume a secretarial title, telling the *New York Times*, "we have a definition and we're fighting for its purity and integrity."[41]

Other secretarial training programs tried to place word processing under the executive secretary's skilled umbrella. The Palmer School in

Philadelphia described use of the word processor as a capability that was not accessible to all. It offered a seminar on word processing so that women could "find out if they have the aptitude for operating a Word Processor."[42]

Surveys revealed that secretaries themselves shared this optimistic perspective about the influence of automation on job prospects and job quality. The majority of secretaries polled by Kelly Services indicated that the advent of word processing was leading to new career opportunities.[43] Professional Secretaries International, the new name in 1981 for the NSA, showed that 87 percent of those surveyed in 1983 believed that automation was having a positive effect on the secretarial profession; 73 percent believed automation was making their jobs more fulfilling.[44] Automation was "creating a whole new career ladder for entry-level office workers to climb," according to PSI president Ina Simpson. Practitioners like Wanda Gant, a senior office systems analyst at Monsanto, claimed that work in word processing promised a distinct path into management. At Monsanto, where entire electronic offices had been installed in about 20 percent of the company, she claimed that a motivated word-processing operator could move into a supervisory position overseeing the word-processing center. From this type of position, she could move to new jobs such as systems training instructor, program designer, systems analyst, and consultant.[45]

Finally, new technology could help to increase clerical wages, according to some consultants. Joan Palmer, a personnel management consultant, claimed that word processing had the potential to upgrade clerical work if labeled a "high-paying skill."[46] Companies hired Palmer to conduct pay equity studies, ensuring that their salaries were equitable and based on standardized criteria. Palmer claimed that clerical wage scales were moving upward because secretaries had taken charge of operating word processors, and managing new technology was traditionally men's work. She theorized, "A lot of the traditional secretarial skills like making contact with the public, using good common sense, organizing meetings, bosses just didn't always appreciate. But there's something about those personal computers that has led to more of an appreciation for the secretaries who use them."[47]

Companies were also reexamining compensation structures for clerical work as automation was reducing the one-to-one ratio of secretary to

manager.[48] Dr. N. Elizabeth Fried, a former secretary who earned a doctorate and became a compensation consultant, helped to lead the charge to
change pay practices for secretaries in the 1980s.[49] Traditionally, companies had graded secretarial jobs "by the organizational level of the manager to whom the secretary reports."[50] According to Fried, employers
should end what she called "rug-ranking," which was the long-standing
practice of basing secretarial pay solely on the level of the manager. Rug-
ranking was so named because the higher the quality of the boss's rug
(indicative of his status in the company), the higher the secretary's pay
grade.[51] Fried believed that actual job content—using factors such as skill,
effort, decision making—should determine pay grades, and that this evaluation system would help many secretaries move up in salary.[52] Destabiliz-
ing the boss-secretary relationship, automation to some extent supported
this transformation away from rug-ranking, but the clerical pay scales still
left most feeling as if they deserved more for their work.

⌛⌛⌛

While some saw word processing as skilled work that would offer increased
pay and promotions, ultimately the gloomy predictions about automation
and secretarial work would prove more accurate. Although automation
had tantalized with prospects of more creative, higher-order secretarial
work, the spread of personal computers undermined, not enhanced, the
status of the secretarial profession. Sure, word processors did away with
correction tapes, correction fluid, and retyping. But the downside of moving to the word processor? "Straight typing seven hours a day," stated a
longtime secretary.[53] The advent of word processing would mean that the
secretary's autonomy and variety would be "taken away from her at a
greater cost than many of us have realized," according to an academic.[54]
Another sociologist explained that word processing "eliminates skills for
the job. And it also eliminates the right to claim mobility and higher salaries based upon growing skills and experience" since the same task was
being performed routinely.[55]

The popular press began to discuss clerical work in terms typically used
to describe blue-collar, industrial labor. As managers were focusing on
increasing clerical output, the automated office had become "the new
factory," according to the *Boston Globe*.[56] The *Los Angeles Times* declared

that automation had regressive implications for work: "The office of the future now looks too often like the factory of the past." An insurance claims examiner at Blue Shield in San Francisco described her work to the newspaper as "very much like an assembly line." The coming of the personal computer had more than doubled managerial expectations of her workload. When she began working at Blue Shield, claims processing was only semielectronic, and supervisors expected her to resolve 116 claims per day. Yet now, with claims fully automated, the standard expectation was to process 350 per day.[57]

Word processing also opened the door for the application of scientific management practices to office work.[58] In his classic *Labor and Monopoly Capital* (1974), activist Harry Braverman maintained that even before widespread use of word processing, management experts had already "erased the distinction between work in factories and work in offices."[59] Relying on data from a number of organizations, the Systems and Procedures Association of America in 1960 had published time values for various types of clerical motions. Its manual included standards for very detailed movements: chair activity (getting up should take 0.033 minutes and turning in a swivel chair 0.009 minutes); filing (opening and closing a file drawer, without selecting a file, should take 0.04 minutes); and "jogging" or aligning a stack of papers (first jog should take 0.006 minutes, second jog 0.009 minutes; pat following jog should take 0.004 minutes, but pat following a pat 0.007 minutes).[60] After the spread of word processing, critics of automation argued that machines were undermining worker autonomy, much as the manufacturing assembly line had routinized industrial labor. Sociologist Daniel Cornfield explained that aspects of Taylorism from the early twentieth century (e.g., time-motion studies) could be found in the automated offices of insurance companies. Increased surveillance of work output meant that managers were relying on more "quantifiable and machine-measured indicators" of productivity.[61]

Word processors transformed the performance evaluation standards of clericals and their work. Before word processors, each boss assessed the performance of his own secretary. Now a group of clericals was accountable to the supervisor of the word-processing center, who could access an output report on each typist. This report reflected that word processing was a "machine-paced job," according to automation experts Jeanne Stellman and Mary Sue Henifin in *Office Work Can Be Dangerous to Your*

Health. They wrote that it was "analogous to the automobile assembly line, where cars come down the line at a prescribed speed and each worker is required to weld his wheel or twist his bolt as the auto passes before him."[62] The emphasis on speed and quantity meant that some clericals disregarded the quality of the finished product if accuracy was not part of the assessment. A former executive secretary turned word processor in the banking industry said that she was evaluated by "the time spent and the total number of keystrokes." So when notes came to her with "wrong spelling, wrong information," she typed exactly what was there and did not take time to correct it for the final document. In her words to Barbara Garson, "Why should I stay two minutes past lunch if they're timing me that way?"[63] Another clerical working in an insurance firm reported anonymously to 9to5 that she felt like she was in grammar school. The word-processing supervisors required that women complete late or absent slips upon their arrival to work. Clericals were to record a proper excuse for the corporate record, and to get the signature of their supervisors.[64]

As more clericals were attached to an electronic workstation instead of a boss, physical and psychological complaints surfaced from all-day use. By 1980, 7 million people, mostly women, operated a VDT.[65] The hazards of repeated use surprised policy makers, employers, and the larger public, who associated work danger with mining or even manufacturing, but not with the office. According to Stellman, a Columbia University professor of public health, the hazards of office work were "less obvious because they [did] not cause an immediate effect." Stellman's pioneering research into the understudied health risks of office work demonstrated that all-day VDT use resulted in a host of negative consequences including increased musculoskeletal problems, increased eye fatigue, decreased job satisfaction, and a decreased sense of general wellness.[66] Industrial psychologist Craig Brod coined the term *technostress* to describe the mental and physical anguish of those adjusting to repeated computer use.[67] An information systems professor told the *Washington Post* that to avoid "cyberphobia—a fear of computers that can cause vertigo, nausea, hysteria and cold sweats," work demands should be decreased while clericals were acclimating to the new arrangement.[68] In response to automation,

9to5 pushed its advocacy further toward the unionization model, given that new concerns were pushing secretarial work further toward industrial labor.

ഇരു

In the 1980s 9to5 devoted resources primarily to two related campaigns: first, as described in chapter 6, to recruiting women into a newly created national union for clerical workers, District 925 of the Service Employees International Union; and, second, to developing Project Health and Safety, which concerned office automation.[69] Karen Nussbaum saw automation as a "window of opportunity" for organizing women workers, believing that the changing nature of office work would encourage the growth of clerical unions.[70] She hoped that 9to5 could move discussions of automation into the broader domain of public debate.[71]

Project Health and Safety had two aims: the first was to collect data about how automation was affecting clericals' health and wellness. Physically, clericals were complaining about eye strain, neck and back pain, and aching wrists from using VDTs all day. 9to5 instituted a national hotline to collect information from VDT operators about their health problems. In one month alone, the hotline received three thousand calls about burning eyes or other problems with vision.[72] The highly routinized nature of the work, coupled with low pay and little chance for upward mobility, was resulting in high levels of reported stress in clerical women.[73]

Second, Project Health and Safety sought to empower clericals to have greater authority over use of the new technology.[74] In April 1980 9to5 issued the first U.S. report to describe automation from the perspective of women office workers. In *Race Against Time*, the organization argued that workers—not just managers and scientists—should make decisions about VDT application. It claimed that managers utilized the machines to increase surveillance and assert control over workers.[75]

The rise of VDTs as standard office equipment—and 9to5's advocacy for those operating them—coincided with the development of a federal organization designed to regulate worker safety, the Occupational Safety and Health Administration (OSHA). Congress had created this Department of Labor agency in 1970 to monitor both private and public workplaces. Its mission was to prevent work-related injuries, illnesses, and occupational fatalities by issuing and enforcing standards for workplace health and safety in tandem with the National Institute for Occupational Safety and Health (NIOSH), a research center established to address similar issues.[76]

Labor interests complained that OSHA was "a toothless tiger" with a light maximum penalty of $1,000 for corporate violations, and that NIOSH was underfunded and had limited resources to conduct research.[77] Most of the focus of occupational safety was on blue-collar work.[78] However, the government did start investigating VDT use, which bolstered 9to5's efforts regarding automation. Even before the launch of Project Health and Safety, NIOSH was attending to workplace stress in offices.[79] NIOSH's research into the negative effects of routinized white-collar labor reported that VDT operators had the highest stress level of any occupational group studied, including air traffic controllers. NIOSH uncovered a strong relationship between job design (repeated performance of a low-skilled task) and job stress. Furthermore, regulating speed of operators, which was intended to boost output, actually was found to decrease workers' productivity over several years.[80] Regarding physical ailments, NIOSH studies linked high rates of musculoskeletal problems (e.g., back and neck pain) with VDT use.[81]

Additional research contended that increasing clericals' safety and comfort would result in higher productivity. In the early 1980s automation expert Marvin Dainoff and his colleagues worked as visiting researchers at NIOSH, ultimately making a case for ergonomics, or the use of science to redesign machines, jobs, and workstations to best fit the human experience. They conducted lab experiments using clericals as subjects and found that workstations with optimal ergonomic design (e.g., adjustable chairs, detachable keyboard, adjustable monitor at eye level, no glare on the screen) resulted in higher productivity. On average, clericals using optimally designed stations enhanced performance in typing tasks by almost 25 percent relative to the control group. In a field study, another specialist surveyed 980 clerical workers in a major insurance company. Three months after the introduction of nonadjustable VDTs, questionnaires revealed a "marked increase in dissatisfaction" as well as back and neck discomfort. Implementation of adjustable workstations increased performance by 10 to 15 percent, such that typing could be performed more quickly. Experts quantified the financial impact of poorly designed workstations at $701 annually per employee; Dainoff responded that an "interesting coincidence that this figure of $701 is close to the current list price of some excellent ergonomic chairs."[82] Psychologist John W. Jones, author of *The Burnout Syndrome*, estimated that stress-related illnesses resulted in corporate costs of $2,298 annually per employee.[83]

Although research teams at NIOSH issued recommendations for improving workstation design, illumination, and vision testing, OSHA did not adopt enforceable standards or mandate these findings.[84] Instead, the federal government used the research to push for voluntary compliance, and it asked employers to institute programs to encourage healthy eating, smoking cessation, and stress management. According to one director in the Department of Health and Human Services, "50 percent of the causes of death are related to health behavior, and, accordingly, worksite health promotion programs have become a more compelling need for us nationally."[85]

9to5, however, continued to lobby the federal government for regulation, pressuring employers and manufacturers to design jobs and apply technology with operators' health and well-being in mind. Judith Gregory, research director at 9to5, used business-friendly reasoning that drew on concepts such as job satisfaction and productivity to make her case. Her testimony before Congress reinforced the connection between automation and worker dissatisfaction. According to Gregory, managers could use the VDT to enhance their current jobs, but for clericals, the VDT "took more and more meaning out of their work." Gregory contended that decreased clerical job satisfaction resulted from a regulated and routinized environment where variety in work duties and contact with other people became less common.[86] She called on the government to help clericals curtail the adverse health effects—stress, visual, musculoskeletal, and nervous system problems—resulting from automation. According to Gregory, "action must be taken *now* before irreparable harm is done to office workers' jobs, health, and quality of working life."[87]

In addition to lobbying the government, 9to5 embarked on its own efforts to influence VDT manufacturers to attend to ergonomic issues in an increasingly competitive space.[88] Knowing that VDT manufacturers wanted to capture as much market share as possible, it launched an Office Machine Design Project to compare different models in terms of ergonomic design and user-friendly features. The group made a conscious choice to have clericals themselves evaluate the machines, while other reports had scientists review the products.[89] It wrote letters to several manufacturers in the Boston area explaining the project, requesting to meet with company representatives and asking for equipment that could be used for testing.[90] The manufacturers were quite hospitable to 9to5's requests to test their products, seeing an opportunity for an endorsement.[91] In its response, Prime Computer was eager to discuss what features clericals would prefer in its future products. Digital Equipment, the largest computer company in Massachusetts, told 9to5 it was considering the development of guidelines to help guide corporations toward responsible introduction of new technology into the workplace.[92]

In August 1982 9to5 released its consumer report, *The Human Factor*, which was the first report of its kind to examine VDTs from users' points of view.[93] Although the organization did not endorse a particular machine, it did provide a list of recommended features that would maximize an operator's health and comfort.[94]

The Human Factor encouraged companies to consider the consequences of scientific management strategies. Instead, manufacturers and employers could increase productivity by ameliorating undue physical and mental job stress.[95] Reports of carpal tunnel syndrome were increasing rapidly, and by the 1990s an estimated two million computer users would experience it. Automation experts claimed that carpal tunnel syndrome alone cost employers an estimated $100 billion a year in combined workers compensation claims and lost work time (a median of thirty workdays lost per person). In addition, some four million VDT workers developed tendinitis.[96] Repetitive strain injuries increased from 18 percent of all occupational illnesses in 1981 to 66 percent by 1999.[97] A strong business case existed for these changes, which aligned with the 9to5 agenda.

While labor and management alike supported improving the ergonomic design of workstations, a more polarizing issue sparked public debate. Walter Kleinschrod, former editor of *Office Administrative and Automation* magazine, who wrote one of the most widely cited books to help managers introduce technology, declared, "Few of OA [office automation]'s issues have been as controversial" as the potential health hazards posed by VDTs to pregnant women.[98] According to a former member of the Office of Technology Assessment, an office of the U.S. Congress, an estimated ten to fifteen million women of childbearing age worked at VDTs in the 1980s.[99] Clusters of pregnant VDT workers were reporting miscarriages, potentially from the radiation emitted from cathode ray tubes (CRTs), which were inside the VDT monitor. At the Defense Logistics Agency in Marietta, Georgia, out of twelve pregnant VDT operators, seven had miscarriages.[100] By 1984 ten clusters of pregnant VDT operators with abnormally high rates of miscarriage had been reported, the smallest group consisting of three pregnant workers and the largest being twenty-four.[101] In a news conference, Nussbaum explained that low-level radiation from VDTs could be the cause.[102]

9to5 publicized adverse pregnancy outcomes throughout the United States and Canada to lobby for government intervention. In particular, it wanted alternate employment offered to pregnant operators along with mandates such as required breaks for all users. It employed an approach that emphasized women's biological difference from men, in an era when most advocates of women's rights at work emphasized equality between the sexes. By the early 1970s, nearly all labor unions had abandoned support for protective labor legislation, gender-specific laws that had arisen early in the twentieth century because of the dangers of industrial work. Such laws shielded women, but not men, from performing heavy lifting on the job. And women, but not men, were banned from working beyond ten hours per day because of their reproductive capabilities and allegedly more delicate natures.[103]

Although 9to5 sought support for protective laws regarding VDT use, the federal government claimed that there was insufficient evidence to establish a causal link between VDT operation and miscarriage. Although NIOSH told 9to5 in 1982 that it would research the possible connection, by 1984 it still had not acted. The director of NIOSH testified before Congress in 1984 that he believed that VDTs were not a dangerous source of radiation. In his opinion, "The VDT revolution in the workplace [had] produced impressively few problems considering the scope of the technological change."[104] 9to5 supporters, both men and women, wrote at least forty letters of complaint to NIOSH, demanding further investigation since millions of women of childbearing age worked daily at VDTs.[105] In 1985 the Office of Technology Assessment reviewed the current research and concluded, "There is at this time no good basis for fear of VDT effects on reproductive processes."[106] 9to5 would not find support through federal channels.

Many clerical workers thought otherwise. 9to5 turned to state governments for remedy, using the issue of pregnancy to try to secure broader regulation of VDT use. While calling for investigation into the radiation issues, it also began campaigns to lobby for state laws to regulate VDT use for all operators in the first half of the 1980s. The efforts to codify protections for VDT use saw mixed success. In Massachusetts, for instance, 9to5 leaders helped write the proposed VDT legislation and met with the bill's sponsors to develop strategies to market the bill and present it on the House and Senate floor.[107] This proposed VDT law provided several protections to workers: advance notice of technology implementation (to affected employees); adjustable chairs, terminal tables, and keyboards; breaks from VDT use; proper lighting; temperature and noise controls; alternate employment for pregnant operators; and employer-paid eye exams.[108]

Yet the Massachusetts bill, like many other state bills through the 1980s, failed to pass in such a stringent form.[109] Some states were able to pass watered-down versions. Seven states and the District of Columbia adopted advisory guidelines, usually applicable to public employees.[110] And Maine, Connecticut, and Rhode Island passed laws calling for further study on the health and safety effects of VDTs but did not require on-site protection of workers.[111] The first bill to pass containing 9to5's recommendations for protecting VDT operators was a local ordinance in Suffolk County, New York, in 1988. The vote was close, as local corporations lobbied strongly against the bill, worried that the measures would prove too costly and deter future business growth. However, the testimony about studies linking miscarriages and VDT use aided the bill's passage. Said one Republican: "That was the real clincher for me. Would you gamble with your child?"[112]

Employers and VDT manufacturers formed alliances to campaign against bills such as the one in Suffolk County.[113] Representative Tom Hayden, sponsor of a bill in California, called the opposition from manufacturers and employers "extremely heavy."[114] Even in Maine, where the bill under consideration was calling for further study only, employers and manufacturers protested. According to the chair of the Labor Committee in the Maine State House of Representatives, "As usual, New England Telephone, Associated Industries of Maine, and the state's largest insurance company Union Mutual violently opposed the bill and conducted intense lobbying against this simple measure."[115] Twenty-two national trade associations, such as the American Bankers Association and the American Insurance Association, formed a lobbying organization, the Coalition for Workplace Technology, to block proposed state bills. This group, created by the Computer Business Equipment Manufacturers Association, helped defeat a number of state bills in 1984 by presenting scientific studies that individuals could remedy the discomfort themselves by blinking frequently to prevent eye strain.[116]

Although some in the business community doubted that VDT use posed substantial hazards, employers capitulated to certain demands to avoid public attention and government intervention. According to one probusiness lobbyist, "The only real danger here is that the terminal might fall on your foot. All of the things they're talking about are comfort concerns. They're trying to mandate employee relations. What if my office chair isn't comfortable? Do I get the Legislature to pass a bill?"[117] A National Association of Manufacturers (NAM) task force reported that because of the number of VDT bills pending in state legislatures, employers should proactively offer solutions to worker discomfort. The task force chairman warned those attending a NAM convention to provide an ergonomically comfortable environment as well as to offer rest breaks or "face mandates from state legislatures that would require impractical solutions."[118] By 1989 several companies, including Federal Express and Aetna Insurance, were preemptively designing more comfortable workstations. These companies believed that yielding to some worker demands would improve employee morale, increase productivity, and help their corporation avoid costly labor and legal entanglements.[119]

In the 1970s a wave of automation changed the structure of the office and the job of the secretary. Initially, the high price of word processors pushed organizations toward centralizing typing into a single department for the entire firm. Private secretaries moved from a seat right outside their bosses' doors to a designated area for VDT operators. As the price of new technology dropped in the 1980s, companies could afford to buy personal computers for a larger segment of employees. Eventually the tide shifted back toward decentralized administrative support, which allowed clericals to abandon the automated pools of highly routinized labor.[120] According to one journalist, the centralization of office automation pleased no one—not boss, and not secretary. Problems that plagued clericals—low job satisfaction, high turnover, work stress, and physical ailments—offset the objectives of increasing productivity and lowering administrative costs.[121] Managers, too, did not like having less control over their work when submitting their typing requests to the pool.[122] Though the boundaries of the centralized support system relaxed by the late 1980s, the practice of assigning each manager a personal secretary never returned. The one-to-one ratio of boss to secretary became more of a one-to-two or even one-to-twenty ratio. A more generalist approach reemerged for those performing secretarial work, although they had more than one boss to please.[123]

Automation allowed some U.S. firms to respond to technological advancement by physically moving clerical labor offshore to Mexico or the Caribbean, and a few to southern and eastern Asia. According to government estimates, the cost of employing an American woman to do data entry would be over $350 per week, whereas the cost of paying a Caribbean woman ranged from $15 to $60 per week.[124] A U.S.-owned airline identified as "Data Air" moved its information processing facilities to Barbados, hiring hundreds of women to enter flight information from ticket stubs into computers. The company estimated that it saved 35 percent on data-entry costs through offshoring.[125]

Besides offshoring, automation facilitated a rise in part-time and temporary labor in the United States, as historian Louis Hyman has described.[126] Though clericals disliked their new routinized jobs, and bosses missed having their own personal assistants, companies reduced their full-time workforces as they experimented with job design and organizational structure to increase productivity.[127] Changes toward precarious labor eliminated health insurance and retirement benefits for the part-time and temporary workers who helped to fill word-processing centers, most of whom were women. In fact, in 1981, 85 percent of the total 3.35 million reported "temps" in the United States were female.[128] Automation did allow "people to work at their own pace at home or away from the office, by connecting portable computer terminals to the office over communications lines," according to the *New York Times*. And those taking advantage of the work-from-home option reported that they liked the increased flexibility.[129] One consultant predicted that eventually, within a few decades, "people won't come to the office at all."[130]

The rise in white-collar automation had different economic implications for employees based on gender and race.[131] Work that women performed continued to be rationalized, their output monitored, and their positions devalued. Men, however, assumed work as computer programmers or analysts, jobs that increasingly held professional or semiprofessional status.[132] Furthermore, women of color were overrepresented in lower-level automated office positions, meaning that they held the most monotonous jobs with the least security. A government report warned that automation could undermine Black women's progress into white-collar work thus far (they had doubled their representation in office work over the span of 1960 to 1980) because automated jobs were susceptible to elimination.[133]

Given the changing nature of secretarial work, some managers worried that automation would result in increased unionization rates among low-paid office workers.[134] Yet the market, not the government and not unions, was ameliorating the physical discomforts resulting from all-day VDT operation. Employers had become motivated to meet the needs of employees. They pushed manufacturers to create work stations that were more comfortable so that employees could be more satisfied and productive.

Yet some women remained sufficiently dissatisfied with pay such that they were interested in what traditional labor organizations could offer. The potential for clerical unionization, and the managerial approaches in response, is the subject of the next chapter. New technology, coupled with the implementation of affirmative action without regard to salary (chapter 4), meant that advancement mechanisms for clerical and professional women were becoming increasingly distinct.

6

COULD PINK-COLLAR WORKERS
"SAVE THE LABOR MOVEMENT"?

I n honor of National Secretaries Week in 1981, the Washington School for Secretaries hosted a discussion of clerical unionization, which one newspaper called "the most explosive and controversial subject concerning secretaries."[1] About a hundred women office workers gathered to discuss the benefits and limitations of joining labor unions as a strategy for higher pay and better promotional opportunities. Opening remarks revealed contrasting approaches—unionization versus professionalization—to the future of clerical work. Jackie Ruff, director of a new national union called District 925, debated Sylvia Cash, director of the trade association Professional Secretaries International (PSI, formerly the National Secretaries Association). Ruff argued that clerical workers could be both union members and professionals. She claimed that "one person can be ignored," while employers had to respond to a union's grievances. According to Ruff, unions raised average pay, which would benefit clericals, as a class of gender-segregated workers. Those working in male-dominated occupations earned more: average annual salaries for manufacturing work were $15,000, but for clerical work, the average was less than $10,000. Ruff believed that the best way to address disparities in pay between traditionally male and traditionally female jobs was for clericals to unionize.[2]

Like Ruff, Cash wanted to improve the pay and status of clerical work. But she believed that unionization would undermine the professional prestige of the occupation. Cash, who sat on the PSI board of directors, listed her problems with unions, starting with the belief that unions "cre-ated an adversarial relationship between management and the employ-ees" that would weaken the "relationship that is necessary between the executive and the professional secretary." Furthermore, she claimed that unions "restrict your freedom" and force professionals to "lose their iden-tity." Because of a union's categorization of employees, Cash stated to those in the audience that each woman would not be "permitted to help your neighbor who may be in a classification higher than your own because a grievance could be filed against you." Last, union contracts specified that "promotions are based on seniority—not on performance or merit. Cash concluded that as part of a union, women would not be rewarded for improving in their jobs, for taking initiative, or for experimenting with new ideas."[3] Gibbs president Lynn Salvage agreed with Cash and the PSI platform. She told the *Chicago Tribune* that unionization of secretaries was not a smart strategy for promotional potential. Salvage believed that "a union would polarize the secretary in terms of management and pose a problem for her or him to move into managerial ranks."[4] Seemingly to sig-nal its opposition to clerical unions, in 1980 the professional association adopted "Free Enterprise" as its Program of the Year topic. Across the globe, all 792 chapters offered "a grassroots educational program about basic economic principles whose understanding is sometimes mired in misconceptions, ignorance, and conjecture," according to a NSA news release.[5]

At issue between those advocating for unionization and those push-ing for professionalization was the question of what type of clerical work-ers represented the future of the secretarial occupation. Union organiz-ers saw the occupational outlook as bleak: VDT operators, facing low pay, lack of autonomy, and unsafe working conditions, represented the next generation. Those in favor of professionalization did not disagree com-pletely. While acknowledging that a growing number of clericals worked automated jobs, PSI wanted to preserve the status distinction between those who operated machines only and those who held more elite posi-tions with varied duties.

While this Washington School debate seemed to be a question of unionization, it also demonstrated the vastly different views of which jobs represented the core of the secretarial occupation. Ruff and Cash were suggesting different remedies because the occupation itself was a broad collection of disparate jobs, all under the umbrella of women's office work. Ruff saw lower-skilled clericals in automated work as fit for unionization, while Cash saw higher-skilled clericals as generalists fit for promotion into management. In reality, most secretarial work by the turn of the twenty-first century would be an alloy of the two flanks. Few clericals worked completely automated jobs and few worked for a single boss. Thus neither unionization nor professionalization would be a perfect fit for clerical work by century's end. But in the 1980s a more stark division between the two flanks was emerging.

Simultaneously, as the status of the occupation itself was in flux in the 1980s, new attention to the state of the employment relationship emerged out of national concern that the United States was losing its place as the world's superpower. Leaders in the private and public sectors became aware of slowing productivity rates in the U.S. economy in contrast to rapid growth that distinguished the Japanese economy. The United States was falling behind other industrialized countries, including the United Kingdom, Canada, France, Germany, and Japan, in its average rates of output per labor hour.[6]

In response, a new trend in personnel practices emerged, known as quality of work life (QWL) initiatives. The idea was that increased job satisfaction would in turn lead to increased economic productivity.[7] The field of QWL, which the first section of this chapter describes, could even be called a movement, according to one management scholar, because of "the appearance of consultants, professional groups, and public and private study centers" across the country.[8] While a few QWL initiatives focused on pay to increase job satisfaction, most emphasized the importance of nonmonetary rewards that would leverage an employee's intrinsic motivation. "Creating more meaningful work," in the words of management scholar Fred K. Foulkes, became an issue of primary concern for public and private entities.[9] Practices grouped under the QWL umbrella fostered cooperation between labor and management to try to remedy turnover, absenteeism, dissatisfaction, and unrest. While some historians have mentioned quality of work life in their accounts of labor's decline, it has been overlooked as an explanatory factor that offered employees and employers a new way forward—in theory even if not in practice.[10]

This focus on labor-management cooperation came at a time when the strength and popularity of private-sector unions was waning. Americans were becoming more skeptical of unions and on average had less confidence in union leaders, who they reported were coercive, than in government or business leaders, according to a major government survey.[11] Academics explained union decline in terms of a souring popular perception. In the 1980s Harvard economist James Medoff revealed that in the public view, unions were closer to monopolies than democracies.[12] While Americans believed in unions as effective vehicles to raise wages, industrial relations experts agreed that "quite clearly that given current circumstances, traditional union-organizing efforts are unlikely to yield substantial new members."[13]

Organizing women, and in particular women office workers, could form the future agenda of labor, according to union experts. The labor movement turned toward addressing the problems facing those in female-dominated occupations, as chronicled by historians Dorothy Sue Cobble, Katherine Turk, and Lane Windham, who uncover an upsurge of activism among women.[14] Service Employees International Union (SEIU) president John Sweeney told a journalist, "Just as industrial workers were the predominant organized groups in the '30s and '40s. . . . I think the clerical and other service workers are going to be the fastest growing areas in the '80s and '90s."[15] Given the public image of unions as top down, organizers needed to convince women that clerical unions could be different. In an era when women were weary of relinquishing autonomy to a male boss (whether in the office or in a union hall), organizers needed to convince women that union membership would result not just in higher pay but also in greater independence.[16]

The founding of a nationwide clerical union, SEIU District 925, in 1981 epitomized the hope, as we will see, that secretaries across a vast spectrum of skill could gravitate toward a single, craft-type of union. Articles from the popular press noted the increasing buzz around white-collar unionization; one newspaper headline asked, "Can women really save the labor movement?"[17] The 9to5 of the 1970s, evidenced by the activities of Women in Publishing, had focused on bridging promotional paths from clerical to managerial work and called for more equitable personnel practices that relied on merit, allowing women to have equal opportunity to advance. Yet the 9to5 of the 1980s focused on automation and unionization, issues that had been of concern to the Fordist factory workers of the past. Labor leaders, organizers, employers, and clerical workers waited to see

if pink-collar unionization would flourish—and if the professionalization of the secretarial ranks would prevail.

⸺ ∞∞ ⸺

Concerns about the slowing productivity rates of the U.S. economy characterized the political climate of the 1970s.[18] Rhetoric from government
officials signaled differing views on how to best increase employee motivation. On the one hand, conservatives shifted the burden of increasing
productivity to the backs of individual workers. President Richard Nixon,
who had convened a national committee to study productivity, asserted
in his Labor Day remarks in 1971 that hard work was a core American
value. Nixon emphasized that each individual's work ethic had serious
consequences for the state of the nation: an "industrious, purposeful
people" had "lifted [America] into the position of the most powerful and
respected leader of the free world today."[19] Other policy makers pointed
to employers and poorly designed jobs as the problem. Senator Edward
Kennedy (D-MA) cosponsored the Worker Alienation Research and Technical Assistance Act of 1972. According to Kennedy, millions "of Americans are alienated because they see their jobs as dead-ends, monotonous
and depressing and without value. And we in the Congress have a responsibility to see what can be done to end that alienation and return the
sense of excitement and adventure that traditionally has characterized our
people." This bill proposed to allocate $20 million for a two-year research
program to investigate the negative effects of and potential remedies for
worker alienation, a term used for employees' detachment from their labor,
as if what they did lacked meaning and purpose. Although the bill died
in committee, it demonstrated the extent to which perceived weakening
of employee motivation and decreasing rates of productivity had become
national concerns worthy of congressional debate.[20]

Others indicted both employers and employees, calling for improved
labor-management relations in the 1970s.[21] Secretary of Commerce
Peter G. Peterson, head of Nixon's productivity initiatives, told a congressional committee that "to be successful such a crusade must unite management and labor."[22] And Nixon's secretary of health, education, and welfare convened a special task force of union and business leaders, resulting
in the widely cited report *Work in America* (1973). It concluded that labor

and management needed to work together to redesign work tasks, "espe-cially since the failure to do so is adding to the tax burden of all Ameri-cans through increased social costs." Reliance on Frederick Winslow Tay-lor's "scientific management" theories had led to workplace problems such as absenteeism, loafing, and attrition. Taylorism discouraged intel-lectual input from lower-level workers, as they were supposed to simply execute tasks while managers did all the higher-level thinking. The task force recommended that workers have greater participation in problem solving and decision making, confirming an earlier line of research by union leader and MIT lecturer Joseph Scanlon and others that supported cooperation and trust between labor and management.[23]

Work in America explained that a new generation had different atti-tudes, aspirations, and values relative to their parents, which meant that they approached work differently too. Younger workers enjoyed higher standards of living and more access to formal education. They prioritized finding work that was interesting, meaningful, and aligned with their social values, perhaps even more so than finding work that paid well.[24] Advertising a job as having decent pay and benefits was no longer enough for New Left activists, according to historian Doug Rossinow, who uncov-ered a quest for authenticity among college students.[25] Public opinion analyst Daniel Yankelovich summarized the changing generational trends as the emergence of a "New Breed" of worker who elevated individualism above all else. Having come of age during the social movements of the 1960s, they had values different from those of their parents. Yankelovich wrote, "They promise to transform the character of work in America in the '80s . . . [refusing] to subordinate their personalities to the work role. To understand this refusal is to grasp the essence of the New Breed's quest for self-fulfillment." Work was a symbolic manifestation of the self, a trend that would fuel perceptions of occupational choice, as we will see in the next chapter.[26]

A wildcat strike represented the spirit of the generation, demonstrat-ing that the quality of a job—not just its wages—undergirded worker dis-satisfaction.[27] The strike was a "collective national symbol for that new breed of worker and [it was] emblematic of a widespread sense of occupa-tional alienation," according to historian Jefferson Cowie. In 1972 mostly young, Black and white male workers, whether members or nonmem-bers of the United Auto Workers (UAW), stood together to protest the acceleration of the assembly line at a General Motors (GM) plant in Lord-stown, Ohio.[28] The press took hold of the three-week strike, portraying the "blue-collar blues" of the workers who longed for meaning in their work and strove for dignity.

GM workers at Lordstown, especially the younger ones, did not neces-sarily see unionization as their remedy. In congressional testimony, the president of Lordstown UAW Local 1112 stated that the men who partici-pated were feeling "apathy—apathy within our union movement towards union leaders and to the Government" because neither seemed to repre-sent their needs. Furthermore, those on strike—union members and nonmembers—prioritized engagement with their job tasks—tasks that were becoming increasingly automated—more so than wages and bene-fits.[29] Following the strike, in 1973, GM and the UAW jointly established a committee of those from labor and management to try to improve employment relations at GM using quality of work life initiatives.[30]

This was just one example of implementing QWL principles, which were spreading throughout organizations in the 1970s. Professor of Orga-nizational Behavior Robert Guest defined QWL as a process whereby "an organization attempts to unlock the creative potential of its people by involving them in decisions affecting their work lives," which would both increase productivity for the organization and improve the fulfillment of individual employees.[31] By 1977 the first annual meeting of the American Quality of Work Life Association took place, where, for two days, labor and management representatives from seventeen organizations discussed QWL initiatives. In most companies, QWL began when management con-vened a committee with representatives from both labor and manage-ment to discuss terms of desired changes and sign an agreement pledg-ing their support.[32] Therefore, on the one hand, QWL programs remained a top-down pursuit, dependent on management to initiate and implement the cooperative process. On the other hand, these programs empowered workers to have a greater voice in decision making.[33] Even if managers ultimately could veto any suggestion of workers, QWL strategies chal-lenged long-standing assumptions about allocating all decision making to those with managerial status, which was integral to Taylorist princi-ples. "The simplistic authoritarianism [of Taylorism] would appear ludi-crous to the young worker who is not the uneducated and irresponsible person on whom Taylor's system was premised," according to sociologist

Harold L. Sheppard in his congressional testimony on worker alienation.[34] After implementing The Power Program, a QWL guide developed by MIT management professors David E. Berlew and Roger Harrison, executives at Polaroid declared that the adversarial relationship between management and labor had become "a pernicious relic of nineteenth-century raw capitalism."[35]

A shift in employee relations was underway. According to "New Industrial Relations" in *Business Week*: "Quietly, almost without notice, a new industrial relations system with a fundamentally different way of managing people is taking shape in the U.S. Its goal is to end the adversarial relationship that has grown between management and labor and that now threatens the competitiveness of many industries."[36] Academics and industrial relations experts debated whether QWL projects were here to stay, and if they had sparked systemic transformation.[37] To be certain, in some workplaces, the most substantive changes involved repainting the lunchroom or providing new trash cans on the plant floor.[38] Yet other QWL projects were reported to be quite effective, resulting in increased job satisfaction and feelings of personal growth, and decreased absenteeism, turnover, and tardiness.[39] Participants at the American QWL conference in 1977 emphasized that increased communication between labor and management reduced hostility between the parties and possibly could lead to profit sharing in the best instances.[40]

———— ✽ ————

Most QWL research and programming focused on the manufacturing sector, traditionally the stronghold of trade unions, where labor-management relations historically had been tense.[41] Yet pink-collar workers increasingly voiced dissatisfaction with automated office work, as the previous chapter illustrated, and the blue-collar blues could become the white-collar woes among office workers. Although the *Work in America* task force mainly focused on the issues faced in manufacturing, it spoke briefly of the problems plaguing the office: "The office today, where work is segmented and authoritarian, is often a factory. For a growing number of jobs, there is little to distinguish them but the color of the worker's collar: computer keypunch operations and typing pools share much in common with the automobile assembly-line."[42] Similarly, in his tome on the degradation of work, author and socialist activist Harry Braverman contended that "the traditional distinctions between 'manual' and 'white-collar' labor . . . represent echoes of a past situation which has virtually ceased to have meaning in the modern world of work."[43] For clerical workers, the VDT "took more and more meaning out of their work," according to 9to5 research director Judith Gregory, a point she emphasized in congressional testimony.[44]

Could solutions designed to remedy dissatisfaction in unionized, blue-collar manufacturing contexts apply to nonunionized, pink-collar office contexts?[45] While office automation received far less attention from academics and practitioners, the QWL movement did influence the nature of office work. For example, dissatisfaction with VDTs, as described in the previous chapter, led to the growth of ergonomics. Heralded as "the cure for computer blues," ergonomics pushed employers to reexamine workstation design to help to relieve eye strain, blurred vision, sore backs, and aching muscles for the more than seven million people employed at VDTs. An industry of ergonomics consultants arose, making claims that investments in ergonomic equipment could offer returns in the range of 96 to 680 percent in first year.[46]

Also, the idea of "job enrichment" replaced the previous shift toward single, repetitive tasks that accompanied VDT implementation. In essence, job enrichment, or completing whole tasks from start to finish, was seen as offering employees more meaningful work, where they could see the results of their labor. In the bestselling exposé *Pink-Collar Workers*, writer Louise Kapp Howe included an account of her experience as an undercover clerical in an insurance company. She reported that job enrichment was in place to try to increase employee satisfaction and prevent turnover. In the group claims department, Howe was told that job design had changed recently and now "each clerk [was] handling the records of individual customers from beginning to end, instead of just fragmented pieces of the job," according to the personnel manager.[47]

Usually the traditional bread-and-butter issue for unions—pay—was not the first step of the QWL process.[48] When Howe asked a personnel manager about raises for clerical workers, the manager distinguished between salary issues and QWL. Higher pay and paths to promotions were not within the realm of job enrichment, according to personnel: "No, those are separate issues; important issues to be sure, but separate issues from what we're talking about here—which is improving the job itself."[49] The nonprofit American Center on the Quality of Worklife recommended, "In the beginning, cosmetic alterations are the easiest and least threatening."[50] Howe noted such cosmetic changes at the insurance firm: the on-site company cafeteria, which served free lunch to all employees, was decorated attractively with an adjoining lounge that contained Ping-Pong and a TV. And the food happened to be much better than the standard institutional fare. Furthermore, the firm offered what Howe called "we're-all-one-big-family activities," such as picnics, employee sporting events, holiday parties, travel clubs, tuition reimbursement, and bowling parties.[51]

Given that QWL processes emphasized labor-management cooperation, some unions struggled to align their strategy and agenda with the changing workplace. "We still need the 'us versus them,'" AFL-CIO president Lane Kirkland stated to the *Boston Globe* in an article entitled "Can Labor Unions Survive?" (1984).[52] A Teamsters leader disagreed, telling the *Globe* that "unions have got to play a different role. . . . The view that participative management is manipulative is old thinking."[53] Either way, the bleak reality for private-sector unions was that they were shrinking. The AFL-CIO reported a significant decline in membership, from 35 percent to below 19 percent from the 1950s to the 1980s. Furthermore, in the 1980s unions reported more illegal discharges, particularly during elections. Unions claimed that employers were becoming less likely to bargain with them and instead would just relocate their operations.[54]

While she was aware of these challenging trends, Karen Nussbaum believed that organizing clericals could save the state of unions. The onset of feminism and the growth of human resource management (HRM), with their promise of expanding career options for women, meant that secretaries had two options—*professionalize or organize*—lest they be left behind in low-paying, dead-end jobs.

As mentioned at the beginning of this chapter, those arguing for professionalization were the leaders of the National Secretaries Association and the Katharine Gibbs School, who interpreted feminism as an opportunity to recast secretaries as part of management. Their approach was to augment formalized training and required certifications.[55] The NSA was not against raises but rather believed that professional status would ensure them. While 9to5 adopted a theme of "Raises Not Roses!" for National Secretaries Week in 1980, the NSA held that secretaries could have both raises and roses. It claimed that 9to5 was using the red rose—the association's initial symbol of the week that had since been discontinued—"contemptuously" and for its own "propaganda." NSA public relations counselor Fran Riley told chapter presidents that within the "office worker organizations (of the type Jane Fonda is supporting)," few members met the NSA definition of a secretary. Rather they had other clerical jobs.[56]

But in Nussbaum's opinion, raises would come through organizing. National Secretaries Week in 1980 was an opportunity to convince women office workers that they were more like the factory workers of the 1930s who had turned to unionizing en masse after getting frustrated with exploitative working conditions.[57] She saw these clericals—those in routinized jobs without upward mobility—as representing the future of secretarial work, work that would be difficult to professionalize. In contrast to those who sought to institute QWL programs to enrich jobs and motivate workers, she embarked on building a unionization movement.

Nussbaum believed that women were changing their attitudes about unions, as evidenced by their willingness to join.[58] As traditional blue-collar industrial unions struggled to maintain political clout and membership numbers in the 1970s, which historian Jefferson Cowie has called the "last days of the working class," more than 50 percent of all new union members in the 1970s were women.[59] If women's issues were made the focal point of an organizing campaign, Nussbaum and others reasoned, then a union election had a greater chance of succeeding.[60] In 1980 the National Labor Relations Board conducted 625 union representation elections among clerical or white-collar employees. Clerical unions won 53.6 percent of their elections, which was better than the average win rate of 45 percent.[61] In speeches and interviews during the 1980s, Nussbaum emphasized that women office workers represented the future of unionization, despite a wave of political and economic conservatism that hindered organizing in the private sector. Nussbaum remembers, "We sailed into the '80s with this enormous momentum."[62]

While major unions had organized clericals before, none had done so by establishing a national clerical workers' division. In the 1960s and 1970s unions that were organizing clericals included Office and Professional Employees International Union, the International Brotherhood of Teamsters, and the Communication Workers of America (CWA). White-collar workers from the public sector were organizing with the American Federation of Government Employees, the National Association of Government Employees, the National Federation of Federal Employees, the National Treasury Employees Union, and AFSCME.[63]

Also, the growing Service Employees International Union (SEIU) was organizing Boston clericals. Local 925 was an SEIU affiliate that Boston 9to5 leaders had begun in 1975 to give bargaining power to workers who wanted to unionize. 9to5 leaders, including Nussbaum, oversaw some of the first 925 campaigns, although the two organizations operated separately. Local 925 won significant battles, including organizing the first university workers in the city (Brandeis), the first major publishing house (Allyn & Bacon), and the first legal services program (Foley, Hoag, & Eliot). Because Local 925 had affiliate status, it operated autonomously and did not have to follow orders from the SEIU national leadership. This affiliate status appealed to clericals who valued independence from central authority, but the freedom meant less funding for campaigns. After assessing the benefits and drawbacks of affiliate status, 9to5 leaders decided they wanted more financial support, which also meant committing more broadly to a national union.[64]

Envisioning a coast-to-coast organizing movement that would augment the increasingly national scope of 9to5, Nussbaum began to search for an international union that could best accommodate an expansive clerical division.[65] Instead of affiliate status, Nussbaum wanted to form a clerical workers' division, or district. A district would have broad reach to organize across the country and would have more access to a national union's financial and human resources. Nussbaum realized that she had some leverage to negotiate for a clerical division. Among labor activists, she had credibility and name recognition, and many unions were hoping to woo 9to5 to increase their membership. Furthermore, 9to5 already was performing consciousness-raising activities and direct action campaigns, meaning that unions would have less work to do on their own. In 1981, 9to5 boasted ten thousand members in thirteen cities although recruiting women of color became a major issue for some affiliates (chapter 7).[66]

Ultimately, Nussbaum aligned with the SEIU to create a national clerical workers' division, District 925, in 1981. The SEIU proved appealing because of its organizing strategy: it launched campaigns in sectors and industries previously not heavily unionized.[67] Already over half of the SEIU's 650,000 members were women, including some 40,000 secretaries and clericals.[68] The national partnership between 9to5 and the SEIU expanded the local alliance that already existed in Boston, where Nussbaum had cofounded 9to5 as well as Local 925. While leaders in CWA and OPEIU courted Nussbaum, in the case of the SEIU, Nussbaum had to wait for confirmation that it wanted to take on a clerical division. In the 1970s national SEIU officials were monitoring the outcomes of Boston Local 925 drives, including one taking place among Boston University librarians, to gauge the potential for large-scale clerical unionization. The SEIU, like many trade unions, had to emphasize winning members and contracts, which meant that national leaders wanted to see proof of victory before committing to a more extensive alliance with Nussbaum.[69] She worried that the SEIU might lose interest if the Boston clerical campaigns were to fail. Nussbaum hoped that the national leaders would take a long-term view of organizing. She wrote that "clericals [would] not be organized in the next year. But the long run investment can't be beat. If the SEIU backs away from clerical organizing now, they [would] be throwing away much more than one local in Boston."[70]

To maintain interest at the national level, Nussbaum pointed to other successful drives that were happening under the auspices of other unions. She wrote to SEIU organizing director John Geagan that the Syracuse University clericals had decided to affiliate with the United Auto Workers, and that the SEIU-affiliated Syracuse librarians were decertifying and joining the UAW, too.[71] Nussbaum wanted to convince Geagan that clerical unions were possible, but she needed his financial assistance. Geagan lent Nussbaum funding for one campaign at the University of Pittsburgh, which had started in the summer of 1977 and promised two thousand potential clerical members.[72] By early 1978 Geagan had granted Nussbaum her own SEIU credit card to support organizing in Pittsburgh, where Local 925 was involved in elections against anti-union administrators.[73] By the fall of 1978, however, the University of Pittsburgh drive had failed, and Geagan curtailed Nussbaum's access to additional funding for ongoing clerical drives. Nussbaum complained to him that office workers in Washington, D.C., Cleveland, Rhode Island, and Los Angeles were contacting her for assistance in unionizing, but she was having to direct them to other unions and institutions. Nussbaum wrote, "Since I couldn't get any authorization from SEIU, I had to advise them to go elsewhere."[74]

Nussbaum called on other women to convince the SEIU leaders—almost all men—that clerical drives were worth the investment. In 1977 she began corresponding with allies who would back the expansion of Local 925 into a national, well-funded sector of the SEIU. Nussbaum aligned with female labor leaders like Elinor Glenn, Rosemary Trump (who would become the first woman on the SEIU Executive Council), and Marilyn Alexander, eliciting their support at a National Coalition of Labor Union Women (CLUW) Convention in Washington, DC, in 1977. They too felt strongly about empowering women as leaders, organizers, and members of the SEIU and other unions.[75] Yet Nussbaum would have to convince the male leaders to invest in her. In her words, "The big hurdle [would] be George," meaning George Hardy, SEIU president from 1971 to 1980.[76] Luckily for Nussbaum, Hardy would retire soon. John Sweeney, who had achieved notoriety as president of a large SEIU local of New York City maintenance workers, was elected president in 1980 and supported Nussbaum's planned clerical division.[77] Given the backing of important female labor leaders and a new SEIU president, Nussbaum's vision of a national clerical union was becoming a reality. Sweeney approved plans for District 925 in 1980.[78]

After Sweeney became SEIU president and approved a clerical division, Nussbaum still needed to negotiate several issues for District 925 to become official. In late 1980 the SEIU was offering 9to5 only half the money that Nussbaum was requesting. Furthermore, Nussbaum was intent on obtaining higher salaries for the 9to5 employees who would be working with District 925.[79] Eventually, the SEIU and 9to5 reached a two-year agreement, whereby Nussbaum was named president of District 925, SEIU's clerical division. Three regional offices were established (East Coast, Midwest, and West Coast), each with a SEIU-funded field organizer. The clerical division was modeled after the SEIU divisions for health care and public employees, both of which were growing rapidly. Technically this clerical division would be an SEIU affiliate so that 9to5, with its expertise in women's issues, could retain influence over structure and operations. But the SEIU agreed to assist 9to5 with funding for organizing campaigns.[80]

To plan when and how to announce the creation of the union, Sweeney and Nussbaum hired public relations professional Ray Abernathy. Abernathy raised the possibility of making a public statement in about a month before an AFL-CIO meeting in Miami so that the story would permeate the conference and dominate the labor press coverage of the meeting. Yet he reasoned that breaking the news in Miami could anger some union leaders who might view Sweeney as the "'new guy on the block' and [the SEIU and 9to5] don't want to appear pushy."[81] To target the mainstream press instead, Abernathy decided to wait an extra week or so (until the end of February 1981) to release the news.[82] Representatives from both the SEIU and 9to5 would be in five major cities (Boston, Washington, D.C., New York, Los Angeles, and San Francisco) for short press conferences on February 24. These concurrent broadcasts would aim to make the announcement major news across the nation. Abernathy provided participants with model answers to many "ticklish subjects," which included why unions had traditionally failed to organize clericals and where the new union would stand on the issue of pay equity. He wanted to create a consistent and advantageous "party line."[83] Abernathy also sought to schedule in-depth interviews with District 925 national leaders on the *Today Show* and *Good Morning America.*[84]

The public announcement of District 925 would coincide with the release of the popular movie *9 to 5* (1980), which was intentional on the part of the SEIU and 9to5. Nussbaum had strategized that she could use the publicity from the film to bolster the impact of announcing the new union.[85] The movie's plot, however, would emphasize some workplace problems and solutions more so than others—and it remained to be seen if *9 to 5* would push audiences toward unionizing.

Filmmaker Colin Higgins gathered material for the storyline by interviewing secretaries, including 9to5 members. Unsurprisingly, in addition to low pay and lack of promotions, sexual harassment emerged as a primary concern.[86] Armed with legal recognition for an age-old problem, women began speaking out about mistreatment in the 1970s. 9to5 supported one of the first grassroots organizations, which had formed in Boston, to combat sexual harassment; eventually it ran a telephone hotline to field questions about job problems including inappropriate sexual conduct. In addition, some trade unions were addressing sexual harassment and its economic implications in their organizing efforts and contract terms.[87] Yet labor and management were not in disagreement here. HRM also made efforts, even if cursory, to ameliorate the problem of sexual harassment. Employers began to devote resources to prevention by way of employee education as to what constituted sexual harassment under the law. Training videos like *Sexual Harassment: That's Not in My Job Description* (1981) and *Power Pinch: Sexual Harassment in the Workplace* (1981) featured scenarios based on real-life situations, which often involved secretaries. While women in blue-collar environments experienced mistreatment, secretaries, in part because of their sheer numbers, became symbolic of the fight against sexual harassment. They were featured prominently in media coverage of the problem.[88] Many of the earliest sexual harassment plaintiffs were Black female office workers who characterized the behavior as a civil rights violation, not an interpersonal issue.[89]

As Higgins was listening to the accounts of sexual harassment and other poor working conditions, he decided to ask the women if they had ever fantasized about killing their bosses. The rapid responses fired at him from the focus group anchored the movie's plot. Higgins remembered, "People couldn't get their stories out fast enough . . . everyone had thought of sticking their boss in the IBM machine at one time or another."[90]

The resulting film featured actress and activist Jane Fonda, along with actress Lily Tomlin and singer Dolly Parton, as secretaries who took revenge against their male-chauvinist boss by kidnapping him and assuming operation of their office. The three women physically tied up their boss, rendering him idle and immobile as they demonstrated their superior ability to run Consolidated Companies. Former and current secretaries loved the film. After seeing the movie, secretaries discussed how they related to certain characters or events. According to one secretary, "When the bosses aren't around, the place runs very smoothly," echoing the message of the film. Others admitted they had felt the temptation "to lock the boss in the closet and throw away the key."[91]

The project was the "brainchild of Miss Fonda," according to reports.[92] She had become interested in the job problems of clericals when Nussbaum, her friend from the antiwar movement, cofounded 9to5. When the film premiered in 1980, the organization boasted ten thousand members across forty-five states. Throughout the 1970s and 1980s, Fonda appeared at 9to5 rallies to bring greater media attention to the organization and its cause.[93] She even held a two-hour workout session at a Danvers, Massachusetts, country club to raise money for 9to5.[94] Although sexism and injustice had inspired the making of the movie, Fonda decided to cast the story as a comedy: "We wanted to make a movie that Joe Blow [would] go see—as far as he's concerned it'll be a really funny movie. But if a secretary goes to see the movie, she's going to identify with it."[95] The movie aspired to have the weight of a documentary—and a social message to the audience—while also enjoying lucrative returns at the box office. One secretary complained that her fiancé found it "inane," to which she retorted, "That is because you're not a secretary."[96]

Although *9 to 5* enjoyed record ticket sales (the movie was the top-grossing comedy of 1980), professional critics gave it mixed reviews. One *New York Times* critic claimed it "began as someone's bright idea [but] then went into production before anyone had time to give it a well-defined personality." Another reviewer found the movie entertaining but claimed it had a "sugar-coated social message," meaning the economic ramifications of sexism were "buried under a pile of sight gags, one-liners, slapstick and general merriment." According to still another reviewer in the radical magazine *Processed World*, "The film's critique of sexual oppression is as shallow as Parton's cleavage is deep."[97]

Some viewers wanted the movie to point clerical workers more overtly toward collective mobilization. Hoping it would serve as "pink-collar workers' call to arms," one secretary expressed disappointment that the film did not "rally the workers" the way she felt *Norma Rae* did.[98] Instead, she perceived the ending of the movie as detached from reality. In how many offices had three secretaries assumed "the power behind the throne," ousting an illegitimate and ineffective manager like Hart? And in how many offices did a rebellious secretary, like Tomlin, earn a promotion to vice president? The movie's main idea, according to one journalist, was that "behind every male mid-level executive sits an exploited female secretary who helped get him where he is. Her reward? A chance to fetch his coffee."[99] In reality, performing well might have meant a lower chance of promotion. In *Men and Women of the Corporation*, sociologist Rosabeth Moss Kanter argued that as secretaries became better at their jobs, they became more indispensable as assistants to others.[100] Author and activist Caroline Bird echoed this. Writing back to an office manager in an advice column, she stated, "You've obviously done too good a job on that sales office, and it is going to take dynamite to blast you out of it."[101] Although Tomlin gained a promotion at the end of the movie, many clericals viewing the film did not experience upward mobility as a reward for their hard work and accomplishments. It was exactly this sense that secretaries remained secretaries—occupationally segregated, without much of a ladder—that spurred interest in the unionization approach over the professionalization approach.

In launching the union, 9to5 leaders emphasized in a press release that their organization had been essential in conceptualization of the *9 to 5* film.[102] A District 925 marketing brochure advertised that 9to5 "most recently [had played] a key role in creating the Jane Fonda film."[103] Abernathy embraced the association, instructing press conference participants to highlight Jane Fonda's previous involvement in the organization. He stated that the new union should welcome "the chance to build public awareness through such things as the movie." And to further promote the union, he instructed press conference participants to divulge talks of a 9to5 television series that might launch given the popularity of the movie.[104] As Abernathy and 9to5 leaders had hoped, articles in national papers discussed the popular movie alongside information about new organizing opportunities for clericals.[105] For instance, Harry Bernstein of the *Los Angeles Times* wrote a March 6 article entitled, "Film 'Nine to Five' [*sic*] Sparks Interest in Unionization of Office Workers."[106]

To its audiences, the SEIU positioned the launch of the clerical division as a response to the unique needs of women; in a press release, it hailed District 925 as a "historical new union alternative linking the women's movement with the trade union movement."[107] Sweeney described the reaction as "overwhelming" since many working women were calling SEIU headquarters and locals to inquire about joining. In fact, the SEIU soon had to create a nationwide, toll-free number to manage these calls better.[108] Jane Fonda taped a television public service announcement about the phone number, which brought in "tons of calls."[109] Organizers discussed strategies to channel the numerous complaints they received into higher union membership numbers. They even considered advertising in popular women's magazines to increase visibility.[110]

Creating a distinct public image for District 925 would be vital to the new organization's success, especially in light of the increasingly negative attitudes about trade unions.[111] Nussbaum was well aware of the need to emphasize the uniqueness of District 925 since office workers were reported to have "outright fear of unions" along with "a belief that unions just aren't for 'us.'" By publicizing the Local 925 campaigns that clericals already had won, Nussbaum aimed to show skeptics that District 925 had the potential to succeed. Furthermore, because 9to5 had built thirteen chapters nationwide, District 925 could use existing channels to its benefit. The idea was that once 9to5 had captured the "attention and allegiance of office workers with a non-threatening but active association," then District 925 could motivate these workers toward unionization. While attempting to woo clericals, Nussbaum and other leaders agreed that a democratic alliance—not a centralized structure—would appeal most. The new union sought to offer autonomy to its locals so that working women could manage their own organizing campaigns and construct their own agendas in each workplace.[112]

This vision of District 925 was what employers, especially banks and insurance companies with high percentages of VDT operators, feared: the growth of clerical unions. Some past trends were supporting their paranoia: federal government data showed that white-collar unionization rates had increased by 46 percent in the 1960s.[113] An article in the *Harvard Business Review* in 1971 predicted that larger numbers of clerical workers would unionize because of negative feelings toward management and their jobs, which provided further impetus for QWL programs. According to over twenty-five thousand workers in more than ninety companies, office workers had more adverse feelings toward their employers than ever before. Workers no longer believed their employers to be fair, and they saw management as impersonal and unresponsive to their needs.[114]

As employers aimed to prevent white-collar unionization and implement QWL programs, a professional category of labor relations consultants, disdainfully referred to as "union busters," grew in scope and visibility. While some had backgrounds in the labor movement, most consultants had worked in management-side labor law and had specialized knowledge of behavioral psychology. They wanted to quell the conflict that inspired union drives, and in some cases they sought to decertify existing unions.[115] According to 925 leader Debbie Schneider, the "rise of the union-busters really came right when we founded District 925 [in the] late 1970s. You couldn't go anywhere without them [even though] it was really a new industry."[116] In the 1980s the labor relations consultancy business grossed an estimated $500 million a year.[117] The AFL-CIO claimed that 75 percent of all white-collar employers were hiring "labor-management consultants."[118] District 925's public relations consultant Ray Abernathy explained, "These companies were willing to spend *anything* to defeat the union and *do* anything to defeat the union."[119] According to labor economist and activist Robert W. Dunn, those opposing office unionization used "briefcases instead of brass knuckles and they [left] no visible marks on their victims."[120] Historian Lane Windham has chronicled the corporate fight against union organizing in the 1970s, explaining that "employers [closed] the door" on activism in the private sector with tactics that were "increasingly sophisticated and effective."[121]

The industry of labor relations consulting gained professional import by appealing to employers' real or imagined anxieties about white-collar unionization. One labor relations consultant warned a room of bank managers: "It's not so much the major unions like the Teamsters or the United Auto Workers that non-unionized employers should worry about. It's the new ones like 925."[122] In addition to convincing management that they were essential, consultants played into conventional wisdom that women could be influenced more easily than men because they constantly craved praise and acceptance.[123] In *Working Woman* magazine, an SEIU union organizer claimed that consultants specialized in "the manipulation of women." Women were expected to be—and often were—accommodating to others, and they had a greater fear of violence, according to several union organizers.[124] One common tactic that consultants used was to train supervisors in how to isolate union supporters.[125] Organizers reported that supervisors would convince the employees who were uninterested in the union to "gang up against a union sympathizer." According to union leaders, this strategy worked with clerical organizing because women were more sensitive than men to social rejection and disapproval.[126]

District 925 leader Doreen Levasseur maintained that labor relations consultants were waging gender-specific "psychological warfare" tailored to fighting clerical unions. She claimed that blue-collar men were unfamiliar with the consultants' ostracism approach: "And I talked to them about some of the tactics that were being used against us in some of these campaigns. And they'd look at us quizzically, like, 'What are you talking about?'" Levasseur recounted that she watched women transition from "feeling strong and like we needed to do something, to feeling like totally terrified to do anything, and paralyzed." She claimed that consultants attempted to persuade women that the union was a "monster" that would control their lives, and they would have to go on strike against their will if they joined.[127]

Whereas union organizers perceived labor relations consultants as convincing women that they would lose autonomy by joining, the consultants usually viewed their work as a type of conflict resolution that benefited employees and employers alike. There were exceptions: Stephen Cabot, nationally recognized as a successful management-side attorney, "was delighted in the phone calls he [was] getting from worried management about white-collar campaigns." He loved being described as "the biggest, no-good, union-busting S.O.B. that ever lived," according to the *Philadelphia Business Journal*.[128] Other consultants, however, shunned the union-busting label and instead saw themselves as promoting QWL practices. They told journalists that they were not trying to punish union sympathizers but rather were advising employers in how to respond to dissatisfied employees. "We teach management to listen," claimed one consultant, viewing himself as a mediator between employee and employer.[129] In another office, consultants had a hand in helping management to implement a suggestion box that would relay employees' ideas to senior executives.[130]

A vice president at Modern Management Methods (3M) described the firm's attitude as "pro-employee."[131] 3M executive Herbert G. Melnick described himself as "a marriage counselor between worker and boss to keep them working positively together so that they [could] have less conflict and more harmony."[132] Yet the AFL-CIO felt differently; it listed 3M as one of its biggest enemies on its "RUB Sheet [Report on Union Busters]," which was a list of consultants and tactics shared with organizers across the nation.[133] On ABC News's *The Last Word*, host Phil Donahue asked Melnick about reports that 3M had engaged in and supported practices that intimidated, threatened, and interrogated employees. Melnick denied any such behaviors.[134]

Whether these consultants saw themselves as pro-employee or antiunion, labor organizers worried that QWL practices, including the use of "quality circles," or regular meetings of labor and management, could appease employees who would have turned to unions otherwise. Increasing communication between employees and employers was a key feature

of the QWL movement—and also happened to quell interest in unionization.[135] A case in point was one of the most notable District 925 victories.
At Equitable Life Insurance in Syracuse, New York, employers installed
VDTs without discussing the change with employees first. Recall from
chapter 5 that 9to5's automation campaign was pushing to give clericals
influence over adoption of new technology. "The overwhelming reason the
workers turned to the union was because of the way automation was
applied to their office," according to union spokeswoman Denise Mitchell.[136] District 925 organizers spent six months meeting with dissatisfied
employees about the heavy-handed implementation of VDTs, among
other issues, resulting in a vote in favor of unionization. Initially Equitable Life refused to recognize the union, which triggered District 925 to
build a coalition of other unions (e.g., AFL-CIO) and feminist organizations (e.g., the National Organization for Women) to boycott the insurance firm for nearly two years.[137]

Eventually Equitable Life was forced to negotiate with District 925,
which resulted in a three-year contract covering fifty-four union members who worked as insurance claims processors and support personnel,
as well as assurance that future drives would not include labor relations
consultants.[138] The contract mandated that VDT operators receive a
fifteen-minute break every two hours as well as have the right to transfer
away from VDT work when pregnant.[139] It also ordered Equitable Life to
make ergonomic changes to workstations, including the institution of
glare-reducing devices, detachable keyboards, and adjustable chairs.[140]

Regarding pay, employees won raises totaling 14 percent over three
years.[141] They also won partial influence over the performance management system. Employees objected to having pay based on factors such as
attitude (as determined by a supervisor).[142] The union contract specified
that appraisal ratings like "works eagerly" and past attendance records
(which could disparately impact primary caregivers) could no longer be
included in the formula used to determine pay. Other types of surveillance remained, however: a computer monitoring program would continue to measure performance, such that speed and accuracy would persist as determinants of pay and promotions.[143] With this victory, District
925 had about six thousand members in total; it had won thirty-five contracts by 1985.[144]

Despite national media coverage of the "first successful unionization of clericals at a major insurance company" in recent history, the victory was short-lived.[145] Equitable Life closed its Syracuse office, giving just cause to fire the unionized workers and dissolve the contract.[146] Yet the union's ephemeral success still managed to concern HR managers in financial services. At a banking industry conference, HR managers worried about the state of white-collar organizing given the recent District 925 election at Equitable Life. Labor relations consultant John Sheridan told them not to worry. Equitable fell to the union because of "bad management," according to Sheridan, and anyone could have organized those women, even Karen Nussbaum, who "doesn't know anything about organizing." What exactly went wrong? Sheridan recounted how Equitable managers introduced VDT equipment in their offices without regard for employee concerns about health and safety. Other experts at the conference agreed that management could have pushed out District 925 if it had allowed employees to participate in the automation process. Prior to installing VDT equipment, an employee grievance system should have been in place, and employee attitudes regarding automation should have been measured by surveys.[147]

To prevent white-collar unionization in banks and insurance companies, labor consultants suggested a range of organizational changes from small perks to raises and promotions. They undermined clerical unions, advertently and inadvertently, with QWL strategies. When a union campaign developed in one office, management purchased new, expensive furniture to create a more pleasant environment.[148] But aesthetic improvements would not be enough to stop unionization in all cases, according to one consultant, who explained that employees of the 1980s, compared to those of earlier decades, were "better educated and more independent. They don't want to take any baloney." Firms had been distributing "pseudo benefits [that] just don't cut water anymore," such as a turkey at Christmas or a holiday party. The best way to preempt unionization, especially in banks and insurance companies where clerical women were "ripe for unionization," was to raise pay and give employees a voice in decision making.[149] Providing raises could weaken union support, as could promoting union sympathizers into supervisory positions, where they would become ineligible for union membership.[150]

Although some anxious employers might offer raises at whispers of unionization, consultants also suggested that support for antidiscrimination policy served as an alternative to adjusting pay scales.[151] Equal employment opportunity practices were promoted as undercutting union appeal. At a Personnel Management Association seminar in Westchester, New York, an employment lawyer contended that personnel managers could "make unions irrelevant by attacking discrimination."[152] When the American Bankers Association held its National Conference on Human Resources in 1984, the rising importance of individual rights based on demographic characteristics like race and gender was evident. Workshops covered the more traditional employment relations issues about unionization and labor law, but sessions were also devoted to trending topics including sexual harassment and affirmative action. Personnel managers reported that they were revisiting their company policies to comply with employee rights based on protected characteristics like gender.[153] Feminist leader Karen Sauvigne once had criticized personnel for failing to intervene in the boss-secretary relationship since it was like a marriage.[154] But now employer attention to such issues negated labor's momentum in the office; a vision of an equitable workplace had emerged whereby workers could thrive without unions.

The concept of labor relations consultants was not new to the 1970s and 1980s: industrialists of the late nineteenth and early twentieth centuries had hired Pinkertons to undermine union campaigns. Yet the notion that unions could cease to exist—especially in those organizations most attentive to employment rights—was new. Some union leaders admitted that organized labor was in decline: one told the *Chicago Tribune* that he could "visualize a day when the union hall [would be] more like a museum than the labor movement's ultimate power center."[155] By the 1980s a vision of a union-free workplace, particularly in the private sector, seemed feasible and perhaps even inevitable.[156] President Ronald Reagan's dismissal of twelve thousand striking air traffic controllers and his decertification of their union greatly weakened the legal rights of workers—both public and private.[157] According to a 1984 *Wall Street Journal* column, managers should take advantage of the president's actions and leverage QWL trends. Yes, a union-free workplace was possible, but employers had to establish "productive relations" with employees and adhere to equal employment opportunity policy to maintain "fairness in all aspects of the employer-employee relationship."[158] HRM programs came to signal corporate commitment to racial and gender equality.[159] According to one scholar, HRM "strikes at the sources which breed unionism to begin with."[160]

While District 925 began with incredible momentum at the start of the 1980s, organizing private-sector offices proved difficult. In 1982, of the 18.5 million U.S. clerical workers, 6.5 percent were unionized (and most of those were working in the public sector).[161] By 1985 the number was a bit higher, but still fewer than 10 percent of all clerical workers were union members. The American Management Association, in an article titled "What Happened to the 'Threat' of White-Collar Unionization?," expressed minimal concern about District 925. Although it had the backing of the SEIU and the momentum of a hit movie, it had "barely gotten off the ground; at the moment, it does not even have an office in New York City, the white-collar capital of the world."[162] To its credit, District 925 had organized six thousand office workers by 1983.[163] By the middle of the 1990s, it had twelve thousand members across the nation.[164] However, its presence in the private sector was weak. According to the Wharton Industrial Research Unit, District 925 had been decertified or lost elections in all but three private-sector organizations during the 1980s.[165]

Why did clerical unionization struggle and fall short? First, clerical unions faced a paradox of looking forward and backward simultaneously, trying to both embrace the benefits and reject the shortcomings of traditional trade unions. Nussbaum and the other leaders of the clerical movement emphasized innovation: these were unions built from the bottom up, responsive to local needs, and democratically led. Yet 925 also wanted to offer the usual union benefits of higher pay and better working conditions. The messaging was, on the one hand, that 925 could give women the economic security enjoyed by previous generations of unionized, blue-collar men. On the other hand, 925 offered something new: it was not top-heavy, power was decentralized, and individual voices were heard. This sell presented some conceptual inconsistencies regarding what a national clerical union would become and what it could accomplish: 925 was described as nothing like the unions of the past while promising to leverage the previous advantages that had sustained those very same unions.

One significant challenge 925 faced was the overall declining popularity of unions. As a leader described, "It was tough because we weren't necessarily responding to an uprising of workers. Several people could want a union in a workplace, but the collective energy sometimes was not there."[166] When District 925 tried to organize Blue Cross Blue Shield in Ohio, employee interest in joining was minimal: "Even management agreement to neutrality does not ensure union success," wrote a scholar in the *ILR Review* of a failed 925 campaign.[167] Economist James Medoff demonstrated that public opinion about unions could determine their success in organizing drives. His findings showed that from 1970 to the mid-1980s, most people surveyed disapproved of unions, viewing them as monopolies, not as democratic forums to express grievances. Furthermore, polling firm Louis Harris and Associates conducted a study showing that those who voted against a union did so almost entirely because they did not believe it could solve their job problems. There was no huge outpouring of hatred and vitriol against unions, according to the Harris poll—just the belief that unions were unhelpful.[168]

Second, as the unionized office seemed less viable moving forward, HRM gained traction as an approach that could appease employers and employees alike. Although the specific agenda of HRM could vary from workplace to workplace, in general it incorporated two trends from the 1970s: labor-management cooperation underlying QWL as well as equal employment opportunity (EEO) motivating Title VII and affirmative action policy.[169] Furthermore, management scholars began stressing the strategic role HR departments could play in shaping a firm's financial success.[170] Leading academics promoted HRM as integral to the health of organizations: "Human resources can make the difference between organizational failure and success," according to psychologist Edgar Schein, who advised executives that HR planning should be part of an organization's strategy.[171] Management professor Fred Foulkes reported in the *Harvard Business Review* that the "personnel department is of increasingly vital importance to the implementation of a company's strategy."[172]

The rise of HRM undercut the reinvention of the labor movement in the office, and in particular the possibilities for clerical unionization across the nation. As employers gave more credence to employee grievances, they could increase employee satisfaction, often without having to raise wages.[173] For example, 3M consultancy had a 98 percent success rate when instituting its QWL programming to prevent unionization.[174] District 925 organizer Jackie Ruff described the difficulty encountered when employers started improving working conditions. Ruff recalled that clericals were determining, "Well, this is a better way to go. I'd rather have a relationship with my employer that is not conflict-ridden, that I don't have to worry that it could be adversarial, and where I'll get some improvement, than to go the other route" (meaning unionization).[175] Harvard University labor economists Richard Freeman and James Medoff attributed "positive labor relations" as a main reason for what they called the "slow strangulation of private-sector unions." The granting of employee requests "attempts to beat unions at their own game by offering unorganized workers much of the benefits of unionism—high wages, good fringe benefits, seniority protection and the like—with none of the associated costs" such as weekly dues, according to Freeman and Medoff. Thomas Kochan, industrial relations professor at Massachusetts Institute of Technology, spoke of "union-substitution," which meant that employers created quasi-union conditions in unorganized workplaces.[176] And interest in the needs of employees even went beyond what unions typically had offered: a workplace wellness movement, which helped to solve some ergonomic issues for clericals in automated jobs (chapter 5), was gaining momentum. Corporate-sponsored programs to curb smoking, promote exercise, and manage stress grew in scale and scope as the Department of Health and Human Services (HHS) urged employers to take action to advance wellness. Health promotion and disease prevention became a "compelling need for us nationally," according to HHS director Michael McGinnis, accounting for half of all deaths in the United States.[177] By the 1990s specific practices like quality circles were waning, but the ideology behind QWL—promoting cooperation, improving job satisfaction, and fostering employee well-being all for the purpose of increasing organizational productivity—had become central to the purpose and agenda of HRM.

Third, District 925 struggled to find a unifying agenda and identity among clerical workers, which meant that appeals to organize them proved difficult. 9to5 and 925 leaders were inspired by the overlap between gender inequality and economic justice at work, and they emphasized issues such as childcare and pay equity, the latter of which posed a "radical threat" to the gendered division of labor, in the words of historian Katherine Turk.[178] But many clericals were not motivated enough by these so-called women's issues to join. Academics who had interviewed District

925 organizers concluded that such issues were "seldom central to a clerical organizing campaign . . . private sector clericals do not view their
workplace concerns from a feminist perspective."[179] Identification with
gender inequity did not prove compelling enough to push most private-
sector clericals toward unionization.

Furthermore, the professional identity of clericals was varied given the
range of jobs classified as clerical work. District 925 was aiming to be a
craft union in which a range of clerical workers came together under one
occupational category. Yet reliance on this sort of shared identity required
clear occupational boundaries, at a time when much was in flux. The status of the work, the nature of the job, and the future of the profession
were all unstable, and to some degree branching off in at least two different directions. Nussbaum saw this type of uncertainty as an advantage
when organizing clerical workers. She had foreseen that office automation
in the 1980s could provide a time-limited "window of opportunity" when
women would be more receptive to collective resistance efforts.[180] But the
fears surrounding automation triggered only interest in clerical unions
and did not result in widespread private-sector membership. With such a
wide range of jobs now in the clerical category, and with the professional
status in question, 9to5's efforts to bring office workers together under a
single banner failed.

Finally, some turned away from unionization to embrace professionalization. They saw executive secretarial positions as possible ladder rungs
for upward mobility. President of Professional Secretaries International
Karen DeMars explained to a journalist, "We are finally getting written
into management, so why should we unionize now?" The National Labor
Relations Board prohibited those with access to confidential material or
who were in a supervisory capacity from unionizing; DeMars claimed that
professional secretaries were in both categories. While "unionization does
make sense for some of them," meaning VDT operators, executive secretaries need not organize.[181] From PSI's perspective, executive secretaries
need not sabotage their careers by joining hands with less skilled laborers who were performing a completely different job.

And maybe DeMars was completely reasonable to view executive secretaries as fit for management. According to social scientist Shoshana
Zuboff in *In the Age of the Smart Machine: The Future of Work and Power*
(1988), the "traditional secretarial skills" that characterized the job of the
executive secretary warranted higher status and higher pay. "Secretaries

who worked for a single boss were required to absorb many subtle responsibilities associated with coordination and communication," according to Zuboff, who relied on sociologist Rosabeth Moss Kanter's description of the secretarial function. The job required the types of problem-solving skills necessary for a managerial role. Executive secretaries accomplished varied tasks and made important decisions just as managers did.[182] Secretarial work involved "social organizational and diplomatic work (connecting people to people)" that could not be automated, according to sociologist Anne Machung.[183] Meanwhile, advocates for clerical unions were emphasizing the similarities between blue-collar and pink-collar labor as they targeted VDT operators. Equating office work with factory labor signaled that the typical clerical worker was unskilled, although many saw themselves otherwise.

Whether they considered themselves skilled or unskilled, younger women and men were beginning to elevate job satisfaction over traditional bread-and-butter issues. Such values undercut the reinvention of the union movement in the office, as a new generation of employees saw themselves as evolving toward meaningful work. One sociologist explained this shift by looking to historical and economic context: "The idea that work should be psychologically fulfilling probably arose when the market became fully monetized, when levels of living were above subsistence, when job choice was possible, and when geographic and occupational mobility became widespread." In other words, peasants did not have the luxury to worry about finding meaningful work because they were concerned with survival.[184] Public opinion analyst Daniel Yankelovich wondered how the workplace could accommodate these changing values: "No question will dominate the workplace in the 1980s more than how to revamp incentives so as to match the motivations of workers."[185] Yankelovich's "New Breed" of worker was the Lordstown striker who valued individualism and shunned bureaucracy—both corporate forms and labor unions. Yet in trying to organize clericals, union leaders were calling for a New Breed of women willing to relinquish some autonomy to gain the protections of a union. Ultimately, most women office workers wanted the same independence—even if precarious—that men had, not the collective benefits that union membership could offer. The final chapter will show how a neoliberal mythology of complete choice regarding occupation and career allowed for the preservation of gender segregation in an EEO-compliant environment.

7

A FEMINIST "BRAND CALLED YOU"

O n January 31, 1986, U.S. District Judge John Nordberg ended twelve years of legal wrangling between the Equal Employment Opportunity Commission and Sears, Roebuck & Company. At issue in the case was whether Sears had demonstrated a pattern of discrimination against women in the hiring and promotional process for commissioned sales employees. The EEOC argued that although women constituted just 27 percent of full-time commission sales hires in the 1970s, they were 61 percent of the applicant pool for these relatively high-paying jobs. It further claimed that Sears had highly subjective hiring processes that pushed women toward noncommission jobs. Challenging the validity of the EEOC's statistical analysis, Sears contended that no proof of discriminatory intent existed. In a decision that was sharply critical of the EEOC's case and quite complimentary of Sears's practices, Nordberg claimed that Sears was not to blame. In fact, he noted that as the second-largest employer of women, Sears was a model for affirmative action.[1]

Given that the Sears-EEOC legal conflict lasted more than a decade, academics and activists had plenty of time to discuss the extent of Sears's culpability—if, in fact, the business was culpable at all. The expert testimony of two feminist historians—one on behalf of Sears and the other on behalf of the EEOC—epitomized this tension about the merits of the case. In support of Sears, Rosalind Rosenberg, professor of history at Barnard College, contended that women preferred certain jobs over others and traditionally had approached their career choices differently from men. Pay disparities and occupational segregation did not necessarily reflect the presence of employer discrimination.[2] Alice Kessler-Harris, then professor of history at Hofstra University, took offense at this reasoning. In her testimony for the EEOC, she claimed that systemic discrimination against women accounted for their underrepresentation in commissioned sales jobs and other higher-paying jobs throughout history. Kessler-Harris did not believe that occupational segregation reflected women's preferences but rather that it resulted from economic, political, and social forces that pushed women out of higher-paid work.[3] Feminist academics and activists tended to align more closely with Kessler-Harris's worldview. A number of scholars criticized Rosenberg in academic and popular pieces, writing in the *New York Times*, the *Chronicle of Higher Education*, the *Nation*, *Ms.* magazine, and *Feminist Studies* that her testimony betrayed to the cause of women's rights.[4] Rosenberg responded that "scholars must not subordinate their scholarship to their politics."[5]

After the trial ended, Rosenberg and Kessler-Harris continued the debate about women's careers in academic journals and the mainstream media. Should Sears have been held liable for the lower representation of women in commission sales jobs? Rosenberg thought that many factors beyond Sears's control accounted for the lack of women in commission sales jobs. She had testified that, from birth, women learned to internalize feminine values, which led them to pursue certain types of work relative to other types.[6] Kessler-Harris, on the other hand, thought that fewer women in certain jobs "can thus only be interpreted as a consequence of employers' unexamined attitudes or preferences," which constituted "the essence of discrimination."[7] Kessler-Harris did not think that businesses should be allowed to justify occupational segregation by claiming that women were not interested in or qualified for certain jobs. While the Chicago chapter of the National Organization for Women tried to address economic justice for all working women in its Sears campaign, ultimately, NOW's activism overlooked those who remained in women's jobs.[8]

Precisely what accounted for occupational segregation, and who was to blame, proved to be a major point of contention between Rosenberg and Kessler-Harris—as well as a topic of continuing debate in the 1980s and beyond. Academic literature began examining various reasons why women did or did not enter into male-dominated jobs. Perhaps employers pushed women toward different jobs; perhaps women preferred them.[9] Kessler-Harris's perspective had focused on the former, the demand side of the labor market, to explain occupational segregation, while Rosenberg focused on the latter, or the supply-side reasons that women were under-represented in traditionally male jobs. In reality, both viewpoints could be true in understanding why women were overrepresented in clerical work despite the achievements of feminism. While employers certainly had a hand in nudging women toward certain office jobs, women might prefer such work if it was flexible and readily available. And the class back-ground of a woman could also determine to what extent she felt comfort-able pushing herself into new territory.[10]

This chapter argues that women's access to managerial careers—and the continued separation between clerical and managerial ladders—bifurcated the feminist agenda in corporate America. Those feminist currents that were elevating equality and individualism fit well with the opening of the managerial ranks to women and the changing nature of white-collar careers. Equal employment opportunity policy eliminated legal barriers such that women—like men—were free, by letter of the law that is, to pursue managerial work, or any other type of work they desired. Whereas women had once faced limited choices after high school or col-lege, with employers overtly telling them no, now they gained the bene-fits, and experienced the burdens, of selecting a job and pursuing a career that best suited their interests, skills, and values. Demographic categories such as race, gender, and class no longer impeded professional opportu-nities, at least explicitly. A major task for the young adult coming of age in the United States was to determine his or her best fit from among a variety of occupational choices. While one's occupation had always had social significance, the promise of equal opportunity, as applied by human resource management, bolstered the belief that one's job, actively chosen by the job holder, served as a reflection of one's inner self.[11] This myth of occupational choice strengthened the ideological alignment between fem-inism and individualism, obscuring the fact that structural barriers, more than personal values, may push people toward certain jobs.[12]

For those entering white-collar work, the changing nature of manage-rial careers bolstered feminist currents that elevated individualism. Whereas young men—and only men—used to be groomed internally for lifetime managerial employment, now global competition, as well as demand for corporate agility and flexibility, threatened permanent job status.[13] A female manager never came to enjoy the security of the "organization man."[14] Women gained access to the managerial ladder as those ladders were weakening, and both men and women were tasked with moving from firm to firm in pursuit of upward mobility.[15] Those interested in advancement had to "increasingly look across companies, as opposed to within them, for opportunities," according to management scholar Peter Cappelli.[16] Historian Sanford Jacoby contended that in the new arrangement, employers shifted a greater share of economic risk to employees.[17] Individuals were forced to navigate across organizations to take charge of their own career advancement.[18] And the extent to which individuals could successfully navigate their careers might vary based on socioeconomic status, research would later show.[19] To navigate career advancement or even career change without an employer's guidance required time, energy, and creativity. According to management scholars, to get a new job without prior experience required "stretchwork," or the bridging of old to new competencies. Stretchwork could involve the rebranding of current skills and experiences or the acquisition of more skills and experiences, both of which required additional resources and could be difficult for those who had begun in stigmatized occupations.[20]

This chapter begins by exploring the idea of occupational choice, literature about the subject, and the growing organizational imperative to match person and job. Then it examines the implications of this rhetoric for those in the secretarial occupation and for women's career advancement in general. It ends by revealing the discontented voices of those who felt left behind by the shifting focus of feminism toward individualism, which tended to mask structural barriers faced in jobs and careers. Evident by the end of the chapter is the fact that certain strains of feminism fit with the rise of "the brand called you," in the words of management consultant and author Tom Peters; but others did not.[21] Corporate feminism came to address the concerns of those white-collar women who had sufficient resources to navigate their own career progression.

Women now were considered full participants in the system of American meritocracy whereby each person was held accountable for his or her own career choice and professional success. The implicit—and sometimes explicit—messaging inquired why a woman would become a secretary if she were free to choose any job. In a *Washington Post* story on National

Secretary's Day, writer Carol Krucoff remarked, "In a modern age of women doctors, lawyers and construction workers . . . women in secretarial jobs face an image problem."[22] Arguably, by the 1990s the secretarial occupation itself became key to understanding the class divide between those who identified with feminism and those who did not. The rise of corporate feminism actually had shifted the burdens—and the benefits—of American individualism onto working women's backs.

The idea of matching person to job was not entirely new, of course. As early as 1909, Frank Parsons, the founder of the vocational guidance movement, developed a new approach to understanding career selection in his book *Choosing a Vocation*. Known as the Trait and Factor Theory of Occupational Choice, Parsons's idea was that a person needed to understand himself first so that he could match his individual traits with the requirements of a job. A better fit between individual and vocation would result in greater satisfaction and success on the job.[23] The field of vocational guidance, or career counseling, continued to develop over the twentieth century, as academics built on Parsons's matching approach.[24] While Parsons had referenced men only, eventually women too needed vocational guidance. In 1960 Harvard psychologist Anne Roe included women in her research on personality and occupation, writing that "an occupation plays a central role in every man's life and in every woman's." She argued for "an intimate relationship between personality (as inferred from tests and life histories) and the choice of vocation, the way in which it was pursued, and its meaning for the subject." Roe claimed that one's occupation could actually have far-reaching effects on the self: an occupation "both reflects personality and affects it."[25] Education scholar Robert Hoppock continued to deepen the person-occupation connection in the 1970s by suggesting that each person should select a job to meet emotional as well as financial needs. Occupation was a means not only of making a living but also of self-fulfillment.[26]

The flourishing of scholarship on vocational guidance eventually gave rise to a new industry of professionals who made "a career of careers," according to *Forbes* magazine.[27] Not knowing which career to choose or trying to switch careers required expert help from psychologists and career consultants. A wave of literature advised and inspired the unemployed and those aspiring for change. Richard Nelson Bolles, a former priest, wrote and self-published a best-selling guide to finding a job titled *What Color Is Your Parachute*. It appeared first in 1970 as a photocopied 182-page booklet to be circulated among unemployed clergy. Bolles was selling so many copies that the book got picked up by Ten Speed Press in 1982, when Bolles also revised it for the general public.[28] According to Bolles, God gave each person special skills; in turn, individuals had a responsibility to learn about which jobs would best match their talents.[29] His rhetoric combined principles from the vocational guidance movement with the Puritan idea of a calling, or pursuit of a mission from God.[30] The book was a best seller for decades, and over the years it grew "like a ramshackle house, adding resources, fine points, numbered lists of tips, personality tests and advice for job-hunting on the Internet," according to the *New York Times*.[31]

Bolles's faith and optimism defied the gloom and realism of widely read sociological literature of the time about class status and career outcomes. In *The Hidden Injuries of Class* (1972), Richard Sennett and Jonathan Cobb contended that societal belief in meritocracy actually undermined the dignity of those who could not achieve professional status. Using their interviews with Boston blue-collar workers—mostly men—the authors argued that in an affluent society like the United States, individuals judged themselves by an arbitrary scale of achievement and then justified their success or failure by where they fell on the scale. Sennett and Cobb explained the belief in this way: "If you have sufficient merit, you rise up through the structure of classes till you reach the level of society your talents permit."[32] Personal lack of career success, therefore, signaled a personal lack of ability. If *What Color Is Your Parachute* provided prescriptions for how to realize your best self, then *The Hidden Injuries of Class* exposed the negative realities of not following—or not being able to follow—such instructions.

The examination of social immobility also pervaded the sociology of education during this period. The publication of *Schooling in Capitalist America* (1976) by Samuel Bowles and Herbert Gintis sparked an outpouring of research on education and inequality. According to the authors' controversial thesis, schooling actually justified class privilege, economic disparities, and occupational segregation by attributing poverty to personal failure. Students came to accept—as the natural order of things—economic inequality under the guise that "job assignment is objective and efficient and, therefore, just and egalitarian (albeit severely unequal)."[33]

Seemingly in response to these critiques, the U.S. Office of Education, which eventually became the Department of Education, began to promote a "career education movement" in the 1970s and 1980s.[34] In an effort to better integrate knowledge about jobs and occupations into primary and secondary school settings, this office conducted research, issued guidelines, and lobbied for legislation. Kenneth Hoyt, an esteemed scholar of school counseling and the Office of Career Education's director, became a leading voice in this movement. He advocated for reform in public education to better connect school to work. For instance, teachers should discuss the occupational implications of a class's subject matter. Hoyt believed that preparing students for the transition to work was crucial, particularly for those not enrolling in four-year college programs.[35]

A growing concern for educators, matching person and job also became a business concern, albeit somewhat in tension with the changing nature of managerial work. As mobility via the external labor market became more common, managers were encouraged to navigate their own job placement and career advancement.[36] Yet the growing field of HRM encouraged organizations, not just individuals, to engage actively in the matching process. Massachusetts Institute of Technology professor Edgar Schein urged businesses to invest in HR planning and development, which would help to align an individual's abilities with an organization's goals. The idea was that satisfied, productive employees would lead to healthier, more effective organizations.[37] HR consultant James W. Walker tasked both individuals and organizations with the responsibility of career advancement. On the one hand, he contended that the modern personnel function of HRM should engage in "managing careers, as opposed to merely staffing jobs," and organizations should provide tools to support individual career development. Yet Walker also noted that individuals were accountable for their own growth: "The responsibility for career planning rests with the employee."[38] Employees needed to know enough about themselves—their preferences, skills, and goals—to effectively utilize organizational resources.

The idea that employees should manage their own career progression aligned nicely with certain branches of feminism that focused on individual fulfillment and equality of opportunity. In 1963 feminist leader Betty Friedan recommended career development for "the problem that has no name" in her best seller *The Feminine Mystique* (chapter 1). In the 1970s and 1980s women were expected to find purpose and meaning through professional pursuits, given that they had the same legal rights afforded to men. Erasing formal barriers thus proved necessary to enacting the belief that women had a vast array of occupational choices and should pursue the career that most satisfied them. This new way of thinking about women and careers destabilized remaining imprints of nineteenth-century separate-spheres ideology, which held that women and men had different social roles.[39] Women now had legal access to the economic pursuits previously preserved for men only.

The proliferation of alternative options partly explained the exodus of women from clerical jobs. Opening previously-restricted occupations had a "tremendous effect" on the secretarial labor market, according to various HR managers who claimed that finding and keeping secretaries was a challenge. Secretaries were reporting low job satisfaction. A National Commission on Women study of clerical women reported that 40 percent would quit their secretarial jobs if they could afford to do so. Sixty percent resented that their jobs were "dead end," citing that they wanted advancement opportunities. Fifty-five percent reported that the pay was far too low. And 41 percent reported that clerical work was boring.[40]

Those who could leave—for an advanced degree or a different profession—did. "It's tough to keep secretaries," a Boston executive lamented to a journalist in 1980. "They pick up the 'go-go' enthusiasm . . . , go back to school, and train themselves for something else."[41] But what determined who stayed and who left? Sociologist Kathleen Gerson's research revealed how structural factors, in particular socioeconomics, limited career mobility. In *Hard Choices* (1985), Gerson interviewed young women and reported that those with college educations not only enjoyed the option to reject secretarial work but were also more likely to articulate a yearning for professional status. She wrote, "The college-educated women gained occupational mobility by changing their jobs or professions, typically from work in a female-dominated occupation to work in a male-dominated one." In other words, women with bachelor's degrees had a greater opportunity to leave clerical work but also expressed a greater desire to leave. In fact, some college women took a secretarial job before "discovering fortuitously that they could hold their own in male occupations," according to Gerson. One woman told her that after working as a secretary for several years, she was dissatisfied and decided to go to medical school. One factor pushing her out of clerical work was its low status: "If you're doing what people regard as an insignificant, stupid job, people will think that you are insignificant and stupid."[42]

Hardly any of the high school–educated women Gerson interviewed were able to move out of clerical jobs once they had begun working in the field after graduation. Without college degrees and bereft of the resources and networks that accompanied a college education, these women faced "constrained" choices, in Gerson's words: "Without economic and educational supports, it is difficult to translate a newfound aspiration into an actual career choice." Women without college degrees had to rely on employer-provided opportunities for training and development, which may or may not allow for advancement into nontraditional fields (chapter 3). Gerson described them as "far more dependent than their college-educated counterparts on the structure of the workplace itself for both the discovery of new insights and access to work that could nourish and support developing capacities." In other words, for those without college degrees, the structure, policies, and culture of the organization itself could constrain them, as they relied on the bureaucratic hierarchy of their current work setting for potential advancement. Although Gerson's college-educated respondents could more independently navigate their careers apart from the organization, high school–educated respondents were typically dependent on the organization itself for promotional opportunities.[43]

Gerson's findings push us to look earlier in the life course for the sources of social immobility: Which women were not going to college and why? Other sociologists were uncovering evidence to answer this question. During high school, the need to become economically self-sufficient could push women of lower socioeconomic status toward vocational training in lieu of college preparation courses. Some research contended that women actively chose secretarial training. In her study of high school students in the 1980s, education scholar Jane Gaskell found that female students were more likely to report that college preparation courses were irrelevant to them if they identified as working class. Instead, they chose to enroll in "business courses" (e.g., typing, bookkeeping) because those classes would help them secure a clerical job after high school. Working-class female students perceived high school business courses as insurance against having to take "dirtier jobs" with lower status (e.g., maids). Also they viewed the office environment as safer than other potential workplaces, disclosing that they wanted to avoid the male-dominated trades because of the prevalence of sexual harassment.[44] While scholars were contending that systemic factors sorted students into different tracks, students themselves claimed to have chosen their own career track. Most female students reported that they were enrolling in their desired courses regardless of opinions of others, including parents or guidance counselors.[45]

Yet by the 1990s sociologist Ivy Kennelly revealed another layer: many secretaries may have imagined themselves doing something else. Her interviews with secretaries showed significant career brainstorming before graduating high school. Many expressed that during high school they had hoped to pursue a different career path, with some citing aspirations to become veterinarians, doctors, or lawyers. Yet due to changing circumstances, such as needing to care for their own children or other family members, they turned to secretarial work after high school. Their dreams to pursue professions requiring higher education were set aside due to economic need.[46] And once in secretarial work, a distinctive class and gender barrier often prevented women from rising to managerial and executive positions. According to one researcher who had examined why women were trying to move out of secretarial work, the job offered little upward mobility. While men could start at lower-status office positions and then gain promotional opportunities "on faith in their potential," women could not use secretarial work as evidence that they had the ability to handle a new job.[47]

Among those who reported the highest job satisfaction were older white women affiliated with the National Secretaries Association, which became Professional Secretaries International in 1981. They saw themselves as taking care of their bosses, reporting that they enjoyed their role of nurturer in the office.[48] Secretarial work, however, was losing its appeal among younger women. According to Fran Riley, spokesperson for 38,000-member National Secretaries Association, "These days, women want to be the boss—or they set their sights on other nontraditional occupations."[49] In fact, according to one survey, only one-third of secretaries under thirty years old reported, with certainty, that they wanted to continue in their present jobs. Mostly they were hoping to move into managerial positions in the future.[50] Therefore, as college-educated women pursued jobs that traditionally had been for men only, secretarial work became a common job for women without college degrees, with age as a determinant of satisfaction in the role.

Given the declining appeal of the work, media reports were emerging from government sources that the demand for secretaries was exceeding the supply. Even with 7 percent unemployment in 1980, the U.S. Department of Labor estimated that 20 percent of secretarial jobs remained unfilled.[51] An annual shortage of sixty thousand secretaries could compound to become as high as six hundred thousand by 1985, according to the Labor Department's predictions.[52] Symbolic of the shortage, a journalist for the *Los Angeles Times* reported that even at the famed Katharine Gibbs School, four secretarial positions remained unfilled in its own executive offices.[53]

This type of scarcity actually benefited those in secretarial positions by elevating wages and increasing job availability. According to the Department of Labor, in 1980 the average salary of a secretary ranged from $11,296 to $17,132, which did not include those classified as "executive assistants," meaning secretaries to company presidents or board chairman. Those jobs could pay $30,000 per year. Each graduate of the Gibbs School reportedly had five to ten job offers, with starting salaries of up to $14,000 per year and sometimes more.[54] Another clerical degree program at a junior college reported that each graduate received at least a dozen job offers.[55] Some newly hired secretaries were offered sign-on bonuses, indicating the extent to which employers were desperate to fill clerical jobs.[56] At Bank of America and Chicago's First National Bank, hiring agents were offering "monetary incentives" to current employees who helped to recruit secretaries to their companies.[57]

Perhaps there was a shortage, but perhaps too there was a mismatch between employers' expectations and candidates' characteristics, qualifications, and skills. Traditionally, hiring managers were choosing from among a pool of college-educated white women, some of whom had additional postcollege clerical training, as explained in chapter 1. The applicant pool was changing, however, and employers started complaining about the qualifications of candidates. When one MIT researcher interviewed HR managers of Boston insurance firms, he received confirmation of a perceived skills shortage in the late 1980s.[58] HR managers complained that applicants lacked necessary academic training. "They make spelling and grammatical errors on their job applications," according to one HR manager. "They are not competent to do the jobs we're seeking to fill."[59] A supervisor of clerical employees spoke of similar complaints: high school graduates of secretarial courses likely "could type 45 wpm [but] they can't spell or punctuate properly." HR consultants recommended to outlets like *Business Week* and *Personnel Journal* that employers should provide more in-house training and development for new hires.[60]

Other experts suggested that the shortage could be alleviated if the job were upgraded and a college degree were preferred or even required. Irol Balsley, a professor of administrative services at the University of Arkansas, Little Rock, cautioned employers against lowering qualifications for secretarial positions. Balsley claimed that firms were too permissive "in their hiring policies among the job levels in the 'office administration cluster.'" She complained that many advertisements had just two requirements: a high school diploma and at least a 50 wpm typing speed. Balsley argued that "the contribution a college-educated secretary can make to executive productivity" had been forgotten in the leniency of the job requirements.[61] Advocates of professionalization warned that hiring secretaries without appropriate credentials could have consequences for organizational effectiveness, since competent secretaries regularly alleviated managerial incompetence.[62]

The National Secretaries Association had two approaches to the secretarial shortage. First, it tried to attract younger, college-educated women to the job by continuing to emphasize stricter use of the term secretary, as described in chapter 5. The secretarial title, according to the NSA, should be reserved for "an executive assistant who possesses a mastery of office skills, demonstrates the ability to assume responsibility without direct supervision, exercises initiative and judgment and makes decisions within the scope of assigned authority."[63] Related to this professionalization point, in 1979 the NSA objected to a television show called *3's a Crowd* that was structured along the lines of *The Newlywed Game. 3's a Crowd* featured secretaries and wives in competition to try to predict an executive's answers to "inane questions," according to NSA public relations counselor Fran Riley. She issued a special memo to members that offered suggestions as to how to best protest the show at the local level. Riley wrote that *3's a Crowd* undermined the professional achievements of secretaries; furthermore, it was aired "at a time when management is having great difficulty in recruiting secretaries, [and] not designed to encourage any human being to be a secretary."[64]

Second, the NSA publicized the flexible and lasting nature of the secretarial job. With a slogan "Secretaries are Forever!" the NSA made two points in a report to division and chapter presidents in 1979: first, professional secretaries still existed despite the onset of "the women's movement" and "word processing." While some aspects of the work were in transition, over many decades the basic function of the secretary had endured through social and technological change. Second, the secretarial job was available to "homemakers" who wanted or needed to go back to work. "Offices everywhere are looking for qualified secretarial personnel. The applicant's maturity is no hindrance, and in many cases is a definite advantage," according to this report. The NSA positioned itself as a resource for those seeking to reenter the workforce.[65] As the NSA was renamed Professional Secretaries International in 1981, the approach remained similar with some shifting terminology. PSI declared that secretaries should now officially be called administrative assistants because they were essential business partners. It claimed that as the ranks of middle management thinned, administrative assistants were taking on an increasing number of skilled tasks.[66]

Recruiting more activists, particularly women of color, to join 9to5 proved challenging during the 1980s. The racial composition of clerical workers was changing: more Black women were entering office jobs, such that by 1980 almost a third of Black women were clericals, up from about 10 percent in 1960.[67] Women of color, however, were not well represented in the 9to5 ranks. Members of the Boston affiliate, almost all white, reported that women of color utilized the 9to5 job counseling telephone hotline but subsequently did not commit to joining the organization.[68] For several years in the 1980s, a 9to5 task force distributed surveys and developed outreach plans to try to recruit more women of color. Outside consultants led "sensitivity training" about race for white 9to5 members.[69] Other actions taken to increase racial and ethnic diversity included featuring more women of color in 9to5 materials; informing clerical colleagues of color about 9to5's platform; distributing 9to5 materials at public transportation stops in Black communities; translating the 9to5 Bill of Rights to Spanish; and focusing on issues determined to be of concern to women of color, such as childcare.[70] With these efforts in place, why were so few women of color interested? According to a 9to5 assessment in 1984, Black women were reluctant to join because they viewed 9to5 women as "radical, Bra Burners, extreme feminists and worse. Many feel they have evolved from this era and are more 'lady like.' Successful women like to "look and feel" their success. They agree with our goals but our approach to the goals they question."[71] Like some white women who were entering new professions, Black women reportedly wanted to "look and feel" their career success, as they were inhabiting different spaces that had excluded their mothers and grandmothers.

Ideological tension permeated career advice to potential and current secretaries amid the flight of college-educated women from clerical work. While some groups, such as District 925, responded by calling for unionization (chapter 6), other associations were emphasizing the professional status of secretaries, as mentioned earlier. The burgeoning field of career consultants and advice literature presented contradictory messaging to secretaries about a variety of issues: how to gain greater respect on the job, how to avoid getting stuck in secretarial work, or how to leave the profession altogether.

The book that best captured the dueling, ambivalent messages—respect us but don't become us—was *Not Just a Secretary: Using the Job to Get Ahead* (1984), by career consultant Jodie Berlin Morrow and editor Myrna Lebov. The book began by declaring that secretaries were "fed up"—and justifiably so. It continued, "This book is geared to secretaries who want to get off a dead-end career track. Some of you may want to move to an entirely new occupation, others may want to move ahead within the secretarial field before advancing into management, still others may simply want to move ahead within the secretarial field." After assuring readers that all secretaries were part of the book's audience, the authors then called them to action: "Now is the time to risk asking for more from a job."[72] While addressing the concerns of those who wanted to remain career secretaries, the book also provided solutions for those trying to get off the clerical ladder. The mixed and multiple messages captured the broader, clashing societal ideas about secretaries in the 1980s.

Essentially, the book revealed the contradictions of applying the main-stream messaging of feminism to the secretarial occupation. An early chapter, "There's Nothing *Wrong* with Being a Secretary," tried to reha-bilitate the stigmatized image. The authors opened with an anecdote to capture the frustration that many secretaries felt. Anne, an executive sec-retary who liked her job, was sitting with her husband's family, listening to her in-laws tell their teenage niece that she should avoid becoming a secretary. The niece, according to her family, should think about going to law school because she was very smart and had career options beyond sec-retarial work. Morrow and Lebov reported that Anne was fuming. And thus began the argument for increased respect for secretarial work. The authors argued that despite conventional wisdom, "a secretarial job is a career, not just a job." "In my seminars," Ms. Morrow continued, "I'll often find people who tell me at the beginning that they don't want to be secre-taries. But when you get down to it and ask them exactly what they want to do, it turns out that some specific aspect of their job is bothering them—not the job itself."[73]

Much of the messaging in the book coached women on how to fully realize their potential—whether that meant remaining a secretary or mov-ing into a different line of work. Morrow and Lebov's book drew on the experiences of secretaries who had "made it" to more rewarding jobs "either inside the secretarial field or out."[74] In a perspective meant to empower the individual—but also shift responsibility to her—Morrow and Lebov claimed that the job was what the person made of it, "depend-ing on what they bring to it and are willing to put up with."[75] Secretaries, according to authors, "lack the confidence to take risks necessary for mov-ing ahead." They must learn to avoid such self-defeating behavior.[76] The authors upended the notion that in a postfeminist era, secretaries were destined to be subordinates. Unlike previous, prefeminism advice that had reinforced the importance of submissiveness (chapter 1), Morrow and Lebov encouraged women to be assertive. Coining the term "entrepre-neurial secretary," Morrow, who gave career workshops to secretaries around the country, encouraged them to "rewrite the rules" if they wanted to escape the secretarial ghetto.[77] The back cover of the book called to potential readers, "if career advancement for secretaries sounds like the impossible dream, you need this book—now."

But exactly how to move ahead? Morrow and Lebov urged women— both those who wanted to remain career secretaries and those who wanted to move into management—to make a "career action plan." This exercise involved doing research on job paths, starting to develop a network, revising a resume, and writing cover letters. To ensure that they were not the ones devaluing their own talents, each secretary should create a "skills inventory" by writing down daily tasks and the knowledge needed to complete them.[78] Those working as secretaries "should recognize the skills that they have—people skills, problem-solving skills, organizational skills—are transferable to other jobs in the company."[79] Morrow and Lebov encouraged women to think about their ideal jobs and dream big— see if any skills could be building blocks for this ideal job.

And readers were counseled to reject the virtue of loyalty, which could stand in the way of career development. "Job-hopping" was no longer condemned, according to Morrow, which also happened to be the reality for managers who were losing long-term job security.[80] Morrow and Lebov advised that in fact, changing jobs, within the company or to a new organization, was a good tactic for career advancement for people at all levels of an organization. Further recommendations included to work for a boss who does not see the secretarial position as dead end. How to determine his views? Try expressing that you want to move up into another division. Does he try to praise you or does he cajole you to stay? And when accepting a new job, women should consider asking for higher pay: "We're not advising you to make exorbitant demands," but research on the salary range is useful.[81]

The ambivalent messaging from Morrow and Lebov—most secretaries are stuck, but the talented ones find a way out—imbued the hit film *Working Girl* (1988), which the screenwriter described as a Horatio Alger story.[82] Melanie Griffith starred as Tess McGill, a working-class secretary for Harvard-trained Katharine Parker (Sigourney Weaver), a Wall Street executive. In the movie, Katharine steals Tess's idea to initiate a corporate merger and begins to implement the plan as her own. But Tess's career takes a fortuitous turn when Katharine takes a leave of absence due to a broken leg. Tess then discards her working-class attire in favor of the expensive clothes from Katharine's closet. She also changes her hair to be shorter and tamer, stating that if "you want to be taken seriously, you need serious hair."[83] An executive colleague, Jack Trainer (Harrison Ford), helps Tess to pursue the merger, to become the boss (with her own secretary), and to expose Katharine's dishonesty. Feminist Susan Faludi criticized the film for several reasons, not least of which is that Jack seems to save Tess (not only by helping her to become the boss but also by marrying her instead of Katharine).[84]

Yet in *Working Girl*, the secretary prevails in a rags-to-riches sort of ending in which luck and merit converge. Most secretaries like Tess are working-class women stuck in a world that devalues them. Without Katharine's credentials and clothes, Tess is given short shrift in the office— that is until Katharine disappears, Tess gets a makeover, and Jack offers Tess some legitimacy. The messaging is that working-class secretaries who attend night school are not taken seriously, even those with intelligence. Tess's exceptional move from secretary to boss is a rare triumph.

While Morrow and Lebov approached the secretary's mobility dilemma with the same optimistic, can-do attitude that was emphasized at the end of *Working Girl*, other career literature warned of the dangers of entering the secretarial abyss in the first place. Prescriptive literature crafted for women who wanted to climb corporate ladders spoke frankly and directly about the dead-end nature of clerical work. In *Games Mother Never Taught You* (1978), Betty Harragan, a longtime member of the National Organization for Women, told women that working was a game and they must learn how to play it. She suggested that women aspiring to advance should draw a pyramid to better understand the company's hierarchy. One of the "unfortunate truths" resulting from this exercise was that "secretarial functions *do not belong anyplace*. These jobs are *outside* the pyramid, nowhere entwined in the network." According to Harragan, too many women were wasting time trying to satisfy the demands of supervisors and operating as "deluded 'Aunt Toms' who thought authority came from longevity or assumed officiousness."[85] Used in undergraduate courses and in business schools, *Games Mother Never Taught You* sold more than one million copies.[86]

Another popular managerial manual reinforced the notion that corporate upward mobility required avoidance of clerical work. After Margaret Hennig and Anne Jardim—the first two women to have received doctorates from the Harvard Business School (HBS)—taught at HBS, they decided that for women to navigate the male-dominated business world, they needed specialized management instruction. Hennig and Jardim launched the first business school for women only (at Simmons College in Boston), attempting to combine the rigorous quantitative courses and case method instruction of HBS with a focus on gender differences in management and organizations.[87] They authored *The Managerial Woman* (1977), based largely on their research in organizational behavior. The book taught women how to not self-sabotage and how to avoid falling into certain patterns that were common to women who were striving to reach the managerial or executive levels. The authors warned against secretarial work, which some women chose after earning a liberal arts degree because it was readily available. Female college graduates had been going "to secretarial school to acquire something they [could] tell themselves *is* a skill because there is a demand for it, it is tangible, it can be used." Secretaries' superiors would praise their accuracy and compliance, but, according to Hennig and Jardim, secretaries were not on promotable tracks, even to "middle management." Annual reviews declared that women in secretarial work were "lacking in management potential" and would remain "terminal in [their] present position," according to their supervisors. Thus secretaries should not mistake consistent praise for promises of promotions.[88]

These distinct lines of thinking—secretarial work as potential entry point in the Morrow and Lebov book, but secretarial work as dead end for Harragan as well as Hennig and Jardim—shared one important message: individual women had the power to determine their own careers. Armed with self-awareness, women should not blame their own lack of mobility on naïveté or institutional barriers. The focus, according to Hennig, should be less on existing structural challenges and more on adapting to the current corporate environment. "The difference between us and the women's movement," she said, "is that they say we have to make men change and we say we have to change first."[89] All three of these popular books encouraged women to adopt the behaviors that had helped men to acquire higher-paid, higher-status positions. Upward mobility required more than competence; it required a strategic plan to navigate organizations and find professional opportunities.

This type of advice in the 1980s, like the advice given to secretaries in the 1950s and 1960s, emphasized the importance of individual responsibility in the making of one's career. In chapter 1 we saw that each woman was to achieve her own success as a secretary, which in part required leveraging her feminine attributes to accommodate her boss's needs. But success in this type of support role was not incompatible with an appropriate exercise of ambition. A lower-level clerical could prove fit for an executive assistant role by demonstrating independent judgment. She could take initiative (within her boundaries) to predict her boss's needs and then act to satisfy them. One book lauded the secretary who could "think for herself and . . . work out problems on her own."[90] Rhetoric about determination and merit characterized career advice to the secretary of the 1950s who faced little criticism of her career choice, arguably because there was little choice.

In the 1980s, however, visible evidence of women like *Working Girl's* Katharine Parker, even if rare, cast smug judgment on the woman who— consciously or not—became a secretary. With other careers available, the secretary faced implicit blame for not having pursued something better. The achievements of feminism actually positioned the secretary to have to defend herself, or to try to rebrand herself into something with more prestige. Through the journey of feminism in the corporation, the secretarial occupation arrived, perhaps, in a place of lower status: jettisoned from the underutilization model of EEO compliance; lacking a standardized, professional credentialing process; struggling for members in its private-sector unions; and absent from the corporate HRM agenda. Yet its role inhabitants were still responsible, somehow, for career advancement and upward mobility—now under a modern rubric of "choice."

This emphasis on individual agency also infused *Working Woman* magazine, established in 1976 as the first magazine explicitly for wage-earning women. It claimed to advise upwardly mobile women, selecting content to appeal to the ambitious female professional. Its editor, Kate Rand Lloyd, wanted to focus on "women who [were] making news and breaking old patterns as they [moved] into and up through the work force."[91] After serving as managing editor of both *Vogue* and *Glamour* magazines, she became editor of *Working Woman* in 1978 when it was bankrupt, just two years after the publication launched.[92] Lloyd shifted its focus toward corporate businesswomen and those who aspired to pioneering positions: the magazine was for women making anywhere "from $6000 to $60,000," as long as readers had "points of view that [aimed] upwards."[93] With this strategy of targeting female professionals, Lloyd enjoyed great success, quadrupling circulation in two years. *Working Woman* became the fastest-growing magazine in 1980. With two million readers that year, a variety of wage-earning women—not just executives—were buying the magazine.[94] Career-development professionals recommended *Working Woman* magazine to those aspiring to better themselves. The magazine coached women on various career-related matters, such as choosing a job, asking for a promotion, and dressing for success.[95]

Despite its vast readership, the magazine clearly had Lloyd's target audience in mind, with advertisements aimed at middle- to upper-class white women like herself. And the featured stories highlighted the careers of such women. In the 1970s *Essence* magazine, known as a broader lifestyle magazine for Black women, began to publish more stories on work and career for those who were making significant moves from "field and kitchen to office."[96] Just a few decades earlier, executive secretarial jobs had been reserved for white women; the few Black women to assume such positions were celebrated in Black newspapers (chapter 1).[97] Furthermore, office work usually offered higher earnings than agricultural or domestic work, contributing to rising relative earnings for Black women in the 1960s, '70s, and '80s.[98] Historian Katherine Turk finds a generational divide in the 1970s among Black women in clerical work: the older women seemed content to stay, but younger women were trying to get out, as evidenced by testimony in the *Sears* case.[99]

By the 1980s, the message to aspiring professional women, both white and Black, was to continue to look upward. In 1984 speakers at Boston's Roxbury Multiserve Community Center told Black clerical women, "to move ahead, not let up on the drive for management level positions and behond [*sic*]," according to 9to5 documents.[100] Career literature echoed this message. Like *Working Woman*, *Essence* warned readers about the dangers of getting stuck in the secretarial role. Both magazines ran articles with similar, and sometimes even identical, content. In fact, some of the articles in *Essence* were reprints of those running in *Working Woman*. Like *Working Woman*, *Essence* magazine ran pieces on "moves you can make to start on your climb from the secretarial pool to the executive suite," as well as "seven ways to move out of the secretarial pool and to supervisory positions."[101] And just as *Working Woman* relied on output from Felice Schwartz's new research organization, Catalyst, *Essence* also included excerpts from Catalyst reports. In the May 1982 issue, one article discussed how to cultivate a bond with your boss, since Catalyst evidence showed that a positive relationship with one's supervisor could lead to career advancement. Yet to some extent the *Essence* personalized the content for the magazine's readership. The author cautioned Black women that sustaining a good working relationship did not have to mean feeling uncomfortable or violated: a Black woman should not have to tolerate sexual harassment from a Black male boss—just as she would not tolerate it from a white male boss.[102]

Thus while the messaging in both magazines was similar, at times *Essence* specifically acknowledged race, noting how certain career issues could have different implications for Black women. They could be more reluctant than White women to initiate a career change, according to experts, because Black women were more likely to lack self-confidence and family resources, as reported by writer Harriet Jackson Scarupa.[103] In another piece, some Black women reported feeling like impostors in a white world. If they did not get a job for which they interviewed, they reasoned that they must not have deserved it. But a psychologist pointed out that Black women had to have abilities superior—not just equal—to those of the other candidates in order to secure the same job as white women. Instead of feeling inferior, Black women should recognize that they had to actually have better experience and performance to be in the position where they sit.[104] Black women might also face disadvantages at work because they were more often the first in their family to secure an office job. *Essence* advised its readers to "learn corporate culture" because "there's a behavior code in corporate America that's not explained in your employee handbook." In fact, understanding the protocols was "subtle and difficult to define unless someone explained them to you." Journalist Betty Winston Bayé noted, "Many of us didn't grow up in families with relatives who worked in white corporations."[105] One expert advised Black women to try to find other Black women to help them. But if none were available, then those wanting to advance should "seek out help wherever you can find it."[106]

Furthermore, *Essence* coached Black women about the difference between a job and a career. A frequent contributor to *Essence*, career counselor Kaaren Johnson, explained that Black women in particular needed more coaching to find their professional calling. Johnson, owner and director of Female Employment Management (FEM), an employment and management service in New York City, helped women, particularly college-educated Black women, in making career changes. Johnson noted, "Black women, especially, have traditionally been conditioned to having a *job*—getting that paycheck—instead of pursuing a *career*. But our horizons are broadening."[107]

Essence, more than *Working Woman*, acknowledged that systemic factors, not just individual preferences, could influence one's occupational choice and career advancement. In the article "Second Careers," Scarupa offered job resources for those with means as well as information about free and reduced-cost services. Kaaren Johnson's for-profit service, FEM, was designed for women with college degrees, and as such, Johnson charged a fee for career counseling, résumé preparation, and career workshops. Yet low-income women and women without college degrees could access other resources: a municipal agency in New York City called Careers for Women, the nonprofit Wider Opportunities for Women, and the nonprofit National Council of Negro Women (NCNW). The NCNW's Women's Center for Education and Career Advancement provided affordable career help, including reduced-cost individual counseling sessions, evening workshops, and a career library. And, the NCNW, in collaboration with Pace University in New York City, offered a joint program that enabled women to earn an associate degree.[108]

Essence signaled to women without college degrees that they could have ambition but might need to be more pragmatic in their choices. Some content echoed the values of individual fulfillment, such as the advice of Johnson's FEM, which told women "to pull together your values, interests, abilities and skills to come up with a profile of who you are."[109] Yet women without college degrees should be more realistic, according to experts. In a career education program for women sponsored by the U.S. Department of Health, Education, and Welfare, speaker Sanita Harper Joyner told women to leverage what they were good at, even if they did not happen to like the activities in which they excelled. Joyner, who served as the project director of Empowerment for Teen Women, advised women without bachelor's degrees to be "aware and realistic about their choices. If there is an oversupply in that field or there are no jobs available, then you are wasting your time pursuing these areas."[110]

While much of the advice to Black women suggested that job seekers, especially those without higher degrees, should approach their searches with pragmatism, select articles encouraged everyone, college degree or not, to "dream big and take risks," according to career counselor and author Beatryce Nivens.[111] At Queens College in New York, she was a counselor in the SEEK program, which advanced qualified high school students who might not attend college otherwise, as well as the chief consultant for New Horizons Educational and Career Consultants. Nivens presented *Essence* readers with a few examples of women who had made transitions, and more were profiled in her book *The Black Woman's Career Guide* (Anchor, 1982). Linda was a secretary who wanted a different job but did not "believe her skills were suitable for anything other than secretarial work." Nivens pointed to this sort of thinking as a common problem. Many women felt hopeless about changing jobs or careers, believing that they were not qualified to transition into something new. However, Nivens encouraged, "Open yourself up to the different opportunities that are available and find something that you are good at doing. Everyone is good at something." For instance, one woman became a photographer because she wanted to "incorporate the way I feel and think into something I could make a living at. A job should be a way of expressing yourself."[112] In another piece for *Essence*, called "Quick and Easy Job Changes," Nivens offered advice specifically for women without college degrees, which she would later present in a book, *How to Change Careers Without Getting More Education* (1990). She offered ideas for dissatisfied clerical workers: consider writing for a magazine as an editorial assistant or take a position as a publicity assistant with a public-relations firm. Other possibilities she mentioned included travel agent, legal assistant, word-processing specialist, sales representative for an office supplies company, computer typesetter, computer graphics worker, court reporter, word-processing business owner, and real estate agent.[113]

Other articles in *Essence* by Bayé detailed stories of upward mobility that required additional educational attainment. Bayé contributed two articles, in 1989 and 1991, about herself and other Black women who had "beaten similar odds" to earn higher degrees and thus "made the move from the secretarial pool to the corner office."[114] She explained her own mental transition from thinking in terms of earning a decent wage to finding a fulfilling career. After graduating from high school, she recalled, "My ambition was to be a secretary. In 1963 my friends and I didn't think about careers; we just wanted jobs that would give us enough money to rent our own apartments, get our hair done every other Friday and go to the Apollo and the Palladium a couple of times a month." Bayé approached secretarial work as an opportunity to learn more about professional possibilities that "the guidance counselors back at Benjamin Franklin High School in East Harlem had never talked about." Growing up in a low-income community, Bayé used secretarial work to gain a more expansive view of career options. Yet secretary was a stop along the way, not her end goal. In her words, she "smashed the mold that existed (and still exists) for kids who grow up in public housing" and made sacrifices to earn her college degree. Although her first newspaper job paid much less than her last secretarial job, she wrote that "I had to go backward before I could go forward."[115]

While both *Working Woman* and *Essence* profiled women who had made the leap out of clerical work (and other female-dominated jobs like teaching), the advice articles cautioned women that the transition could be difficult. Readers needed to understand that employers might view clerical work as unrelated to management. *Essence* advised its readers against listing job titles on résumés if their previous work experience was clerical. In an article entitled "Resumes: Tooting Your Own Horn," an *Essence* writer advised readers that "if that last job happened to be secretarial or clerical, a prospective employer might decide to give you a typing test 'just for the record'—and you'd be back at square one before you began."[116] In *Working Woman*, former teacher Judy Boston revealed that her search for a new career began when she read *What Color Is Your Parachute?*[117] The book helped her to determine that she wanted a job that offered more "money and power," but when she sent out résumés, "she discovered that being an ex-teacher was worse than having no experience at all." According to Boston, who eventually found a new, commission-based job selling advertising space, she had to hide the fact that she had been a teacher, "as though it were a communicable disease."[118] In another *Working Woman* article, career advisers reinforced the idea that job seekers hoping to transition into management should minimize their secretarial experience. One career counselor advised a secretary who was applying to managerial positions to emphasize certain skills on her résumé that related to management competencies but to "underplay the secretarial role" itself.[119]

Numerous letters to the editor—which were not published in *Working Woman* but preserved in the Smith College archives—challenged the magazine's narrow definition of success in the workplace. While inspiring stories celebrated the pioneering women who were entering new territory like the C-suite, some women complained that the magazine overlooked the needs of women in female-dominated jobs. One clerical employee who worked in a small office said that she used to subscribe to *Working Woman* but the magazine did not help her daughter (a nurse), her daughter-in-law (a teacher), or herself (a clerical) with their problems of being overworked, underpaid, and trying to "hold our lives and our families together."[120] Another letter complained, "The title of your magazine, WORKING WOMAN, indicated to me that it was addressing the issues of working women everywhere," but in fact, this reader, a government clerk, felt "slighted" and "inadequate" by the articles addressed to corporate women who earned "'big money'" and traveled extensively. She asked the magazine to "address the issues of thousands of women like me who are in hi [*sic*] pressure jobs with low pay, and low rewards. We are a very dedicated group of women, and I don't think we should go unrecognized."[121] A similar clerical complaint stated:

> Your magazine has forgot [*sic*] about the other side of our working women. I mean the secretaries, Accounting Assistants, hotel carriers, telephone operators, Sales clerks, Bus drivers, Word Processors, oh! Do you get the idea. I consider my self [*sic*] a professional and a career woman in every respect bringing up my children and being able to deal with people on all levels of society. You make me feel that your magazine is geared to college grads, MBA people only.[122]

This woman was demanding that the magazine recognize the talents of women who were struggling to support their families on meager wages. She thought they deserved the same respect that was granted to "college grads, MBA people." Another secretary, frustrated by the status of secretarial work, asked, "Why is it that all the books and magazine articles on job-hunting automatically assume we all want executive positions?" She had enjoyed being a secretary and thought she was very good at it. She believed that secretaries were "so important to the world of business" that business would be "paralyzed" without them.[123] These readers wanted the magazine to address problems facing gender-segregated workers and underscore the value of support positions, but *Working Woman* was emphasizing the concerns of more credentialed women who were striving for professional mobility in what used to be a man's world.

Other clerical workers admitted that they were reading *Working Woman* solely because it was one of the only national magazines, besides *Essence* and another magazine called *Savvy*, that addressed women's careers. But many were finding that the content was not relevant to them. One clerical employee told the magazine that it should address more than "corporate gamesmanship" for the professional, upwardly mobile woman, referencing the magazine's similarity to books such as Betty Harragan's *Games Mother Never Taught You.*[124] Another woman from Georgia, who in 1983 was making less than $10,000 per year in her office job, criticized a salary negotiation article by Harragan. This worker said that unlike the concerns of women with four-year degrees and professional contacts, "the name of the game [for her was] income to keep alive versus no job and bare subsistence on welfare."[125]

Some women also noticed that the advice in *Working Woman* did not address additional challenges they faced based on their class, race, or age. The content in *Essence* seemed to acknowledge that not all women began their careers with college degrees. But as a single mother noted in an unpublished letter, *Working Woman* did not address financial and educational issues for those without advanced degrees who had not been working in the "great positions we all wish for." A clerical worker for fifteen years, she was trying for "something better" and planning to enroll in school to earn an associate degree. Yet at this point she worked "to put food on the table and pay the rent."[126] A woman of color complained that *Working Woman* "focuses almost exclusively on white women, seemingly ignoring that minority women are a part of its readership."[127] Another woman told the magazine to "try to print some articles on what the 'poor' class are wearing and how to get *that* job after one reaches the 30–40 age bracket."[128] Echoing similar sentiments, a clerical worker called for the magazine to approach the issues of older women who lacked college educations. This single mother in her forties had been a secretary for twenty-five years. Working toward an associate degree in management, she was hoping to advance to a more "responsible and rewarding" position. Unsurprisingly, an editor had written a big "NO" in red ink on the top, signaling that the letter would not appear in the magazine. The problems of older women without college degrees apparently did not represent the magazine's brand, which aimed to feature articles for and about professional women who were "movers and shakers," in the words of Kate Rand Lloyd, the magazine's editor.[129]

Clerical workers were becoming increasingly aware of the devaluation of their jobs in a world where women, by law, had equal opportunity to pursue any job that was available to men. *Working Woman* and other advice literature bolstered a type of corporate feminism that attended to the needs of professional women who were eager to move into new spaces. Clericals became ashamed to say that they were secretaries when asked about what they did, even though, according to one woman, there was no reason to feel embarrassed about hard work.[130] These sentiments of shame seemed warranted given that some feminist comments positioned career advancement as avoidance and rejection of clerical work. *Working Woman*'s Lloyd, in remarks at a women's conference, described all secretaries as suffering from a "terminal illness" because their jobs depended on pleasing other people. In her view, secretaries had to prioritize likability over ambition, which had kept them from achieving success in the workforce.[131]

In *The Assistant: New Tasks, New Opportunities* (1982), HR consultant Elizabeth R. Murphy revealed some hard truths regarding questions she had received when leading secretarial training programs. The most common question she entertained: how to get out of the secretarial field. Women complained to her that every time they tried to interview for a new, nonclerical position, hiring managers offered them a secretarial position instead. Murphy answered: "First, stop telling them you *are* a secretary." She emphasized that obtaining a different title, such as "administrative assistant, or assistant to, or assistant manager, or research specialist," was very important because "these titles carry a different connotation from secretary. I'm not downgrading secretaries. I'm saying that if you want to do something different, your first step may be to get a different title."[132] The myth of occupational choice imbued Murphy's advice. As women gained the privilege of choosing a career, their identity and status ultimately depended on that initial choice, one that seemed to be completely their own. But in reality, a woman's job after high school (or even following college) often reflected her broader socioeconomic situation. Structural factors still mattered in terms of job choice and career advancement. Yet a growing body of advice literature, particularly literature targeted toward women, emphasized the power of the individual, regardless of circumstances, to change her own situation.

The conjunction of several factors—the long-standing ideology of American individualism, the codification of legal equality, and the institutionalization of seemingly merit-based HR practices—fractured the feminist movement at work. The concerns of some working-class women (i.e., domestic workers and home health care workers) who faced financial insecurity and unsafe working conditions moved to the forefront of the labor movement.[133] The problems of managerial and executive women shifted to the corporate agenda, as the issues facing women in leadership positions gained the attention of investors and board directors. Many corporations actively recruited the most talented women and underrepresented men for executive roles, as HR managers and consultants argued that diverse organizations enjoyed competitive advantages.[134]

Secretaries inhabited a liminal space, between the concerns headlining the labor movement and the issues facing the executive woman. They had not rushed to unionize in the 1980s, leery to abandon the promise of promotion, lower the status of white-collar work, and unify with others across a massive and diverse occupational category. But stigmatized by the connotations of their job titles, secretaries struggled to compete in the merit-based workplace, and they often got "locked into the 'secretarial image,'" according to Morrow and Lebov. The authors of *Not Just a Secretary* continued to broadcast warnings that had been issued before: consummate performance in a secretarial job actually did not ensure mobility out of the position.[135]

In 1981 *The Working Woman Success Book* declared to managerial women what secretaries already knew: hard work was not enough. The editors of *Working Woman* magazine explained: "A growing number of women moving up in the work world are finding that strategy, not talent, is the deciding factor in moving toward higher, better-paid positions."[136] Decades later such advice remained relevant for career advancement. In her multimillion bestseller *Lean In: Women, Work, and the Will to Lead* (2013), Sheryl Sandberg counseled professional women in adjusting their interpersonal behavior and self-perception, arguing that "leaning in" could help them get ahead.[137] While citing the latest social science research, Sandberg, then the chief operating officer for Facebook, was offering recommendations similar to those that had imbued the advice literature of the 1970s and 1980s. The first generation of female managers could ascend into higher-status corporate positions by learning "the rules of the game," in the words of Betty Harragan in 1977. Even the Philadelphia chapter of the National Secretaries Association considered hosting a Secretaries Week event in 1977 to view *Pack Your Own Chute*, a motivational film about a parachute jump that forwarded broader themes of individualism, autonomy, and independence.[138]

The victories of women at the top, which journalist Dawn Foster's *Lean Out* calls a "feminism of the 1%," did not always represent "a victory for women as a whole."[139] And to get to the top, Sandberg no longer had to instruct twenty-first-century women that career mobility relied on avoidance of secretarial work. Professional women now knew that the traits that had long been associated with a secretary—nurturing, obedient, and submissive—would not give them an edge in the current corporate climate. By the 1990s, contrasting images of working women in corporate America had emerged: some seemed to have chosen secretarial work, which remained stigmatized as inferior, while the more visible and celebrated women were striving for the highest leadership positions in male-dominated spaces.

EPILOGUE

In exit polls for the 2016 presidential election, white women without college degrees reported that they favored Republican candidate Donald Trump over Democratic candidate Hillary Clinton by a ratio of almost two to one. Sixty-one percent voted for Trump while 34 percent voted for Clinton.[1] Understanding why white working-class women did not support a female candidate (who could have been the first female president in U.S. history) requires us to overcome "class cluelessness," in the words of legal scholar Joan Williams.[2] Williams explains in *White Working Class* that Americans who are part of a "professional-managerial elite" think that all women aspire to do men's work. Many working-class women, however, would like to "invest more of their identity in family." Furthermore, the pink-collar career trajectories of many white working-class women remained similar to those of their mothers. Feminism may have been pivotal in changing opportunities and outcomes for college-educated women like Hillary Clinton, but it did not—at least not as overtly or explicitly—have such an impact on less privileged women. White working-class women, like their mothers, never had the choice to stay home and bake cookies, an option Clinton publicly disparaged in 1992.[3]

This is not to say that white working-class women who were secretaries, executive assistants, clerks, bookkeepers, typists, and receptionists were not influenced by feminism or that they did not contribute to social progress, just that their career paths remained remarkably similar before and after the feminist movement of the 1960s and 1970s. Women of color gained new opportunities to move into office work, albeit in lower-status, lower-paid jobs. Those who earned advanced degrees became eligible to be the boss, although they faced significant hurdles posed by the intersections of their gender and racial identities.[4] But gender segregation has remained strong among those working in jobs—both inside and outside of the office—that do not require a college degree. Men still dominate the highest-paid trades: only 9 percent of construction workers are women.[5] As historian Katherine Turk explains, "The relationship between sex and class in the American labor force had been reworked" in the age of gender equality. Occupational segregation had become a class-based issue.[6] The continued labor market segregation of women without college degrees had fallen through the feminist cracks.

And, of course, clerical work, the lowest-status form of white-collar labor, has remained dominated by women.[7] Yet women in these jobs, due to the size and variability of the occupational category, arguably have weak ties to their professional identity.[8] Karen Nussbaum recalled of the struggle to unionize clericals, "You can't organize people who hate themselves for what they're doing. You can't organize around the desire to be doing something else because those people will only try to get out of that work situation."[9] Indeed, Nussbaum had accurately assessed the way a large group of women felt about their jobs. Perhaps the attack on certain gendered aspects of the job—making coffee, serving lunch, running personal errands—had had the unintended consequence of corroding respect for the secretarial job itself. And women's access to a wider variety of career choices, thanks to barriers against overt discrimination, reinforced the American myth of meritocracy. Still, class privilege gave some women greater knowledge and capital to navigate their professional paths.

By the end of the twentieth century, a person's job—or lack of one— perhaps more than any other factor, could bolster or undermine self-esteem. In a culture of "meritocratic individualism," according to sociologist Katherine Newman, those without economic security tended to blame themselves.[10] Self-blame also accompanied job searching, piercing those who were unemployed and seeking work but coming up short.[11] The linking of one's job with one's true self "channeled the counterculture value of self-fulfillment back into the productive spheres—back into the workplace," according to sociologist Micki McGee in *Self-Help, Inc.: Makeover Culture in American Life.*[12]

This self-blame that plagued those performing unfulfilling jobs or those without jobs was not completely new, as Americans had always valued work ethic as a key component of moral character.[13] Historian Pamela Laird makes this point masterfully in *Pull*, as she accounts for the distinctly American nature of the stories we tell about business success.[14] But since the 1990s the refrain of finding one's passion through paid employment, or "the productive spheres," in the words of McGee, has become stronger than ever.[15] In books like *Do What You Love and the Money Will Follow*, author and psychologist Marsha Sinetar declared an end to the Monday morning blues; finding one's "passion" was a source of liberation.[16] But each person had an individual responsibility to find that passion; the employee, not the employer, managed her own career. Therefore lack of a job, or even lack of a fulfilling job, signaled poor management of the self.[17] In 1997 author and management consultant Tom Peters famously elevated this self-management of career. Writing in *Fast Company*, Peters advised that individuals should reject dependence on any single organization: "You don't 'belong to' any company for life, and your chief affiliation isn't to any particular 'function.' You're not defined by your job title . . . starting today you are a brand."[18]

The problem with this way of thinking was that, unfortunately, secretaries were defined by their job titles and by the historical connotations of the role. With the rise of feminism, secretarial work became "dirtier" in the sociological sense: the job lost esteem and prestige, and those doing it became more stigmatized.[19] Consequently, secretaries had difficulty rebranding themselves into something new. The unraveling of the boss-secretary relationship (chapter 1) and the rise of occupational choice for women (chapter 7) left clerical women in a precarious situation regarding their own brand management. Yes, they had become administrative assistants, in what was perhaps an effort to increase the status of the role and to detach the job from its gendered history. Still, administrative assistants faced substantial barriers if they wanted to advance beyond their present job category. A recasting of clerical experience for other types of white-collar jobs proved practically impossible, which explains why so much career advice literature recommended avoidance (chapter 7). Thus while secretaries in the 1950s had little upward mobility, they could still possess ambition (chapter 1). The secretaries of the 1990s also lacked upward mobility but additionally had trouble claiming that they were ambitious amid all the other job options available. Armed with legal equality and career advice, secretaries could find their passion, if only they so desired.

In *She Come by It Natural*, journalist Sarah Smarsh identifies an "unnamed sort of feminism" among working-class, rural women who have been "economically disenfranchised." Looking beyond the more conventional feminist channels that brought us Hillary Clinton, Smarsh points to Dolly Parton, a "female boss" of her own cultural territory. Despite Parton's reluctance to claim the feminist label for herself, Smarsh contends that the music superstar is in fact a feminist icon. She embodies the grit of many working-class women: "The fight to merely survive is a declaration of equality that could be called 'feminist.'"[20] Parton, with her eye-catching hair and bedazzled clothes, arguably has represented a feminism more fit for the rural masses. And as Doralee in the movie *9 to 5*, Parton played a role that many women understood: she was a secretary who endured sexual harassment because she needed a paycheck. The movie's widespread appeal in the early 1980s pushed viewers to imagine that feminism could have been more expansive and able to address the concerns of working women from top to bottom of the corporate hierarchy. Instead, by the 1990s corporate feminism had not become a vertical type of feminism inclusive of class and occupational difference. Some key constituencies benefited more than others, and therefore what has become corporate feminism happened to overlook the occupation most common for women: the secretary.

ACKNOWLEDGMENTS

S o many individuals and institutions have supported the writing of this book, and I am grateful to have space to thank them for believing in me and in this story.

I could not have received better graduate training than I did at the University of Virginia. My advisor Cindy Aron imparted an intersectional approach to gender as an analytical category, which shaped my thinking about the past and present status of women at work. She cultivated my interest in female-dominated jobs and encouraged me to examine clerical work, a massive but understudied occupational category in modern American history. Grace Hale, Charles McCurdy, and Allan Megill opened my mind to the method and writing of history. They taught me how to evaluate sources and construct an evidence-based narrative.

Nothing in the history of gender and work becomes a scholarly contribution without the imprint of Eileen Boris, whose mentorship to junior scholars is truly unmatched. Her extensive comments propelled this project forward; her intellectual prowess in this field is behind many projects, including this one.

Having senior colleagues at Cornell who believed in my scholarship inspired me to persist amid moves and turns in my career. Diane Burton, whose brilliance reaches beyond disciplinary boundaries, is an exemplary mentor and friend; her kindness and wisdom are largely responsible for any professional successes I enjoy. The intellectual guidance and unwavering support of Rose Batt and Pam Tolbert have backed my scholarly development, and they have enriched my thinking about gender, employment, and occupations. Other Cornell colleagues who saw promise in this project (and in me) include Jeff Cowie, Adam Litwin, and Ben Rissing, as well as Cornell alum Leona Barsky. Academic friends from across several institutions were also supportive: Rachel Aleks, Elena Belogolovsky, Vanessa Bohns, Christy Chapin, Steph Creary, Todd Dickey, Susan Fleming, Kristina Harris, Amy Jacobs, Jessica Kennedy, Andrew McGee, Betsy More, Jamie Perry, Ellie Shermer, Phoebe Strom, and Megan Stubbendeck. At Darden, I have benefited greatly from conversations with Ming-Jer Chen, Mary Margaret Frank, Ed Freeman, and Bobby Parmar, whose interest in my success has proven vital during the vicissitudes of academic life. Nancy Rothbard at Wharton—as well as current Darden colleagues like Tatiana Batova, Brian Moriarty, Marc Modica, Anthony Palomba, Lili Powell, and June West—have supported my professional development and welcomed me into new spaces. Research collaborations with Rolv Petter Amdam, Jirs Meuris, Kendall Park, and Mike Roach have expanded my knowledge of management and organizations, which has positively influenced the final draft of this book.

The publication of this book would not have been possible without the generous sponsorship of Melissa Thomas-Hunt, whose exceptional intelligence as a scholar and a practitioner have gifted her with the ability to support and enrich so many lives, including mine. She bolstered my career at pivotal points, providing me with the opportunity to revise this manuscript and to pursue new avenues for thinking about gender, diversity, and inequality at work. Her wisdom and energy are contagious, and I become a better person with each interaction I have with her.

Stephen Wesley provided thoughtful guidance through the peer-review and editing process. Bethany Moreton's keen insights and invaluable suggestions pushed this narrative to engage more deeply in historical conversations. Louis Hyman has supported this work for many years, first at Cornell and then as an academic editor at Columbia. I am honored to have these two distinguished experts in the history of capitalism behind this project.

Pamela Haag's development of this book transformed the argument's presentation and structure, and she is truly a literary genius. Silvia

Benvenuto, Jane Haxby, and Anita O'Brien applied their mastery of language to improve the prose and finalize the manuscript. In addition, I have gained crucial research assistance from Alexandra King, Henry Marshall, Ryan Purcell, and Kwelina Thompson. Melanie Sobocinski gave me tools to reengage in book revisions amid life's interruptions.

As a gender historian, I believe the separation between home and work is quite fictive, and thus I am grateful to Amanda Molinari and Sheila Parker, who gave me cognitive freedom to engage in this project.

I thrive from a lifetime of support from my parents Adele and Bill, siblings Jeff, Jennifer, and Andrea, and their spouses Juliana, Lee, and Lynn. Also important has been the backing of Donna, Larry, Jeannine, Damian, Nathan, Tyler, and Justin. The love of my niece and nephews, Jack, Nate, Will, Ellen, and Andrew, rejuvenates me and enriches my life tremendously. I am grateful to have the gift of Lila and Derek in my life, and to share a love of Alex with them. Alex has brought me more joy than I could ever imagine. He provides a type of love and happiness that allows me to fully engage in all parts of life.

This book is dedicated to Rob, whose determination and bravery are inspirational to me; his areas of strengths are my points of weakness.

ARCHIVES AND REPOSITORIES

9to5 Records

9to5, National Association of Working Women (U.S.), Records, 1972–1980, 79-M16–81-M121, Schlesinger Library, Radcliffe Institute, Harvard University, Cambridge, Mass.

9to5 Additional Records A

9to5, National Association of Working Women (U.S.), Additional records, 1972–1986, 88-M96–89-M104, Schlesinger Library, Radcliffe Institute, Harvard University, Cambridge, Mass.

9to5 Additional Records B

Additional records of 9 to 5, National Association of Working Women (U.S.), 1972–1985, 82-M189-86-M213, Schlesinger Library, Radcliffe Institute, Harvard University, Cambridge, Mass.

Black Women Oral History Project

Interviews, 1976–1981, Schlesinger Library, Radcliffe Institute, Harvard University, Cambridge, Mass.

Harvard Union Records

Harvard Union of Clerical and Technical Workers, Records, 1967–2005, Schlesinger Library, Radcliffe Institute, Harvard University, Cambridge, Mass.

KGS Records

Katharine Gibbs School Records, John Hay Library Special Collections, Brown University, Providence, R.I.

Massachusetts History Workshop Records	Massachusetts History Workshop Records, 1980–1984, MC365, Schlesinger Library, Radcliffe Institute, Harvard University, Cambridge, Mass.
NSA, Philadelphia Records	National Secretaries Association, Philadelphia Chapter Records, accession no. 478, Special Collections Research Center, Temple University Libraries, Philadelphia, Pa.
Polaroid Corporation Administration Records	Polaroid Corporation Administrative Records, Baker Library Historical Collections, Harvard Business School, Cambridge, Mass.
SEIU District 925 Collection	SEIU District 925 Collection, Walter P. Reuther Library, Wayne State University, Detroit, Mich.
SEIU District 925 Legacy Project	SEIU District 925 Legacy Project, Walter P. Reuther Library, Wayne State University, Detroit, Mich.
Voices of Feminism Oral History Project	Voices of Feminism Oral History Project, Sophia Smith Collection of Women's History, Smith College, Northampton, Mass.
Women's Action Alliance Records	Women's Action Alliance Records, Sophia Smith Collection of Women's History, Smith College, Northampton, Mass.
Working Woman magazine, Letters to the Editor	*Working Woman* magazine, Letters to the Editor, 1981–1983, unprocessed, location 58A, acc. 83-60, Sophia Smith Collection of Women's History, Smith College, Northampton, Mass.
Tepperman Papers	Jean Tepperman Papers, Schlesinger Library, Radcliffe Institute, Harvard University, Cambridge, Mass.

NOTES

INTRODUCTION

1. Gloria Steinem, "The Politics of Women," commencement speech, Smith College, Northampton, Mass., May 29, 1971, originally broadcast on WFCR's Five College Forum; Kristen Richard, NPR, August 1, 2016, https://digital.nepr.net/audiofiles/2016/08/01/gloria-steinem-on-the-politics-of-women/.
2. Jean Caldwell, "Gloria Steinem Says at Smith, the College Is Not Ready for Males," *Boston Globe*, May 31, 1971.
3. Ruth Rosen, *The World Split Open: How the Modern Women's Movement Changed America* (New York: Penguin, 2000).
4. Katherine Turk, *Equality on Trial: Gender and Rights in the Modern American Workplace* (Philadelphia: University of Pennsylvania Press, 2016); Nancy MacLean, *Freedom Is Not Enough: The Opening of the American Workplace* (New York and Cambridge, Mass.: Russell Sage Foundation and Harvard University Press, 2006); Alice Kessler-Harris, *In Pursuit of Equity: Women, Men, and the Quest for Economic Citizenship in 20th-Century America* (New York: Oxford University Press, 2001).
5. Judith B. Bremner, "Black Pink Collar Workers: Arduous Journey from Field and Kitchen to Office," *Journal of Sociology & Social Welfare* 19, no. 3 (1992); Mary C. King, "Black Women's Breakthrough Into Clerical Work: An Occupational Tipping Model," *Journal of Economic Issues* 27, no. 4 (1993): 1097–1125; Jacqueline Jones, *Labor of Love, Labor of Sorrow* (New York: Basic Books, 1985).
6. Claudia Goldin and Lawrence Katz, "The Power of the Pill: Oral Contraceptives and Women's Career and Marriage Decisions," *Journal of Political Economy* 110, no. 4 (2002): 730–70.
7. Laurie Johnston, "Women's Caucus Has a New Rallying Cry: 'Make Policy, Not Coffee,'" *New York Times*, February 6, 1972.

8. Robin Morgan, *Going Too Far: The Personal Chronicle of a Feminist* (New York: Random House, 1977), 65.

9. Mitra Toossi and Teresa L. Morisi, "Women in the Workforce Before, During, and After the Great Recession," U.S. Bureau of Labor Statistics, July 2017, https://www.bls.gov /spotlight/2017/women-in-the-workforce-before-during-and-after-the-great-recessi on/pdf/women-in-the-workforce-before-during-and-after-the-great-recession.pdf; Nathan Yau, "Most Female and Male Occupations Since 1950," FlowingData, September 11, 2017, https://flowingdata.com/2017/09/11/most-female-and-male-occupations -since-1950/. In 1950 the greatest number of working women (1.7 million) belonged to the census category of "stenographers, typists, or secretaries"; in 2010 the census category of "secretaries and administrative assistants" represented the most common job for women (almost four million women). See Annalyn Kurtz, "Why Secretary Is Still the Top Job for Women," CNN Business, January 31, 2013, https://money.cnn .com/2013/01/31/news/economy/secretary-women-jobs/index.html.

10. For scholarship showing the ways that feminist ideas sparked rebellion among working women, see Dorothy Sue Cobble, *The Other Women's Movement: Workplace Justice and Social Rights in Modern America* (Princeton, N.J.: Princeton University Press, 2004). On service-sector women workers in the 1970s, see Cobble, "'A Spontaneous Loss of Enthusiasm': Workplace Feminism and the Transformation of Women's Service Jobs in the 1970s," *International Labor and Working-Class History* 56 (Fall 1999): 23–44. About home health care workers, see Eileen Boris and Jennifer Klein, *Caring for America: Home Health Workers in the Shadow of the Welfare State* (New York: Oxford University Press, 2012). Also see chapters about pink-collar workers in Turk, *Equality on Trial*; Lane Windham, *Knocking on Labor's Door: Union Organizing in the 1970s and the Roots of a New Economic Divide* (Chapel Hill: University of North Carolina Press, 2017); Dennis Deslippe, *Rights, Not Roses: Unions and the Rise of Working-Class Feminism* (Urbana: University of Illinois Press, 2000); Kathleen Barry, *Femininity in Flight: A History of Flight Attendants* (Durham, N.C.: Duke University Press, 2007); and Nancy MacLean, "The Hidden History of Affirmative Action: Working Women's Struggles in the 1970s and the Gender of Class," *Feminist Studies* 25, no. 1 (1999): 42–78.

11. I use the "second-wave" terminology, coined in Martha Weinman Lear, "The Second Feminist Wave," *New York Times Magazine*, March 10, 1968, and I address this choice later in this introduction.

12. Frank Dobbin, *Inventing Equal Opportunity* (Princeton, N.J.: Princeton University Press, 2009).

13. *Report of the Commission on the Status of NSA*, November 8, 1968, pp. 2–3, box 6, folder 27, NSA, Philadelphia Records.

14. *Report of the Commission on the Status of NSA*, 3.

15. Luc Boltanski and Eve Chiapello, *The New Spirit of Capitalism*, trans. Gregory Elliott, rev. ed. (1999; New York: Verso, 2005).

16. In 1997 author and management consultant Tom Peters used the language of branding for careers: "You don't 'belong to' any company for life, and your chief affiliation isn't

to any particular 'function.' You're not defined by your job title . . . starting today you are a brand." Peters, "The Brand Called You," *Fast Company*, August 31, 1997, 83.

17. Pamela Walker Laird, *Pull: Networking and Success Since Benjamin Franklin* (Cambridge, Mass.: Harvard University Press, 2007).

18. See Nancy Fraser, "Feminism, Capitalism, and the Cunning of History," *New Left Review* 56 (March–April 2009): 97–117. On occupational choice, see Peter M. Blau, John W. Gustad, Richard Jessor, Herbert S. Parnes, and Richard C. Wilcock, "Occupational Choice: A Conceptual Framework," *ILR Review* 9, no. 4 (July 1956): 531–43; Ofer Sharone, "Constructing Unemployed Job Seekers as Professional Workers: The Depoliticizing Work-Game of Job Searching," *Qualitative Sociology* 30 (2007): 403–16; Steven Vallas and Andrea Hill, "Reconfiguring Worker Subjectivity: Career Advice Literature and the 'Branding' of the Worker's Self," *Sociological Forum* 33 (2018): 287–309.

19. A robust literature in the social sciences also reveals the ways in which the unraveling of stable employment relationships and the decline of internal labor markets have influenced work and the economy. Gerald F. Davis, *The Vanishing American Corporation Navigating the Hazards of a New Economy* (New York: Barrett-Kohler, 2016); Arne Kalleberg, *Good Jobs, Bad Jobs: The Rise of Polarized and Precarious Employment Systems in the United States, 1970s to 2000s* (New York: Russell Sage Foundation, 2011); Eileen Appelbaum and Rosemary Batt, *The New American Workplace* (Ithaca, N.Y.: ILR Press, 1994); Thomas Kochan, Harry Katz, and Robert McKersie, *The Transformation of American Industrial Relations* (New York: Basic Books, 1986); Thomas Kochan and Lee Dyer, *Shaping the Future of Work: A Handbook for Action and a New Social Contract* (Cambridge, Mass: MITx Press, 2017).

20. For an account that presents these changes as more contingent, see Louis Hyman, *Temp: How American Work, American Business, and the American Dream Became Temporary* (New York: Viking, 2018).

21. For women, long-standing notions about the family wage ideal had relegated them to lower-paid jobs and seasonal work, justifying lower compensation as appropriate and fair because of their dependent status. Alice Kessler-Harris, *Out to Work: A History of Wage-Earning Women in the United States* (New York: Oxford University Press, 2003).

22. Davis, *Vanishing American Corporation*. Queueing theory holds that as men move toward more entrepreneurial ventures and more lucrative fields, women gain access to the jobs and occupations that men have left behind. Barbara Reskin and Patricia Roos, *Job Queues, Gender Queues: Explaining Women's Inroads Into Male Occupations* (Philadelphia: Temple University Press, 1990).

23. William H. Whyte, *The Organization Man* (New York: Simon & Schuster, 1956).

24. Paula England, *Comparable Worth: Theories and Evidence* (New York: Transaction Publishers, 1992); Ronnie J. Steinberg, "Comparable Worth in Gender Studies," in *International Encyclopedia of the Social and Behavioral Sciences*, ed. Neil Smelser and Paul Baltes (Amsterdam: Elsevier, 2001), 2293–397.

25. Mary Ann Cejka and Alice Eagly, "Gender-Stereotypic Images of Occupations Correspond to the Sex Segregation of Employment," *Personality and Social Psychology Bulletin* 25, no. 4 (1999): 413–23.

26. Tak Wing Chan, "Revolving Doors Reexamined: Occupational Segregation Over the Life Course," *American Sociological Review* 64, no. 1 (February 1999): 86–96.

27. MacLean, *Freedom Is Not Enough.*

28. James W. Walker, *Human Resource Planning* (New York: McGraw Hill, 1980). According to Walker, "While much attention has been devoted to recruitment and selection, less attention has been given the way employees are promoted or transferred among jobs in a company" (261). EEO demands have focused on external hiring more than internal, leaving the promotional process up to employer discretion.

29. Important contributions regarding clerical work before World War II include Cindy S. Aron, *Ladies and Gentlemen of the Civil Service: Middle-Class Workers in Victorian America* (New York: Oxford University Press, 1987); Margery W. Davies, *Women's Place Is at the Typewriter: Office Work and Office Workers,1870–1930* (Philadelphia: Temple University Press, 1982); Ileen DeVault, *Sons and Daughters of Labor: Class and Clerical Work in Turn-of-the-Century Pittsburgh* (Ithaca, N.Y.: Cornell University Press, 1990); Sharon Hartmann Strom, *Beyond the Typewriter: Gender, Class, and the Origins of Modern American Office Work, 1900–1930* (Urbana: University of Illinois Press, 1992).

30. Segregation declined by 13 percentage points in the twenty years between 1970 and 1990, but by only 3 percentage points over the next twenty years, with some variation by race. According to this report, since 1950 the percentage of men working in clerical careers, relative to that of women, has not budged. Slightly more men have entered teaching and nursing. Kim A. Weeden, Mary Newhart, and Dafna Gelbgiser, *State of the Union 2018: Occupational Segregation, Pathways Poverty and Inequality Report* (Stanford Center on Poverty and Inequality), 31, https://inequality.stanford.edu/sites/default/files/Pathways_SOTU_2018_occupational-segregation.pdf. There is some evidence, however, that occupational segregation in clerical work has been declining. Using data from 1990 to 2016, an economist finds that men have been entering service and clerical occupations due to decreasing opportunities in blue-collar work. Their entrance is crowding out some lower-educated women. See Joana Duran-Franch, "Oh, Man! What Happened to Women? The Blurring of Gender-Based Occupational Segregation," working paper (July 2021), https://drive.google.com/file/d/1H2XWd5WPqRPeBrlqbWMQfrO3pryxBZ2H/view.

31. Paula England, "The Gender Revolution Uneven and Stalled," *Gender & Society* 24, no. 2 (April 2010): 149–66. Working-class women, for various reasons, are more likely to remain in female-dominated work, so the higher-paid blue-collar trades remain heavily male.

32. Economists Francine Blau and Lawrence Kahn find that the sorting of men and women into different occupations (whether by choice or as a result of discrimination) is the single greatest factor accounting for the gender pay gap, comprising over 30 percent of the overall wage differential. Blau and Kahn, "The Gender Wage Gap: Extent, Trends, and Explanations," *Journal of Economic Literature* 55, no. 3 (2017): 789–865.

33. Weeden, Newhart, and Gelbgiser, *State of the Union 2018*, 32.

34. For instance, about the environmental movement, see Andrew J. Hoffman, "Shades of Green," *Stanford Social Innovation Review* 7, no. 2 (Spring 2009): 40–49.

35. See Emilio Castilla and Stephen Benard, "The Paradox of Meritocracy," *Administrative Science Quarterly* 55, no. 4 (2010): 543–676; Lauren Edelman, *Working Law: Courts, Corporations, and Symbolic Civil Rights* (Chicago: University of Chicago Press, 2016); Pamela Tolbert and Emilio Castilla, "Introduction to a Special Issue on Inequality in the Workplace," *ILR Review* 70, no. 1 (2017): 3–15; Frank Dobbin and Alexandra Kalev, "Why Diversity Programs Fail," *Harvard Business Review*, July–August 2016, https://hbr.org/2016/07/why-diversity-programs-fail; and Turk, *Equality on Trial*.

36. Dorothy Sue Cobble, Linda Gordon, and Astrid Henry, *Feminism Unfinished: A Short, Surprising History of American Women's Movements* (New York: Norton, 2014); Annelise Orleck, *Rethinking American Women's Activism* (New York: Routledge, 2014).

37. Susan Hartmann, *The Other Feminists* (New Haven, Conn.: Yale University Press, 1998); Nancy Gabin, *Feminism in the Labor Movement* (Ithaca, N.Y.: Cornell University Press, 1990); Cobble, *Other Women's Movement*; Annelise Orleck, *Common Sense and a Little Fire: Women and Working-Class Politics in the United States, 1900–1965* (Chapel Hill: University of North Carolina Press, 1995); Boris and Klein, *Caring for America*.

38. Cynthia Harrison, *On Account of Sex* (Berkeley: University of California Press, 1988); Leila J. Rupp and Verta Taylor, *Survival in the Doldrums* (New York: Oxford University Press, 1987).

39. Annelise Orleck, *Storming Caesars Palace: How Black Mothers Fought Their Own War on Poverty* (Boston: Beacon Press, 2005); Premilla Nadasen, *Welfare Warriors: The Welfare Rights Movement in the United States* (New York: Routledge, 2005); Felicia Kornbluh, *The Battle for Welfare Rights: Politics and Culture in Modern America* (Philadelphia: University of Pennsylvania Press, 2007).

40. Cobble, *Other Women's Movement*; Windham, *Knocking on Labor's Door*; Turk, *Equality on Trial*.

41. See chapters 1 and 2. Some activists working to increase rights and respect for secretaries made clear that they did not consider themselves part of the feminist movement, which prioritized the concerns of white middle-class women. They even cautioned other activists against being viewed as part of the movement, ostensibly because other secretaries would perceive them as less relatable.

42. Cobble, *Other Women's Movement*; Windham, *Knocking on Labor's Door*.

43. Boris and Klein, *Caring for America*; Dorothy Sue Cobble, *Dishing It Out: Waitresses and Their Unions in the Twentieth Century* (Champaign: University of Illinois Press, 1991); Premilla Nadasen, *Household Workers Unite: The Untold Story of African American Women Who Built a Movement* (Boston: Beacon Press, 2015); Barry, *Femininity in Flight*.

44. John J. Sweeney and Karen Nussbaum, *Solutions for the New Work Force: Policies for a New Social Contract* (Santa Ana, Calif.: Seven Locks Press, 1989); Dan Clawson, *The Next Upsurge: Labor and the New Social Movements* (Ithaca, N.Y.: ILR Press, 2003).

45. Sexual harassment is rarely mentioned in the archives, although its absence from the historical record does not imply it was not happening. Perhaps it was so common that it was rarely recorded. Or perhaps in the 1970s and 1980s, despite the codification of sexual harassment as a type of sex-based discrimination under Title VII and before the

far-reaching effects of the Anita Hill–Clarence Thomas hearings, sexual harassment remained a taboo subject. Many women office workers may not have voiced complaints (to their HR managers, union organizers, professional associations, or the government) to avoid social stigmatization and risk of job loss. We can assume by the reportedly high turnover rates in clerical work that many women might have confronted sexual harassment by finding new jobs (although I did not find explicit evidence of this connection in the archives). For an excellent book on sexual harassment in office work, see Julie Berebitsky, *Sex and the Office: A History of Gender, Power, and Desire* (New Haven, Conn.: Yale University Press, 2012). Pregnancy leave is also rarely mentioned in the historical archives, likely because much of the collective activism of secretaries in the 1980s concerned other issues, such as automation and unionization. Comparable worth is not included extensively because the narrative centers activism in the private sector (and much of the activism on behalf of comparable worth occurred in the public sector). Despite the movement for comparable worth in the 1980s, which made some inroads in the public sector, women in the private sector had little recourse in the face of unfair pay scales other than through collective bargaining. See Linda M. Blum, *Between Feminism and Labor: The Significance of the Comparable Worth Movement* (Berkeley: University of California Press, 1991), and chapter 4 regarding the failure of affirmative action to account for salary.

46. Nancy Hewitt, ed., *No Permanent Waves: Recasting Histories of U.S. Feminism* (New Brunswick, N.J.: Rutgers University Press, 2010); Sara M. Evans, *Tidal Wave: How Women Changed America at Century's End* (New York: Free Press, 2003).

47. There is a rich literature about negative connotations of the feminist label despite public beliefs in favor of equality. See Debra Baker Beck, "The 'F' Word: How the Media Frame Feminism," *NWSA Journal* 10, no. 1 (Spring 1998): 139–53; Pamela Aronson, "Feminists or 'Postfeminists'?: Young Women's Attitudes Toward Feminism and Gender Relations," *Gender and Society* 17, no. 6 (December 2003): 903–22; Janice McCabe, "What's in a Label? The Relationship Between Feminist Self-Identification and 'Feminist' Attitudes Among U.S. Women and Men," *Gender and Society* 19, no. 4 (August 2005): 480–505; Pia Peltola, Melissa A. Milkie, and Stanley Presser, "The 'Feminist' Mystique: Feminist Identity in Three Generations of Women," *Gender and Society*, 18, no. 1 (February 2004): 122–44; Kay Schaffer, "Scare Words: 'Feminism,' Postmodern Consumer Culture and the Media," *Journal of Media & Cultural Studies* 12, no. 3 (1998): 321–34; Amanda D. Lotz, "Communicating Third-Wave Feminism and New Social Movements: Challenges for the Next Century of Feminist Endeavor," *Women and Language* 26, no. 1 (2003): 2–9; and Loreen N. Olson, Tina A. Coffelt, Eileen Berlin Ray, Jill Rudd, Renée Botta, George Ray, and Jenifer E. Kopfman, "'I'm All for Equal Rights, but Don't Call Me a Feminist': Identity Dilemmas in Young Adults' Discursive Representations of Being a Feminist," *Women's Studies in Communication* 31, no. 1 (2008): 104–32.

48. "Doris and Glennis Speaking," *The Willmar 8*, directed by Lee Grant, produced by Mary Beth Yarrow and Julie Thompson (1980), transcript, http://newsreel.org/transcripts/The -Willmar-8-transcript.pdf, 15–16.

49. *The Willmar 8*, 24.

50. Judy Blemesrud, "Secretary Image: A 'Tempest in a Typewriter?,'" *New York Times*, March 7, 1972.

51. Rosen, *World Split Open*, 205.

52. Patricia Bradley, *Mass Media and the Shaping of American Feminism, 1963–1975* (Jackson: University Press of Mississippi, 2003).

53. Kathryn Cirksena and Lisa Cuklanz, "Male Is to Female as ____ Is to ____: A Guided Tour of Five Feminist Frameworks for Communication Studies," in *Women Making Meaning: New Feminist Directions in Communication*, Routledge Library Editions: Communication Studies 10, ed. Lana F. Rakow (New York: Routledge, 1992), 37; John Fiske, *Television Culture* (New York: Routledge, 1987); Marilyn Crafton Smith, "Feminist Media and Cultural Politics," in *Women in Mass Communication*, 2nd ed., ed. Pamela J. Creedon (Newbury Park, Calif.: SAGE, 1992), 61–83.

54. Susan J. Douglas, *Where the Girls Are: Growing Up Female with the Mass Media* (New York: Three Rivers Press, 1994); Bonnie J. Dow, *Watching Women's Liberation, 1970: Feminism's Pivotal Year on the Network News* (Urbana: University of Illinois Press, 2014).

55. Carol Hanisch, "Struggles Over Leadership in the Women's Liberation Movement," in *Leadership and Social Movements*, ed. Colin Barker, Alan Johnson, and Michael Lavalette (New York: Palgrave, 2001), 80.

1. FEMINIST OR SECRETARY?

1. Deirdre Carmody, "General Strike by U.S. Women Urged to Mark 19th Amendment," *New York Times*, March 21, 1970.

2. David M. Dismore, "When Women Went on Strike: Remembering Equality Day, 1970," *Ms.* magazine blog, August 26, 2010, http://msmagazine.com/blog/2010/08/26/when-women-went-on-strike-remembering-equality-day-1970/.

3. Ruth Rosen, *The World Split Open: How the Modern Women's Movement Changed America* (New York: Penguin, 2000), 92–93; Flora Davis, *Moving the Mountain: The Women's Movement in America since 1960* (New York: Simon & Schuster, 1991), 114–16. According to Rosen, under Friedan's leadership, feminists declared that the Women's Strike had three main issues: the right to abortion, the right to childcare, and equal opportunity in education and employment.

4. "Women's Lib . . . Strike to Highlight Political Objectives," *Hartford Courant*, August 25, 1970.

5. "Women's Strike Tomorrow to Feature Varied Tactics," *Baltimore Sun*, August 25, 1970; "Women Rightists Plan for March," *Hartford Courant*, August 6, 1970.

6. Martha Weinman Lear, "The Second Feminist Wave," *New York Times Magazine*, March 10, 1968.

7. Rosen, *World Split Open*, 92.

8. "Friedanisms! 'I am speaking for the truly silent majority.' 'Many people think men are the enemy . . . man is not the enemy! he is the fellow victim,'" *New York Times*, November 29, 1970.

9. Susan J. Douglas, *Where the Girls Are: Growing Up Female with the Mass Media* (New York: Three Rivers Press, 1994).

10. Bonnie J. Dow, *Watching Women's Liberation, 1970: Feminism's Pivotal Year on the Network News* (Urbana: University of Illinois, 2014).

11. Rosabeth Moss Kanter, *Men and Women of the Corporation* (New York: Basic Books, 1977), 27.

12. Ideal skills changed over time depending on changing office technology. See chapter 5.

13. The Gibbs family sold the school in 1968, and it remained in corporate ownership until closing in 2011. Rose A. Doherty, *Katharine Gibbs: Beyond White Gloves* (Scotts Valley, Calif.: CreateSpace Independent Publishing Platform, 2014), 2, 25, 46. I rely heavily on Doherty, who began her career as an English teacher at Gibbs, then assumed a position as an academic dean, and was a member of the board until the Gibbs School closed in 2011.

14. Paulina Bren, *The Barbizon: The Hotel That Set Women Free* (New York: Simon & Schuster, 2021).

15. The Gibbs School distinguished itself as a more exclusive program than the clerical training classes in public school systems. Historian Ileen DeVault examines an earlier, pre-Gibbs era of clerical education in the public school system, from 1890 to 1903. She explores the life choices and career paths of students in the Pittsburgh Central High School's Commercial Department (clerical training), concluding that pursuit of clerical work had ambiguous meanings within the working class based on factors like ethnicity, gender, and social class. Devault, *Sons and Daughters of Labor: Class and Clerical Work in Turn-of-the-Century Pittsburgh* (Ithaca, N.Y.: Cornell University Press, 1990).

16. Doherty, *Katharine Gibbs*, 32–36. By the 1970s more than 25 percent of Gibbs students entered with two or more years of college. David Gumpert, "Women's Liberation Has All but Bypassed the Katy Gibbs Chain," *Wall Street Journal*, March 15, 1974.

17. KGS catalog 1922–23, box 5, folder 44, KGS Records.

18. "Nobody Ever Called Her Katie," *Gibbsonian*, 1985, p. 6, box 5, folder 44, KGS Records. Also see Doherty, *Katharine Gibbs*, 21, 37.

19. Jane See White, "The Growing Secretarial Shortage," *Los Angeles Times*, December 16, 1981.

20. KGS catalog 1927, box 5, folder 44, KGS Records.

21. Gumpert, "Women's Liberation."

22. White, "Growing Secretarial Shortage."

23. Gumpert, "Women's Liberation."

24. Carol Kleinman, "When Hotpants Hit the Office," *Chicago Tribune*, April 29, 1971.

25. "Katie Gibbs Grads Are Secretarial Elite," *Business Week*, September 2, 1961, 42.

26. Doherty, *Katharine Gibbs*, 1–3, 28–30, 42–45.

27. "The Private Secretary: Her Qualifications and Requirements," Katharine Gibbs School, 1959, pp. 5–7, box 4, subseries 5, KGS Records.

28. "The Private Secretary," 4.

29. White, "Growing Secretarial Shortage."

30. Doherty, *Katharine Gibbs*, 4, 147.

31. White, "Growing Secretarial Shortage."

32. Doherty, *Katharine Gibbs*, 4, 118.

33. Martha Weinman Lear, "The Amanuensis: Evolution and Revolution of the Secretary Over Half a Century," *New York Times*, October 15, 1961; Clare M. Reckert, "Publisher in Bid for Gibbs School," *New York Times*, June 30, 1968.

34. Gumpert, "Women's Liberation," 1.

35. Nell Braly Noyes, *Your Future as a Secretary* (New York: Richards Rosen, 1970), 60–61.

36. Quoted from Nellie Hardy, *The Secretary*, October 1962, in Lucy Graves Mayo, *You Can Be an Executive Secretary* (New York: Macmillan, 1965), 190.

37. Noyes, *Your Future as a Secretary*, 62. By 1970 more than five thousand secretaries had achieved the CPS rating.

38. *Report of the Commission on the Status of NSA*, November 8, 1968, p. 7, box 6, folder 27, NSA, Philadelphia Records.

39. Noyes, *Your Future as a Secretary*, 60–61.

40. Historian Barbara Welter first described what would be known as separate-spheres ideology, meaning that women had their own sphere or domain of influence over the domestic realm while men took charge in the more public arenas of politics and commerce. Because women were believed to have distinct innate abilities relative to men, they were to honor their roles as wives and mothers by cultivating four traits (piety, purity, submissiveness, and domesticity), which would contribute to the well-being of their families and the larger society. Barbara Welter, "The Cult of True Womanhood: 1820–1860," *American Quarterly* 18, no. 2 (1966): 151–74. Also see Nancy F. Cott, *The Bonds of Womanhood: "Woman's Sphere" in New England, 1780–1835* (New Haven, Conn.: Yale University Press, 1997); and Linda K. Kerber, "Separate Spheres, Female Worlds, Woman's Place: The Rhetoric of Women's History," *Journal of American History* 75, no. 1 (1988): 9–39.

41. Marie Lauria, *How to Be a Good Secretary* (New York: Fell, 1969), 24–35.

42. Lauria, 30–32, 60–61.

43. Noyes, *Your Future as a Secretary*, 139–40.

44. Patricia Flynn, *So You Want to Be an Executive Secretary* (New York: Macfadden Books, 1963), 13.

45. Mayo, *You Can Be an Executive Secretary*, 234.

46. "The Private Secretary," 11.

47. Bernice C. Turner, *The Private Secretary's Manual*, 3rd ed. (Englewood Cliffs, N.J.: Prentice-Hall, 1963), 225.

48. Flynn, *So You Want to Be an Executive Secretary*, 75.

49. Lauria, *How to Be a Good Secretary*, 30–32, 40, 28.

50. Flynn, *So You Want to Be an Executive Secretary*, 126, 158.

51. Lauria, *How to Be a Good Secretary*, 30–32, 52–54, 38–39.

52. Helen Whitcomb and John Whitcomb, *Strictly for Secretaries*, rev. ed. (New York: Mcgraw-Hill, 1965), 125, 124.

53. Lauria, *How to Be a Good Secretary*, 25
54. Lauria, 26.
55. Whitcomb and Whitcomb, *Strictly for Secretaries*, 112.
56. Turner, *Private Secretary's Manual*, 220, 222, 232.
57. Turner, 232.
58. Lauria, *How to Be a Good Secretary*, 51.
59. Flynn, *So You Want to Be an Executive Secretary*, 75.
60. Remington Rand, *How to Be a Super-Secretary* (New York: Remington Rand, 1951).
61. "A Model Secretary," *LIFE Magazine*, March 12, 1951. The secretarial school was called Wright MacMahon Secretarial School.
62. Mayo, *You Can Be an Executive Secretary*, 131.
63. Mayo, 142.
64. Whitcomb and Whitcomb, *Strictly for Secretaries*, 33.
65. Mayo, *You Can Be an Executive Secretary*, 130.
66. Evelyn G. Day, ed., *Secretaries on the Spot: A Collection of Actual Secretarial Problems and How They Were Solved* (Kansas City, Mo.: National Secretaries Association International, 1961), 5, 3.
67. "International Secretary of the Year," NSA Reports no. 3, October 1979, box 6, folder 32, NSA, Philadelphia Records.
68. Noyes, *Your Future as a Secretary*, 82–84; Whitcomb and Whitcomb, *Strictly for Secretaries*, 24; Mayo, *You Can Be an Executive Secretary*, 19.
69. Flynn, *So You Want to Be an Executive Secretary*, 68.
70. Whitcomb and Whitcomb, *Strictly for Secretaries*, 51.
71. Mayo, *You Can Be an Executive Secretary*, 122.
72. Flynn, *So You Want to Be an Executive Secretary*, 69.
73. Whitcomb and Whitcomb, *Strictly for Secretaries*, 33.
74. Flynn, *So You Want to Be an Executive Secretary*, 70–71.
75. Mayo, *You Can Be an Executive Secretary*, 143.
76. Turner, *Private Secretary's Manual*, v.
77. Noyes, *Your Future as a Secretary*, 97.
78. Doherty, *Katharine Gibbs*, 126
79. Mayo, *You Can Be an Executive Secretary*, v.
80. Lauria, *How to Be a Good Secretary*, 36, 5–6
81. Flynn, *So You Want to Be an Executive Secretary*, 121.
82. Whitcomb and Whitcomb, *Strictly for Secretaries*, 160.
83. Flynn, *So You Want to Be an Executive Secretary*, 82, 1, 21.
84. Lauria, *How to Be a Good Secretary*, 37
85. Noyes, *Your Future as a Secretary*, 108, 98.
86. Turner, *Private Secretary's Manual*, 227.
87. Whitcomb and Whitcomb, 152, 153.
88. Flynn, *So You Want to Be an Executive Secretary*, 19.
89. Whitcomb and Whitcomb, *Strictly for Secretaries*, 14–15.
90. Mayo, *You Can Be an Executive Secretary*, vi, 7, 240.

91. Aligning suburban homes with "concentration camps" comes from Betty Friedan, *The Feminine Mystique* (New York: Norton, 1963), 294.

92. Rosabeth Moss Kanter, "Where You Stand in the Power Play," *Working Woman* 2, no. 10 (October 1977): 29. Finette McCotter, a Katharine Gibbs graduate, had worked as a secretary for ten years and claimed she wanted to be called a secretary, not an administrative assistant: "People are always trying to promote me . . . I love what I am doing."

93. Carol Hanisch, "A Critique of the Miss America Protest," 1968, http://carolhanisch.org /CHwritings/MissAmericaProtestCritique.pdf.

94. Lear, "Second Feminist Wave."

95. Julie Berebitsky, *Sex and the Office: A History of Gender, Power, and Desire* (New Haven, Conn.: Yale University Press, 2012), 209–10.

96. Lear, "Second Feminist Wave."

97. Judy Blemesrud, "Secretary Image: A 'Tempest in a Typewriter'?," *New York Times*, March 7, 1972.

98. As early as the 1930s, cultural messages (advertising, novels, movies, comic books) started to depict secretaries as undermining companionate marriage. At times in these representations, secretaries actively used their sexual appeal to tempt married men; in other cases, bosses used their institutional power to force secretaries to submit to their sexual needs. Berebitsky, *Sex and the Office*, 117–40.

99. Helen Gurley Brown angered progressive and conservative women alike with her calls for women to use their sexuality to get ahead at work. Brown's advice to women in her own books and her influence as the founding editor of *Cosmopolitan* alienated both new feminists and old-fashioned Gibbs School teachers. In *Having It All: Love Success, Sex, Money, Even If You're Starting with Nothing* (New York: Simon & Schuster, 1982), Brown wrote: "Does a *man* ever have to choose between being a totally sexual person and loving his work? Of course not, and neither do *you*! You can put love of men *and* love of work first" (19). Brown did not see work and sex as incompatible priorities for women. She claimed that women had to have the requisite "talent and brains" to advance but also could make use of their own sexuality. She countered the Victorian-inspired ideals of the Gibbs School: that a secretary should remain untarnished and chaste if she were to leave her job to become a wife.

100. Brown refers to herself as a "devout feminist" in an interview on CNN in 1996. Emanuella Gringberg, "Helen Gurley Brown's Complicated Feminist Legacy," August 19, 2012, https://www.cnn.com/2012/08/17/living/helen-gurley-brown-legacy/index.html.

101. "Don't sex around in your bread-and-butter bailiwick. Call it prudish, reactionary or unhip. I'll still swear by that commandment. Define the parameters of your professional circle and draw the line on sexual adventure right there." Letty Cottin Pogrebin, *How to Make It in a Man's World* (Garden City, N.Y.: Doubleday, 1970), 168. In *Getting Yours: How to Make the System Work for the Working Woman* (New York: McKay, 1975), Pogrebin claimed that women who used their sexuality to try to get ahead at work were suggesting that "a woman couldn't possibly have achieved success by virtue of her superior ability and hard work" (89). Women should avoid mixing sex and work, and

trying to exploit their own attractiveness, so that colleagues would stop reading "sex into every male/female encounter" in the workplace (88).

102.   Mayo, *You Can Be an Executive Secretary*, 231, 232, 117.

103.   Mayo, 117.

104.   George Gallup, "Office Rated Best Husband Hunting Group in the U.S.," *Washington Post*, May 12, 1952.

105.   Lear, "Amanuensis."

106.   Sheila Cronan, "Marriage," in *Radical Feminism: The Book*, ed. Anne Koedt, Ellen Levine, and Anita Rapone (New York: Times Books, 1973). Others included Judith Brown, Marlene Brown, Andrea Dworkin, and Germaine Greer.

107.   Alice Echols, *Daring to Be Bad: Radical Feminism in America 1967–1975* (Minneapolis: University of Minnesota Press, 1989), 178.

108.   Turner, *Private Secretary's Manual*, 228, 229.

109.   Lillian Doris and Besse May Miller, *Complete Secretary's Handbook* (Englewood Cliffs, N.J.: Prentice-Hall, 1951), 367, 369–70, 372.

110.   Whitcomb and Whitcomb, *Strictly for Secretaries*, 99.

111.   Whitcomb and Whitcomb, 112.

112.   White, "Growing Secretarial Shortage."

113.   Noyes, *Your Future as a Secretary*, 100, 103.

114.   W. H. Whyte, "The Wives of Management," *Fortune* 44 (October 1951): 86.

115.   Noyes, *Your Future as a Secretary*, 97.

116.   Flynn, *So You Want to Be an Executive Secretary*, 153.

117.   Pat Mainardi, "The Politics of Housework," in *Sisterhood Is Powerful: An Anthology of Writings from the Women's Liberation Movement*, ed. Robin Morgan (New York: Vintage Books, 1970), 447–54.

118.   Kessler-Harris, introduction, *In Pursuit of Equity*, 3–18.

119.   Betty Friedan, *The Feminine Mystique* (New York: Norton, 1963), 307, 309.

120.   Miriam Gilbert, "Women in Medicine," in *Sisterhood Is Powerful*, 63.

121.   Mayo, *You Can Be an Executive Secretary*, 5.

122.   Mayo, 6.

123.   Jean Caldwell, "Gloria Steinem Says at Smith, the College Is Not Ready for Males," *Boston Globe*, May 31, 1971.

124.   In "The Secretarial Proletariat," Judith Ann Duffett warns against this notion that secretaries are unaware of their own oppression. Yet she acknowledges the belief that many held about secretaries and false consciousness. "Maybe some readers of this article will think that I was unusual among clerical workers because I knew that I was being exploited and rebelled against it. Maybe some of you think that most clerical workers accept and even like their lot and don't care about changing it. But it's not true." Judith Ann Duffett, "The Secretarial Proletariat," in *Sisterhood Is Powerful*, 100.

125.   Carol Hanisch, "The Personal Is Political: The Women's Liberation Movement Classic with a New Explanatory Introduction," 1969, 2006, http://www.carolhanisch.org /CHwritings/PIP.html.

126. Rosen, *World Split Open*, 160. Reported correctly by the *New York Times* on the day of the protest but a few weeks later referenced as bra burning.

127. bell hooks, *Feminist Theory: From Margin to Center* (Boston: South End Press, 1984), 2–3.

128. Seminal feminist theory by women of color includes collections such as Beverly Guy-Sheftall, ed., *Words of Fire: An Anthology of African-American Feminist Thought* (New York: New Press, 1995); and Cherrie Moraga and Gloria Anzaldúa, eds., *This Bridge Called My Back: Writings by Radical Women of Color* (New York: Kitchen Table Women of Color Press, 1984).

129. Jacqueline Jones, *Labor of Love, Labor of Sorrow* (New York: Basic Books, 1985).

130. Timothy J. Minchin, *Hiring the Black Worker: The Racial Integration of the Southern Textile Industry, 1960–1980* (Chapel Hill: University of North Carolina Press, 1999), 161–204.

131. James Booker, "High City Official Turns Down Negro Secretary," *New York Amsterdam News*, June 8, 1963.

132. Katherine Turk, *Equality on Trial: Gender and Rights in the Modern American Workplace* (Philadelphia: University of Pennsylvania Press, 2016), 37.

133. Judith B. Bremner, "Black Pink Collar Workers: Arduous Journey from Field and Kitchen to Office," *Journal of Sociology & Social Welfare* 19, no. 3 (1992): 16–17.

134. Dorothy Irene Height, Black Women Oral History Project, Schlesinger Library.

135. Era Bell Thompson, Black Women Oral History Project, Schlesinger Library.

136. "Negro Secretary to Dever First of Race So Honored," *Daily Boston Globe*, June 12, 1951; "Massachusetts Governor Names Negro Secretary," *New York Herald Tribune*, June 12, 1951.

137. "State Labor Head Hires Negro Secretary," *Chicago Defender*, February 14, 1961.

138. "First Negro in Lake Shore Chapter of National Secretaries Association," *Chicago Defender*, June 15, 1963.

139. "Tennessee Congressman Hires a Negro Secretary," *Wall Street Journal*, June 19, 1963.

140. "Fla. VA Hires First Negro Secretaries," *Chicago Defender*, June 18, 1963.

141. "Zanuck Hires Negro Secretary," *Chicago Defender*, October 23, 1962.

142. Annelise Orleck, *Common Sense and a Little Fire: Women and Working-Class Politics in the United States, 1900–1965* (Chapel Hill: University of North Carolina Press, 1995); Dorothy Sue Cobble, *The Other Women's Movement: Workplace Justice and Social Rights in Modern America* (Princeton, N.J.: Princeton University Press, 2004); Lane Windham, *Knocking on Labor's Door: Union Organizing in the 1970s and the Roots of a New Economic Divide* (Chapel Hill: University of North Carolina Press, 2017).

143. Linda Charlton, "Women March Down Fifth in Equality Drive," *New York Times*, August 27, 1970.

144. Doherty, *Katharine Gibbs*, 157.

145. "The Death of the Dead-End Secretary," advertisement for Redactron, *New York*, December 20, 1971, 21.

146. Laurie Johnston, "Women's Caucus Has a New Rallying Cry: 'Make Policy, Not Coffee,'" *New York Times*, February 6, 1972.

147.   Douglas, *Where the Girls Are.*

148.   Dagmar Miller, "Not JUST a Secretary," *Washington Post*, November 14, 1971.

2. AT THE INTERSECTION OF SEX EQUALITY
AND ECONOMIC JUSTICE

1.   Dorothy Sue Cobble, *Dishing It Out: Waitresses and Their Unions in the Twentieth Century* (Champaign: University of Illinois Press, 1991), 201.

2.   Robin Freedberg, "Waitresses Strike Against Square Regular," *Harvard Crimson*, June 15, 1972, http://www.thecrimson.com/article/1972/6/15/waitresses-strike-against -square-regular-pa/.

3.   The following works detail some of the women who did join the labor movement in their fight against sex discrimination: Annelise Orleck, *Common Sense and A Little Fire: Women and Working-Class Politics in the United States, 1900–1965* (Chapel Hill: University of North Carolina Press, 1995); Dorothy Sue Cobble, *The Other Women's Movement: Workplace Justice and Social Rights in Modern America* (Princeton, N.J.: Princeton University Press, 2004); Lane Windham, *Knocking on Labor's Door: Union Organizing in the 1970s and the Roots of a New Economic Divide* (Chapel Hill: University of North Carolina Press, 2017); and Katherine Turk, *Equality on Trial: Gender and Rights in the Modern American Workplace* (Philadelphia: University of Pennsylvania Press, 2016). For a summary, see Allison Elias, *Nevertheless, They Persisted: Feminisms and Continued Resistance in the U.S. Women's Movement*, ed. Jo Reger (New York: Routledge, 2019), 204–20.

4.   "Karen Nussbaum: In Conversation with Dorothy Sue Cobble and Alice Kessler-Harris," in *Talking Leadership: Conversations with Powerful Women*, ed. Mary S. Hartman (New Brunswick, N.J.: Rutgers University Press, 1999), 136, 137.

5.   Angela Taylor, "Pants Suits for the City Stir Debate," *New York Times*, August 20, 1964. Women in the new feminist era questioned appropriate office attire, asking why corporate policies mandated skirts, with some arguing that this policy existed just so that men could enjoy seeing a woman's legs. Yet other women acknowledged that they liked wearing skirts because they were more slimming than pants or because they were more feminine than pants (and pants were for men).

6.   Kathi Roche, "The Secretary: Capitalism's House Nigger," Pittsburgh, Pa., 1975, Women's Liberation Movement Print Culture, Atlanta Lesbian Feminist Alliance (ALFA) Archives, Duke University, https://idn.duke.edu/ark:/87924/r3rxox. Ruhi Khan addresses whether slavery should be invoked to bring visibility to the issues of white feminists in "How White Feminists and Elites Appropriated Slavery, and Still Do," London School of Economics blog, October 1, 2020, https://blogs.lse.ac.uk/medialse/2020 /10/01/how-white-feminists-and-elites-appropriated-slavery-and-still-do/.

7.   This book references the left-leaning movements of the 1960s because these were the ones in which Nussbaum and other 9to5 members were engaged. Recent work,

however, challenges the idea that the 1960s was a time of rebellion for the Left only. Beginning in the 1950s, white middle-class Americans from the Left and the Right began to "romanticize the outsider." Political conservatives and Christian evangelicals, as well as students in the New Left, could claim outsider status to assert new identities and exist as part of an emerging collective milieu. Grace Elizabeth Hale, *A Nation of Outsiders: How the White Middle Class Fell in Love with Rebellion in Postwar America* (New York: Oxford University Press, 2011). Also on the 1960s, see two collections: Alexander Bloom and Wini Breines, eds., *"Takin' It To the Streets": A Sixties Reader*, 2nd ed. (New York: Oxford University Press, 2002); David Farber, ed., *The Sixties: From Memory to History* (Chapel Hill: University of North Carolina Press, 1994).

8. Karen Nussbaum, interview by Ann Froines, Washington, D.C., November 16, 2006, SEIU District 925 Legacy Project.

9. Karen Nussbaum to Dick Cordtz, June 19, 1981, box 4, folder 7, SEIU District 925 Collection; Virginia Groark, "Annette Nussbaum, 79: Activist, Fun-loving Mom, Grandma," obituary, *Chicago Tribune*, April 7, 2003.

10. Karen Nussbaum, Voices of Feminism Oral History Project, Sophia Smith Collection, 1, 5–7.

11. Nussbaum, interview by Ann Froines.

12. "Nussbaum," in *Talking Leadership*, 137.

13. Nussbaum, Voices of Feminism Oral History Project, 9–11, 14–15. In the body of literature about women in mixed-gender organizations of the New Left and the civil rights movement, scholars and participant-writers have explained that the structure of these organizations often did not foster women's leadership. These associations often propelled traditional gender roles for men and women. Men led the organizations and created the strategies while they relied on women for day-to-day administrative tasks that kept the groups functioning. Many women became more aware of gender-based oppression through the pursuits of the New Left, leading them to embrace women-only groups for progressive activities and discussion. See, for instance, Alice Echols, *Daring to Be Bad: Radical Feminism in America 1967–1975* (Minneapolis: University of Minnesota Press, 1989), 23–50; Robin Morgan, ed., *Sisterhood Is Powerful: An Anthology of Writings from the Women's Liberation Movement* (New York: Vintage Books, 1970); Sara Evans, *Personal Politics: The Roots of Women's Liberation in the Civil Rights Movement and the New Left* (New York: Random House, 1979). Evans argues that as SNCC and SDS replicated the inequitable gender norms that were found in the broader society, female activists challenged gender-based oppression by creating a women's liberation movement.

14. Judy Nicol, "U.S. Student's Close-Up of Cuba," *Los Angeles Times*, August 16, 1970.

15. Nussbaum, Voices of Feminism Oral History Project, 10, 12–14.

16. Nicol, "U.S. Student's Close-Up of Cuba."

17. "Nussbaum," in *Talking Leadership*, 137.

18. Nussbaum, interview by Ann Froines.

19. Nussbaum, Voices of Feminism Oral History Project, 14.

20. Nussbaum, Voices of Feminism Oral History Project, 18; "Tess Ewing," Cambridge Women's Heritage Project, Cambridge Women's Commission and Cambridge Historical Commission, https://www2.cambridgema.gov/Historic/CWHP/bios_e.html.

21. Nussbaum, Voices of Feminism Oral History Project, 14–15. Nussbaum provided the example of a woman in Boston who had offered karate lessons to help other women become physically and emotionally stronger.

22. Although Bread and Roses was short-lived (1969–1971), the organization participated in several activities in Boston, including studying women's history, lobbying for a women's center, and advocating for equal pay. It split because some women wanted to prioritize class inequality while others perceived sex as the main source of oppression. See Priscilla Long, "We Called Ourselves Sisters," in *The Feminist Memoir Project: Voices from Women's Liberation*, ed. Rachel Blau Duplessis and Ann Snitow (New York: Crown, 1998), 324–37. Cell 16 believed that women should liberate themselves from gender stereotyping by not wearing makeup or conforming to feminine fashion norms, and that they should abstain from sex with men to spend time on pursuits that would promise lasting social and cultural value. For more on the theory and actions of Cell 16, see Echols, *Daring to Be Bad*, 139–202. On the women's collective that wrote a pamphlet that eventually became *Our Bodies, Ourselves* (New York: Simon & Schuster, 1973), see Kathy Davis, *The Making of Our Bodies, Ourselves: How Feminism Travels Across Borders* (Durham, N.C.: Duke University Press, 2007), which uses the records of the Boston Women's Health Book Collective from the Schlesinger Library.

23. Nussbaum, interview by Ann Froines.

24. Nussbaum, Voices of Feminism Oral History Project, 19–20.

25. "Nussbaum," in *Talking Leadership*, 136–37.

26. "Nussbaum," in *Talking Leadership*, 138.

27. Other labor organizations that focused on clerical workers at this time included Union WAGE, an organization on the West Coast; the Harvard Union of Clerical and Technical Workers; District 65, a national union that later became part of the UAW; and the Office and Professional Employees International Union.

28. Doreen Levasseur, interview by Ann Froines, Braintree, Mass., February 23, 2005, SEIU District 925 Legacy Project; David S. Broder, *Changing of the Guard: Power and Leadership in America* (New York: Simon and Schuster, 1980), 144–45.

29. Morgan, *Sisterhood Is Powerful*; Evans, *Personal Politics*.

30. Ellen Cassedy, interview by Ann Froines, Washington, D.C., November 6, 2005, SEIU District 925 Legacy Project. Although they shared many similar values, Nussbaum and Cassedy had vastly different temperaments and personalities. Whereas Nussbaum was a natural leader who was eager to take action, Cassedy describes herself as "developing new muscles and going against the grain of what [she'd] been brought up to do" in her work on behalf of 9to5. As a child she was afraid to call a theater to inquire about the time of a movie, usually employing the aid of a written script. In college she began to feel more comfortable asserting herself in the Berkeley atmosphere.

31. For memos and newsletters of the Harvard Office Workers' Group (HOWG), see box 18, folder 14, Harvard Union Records.

32. Ellen Cassedy, Karen Nussbaum, and Debbie Schneider, interview by Ann Froines, Washington, D.C., November 1, 2005, SEIU District 925 Legacy Project. According to Nussbaum (transcript, 1), not all of the initial ten women worked at Harvard. One was a secretary in a shoe factory, another in a hospital, a couple in universities, and some in insurance companies.

33. "Nussbaum," in *Talking Leadership*, 138.

34. "High Prices-Low Wages," 9to5 newsletter for Boston area workers, vol. 1, no. 4 (Summer 1973), box 1, folder 20, SEIU District 925 Collection.

35. "Nussbaum," in *Talking Leadership*, 139. The memo claimed that men interrupted female office workers during their lunch hours, expecting them to make photocopies on demand. Women working in labs routinely were denied promotions to the position of research assistant, although they did the same work as male research assistants. Lastly, the memo demanded significant raises of $1,000 (which was about a 20 percent increase) for many female-dominated roles.

36. "Nussbaum," in *Talking Leadership*, 138–39.

37. For other works on the Harvard clerical organizing movement, see John Hoerr, *We Can't Eat Prestige: The Women Who Organized Harvard*, Labor and Social Change series (Philadelphia: Temple University Press, 1997); Robert D. Putnam and Lewis M. Feldstein, "The Harvard Union of Clerical and Technical Workers," in *Better Together: Restoring the American Community* (New York: Simon & Schuster, 2003), 166–85; John Trumpbour, ed., *How Harvard Rules: Reason in the Service of Empire* (Boston: South End Press, 1989).

38. "G.A.I.U. on Strike!," c. 1974, box 18, folder 14, Harvard Union Records. Also see John P. Hardt, "Harvard's Unions: The Printers Ask for More Money," *Harvard Crimson*, June 13, 1974.

39. *Harvard Crimson*, June 4, 1976, MC 624, box 21, folder 6, Harvard Union Records. Dining hall employees were part of the Local 26 chapter of the Hotel, Restaurant, and Institutional Employees Union.

40. "Personnel Matter in Progress," *Harvard Crimson*, October 19, 1974. Representatives from the HEOC and the association for medical employees attended one of the first 9to5 conferences for university workers in 1974. See Natalie Wexler, "Boston Conference Seeks to Organize University Workers," *Harvard Crimson*, October 5, 1974. Articles about and documents from the HEOC can be found in box 18, folder 13, Harvard Union Records.

41. Hoerr, *We Can't Eat Prestige*.

42. "The Fourth Estate," *HBS Staff Association News*, no. 7, May 25, 1973; "Memo to Faculty/Staff Advisory Committee on Conditions of Work and Employment from Task Force on Perquisites Re: Outline Submitted for Suggestions and Comments," May 8, 1974; "Statement of Purpose and Goals, 1973," all in MC624, box 18, folder 14, Harvard Union Records.

43. *Coffee Break*, newsletter of Boston University workers, vol. 1, no. 3, July 1974, box 7, folder 29, SEIU District 925 Collection.

44. "Where Are All the Women at Harvard?" 1974, MC624, box 18, folder 13, Harvard Union Records.

45. Robin Freedberg, "Women Form Employee Group in Atmosphere of Tense Distrust,"
     Harvard Crimson, June 14, 1973; "Affirmative Action," letter to the editor from copresi-
     dent of Graduate Women's Organization, *Harvard Crimson*, July 31, 1973. Thirty-three
     female faculty members and administrators started meeting and formed what became
     known the next year as WEH.
46. Freedberg, "Women Form Employee Group in Atmosphere of Tense Distrust."
47. "University Women Lay Foundation for Organization," *Harvard Crimson*, May 18, 1973.
48. Nussbaum, Voices of Feminism Oral History Project, 20, 19, 22.
49. Bob Greene, "Secretary's 'Duty' Leaves a Bitter Taste," *Chicago Tribune*, August 1, 1988.
50. "Secretaries Are Forever!" NSA Reports no. 4, November 1979, box 6, folder 32, NSA,
     Philadelphia Records.
51. Cassedy, Nussbaum, and Schneider, interview by Ann Froines, transcript, 3.
52. "Nussbaum," in *Talking Leadership*, 138.
53. Draft of speech for National Convention, 1978, carton 2, folder 65, 9to5 Records.
54. Pat Mainardi, "The Politics of Housework," in *Sisterhood Is Powerful*, 447–54.
55. Karen Nussbaum, Ellen Cassedy, Marilyn Albert, and Penny Kurland were four of the
     ten, but I have not found the other names in the archives or oral histories.
56. Cassedy, interview by Ann Froines; Brochure for Women's Assembly on April 29, car-
     ton 1, folder 3, 9to5 Records. Issues at the Women's Assembly conference included win-
     ning girls at a local high school the right to wear slacks, supporting a local strike of
     waitresses at Cronin's Restaurant, and trying to establish women's history courses and
     a women's center at a local college.
57. Cassedy, interview by Ann Froines.
58. Karen Nussbaum, speech, 1973, carton 2, folder 47, 9to5 Additional Records A.
59. Cassedy, interview by Ann Froines.
60. Cassedy, Nussbaum, and Schneider, interview by Ann Froines.
61. Cassedy, interview by Ann Froines; Nussbaum, Voices of Feminism Oral History Proj-
     ect, 23.
62. Box 1, folder 20, SEIU District 925 Collection. The early issues of the 9to5 newsletter
     did not hide 9to5's allegiances to other social movements. The first newsletter, Decem-
     ber 1972/January 1973, included an article, "Some Costs to the War," that criticized the
     Nixon administration's fiscal policies. The second newsletter ran pieces about a cease-
     fire agreement in Vietnam and an advocacy organization called the Indochina Peace
     Campaign. By the third issue, 9to5 was encouraging readers to boycott lettuce on behalf
     of the United Farm Workers and reporting on the conditions of the jails for prisoners
     of war in Saigon. Soon, 9to5 narrowed its focus.
63. Previous histories of clerical work in the early twentieth century also have demonstrated
     diversity in demographic factors like race, ethnicity, class, and education. Lisa M. Fine,
     The Souls of the Skyscraper: Female Clerical Workers in Chicago, 1870–1930, Women of
     Letters series (Philadelphia: Temple University Press, 1990); Ileen DeVault, *Sons and
     Daughters of Labor: Class and Clerical Work in Turn-of-the-Century Pittsburgh* (Ithaca,
     N.Y.: Cornell University Press, 1990).

64. Cassedy, Nussbaum, and Schneider, interview by Ann Froines.

65. To show that Boston clerical workers made substandard wages relative to clericals in other major U.S. cities, 9to5 issued many reports on wages and the cost of living. For instance, in 1977, using a poverty line of $6,200, over 50 percent of file clerks in the Boston insurance industry (chapter 4) made less than poverty-level wages. "Office Work in Boston: A Statistical Study," by 9to5 Organization for Women Office Workers, box 5, folder 127, 9to5 Records.

66. Box 1, folder 20, SEIU District 925 Collection.

67. Joyce C. Weston, "Girls Till We Retire," 9to5 newsletter for Boston area office workers, vol. 1, no. 4 (Summer 1973), box 1, folder 20, SEIU District 925 Collection.

68. "Working Downtown," 9to5 newsletter for Boston area office workers, vol. 1, no. 1 (December 1972/January 1973), box 1, folder 20, SEIU District 925 Collection.

69. "Hospitality," 9to5 newsletter for Boston area office workers, vol. 1, no. 2 (February/March 1973), box 1, folder 20, SEIU District 925 Collection.

70. "Every Morning . . . ," 9to5 newsletter for Boston area office workers, vol. 1, no. 1 (December 1972/January 1973), box 1, folder 20, SEIU District 925 Collection.

71. "What's Happening . . . ," 9to5 newsletter for Boston area office workers, vol. 1, no. 4 (Summer 1973), box 1, folder 20, SEIU District 925 Collection.

72. 9to5 newsletter for Boston area office workers, vol. 2, no. 1 (December 1973/January 1974), box 1, folder 20, SEIU District 925 Collection.

73. Karen Nussbaum, speech, 1974, carton 2, folder 47, 9to5 Additional Records A.

74. Joan Quinlan, 9to5 Leader, speech, carton 2, folder 47, 9to5 Additional Records A.

75. According to the Jewish Women's Archive, Heather Booth founded movements for women's rights on college campuses and began JANE, an early organization for abortion counseling. "Feminism," Jewish Women's Archive, https://jwa.org/feminism, accessed October 1, 2021.

76. Heather Tobis Booth, interview by Stacey Heath, May 17, 2006, SEIU District 925 Legacy Project, http://reuther.wayne.edu/files/LOH000682.02.00.0.00.00.00.pdf.

77. Cassedy, interview by Ann Froines.

78. 9to5 newsletter for Boston area office workers, vol. 2, no. 1 (December 1973/January 1974), box 1, folder 20, SEIU District 925 Collection.

79. Although the Coalition of Labor Union Women (CLUW) was founded in 1974 at almost the same time as 9to5, Nussbaum and Cassedy remember that they were trying to create something different from CLUW, which they perceived as trapped within the male-dominated union movement. In their oral histories, Nussbaum and Cassedy claim that various factors made their strategies and goals different. CLUW was run by women a generation older, and 9to5 sought to have its own base from which women could rise to top leadership positions. Nussbaum and Cassedy set out to "transform the labor movement," while they perceived CLUW as quickly becoming "a bureaucratic labor organization that was captured by the AFL-CIO as opposed to changing, transforming the AFL-CIO." Cassedy, Nussbaum, and Schneider, interview by Ann Froines.

80. Cassedy, Nussbaum, and Schneider, interview by Ann Froines.

81. Nussbaum, interview by Ann Froines.

82. Cassedy, Nussbaum, and Schneider, interview by Ann Froines. Also see Ann Elizabeth Donner, "The Future of Women Office Workers in Trade Unions," 1981, 47, MC365, folder 9, Massachusetts History Workshop Records.

83. Nussbaum, speech, 1974. About 120 women attended this public forum.

84. 9to5, "Statistical Study of Boston Area Employment," 9to5 Organization for Women Office Workers, November 1973, 79-M16-81-M121, box 5, folder 127, 9to5 Records.

85. 9to5 reported that 41 percent of Boston's women worked for wages.

86. 9to5 newsletter for Boston area office workers, vol. 2, no. 1 (December 1973/January 1974), box 1, folder 20, SEIU District 925 Collection.

87. "9to5 Job Survey," 9to5 Organization for Women Office Workers, 1973–1974, 79-M16-81-M121, carton 2, folder 74, 9to5 Records. In addition, on the second page, employees could provide their addresses if they wanted to request more information about the organization.

88. Only one respondent reported no complaints with her job at Gillette. Many respondents did not write comments, but they did check certain issues as being workplace problems. A few said that they liked their current positions better than past positions but still had many issues in their workplaces.

89. Nancy Woloch, *A Class by Herself: Protective Laws for Women Workers, 1890s–1990s* (Princeton, N.J.: Princeton University Press, 2015).

90. "9to5 Job Survey." Among clerical workers who marked that they faced sex discrimination, one temporary agency worker wrote that "sex discrimination goes hand in hand with secretarial work." Another secretary noted, "No women in higher levels, yet we represent approx. 80% of workers at home office which is where I'm employed." Still another clerical who worked at Gillette reported that "most executives are men. I only know of two women supervisors in this whole division."

91. Although many completed surveys are included in the 9to5 papers at the Schlesinger Library, no tally sheet existed, compelling me to make my own conclusions from my observations. Folder 74 contained at least twenty-five completed surveys.

92. The Ritz Carlton clerical stated that she made $120 per week and did not receive cost-of-living raises. Furthermore, she disliked the dress code policy enough to write "a woman cannot wear pants" in her survey comments, although she did not mark sex discrimination as a workplace problem. This clerk's responses indicated that enforcement of traditional gender norms about masculinity and femininity—even if undesirable—existed beyond the boundaries of what constituted sex discrimination.

93. The organization would spread to thirteen cities across the United States and boast upward of ten thousand members at its peak in 1981, according to Lorraine Sorrel, "Working Women Organize 925," *Off Our Backs* 11, no. 4 (April 30, 1981): 8. However, given that millions of women worked in clerical jobs, the membership rate for 9to5 was low relative to total workers in the category.

94. Publishing clerical, box 1, folder 7, Tepperman Papers.

95. Ann Crittenden, "Interest in Unionizing Increases Among Female Office Workers," *New York Times*, July 9, 1979.

96. Jean Tepperman, interview with Travelers Insurance employee, no. 17, 1974–1975, MC366, box 1, folder 4, Tepperman Papers.

97. Of course, pay was a gendered issue but not as obviously so as other issues that were explicitly about gender differences. 9to5 would wage many campaigns regarding pay equity to suggest that the low salaries of clerical workers were a gender issue.

98. Box 2, folder 11, no. 46, Tepperman Papers.

99. Insurance worker, August 24, no. 10, Tepperman Papers.

100. Karen Nussbaum and others, "Good speeches," 1978, no date, carton 2, folder 47, 9to5 Additional Records A.

101. Amy E. Weisman, "9 to 5: Organization for Women Office Workers and Local 925: An Organizing Duo with New Hope for Office Workers," Spring 1981, 10, carton 2, folder 58, 9to5 Additional Records A.

102. Carton 17, folder 1081, 9to5 Additional Records B.

103. Weisman, "9 to 5: Organization for Women Office Workers and Local 925."

104. Donner, "Future of Women Office Workers in Trade Unions," 43. When collecting and analyzing these survey responses, 9to5 leaders claimed they had three motives: first, to learn more about office workers' concerns; second, to increase workers' self-awareness by having them think and write about their job problems; third, to start to form a base of support by spreading the 9to5 name.

105. Tepperman, interview with Travelers Insurance employee, no. 17.

106. Jean Tepperman, interview with Macmillan employee, no. 24, 1974–1975, MC366, box 1, folder 6, Tepperman Papers.

107. Janet Selcer, interview by Ann Froines, February 1, 2005, SEIU District 925 Legacy Project.

108. Carol Krucoff, "Careers: Take a Memo . . . It's National Secretary's Day," *Washington Post*, April 23, 1980.

109. Selcer, interview by Ann Froines, 4.

110. Strategies of 9to5 have been compared with and contrasted to those of the Women's Trade Union League of the early twentieth century because both sought to improve working conditions through organizing working women and bringing greater public awareness to their problems. Donner, "Future of Women Office Workers in Trade Unions," 48.

111. Turk, *Equality on Trial*. Dorothy Sue Cobble, Sara Evans, Ruth Rosen, Annelise Orleck, Serena Mayeri, Eileen Boris, and Kathleen Barry have written about women and their changing attitudes. Their work provides a variety of perspectives about the women's movement of the 1960s and 1970s, demonstrating that both those who organized into markedly feminist associations and those advocating for their own rights apart from the mainstream movement contributed to increased progress and opportunities for women. Furthermore, when publicly defining "sex discrimination," the federal

government could not always settle on boundaries of legal and illegal. It did not vigorously monitor Title VII of the Civil Rights Act of 1964, which outlawed private employment discrimination based on sex, race, and religion, among other characteristics. By the early 1970s the Equal Employment Opportunity Commission, which was established by the Civil Rights Act of 1964 to interpret and enforce Title VII, was burdened with several problems preventing efficient operation, including a backlog of cases and an inability to enforce its decisions. See Alfred W. Blumrosen, "Labor Arbitration, EEOC Conciliation, and Discrimination in Employment," *Dispute Resolution Journal* 24, no. 2 (1969): 88–105.

3. THE PROGRESSIONAL AND PROFESSIONAL PATHS INTERTWINED

1. "9to5 Job Survey," 9to5 Organization for Women Office Workers, 1973–1974, carton 2, folder 74, 9to5 Records. The quote in the title of this chapter is from Lynn Salvage, as quoted in Barbara Brotman, "Katharine Gibbs School: From 'Educated Women' to 'Office Teams,'" *Chicago Tribune*, November 30, 1980.
2. Carol Krucoff, "Careers: Take a Memo . . . It's National Secretary's Day," *Washington Post*, April 23, 1980.
3. Rose A. Doherty, *Katharine Gibbs: Beyond White Gloves* (Scotts Valley, Calif.: CreateSpace Independent Publishing Platform, 2014), 173. Macmillan bought the Katharine Gibbs School from the Gibbs family in 1968.
4. Brotman, "Katharine Gibbs School."
5. Thomas A. DiPrete and Whitman T. Soule, "Gender and Promotion in Segmented Job Ladder Systems," *American Sociological Review* 53, no. 1 (February 1988): 26–40; J. N. Baron, A. Davis-Blake, and W. T. Bielby, "The Structure of Opportunity: How Promotion Ladders Vary Within and Among Organizations," *Administrative Science Quarterly* 31 (1986): 248–73; Paul Osterman, "Sex Discrimination in Professional Employment: A Case Study," *ILR Review* 32, no. 4 (July 1979): 451–64; Paul Osterman and M. Diane Burton, "Ports and Ladders: The Nature and Relevance of Internal Labor Markets in a Changing World," in *The Oxford Handbook of Work and Organization*, ed. Stephen Ackroyd, Rosemary Batt, Paul Thompson, and Pamela S. Tolbert (Oxford: Oxford University Press, 2005), 426–47.
6. Anthony Chen, *The Fifth Freedom: Jobs, Politics, and Civil Rights in the United States, 1941–1972* (Princeton, N.J.: Princeton University Press, 2009); Nelson Lichtenstein, *State of the Union: A Century of American Labor* (Princeton, N.J.: Princeton University Press, 2002).
7. Katherine Turk, *Equality on Trial: Gender and Rights in the Modern American Workplace* (Philadelphia: University of Pennsylvania Press, 2016); Alice Kessler-Harris, *In Pursuit of Equity: Women, Men, and the Quest for Economic Citizenship in 20th-Century America* (New York: Oxford University Press, 2001).

8. Executive Order 11375 added "sex" to the list of protected classes outlined in 11246, and women became a category of workers entitled to affirmative action guidelines. Yet the affirmative action guidelines had been created with Black men in mind. Serena Mayeri, *Reasoning from Race: Feminism, Law, and the Civil Rights Revolution* (Cambridge, Mass.: Harvard University Press, 2011).

9. Lyndon B. Johnson, "To Fulfill These Rights," commencement address at Howard University, June 4, 1965.

10. Frank Dobbin, *Inventing Equal Opportunity* (Princeton, N.J.: Princeton University Press, 2009); Lauren B. Edelman, "Legal Ambiguity and Symbolic Structures: Organizational Mediation of Civil Rights Law," *American Journal of Sociology* 97, no. 6 (May 1992): 1531–76; Chen, *Fifth Freedom*; Hugh Davis Graham, *The Civil Rights Era: Origins and Development of National Policy, 1960–1972* (New York: Oxford University Press, 1990).

11. John Tebbel, *Between Covers: The Rise and Transformation of Book Publishing in America* (New York: Oxford University Press, 1987), 85.

12. Lewis A. Coser, Charles Kadushin, and Walter W. Powell, *Books: The Culture and Commerce of Publishing* (New York: Basic Books, 1982).

13. Barbara F. Reskin and Patricia A. Roos, *Job Queues, Gender Queues: Explaining Women's Inroads into Male Occupations* (Philadelphia: Temple University Press, 1990), 94.

14. Coser, Kadushin, and Powell, *Books*, 15.

15. Ethel Strainchamps, ed., *Rooms with No View: A Woman's Guide to the Man's World of the Media* (New York: Harper & Row, 1974), 153.

16. Strainchamps, 191.

17. John Tebbel, *A History of Book Publishing in the United States*, vol. 4: *The Great Change, 1940–1980* (New York: Bowker, 1981), 727.

18. Strainchamps, *Rooms with No View*, 152.

19. Strainchamps, 173; based on Norton Publishing information.

20. Publishing clericals working in Boston often had bachelor's degrees in English, and some had graduated from elite undergraduate programs at Duke, Pomona, Berkeley, Cornell, Boston University, and Columbia. A few had started graduate work at MIT, Columbia, or Harvard before entering the publishing industry. Information on education was gathered from selected returned surveys in the Women in Publishing (WIP) Wage Survey, carton 2, folders 79 and 80, 9to5 Records.

21. Marcia Millman and Rosabeth Moss Kanter, *Another Voice: Feminist Perspectives on Social Life and Social Science* (Norwell, Mass.: Anchor Press, 1975), 50.

22. Osterman, "Sex Discrimination in Professional Employment."

23. Strainchamps, *Rooms with No View*, 154–55.

24. Reskin and Roos, *Job Queues, Gender Queues*, 96.

25. Strainchamps, *Rooms with No View*, 155.

26. Ann Geracimos, "Women in Publishing; Where Do They Feel They're Going?," *Publishers Weekly*, November 11, 1974, 26.

27. Junko Onosaka, *Feminist Revolution in Literacy: Women's Bookstores in the United States* (New York: Routledge, 2006).

28. Strainchamps, 147–49, 153, 191.

29. Strainchamps, 147.

30. Reskin and Roos, *Job Queues, Gender Queues*, 95.

31. Coser, Kadushin, and Powell, *Books*, 156–57.

32. Anita D. McClellan, "An 'Unpaid-for Education': A Feminist Labor Organizer in Boston Publishing," *Frontiers: A Journal of Women's Studies* 10, no. 3 (1989): 16–21.

33. Selected survey, WIP Job Training Questionnaire, carton 2, folder 81, 9to5 Records. She jokingly remarked that perhaps being a secretary was Allyn & Bacon's idea of a training program for female employees since a formal one did not exist.

34. Jean Tepperman, interview with associate editor at Harper and Row, no. 28, 1974–1975, MC 366, box 1, folder 7, Tepperman Papers.

35. Jean Tepperman, interview with credit analyst from Harper and Row, no. 27, 1974–1975, MC 366, box 1, folder 7, Tepperman Papers.

36. Jean Tepperman, interview with production editor at Macmillan, no. 23, 1974–1975. MC 366, box 1, folder 6, Tepperman Papers.

37. Michael Korda, "Some Crazy/Practical Ideas on Moving Up from a Secretarial Job," *Glamour*, April 1978, 224. Korda stated that staying in the same position would not lead to growth. He warned, "*Don't* get yourself assigned to one person and stick there."

38. Strainchamps, *Rooms with No View*, 192.

39. Geracimos, "Women in Publishing," 22–27; Strainchamps, *Rooms with No View*, 159.

40. Geracimos, 23, 26.

41. Geracimos, 22; Barbara A. Bannon, "Joan Manley," *Publisher's Weekly*, March 4, 1974, 8.

42. Bannon, "Joan Manley," 8, 9.

43. William Targ, "One Man's View of 'Women in Publishing,'" *Publishers Weekly*, December 2, 1974, 11–12.

44. Geracimos, "Women in Publishing," 24.

45. Strainchamps, *Rooms with No View*, 166; "Alumnae Achievement Awards 1982: Genevieve Young '52," Wellesley College, https://www.wellesley.edu/alumnae/awards /achievementawards/allrecipients/genevieve-young-52.

46. Geracimos, "Women in Publishing," 24.

47. Geracimos, "Women in Publishing," 23, 27.

48. Strainchamps, *Rooms with No View*, 157.

49. Lee Smith, "The Fight to Organize Book Publishing in New York," *Party Builder: Socialist Workers Party Organizational Discussion Bulletin* 8, no. 5 (August 1974): 18, https:// www.marxists.org/history/etol/document/swp-us/idb/party-builder/v08n5-aug-1974 -SWP-part-build.pdf.

50. Tepperman, interview with associate editor, no. 28. During the Great Depression, workers at Macmillan joined Local 18 of the United Office and Professional Workers of America (UOPWA), a union that grew out of the Book and Magazine Guild in New York. The professionals in the guild decided to affiliate with the UOPWA to get the benefits associated with unionization, since most were low paid and seeking promotions. See Jean Tepperman, interview with unionized publishing worker in the UOPWA, no. 22, 1974–1975, MC 366, box 1, folder 6, Tepperman Papers.

51. Strainchamps, *Rooms with No View*, 156.
52. Tepperman, interview with credit analyst from Harper and Row, no. 27. Also see Tepperman, interview with associate editor, no. 28; Jean Tepperman, interview with District 65 organizer in law office, no. 45, 1974–1975, MC 366, box 2, folder 11, Tepperman Papers.
53. Tepperman, interview with credit analyst, no. 27. Also see Tepperman, interview with associate editor, no. 28.
54. Strainchamps, *Rooms with No View*, 154.
55. Strainchamps, 156.
56. Tepperman, interview with associate editor, no. 28. Most of the committee's actions, such as having the women's committee sponsor a talent show and a festival, were intended to increase company morale. Thus editorial and managerial employees with substantial complaints against Harper's practices were not able to work effectively through the women's committee.
57. Strainchamps, *Rooms with No View*, 157.
58. Tepperman, interview with associate editor, no. 28.
59. Coser, Kadushin, and Powell, *Books*. As conglomerates took hold of some of the most notable publishing houses, including Harper, publishing executives suddenly began to shoulder all the shareholder pressures affecting executives in steel or oil.
60. "Professionals in Unions Cite Old Reasons: Pay, Security," *New York Times*, July 28, 1974; "Book Biz Getting Organized?," *New York Magazine*, July 8, 1974, 72.
61. Tepperman, interview with credit analyst, no. 27. Clericals in the Scranton warehouse had little interest in unionizing, and this credit analyst complained about the level of interest of those in the New York office as well.
62. Tepperman, interview with credit analyst, no. 27.
63. Tepperman, interview with associate editor, no. 28.
64. Fred Ferretti, "Going Out Guide," *New York Times*, June 25, 1974.
65. "Professionals in Unions Cite Old Reasons"; "Book Biz Getting Organized?"
66. Interviewees no. 27 (the credit analyst from Harper and Row) and no. 28 (the associate editor at Harper and Row) both cited that the strike most likely ended because the American Library Association Convention, to be held in New York in a matter of days, was fast approaching, causing Harper executives to want to end the strike by the time the convention started. Two of those in charge of the Harper and Row exhibit were on strike, and Harper executives needed them to work at the convention. Also, the convention was to be held in a hotel that was a couple of blocks from the Harper and Row office, and executives did not want the convention attendees to witness the strike. Last, the Harper and Row social events were supposed to be held in the Harper offices, and the librarians publicly stated that they would not cross picket lines to attend. Regarding union affiliation, the associate editor stated that she preferred District 65 to the OPEIU because Margie Albert (District 65 leader) seemed very genuine. She did not like the "union people who make up the union offices" of the AFL-CIO (of which the OPEIU was a part) and thought that many labor unions became "a big business" in themselves and thus were not helpful to workers' needs. See Tepperman, interviews with

credit analyst, no. 27, and associate editor, no. 28. According to a legal secretary in New York, Harper and Row chose District 65 after forming an ad hoc city committee of publishing employees who had supported the Harper strike. Three weeks after the strike, Harper activists gathered their supporters to discuss the possibility of organizing the entire industry. This committee investigated different unions, including District 65, the Newspaper Guild, and the Office and Professional Employees, and thought that District 65 was the most appropriate choice. Harper workers joined District 65 because it promised to create a publishing division while also ensuring immediate funding and emphasis on organizing. See Tepperman, interview with District 65 organizer in law office, no. 45.

67. Tepperman, interview with associate editor, no. 28. Even following the strike, the clericals in royalties declined to meet with the union to voice opinions about the proposed contract. Tepperman, interview with credit analyst, no. 27. Clericals in the Scranton warehouse had little interest in unionizing, and this credit analyst complained about the interest of those in the New York office as well.

68. Tepperman, interview with associate editor, no. 28. The pay raises were not 20 percent but were $5 or $7 (per week) increases every six months.

69. Tebbel, *History of Book Publishing in the United States*, 4:141.

70. Tepperman, interview with associate editor, no. 28.

71. I give credit here to my developmental editor Pamela Haag for "vertical feminism."

72. Smith, "The Fight to Organize Book Publishing in New York," 18.

73. Jean Tepperman, interview with assistant vice president at Macmillan, no. 24, 1974–1975, MC366, box 1, folder 6, Tepperman Papers.

74. Janet Schulman, "Looking Back: The 1974 Macmillan Massacre," *Publishers Weekly*, April 10, 2008, http://www.publishersweekly.com/pw/by-topic/childrens/childrens -industry-news/article/15635-looking-back-the-1974-macmillan-massacre.html; Tepperman, interview with assistant vice president, no. 24. The women's group formed in 1973, as female employees in the school division began to gather facts about discriminatory practices such as wage differentials between men and women and a lack of standard personnel policies, which disadvantaged them.

75. Smith, "The Fight to Organize Book Publishing in New York," 17.

76. The chief complaints included lack of maternity benefits, unequal pay, differential hiring practices, and distinct promotional tracks for men and women. Schulman, "Looking Back." The women's grassroots efforts coincided with New York attorney general Louis Lefkowitz's investigation of the employment practices at several publishing houses. He subpoenaed personnel and payroll records to examine the pattern of hiring and employment at these companies. Tepperman, interview with assistant vice president at Macmillan. Lefkowitz was investigating other New York publishing houses as well, such as McGraw-Hill and Harcourt Brace Jovanovich, and was not investigating Macmillan only in response to the protests. Also, forty-four women from Macmillan signed their names to the complaint filed with the New York State Division of Human Rights. (The Tepperman transcript names the "U.S. Commission of Human Rights" as the body of redress, but I found elsewhere that the charges in 1974 were at the state level

only. See "Four Women Bring Class Suit Against Macmillan," *Publishers Weekly*, 1974, carton 2, folder 39, 9to5 Records.)

77. Tepperman, interview with production editor at Macmillan, no. 23.

78. "A Discrimination Suit at Macmillan," *Washington Post*, September 21, 1974.

79. "Discrimination Suit at Macmillan"; Schulman, "Looking Back."

80. The policy claimed that there was not a problem with the distribution of women and racial minorities at Macmillan, but if there were it would be hard to assess because statistics were not available that would allow Macmillan to compare its demographic distribution to that of similar companies in New York. Tepperman, interview with production editor at Macmillan, no. 23. According to Tepperman's interview with another Macmillan employee (no. 24), Macmillan tried to avoid setting goals and timetables for a period by claiming that the company no longer had $50,000 worth of contracts with the Department of Defense, but after the attorney general's investigation, the company had to comply with the regulations. Tepperman, interview with assistant vice president, no. 24. The affirmative action officer happened to be a Black woman.

81. Tepperman, interview with production editor, no. 23.

82. Tepperman, interview with assistant vice president, no. 24.

83. Tepperman, interview with production editor, no. 23.

84. Smith, "The Fight to Organize Book Publishing in New York," 17.

85. Tepperman, interview with assistant vice president, no. 24. District 65 of the Distributive Workers of America, led by labor feminist Margie Albert, was the other union that was organizing in the publishing industry in New York at this time. Martin Waldron, "Two Unions Step Up Organizing Drives at Book Publishers Here," *New York Times*, October 15, 1975. District 65 was known to empower women workers and instill leadership skills in them.

86. Smith, "The Fight to Organize Book Publishing in New York," 17.

87. Tepperman, interview with production editor, no. 23. Genteel was actually written as "gentile" in the transcription of the interview in the Tepperman Papers. But within the context of the interview, genteel makes more sense.

88. Tepperman, interview with assistant vice president, no. 24; Waldron, "Two Unions Step Up."

89. Tepperman, interview with production editor, no. 23.

90. Paul L. Montgomery, "Macmillan Book Divisions Sharply Cut Their Staffs," *New York Times*, October 15, 1974.

91. Eleanor Blau, "Two Editors Quit Macmillan in Protest," *New York Times*, October 16, 1974.

92. Montgomery, "Macmillan Book Divisions Sharply Cut Their Staffs."

93. Blau, "Two Editors Quit Macmillan in Protest"; Paul L. Montgomery, "N.L.R.B. Studies Macmillan Ousters," *New York Times*, October 22, 1974. Macmillan executives attributed the dismissals to fiscal planning as they were preparing their 1975 budget, claiming that they were firing the fewest number of employees to exercise caution given the "general economic forecast for the next year." However, Macmillan sales and revenues increased in 1974 from their 1973 levels, leading employees to believe that other

factors accounted for the dismissals. See Montgomery, "Macmillan Book Divisions Sharply Cut Their Staffs."

94. Schulman, "Looking Back."

95. After the firings at Macmillan in 1974, some of the most active members of the women's group joined the union effort. Tepperman, interview with assistant vice president, no. 24.

96. Schulman, "Looking Back."

97. Blau, "Two Editors Quit Macmillan in Protest."

98. Schulman, "Looking Back."

99. Montgomery, "N.L.R.B. Studies Macmillan Ousters."

100. Tepperman, interview with production editor, no. 23. When the interview was conducted in the mid-1970s, the subject was waiting to hear from the labor board concerning union recognition and reinstatement of fired employees. Workers from almost all departments—maintenance, mailroom, finance, art and production, clerical, and editorial—had been fired and also had participated in the strike.

101. Schulman, "Looking Back"; Tepperman, interview with production editor, no. 23; Montgomery, "N.L.R.B. Studies Macmillan Ousters."

102. Schulman, "Looking Back"; Montgomery, "N.L.R.B. Studies Macmillan Ousters."

103. Montgomery, "N.L.R.B. Studies Macmillan Ousters."

104. Schulman, "Looking Back"; Leonard S. Marcus, *Minders of Make-Believe: Idealists, Entrepreneurs, and the Shaping of American Children's Literature* (New York: Houghton Mifflin, 2008), 267–69.

105. Schulman, "Looking Back."

106. "Beacon Press Team Keeps Agency Shop," News from Local 925, April 1980, box 7, folder 25, SEIU District 925 Collection. Half of an employee's tuition reimbursement would now be made halfway through a semester, with the balance paid on completion of the course. Beacon also agreed to bring long-term workers, whose pay had fallen behind the cost of living, closer to the pay range of newer employees.

107. News from Local 925, March 7, 1982, box 7, folder 25, SEIU District 925 Collection. They gained a 1 percent merit pool raise, which was evenly divided. They added a prescription plan to their health benefits and rejected the addition of management's proposed procedure of new performance reviews. News from Local 925, vol. 3, no. 3, August 1982, box 7, folder 25. Local 925 was still securing contracts at Beacon by 1985, with raises at 5 percent across the board, and 2 percent merit. News from Local 925, vol. 5, no. 1, March 1985, box 7, folder 25.

108. News from Local 925, vol. 2, no. 2, June 1980, box 7, folder 25. Employees picketed on May 1, 1980, from 7:30 A.M. to 1:30 P.M., at which time employees returned to work.

109. "Women in Publishing Announces Fall Program," press release, October 24, 1974, box 5, folder 118; Ellen Cassedy, letter to Leslie Max, August 14, 1974, carton 1, folder 27; Reskin and Roos, *Job Queues Gender Queues*, 105. There was also a group in Chicago called Women in Publishing, which seems not to be directly associated with the Boston group.

110. When founded, WIP stated that its goals were to collect information about women working in publishing firms in the Boston area, to aid women in solving problems at

those companies, and to investigate affirmative action in publishing houses and bring about compliance with the law. Women in Publishing at Boston Globe Book Festival, press release, September 30, 1974, box 5, folder 118.

111. Minutes, Minority Task Force, February 11, 1982, carton 5, folder 171, 9to5 Additional Records A.

112. McClellan, "Unpaid-for Education," 19.

113. Tepperman, interview with associate editor, no. 28. Even among the clericals, they are "also very involved with being professionals and not blue collar, nothing to do with unions because that's blue collar."

114. McClellan, "Unpaid-for Education," 19.

115. McClellan, "19.

116. When founded, WIP stated its goals as being to collect information about women working in publishing firms in the Boston area, to aid women in solving problems at those companies, and to investigate affirmative action in publishing houses and bring about compliance with the law. WIP at Boston Globe Book Festival, press release, September 30, 1974.

117. WIP, 9to5 Organization, "Women in the Boston Area Publishing Industry: A Status Report," March 1975, box 5, folder 127, 9to5 Records. This report also contained information about implementing affirmative action policies, which will be discussed in chapter 4.

118. WIP, "Women in the Boston Area Publishing Industry."

119. WIP, 9to5 Organization, "A Comparison of Benefits and Employment Policies at Boston Area Publishing Houses," Summer 1975, box 5, folder 127, 9to5 Records.

120. "Women in Publishing Presents Dubious Distinction Awards to Boston Publishing Firms," WIP press release, June 26, 1975, box 5, folder 126, 9to5 Records.

121. "Five Boston Publishers Accused of Sex Discrimination," BP Report on the Business of Book Publishing, December 1, 1975, box 5, folder 118, 9to5 Records. After almost a decade of legal wrangling, Allyn & Bacon and Addison-Wesley reached costly settlements with government authorities. See Anson Smith, "Job Bias Settlements Costly for Publishers," Boston Globe, January 22, 1981.

122. Danlia Quirk, ed., "Addison-Wesley, Allyn & Bacon, Houghton Hit with Discrimination Charges," Educational Marketer: Newsletter for Sales, Marketing and Advertising Executives in Educational Publishing, Materials and Equipment Companies 8, no. 3, December 1, 1975, box 5, folder 118, 9to5 Records.

123. "Attorney General and 9to5 Charge Publishing Companies with Discrimination," 9to5 press release, November 21, 1975, box 5, folder 126, 9to5 Records.

124. Susan Trausch, "Three Publishers Named in Discrimination Action," Evening Globe, December 3, 1975, box 5, folder 118, 9to5 Records.

125. Trausch, "Three Publishers Named in Discrimination Action"; "Bias Charge Is Filed Against 3 Publishers in the Boston Area," Wall Street Journal, December 4, 1975, box 5, folder 118, 9to5 Records.

126. "Five Boston Publishers Accused of Sex Discrimination," BP Report.

127. Quirk, "Addison-Wesley, Allyn & Bacon, Houghton Hit with Discrimination Charges."

128.   Suggestions for Job Postings from Meeting for Houghton Mifflin Women, March 10, 1976, carton 15, folder 931, 9to5 Records. WIP wanted skills, experience, salary, and the job description to be clear on the announcements, which they wanted to be posted internally for two weeks.

129.   Women in Publishing report from HMCO meeting, September 1976, carton 15, folder 931, 9to5 Records.

130.   Settlement agreement and plaintiff's statement in Nancy Garden, Linda Cox, Emily Shenk, Sandra Wright, Linda Krupp-Tong v. Houghton-Mifflin Company, December 22, 1977, carton 15, folder 935, 9to5 Records.

131.   Irene of HMWomen to Ellen Cassedy, "Commend-Recommend List," May 24, 1976, carton 15, folder 932, 9to5 Records. Salary scales were adjusted in January 1975.

132.   Strainchamps, *Rooms with No View*, 154.

133.   Information Science Incorporated and Humanic Designs Division, *How to Eliminate Discriminatory Practices: A Guide to EEO Compliance* (New York: AMACOM, 1975), 56.

134.   Jennie Farley, *Affirmative Action and the Woman Worker: Guidelines for Personnel Management* (New York: AMACOM, 1979), 29–34, 38, 39–40. Farley suggested that personnel keep records of the sex and race of applicants so that applicants who were not selected for one job could be considered for future openings.

135.   McClellan, "Unpaid-for Education," 18.

136.   "Boston Women in Publishing Hails Job Posting Efforts," in "The Week," ed. Madalynne Reuter, *Publishers Weekly*, October 11, 1976, 18, carton 2, folder 43, 9to5 Records.

137.   "Boston Women in Publishing Hails Job Posting Efforts."

138.   Paul Osterman also makes an argument for investment in training as increasing firm productivity and efficiency; he finds that more women quit at firms with fewer internal opportunities. Osterman, "Affirmative Action and Opportunity: A Study of Female Quit Rates," *Review of Economics and Statistics* 64, no. 4 (November 1982): 611.

139.   Women in Publishing, Issue Campaign Proposal: Job Posting & Job Description, [1975], carton 2, folder 43, 9to5 Records.

140.   Women in Publishing, Issue Campaign Proposal.

141.   Women in Publishing Hails Job Posting Improvements, press release, September 24, 1976, box 5, folder 126, 9to5 Records; Women in Publishing, Issue Campaign Proposal.

142.   Women in Publishing Hails Job Posting Improvements.

143.   Chen, *The Fifth Freedom*.

144.   "Boston Women in Publishing Hails Job Posting Efforts."

145.   Women in Publishing Job Posting Campaign, summary, June 17, 1976, carton 2, folder 43, 9to5 Records.

146.   "Boston Women in Publishing Hails Job Posting Efforts."

147.   Paul Osterman wrote, "There are no direct data on costs of compliance, on how expensive it is to introduce a job posting system or to alter promotional patterns" because the cost of job posting is so minimal that no one was discussing it. Osterman, "Affirmative Action and Opportunity," 605.

148. Osterman, 611; According to Osterman, job posting would allow for internal promotions from one job function to another. Most likely the association between greater enforcement activities of the OFCCP and lower female quitting rates could be attributed to opportunities for internal promotion.

149. McClellan, "Unpaid-for Education," 18.

150. Jean Tepperman, interview with associate editor at Houghton Mifflin, no. 26, 1974–1975, MC366, box 1, folder 7, Tepperman Papers.

151. Jean Tepperman, interview with organizer of Black Employee Committee at Houghton Mifflin, no. 25, 1974–1975, MC366, box 1, folder 7, Tepperman Papers.

152. Strainchamps, *Rooms with No View*, 159.

153. Heidi Hartmann, "Internal Labor Markets and Gender: A Case Study of Promotion," in *Gender in the Workplace*, ed. Clair Brown and Joseph Pechman, (Washington, D.C.: Brookings Institution, 1987), 59–105.

154. Tepperman, interview with associate editor at Harper and Row, no. 28.

155. Strainchamps, *Rooms with No View*, 148, 151.

156. WIP, 9to5 Organization, introduction to *Publishing Salaries in the Boston Area: A Comparison Report*, February 1977, box 5, folder 127, 9to5 Records.

157. Geracimos, "Women in Publishing," 27.

158. Strainchamps, *Rooms with No View*, 141.

159. WIP, 9to5 Organization, *Publishing Salaries in the Boston Area: A Comparison Report*, February 1977, box 5, folder 127, 9to5 Records. National salary data obtained from the Association of American Publishers in the 9to5 report.

160. WIP, Preliminary Fact Sheet . . . and This Is Only the Beginning! [March 1975], carton 2, folder 52, 9to5 Records. While publishing executives claimed that their profits were insecure in an increasingly unstable industry, in 1975 WIP maintained that sales numbers and stock prices had risen significantly for most area firms in 1973 and 1974. In 1977 WIP again emphasized low wages, highlighting the lower earnings of publishing employees relative to teachers. See WIP, *Publishing Salaries in the Boston Area*.

161. This is the equity theory of compensation that was advanced in the 1960s.

162. WIP, introduction to *Publishing Salaries in the Boston Area*.

163. McClellan, "Unpaid-for Education," 20.

164. On the development and implementation of sex-based policies and formal equality, see Mayeri, *Reasoning from Race*; Deborah Dinner, "The Costs of Reproduction: History and the Legal Construction of Sex Equality," *Harvard Civil Rights-Civil Liberties Law Review* 46 (2011): 415–95; Cary C. Franklin, "Inventing the 'Traditional Concept' of Sex Discrimination," *Harvard Law Review* 125, no. 6 (April 20, 2012): 1307; Turk, *Equality on Trial*.

165. Information on education gathered from selected returned surveys, WIP Wage Survey.

166. WIP, *Publishing Salaries in the Boston Area*, exhibit 4.

167. Tepperman, interview with associate editor, no. 28.

168. WIP, Job Training Program (draft), May 1977, carton 2, folder 44, 9to5 Records. Although no record exists of publishing houses employing 9to5 as a consultant, more

important is that WIP thought that managers should use its expertise to comply with affirmative action guidelines.

169.   I gathered from reading employee responses to the surveys that this was the purpose of hiring the Hay Consultants. WIP, survey on job posting at Houghton Mifflin, February 1976, carton 15, folder 936, 9to5 Records.

170.   The issue of misalignment between job titles and job descriptions, as well as discontentment due to low salaries, had motivated a failed unionization effort among many women workers in 1970. In 1974 Houghton management was also facing the state attorney general in a lawsuit over race and sex discrimination.

171.   WIP, survey on job posting at Houghton Mifflin.

172.   Joan Quinlan, handwritten notes, 9to5 with HM employees, July 17, 1978, carton 15, folder 932, 9to5 Records.

173.   Houghton Mifflin Company, "Personnel Policy," "A Summary of Our Salary Administration Program," "Organization of the Houghton Mifflin Company," and "Summary of Training Activities," 1978–1979, carton 15, folder 937, 9to5 Records.

174.   "Beacon Press Team Keeps Agency Shop."

175.   Peter B. Olney, Jr., president of Olney Association Inc. Management Consultants, letter marked "Personal/Confidential" to Mr. Wells Drorbaugh, Director of Beacon Press, September 26, 1975, box 7, folder 28, 9to5 Records. In fact, 9to5 argued that Boston wages were significantly lower than office workers' wages in other large cities like New York and Chicago, but the consultant said that was acceptable as long as Beacon wages were competitive with other Boston-area employers: "[Actual] salaries paid reflect supply and demand conditions in the local labor market," and salary equity did not require Beacon management to bring its employees' salaries in line with those of other cities regardless of the high cost of living in Boston.

176.   WIP, 9to5 Organization, "What Beacon Press Employees Have Gained Since August 1975," February 26, 1976, box 7, folder 28, 9to5 Records.

177.   Ronnie J. Steinberg, "Social Construction of Skill: Gender, Power, and Comparable Worth," *Work and Occupations* 17, no. 4 (1990): 458.

178.   Ellen Cassedy, memo to WIP Job Training Committee, "re: Work to be done following meeting of December 2," December 16, 1976, carton 2, folder 44, 9to5 Records. WIP wanted to gauge the opportunities available across firms for different job categories, including clerical, editorial, production, art, design, marketing, business administration, copy writing, and management.

179.   Strainchamps, *Rooms with No View*, 172, 153.

180.   Coser, Kadushin, and Powell, *Books*, 156.

181.   Cassedy, memo, December 16, 1976.

182.   WIP, typed charts detailing job training practices of publishing houses in Boston, carton 2, folder 44, 9to5 Records.

183.   WIP, Totals of Women in Publishing Job Training Questionnaire, carton 2, folder 44, 9to5 Records. Employees responded that they wanted more in-house courses and revealed that they would be more likely to stay at their companies if more

career training were offered. They also reported that their companies did not provide them with information about external education and training offerings at local schools and expressed interest in industry-wide training programs to teach specific skills.

184.   WIP, Job Training Questionnaire, selected surveys, carton 2, folder 81, 9to5 Records.

185.   HMCO Personnel Meeting, Subject: Job Training, August 9, 1976, carton 15, folder 931, 9to5 Records.

186.   WIP report from HMCO meeting.

187.   Geracimos, "Women in Publishing," 26.

188.   WIP, Job Training Proposals, June 1977, carton 2, folder 44, 9to5 Records.

189.   Geracimos, "Women in Publishing," 25.

190.   WIP, Job Training Proposals.

191.   WIP, Job Training Proposals.

192.   Pat Cronin, chairwoman of Women in Publishing, letter to personnel managers, June 10, 1977, carton 2, folder 81, 9to5 Records.

193.   Ellen Cassedy, "9to5 Presents Publishing Industry with Model Job Training Program," press release, June 24, 1977, box 5, folder 126, 9to5 Records.

194.   WIP, Job Training Proposals.

195.   Farley, *Affirmative Action*, 74, 75. A Bank of America affirmative action seminar reaffirmed that whether women developed a drive to pursue promotions often rested on whether supervisors gave them the confidence and guidance necessary to aspire for management. See Suki Cathy, "Bank of America's AA Seminar," in *Affirmative Action for Women: A Practical Guide for Women and Management*, ed. Dorothy Jongeward and Dru Scott (New York: Addison-Wesley, 1973), 190–91.

196.   Farley, *Affirmative Action*, 77–78.

197.   Strainchamps, *Rooms with No View*, 146.

198.   Strainchamps, 154.

199.   Geracimos, "Women in Publishing," 24.

200.   Geracimos, 23.

201.   Information Science Incorporated and Humanic Designs Division, *How to Eliminate Discriminatory Practices*, 67–68.

202.   Paul Ryan, "Job Training, Employment Practices, and the Large Enterprise: The Case of Costly Transferable Skills," in *Internal Labor Markets*, ed. Paul Osterman (Cambridge, Mass.: MIT Press, 1984), 195–96.

203.   Emilio Castilla and Stephen Benard, "The Paradox of Meritocracy," *Administrative Science Quarterly* 55, no. 4 (2010): 543–676.

204.   Geracimos, "Women in Publishing," 25; Coser, Kadushin, and Powell, *Books*, 172.

205.   Coser, Kadushin, and Powell, *Books*, 172.

206.   Information Science Incorporated & Humanic Designs Division, *How to Eliminate Discriminatory Practices*, 70.

207.   Emilio Castilla, "Meritocracy," in *Sage Encyclopedia of Political Behavior*, ed. Fathali M. Moghaddam (Thousand Oaks, Calif.: SAGE Publications, 2017).

4. OVERUTILIZED AND UNDERENFORCED

1. Nancy MacLean, *Freedom Is Not Enough: The Opening of the American Workplace* (New York and Cambridge, Mass.: Russell Sage Foundation and Harvard University Press, 2006).

2. Frank Dobbin, *Inventing Equal Opportunity* (Princeton, N.J.: Princeton University Press, 2009). Dobbin argues that personnel took charge at a time of declining union power, and "what personnel made popular gradually became lawful" (5). The courts have fostered similar equal opportunity policies across firms and industries by upholding the "best practices" of prominent employers. Also see Benton Williams, "AT&T and the Private-Sector Origins of Private-Sector Affirmative Action," *Journal of Policy History* 20, no. 4 (2008): 542–68.

3. Minutes of Executive Board, November 17, 1975, carton 1, folder 6, 9to5 Records.

4. 9to5, *Women's Insurance News* 1, no. 1, [1976], carton 3, folder 111, 9to5 Additional Records A.

5. Karen Nussbaum, speech, 1976, carton 1, folders 3 and 18, 9to5 Records.

6. 9to5 National Association of Working Women, *Hidden Assets: Women and Minorities in the Banking Industry*, February 1980, 8, carton 5, folder 172, 9to5 Additional Records A.

7. Pamela Walker Laird, *Pull: Networking and Success Since Benjamin Franklin*, Harvard Studies in Business History (Cambridge, Mass: Harvard University Press, 2006).

8. Hugh Davis Graham, *The Civil Rights Era: Origins and Development of National Policy, 1960–1972* (New York: Oxford University Press, 1990), 413.

9. Leah Platt Boustan and William J. Collins, "The Origin and Persistence of Black-White Differences in Women's Labor Force Participation," in *Human Capital in History: The American Record*, ed. Leah Platt Boustan, Carola Frydman, and Robert A. Margo (Chicago: University of Chicago Press, 2014), 212.

10. Claudia Goldin, "The Quiet Revolution That Transformed Women's Employment, Education, and Family," *American Economic Review* 96, no. 2 (May 2006), 13. Also, universities with public funding were required to encourage women to take part in nontraditional majors.

11. The Index of Segregation decreased from 67.68 in 1970 to 52.98 in 1990. Changes in the sex composition within occupations—principally due to the entry of women into traditionally male jobs—accounted for two-thirds to three-quarters of the decline in segregation. While in 1970, 71 percent of men and 55 percent of women worked in jobs where individuals of the same sex comprised the overwhelming majority (80 percent or more) of workers, by 1990 this was true of only about two-fifths of men and one-third of women. Francine Blau, Patricia Simpson, and Deborah Anderson, "Continuing Progress? Trends in Occupational Segregation in the United States Over the 1970s and 1980s," *Feminist Economics* 4, no. 3 (Fall 1998): 29–71. The gender wage gap narrowed from almost 60 cents to a man's dollar in 1970 to 72 cents to a man's dollar in 1990. "Number and Real Median Earnings of Total Workers and Full-Time, Year-Round Workers by Sex and Female-to-Male Earnings Ratio: 1960–2013," U.S. Census Bureau,

Income and Poverty in the United States, https://www2.census.gov/library/publications /2014/demographics/p60-249.pdf.

12. Dorothy Sue Cobble, introduction to *The Sex of Class: Women Transforming American Labor*, ed. Dorothy Sue Cobble (Ithaca, N.Y.: ILR Press, 2007), 2.

13. Blau, Simpson and Anderson, "Continuing Progress?" The percentage of women who worked as secretaries actually increased: 98 percent in 1970 to 99 percent in 1980 and 1990. Typists went from 95 percent in 1970 to 97 percent in 1980 and 94 percent in 1990, and bookkeepers went from 81 percent in 1970 to 90 percent in 1980 and 1990.

14. Christine Jolls, "Accommodation Mandates," *Stanford Law Review* 53 (2000): 292–95. By 1990 seven jobs remained more than 95 percent female: secretaries (98.7%), dental hygienists (98.4%), prekindergarten and kindergarten teachers (97.8%), childcare workers in private households (97.3%), dental assistants (97.1%), receptionists (95.7%), and childcare workers other than in private households (95.6%).

15. According to the U.S. Census, 0.8 percent of Black working women and 1.0 percent of white working women were in the skilled trades in 1972; by 1992 their numbers had inched up to 2.3 percent of Black working women and 2.1 percent of white working women. See Nancy MacLean, "The Hidden History of Affirmative Action: Working Women's Struggles in the 1970s and the Gender of Class," *Feminist Studies* 25, no. 1 (Spring 1999): 57.

16. Other histories explore fair employment practices before affirmative action had fully materialized. Historian Jennifer Delton argues that corporate actors, not just civil rights activists and policy makers, promoted equal employment opportunities based on race long before the affirmative action directives of the 1960s and 1970s. Jennifer Delton, *Racial Integration in Corporate America, 1940–1990* (New York: Cambridge University Press, 2009). Sociologist Anthony Chen traces the roots of affirmative action policy to the 1940s, exploring debates about the role of government in job discrimination. Anthony Chen, *The Fifth Freedom: Jobs, Politics, and Civil Rights in the United States, 1941–1972* (Princeton, N.J.: Princeton University Press, 2009).

17. MacLean, *Freedom Is Not Enough*.

18. Dennis Deslippe, *Protesting Affirmative Action: The Struggle Over Equality After the Civil Rights Revolution* (Baltimore: Johns Hopkins University Press, 2012). Deslippe addresses affirmative action in higher education as well as in the police force.

19. Katherine Turk, *Equality on Trial: Gender and Rights in the Modern American Workplace* (Philadelphia: University of Pennsylvania Press, 2016).

20. Rosabeth Moss Kanter, *Men and Women of the Corporation* (New York: Basic Books, 1977); Allison Elias, "Learning to Lead: Women and Success in Corporate America," *Business and Economic History—Online* 13 (2015).

21. The Department of the Treasury, for instance, monitored its own contracts with private banks. Dean J. Kotlowski, *Nixon's Civil Rights: Politics, Principle, and Policy* (Cambridge, Mass.: Harvard University Press, 2002); Nathan Glazer, *Affirmative Discrimination: Ethic Inequality and Public Policy* (New York: Basic Books, 1975).

22. Pauli Murray, "Economic and Educational Inequality Based on Sex: An Overview," *Valparaiso University Law Review* 5, no. 237 (1971): 237–80.

23. Advisory Commission on Intergovernmental Relations, *The Evolution of a Problematic Partnership: The Feds and Higher Education* (Washington, D.C.: Advisory Commission on Intergovernmental Relations, 1981): 41–43; Max Frankel, "Johnson Signs Order to Protect Women in U.S. Jobs from Bias," *New York Times*, October 14, 1967. The women's groups lobbied the Department of Housing, Education, and Welfare (HEW), the government agency that held university contracts.

24. *A Matter of Simple Justice: The Report of the President's Task Force on Women's Rights and Responsibilities*, U.S. President's Task Force on Women's Rights and Responsibilities, April 1970 (Washington, D.C.: U.S. Government Printing Office, 1970), 18.

25. Marylin Bender, "Corporate Tokenism for Women? 3 Companies Name Them Assistant Secretary," *New York Times*, February 20, 1972.

26. Kotlowski, *Nixon's Civil Rights*, 243–44.

27. Graham, *Civil Rights Era*, 412–13. Graham observed that the directive "was officially promulgated to a non-observant nation," meaning many employers and employees overlooked or even underestimated its potential significance.

28. Jean Tepperman, interview with organizer of Black Employee Committee at Houghton Mifflin, no. 25, 1974–1975, MC366, box 1, folder 7, Tepperman Papers.

29. Carol S. Greenwald, *Banks Are Dangerous to Your Wealth* (Englewood Cliffs, N.J.: Prentice-Hall, 1980), 10–11.

30. Former in-house counsel of MNE in 1980s, interview with author, January 21, 2016.

31. See Patricia J. Snider, "External Data for Affirmative Action Planning," in *Affirmative Action Planning*, ed. George Milkovich and Lee Dyer (New York: Human Resource Planning Society, 1979), 5–14.

32. Snider, 6.

33. Karen Nussbaum, "Women at Work" (speech), May 23, 1978, 88-M96-86-M104, carton 2, folder 47, 9to5 Additional Records A.

34. 9to5, "Enforcement Research Committee Report" concerning affirmative action, [early 1980s], carton 4, folder 144, 9to5 Additional Records A. Although most women in 9to5 were white (see chapter 7 for difficulties recruiting women of color), the group recognized that women of color faced discrimination "both by sex as well as race . . . [and we] need to united all discriminated women if we ever plan to eliminate sex discrimination." The median annual salary for Black women in Boston insurance companies was $3,672 in the early 1980s.

35. 9to5, *Women's Insurance News* 1, no. 1, [1976].

36. Jerry Newman and Frank Krzystofiak, "Toward Internal Availability: Intra-Organizational Roadmaps," in *Affirmative Action Planning*, ed. George Milkovich and Lee Dyer (New York: Human Resource Planning Society, 1979), 32–33.

37. Bender, "Corporate Tokenism for Women?"

38. Susan Davis, "Law and Revised Order 4: Showdown on Sex Discrimination," *Chicago Tribune*, February 4, 1972.

39. "Management: Therapy for Sexists," *Time*, September 2, 1974.

40. Barbara Boyle, "Equal Opportunity for Women Is Smart Business," *Harvard Business Review*, May–June 1973, 85, 91, 92.

41. In publishing houses more than in other industries, women clerical workers were able to win tangible victories. As discussed in chapter 3, a particular committee of 9to5, Women in Publishing, worked to improve pay and advancement for women in the field.

42. 9to5, Attachment to Demands to SSA, January 27, 1977, carton 16, folder 1033, 9to5 Additional Records B.

43. 9to5, "Statistical Study of Boston Area Employment," November 1973, box 5, folder 127, 9to5 Records.

44. P. C. Krist, executive vice president of Mobil, Women at Work Exposition, October 1979, box 93, folder 3, Women's Action Alliance Records, Sophia Smith Collection.

45. Polaroid Corporation Corporate Services Division, "Affirmative Action Plan," July 1979 to July 1980, HR-18, I.388, Polaroid Corporation Administration Records. For employee complaints about external hiring, see Minutes from Employees Committee-Personnel Policy Committee meetings, April 15, 1976, and May 20, 1976, HR-5, I.377, Polaroid Corporation Administration Records. See March 31, 1977, meeting, HR-5, I.377, Polaroid Corporation Administration Records for Employees Committee slide show presentation on the problems of external hiring.

46. Helen Fogel, "Order 4 Opens Doors for Women in Industry," *Chicago Tribune*, February 13, 1972.

47. Carol Kleinman, "Local Companies Swing Into Action on Female Equality," *Chicago Tribune*, February 13, 1972.

48. Honeywell Affirmative Action Plan, 1974, carton 3, folder 92, 9to5 Records.

49. Honeywell Affirmative Action Plan, 1974. Overall, women constituted 87 percent of its office workforce.

50. Dorothy G. Curnane, manager of personnel and EEO coordinator, "Affirmative Action Program," Cabot Corporation of Boston, May 1, 1976, carton 16, folder 1037, 9to5 Additional Records B.

51. Evelyn Ray, EEO compliance at Norton Simon, Women at Work Exposition, October 1979, box 92, folder 31, Women's Action Alliance Records.

52. Mary Ralston, "Myths That Hold Back Miss, Ms., and Mrs.," *Wisconsin Academy Review* 20, no. 2 (Spring 1974): 30.

53. Boyle and her receptionist, quoted in Ralston, 30.

54. Neil C. Churchill and John K. Shank, "Affirmative Action and Guilt-Edged Goals," *Harvard Business Review*, March–April 1976, 112.

55. Churchill and Shank, 113.

56. Churchill and Shank, 116.

57. Jonathan S. Leonard, "The Impact of Affirmative Action on Employment," *Journal of Labor Economics* 2, no. 4 (October 1984): 447. Only 26 of the establishments were barred from bidding on government contracts, and 331 had to provide back pay totaling $61 million. In his article in 1985, Leonard indicated that establishments seemed to be randomly chosen, citing an OFCCP officer who explained that because he had a summer cottage on the beach, in the summer he reviewed establishments near the ocean. Jonathan S. Leonard, "Affirmative Action as Earnings Redistribution: The Targeting of Compliance Reviews," *Journal of Labor Economics* 3, no. 3 (July 1985): 374, 387.

58. Letter from Nancy Farrell, 9to5 chairwoman, to other activists (mailing list of activist groups attached to the letter), July 1, 1977, carton 3, folder 106, 9to5 Records.

59. Rodney Alexander and Elisabeth Sapery, *The Shortchanged: Minorities and Women in Banking* (New York: Dunellen, 1973).

60. Mark McColloch, *White-Collar Workers in Transition: The Boom Years, 1940–1970* (Westport, Conn.: Greenwood, 1983).

61. Gayle Graham Yates, *What Women Want: The Ideas of the Movement* (Cambridge, Mass.: Harvard University Press, 1975), 47; Barbara J. Love, ed., *Feminists Who Changed America, 1963–1975* (Urbana: University of Illinois Press, 2006), 233.

62. Greenwald, *Banks Are Dangerous to Your Wealth*, 8.

63. Allison Elias, "'Measured By Two Yardsticks': Women in Bank Management Training, 1960s–1990s," *Management & Organizational History* 15, no. 2 (2020): 132–53.

64. Letter from Peg Terry, 9to5 Boston, to Massachusetts Special Legislative Committee on Affirmative Action, August 13, 1976, carton 3, folder 116, 9to5 Records. For more on economic inequality facing Black and Latina women in the 1960s to 1990s, see Irene Brown, ed., *Latinas and African American Women at Work: Race, Gender, and Economic Inequality* (New York: Russell Sage Foundation, 1999).

65. Letter from Peg Terry, 9to5 Boston, to Massachusetts Special Legislative Committee on Affirmative Action, August 13, 1976, carton 3, folder 116, 9to5 Records.

66. Letter from Bill Owens, Senate chairman, and Raymond Jordan, House chairman, Massachusetts legislature, to Janet Selcer, 9to5, October 4, 1976, carton 3, folder 116, 9to5 Records. The letter established that Selcer would testify on October 12 as part of the Massachusetts Public Hearing on Affirmative Action.

67. Draft of 9to5 remarks to the Massachusetts State House Public Hearing on Affirmative Action, 1976, carton 3, folder 116, 9to5 Records.

68. The Dukakis administration had advanced equal employment opportunity at the state level by issuing a new executive order in 1975 that added sex, age, and national origin to the list of categories protected from discrimination in public employment, schools, accommodations, and housing. Michael Dukakis, governor, Executive Order No. 116 (Revising and Amending EO 74), May 1, 1975, https://www.mass.gov/executive-orders/no-116-governors-code-of-fair-practices. Along with the Congressional Black Caucus, 9to5 lobbied Dukakis to issue Executive Order 116, which, in addition to prohibiting discrimination, called for state agencies to formulate affirmative action plans within 30 days. While Dukakis was in office, his administration, in general, supported "the goals of 9to5 without reservation," including 9to5's push to allocate more money to the Massachusetts Commission Against Discrimination during a time when Massachusetts was having budget concerns. John R. Buckley, Massachusetts state representative, letter to Fran Cicchetti, 9to5 leader, December 26, 1974, carton 16, folder 1028, 9to5 Additional Records B. 9to5 complained that after Governor Dukakis left office and was replaced by a Republican in 1979, MCAD became increasingly understaffed and underfunded, and it was led by officials who were only nominally committed to affirmative action. See Affirmative Action in Banking and Insurance—Position Paper, [1982/1983], carton 16, folder 1033, 9to5 Additional Records B.

69. Karen Nussbaum, speech, 1976, carton 1, folder 3, 9to5 Records.

70. Greenwald, *Banks Are Dangerous to Your Wealth*, 7.

71. Alexander and Sapery, *Shortchanged*, 5.

72. Greenwald, *Banks Are Dangerous to Your Wealth*, 8.

73. Greenwald, 9.

74. Ruth Olds, banking chair, 9to5, letter to Weldon J. Rougeau, director of OFCCP, December 18, 1979, carton 16, folder 1028, 9to5 Additional Records B.

75. Olds to Rougeau, December 18, 1979.

76. Greenwald, *Banks Are Dangerous to Your Wealth*, 10–11, 17.

77. Alexander and Sapery, *Shortchanged*, 34.

78. Jean Tepperman, interview with associate editor at Houghton Mifflin, no. 26, 1974–1975, MC366, box 1, folder 7, Tepperman Papers.

79. Alexander and Sapery, *Shortchanged*, 34.

80. Greenwald, *Banks Are Dangerous to Your Wealth*, 20. Greenwald conducted studies on affirmative action in 1976 and 1978, charging banks with discriminatory hiring and employment practices. This survey focused not only on the number of women and underrepresented men in certain job categories but also on whether women and underrepresented men with comparable experience and education were receiving the same pay as white men.

81. 9to5, Chronology of Events, [1979], 88-M96-89-M104, carton 4, folder 119, 9to5 Additional Records A.

82. Anson Smith, "Legislator Wants Look at Bank Study," *Boston Globe*, February 9, 1979, carton 4, folder 119, 9to5 Additional Records A.

83. Smith, "Legislator Wants Look at Bank Study."

84. William Proxmire, chairman of Senate Banking, Housing, and Urban Affairs Committee, letter to the Honorable Ray Marshall, Secretary of Labor, January 4, 1979, carton 4, folder 119, Additional Records A.

85. "9to5's Claims Substantiated by Greenwald Survey," Contact: Anne Serino, Joan Quinlan, press release, January 3, 1979, carton 4, folder 119, 9to5 Additional Records A.

86. 9to5, Chronology of Events [1979].

87. "9to5's Claims Substantiated by Greenwald Survey."

88. Weldon J. Rougeau, OFCCP director, letter to Joan Quinlan, 9to5, January 29, 1979, carton 4, folder 119, 9to5 Additional Records A.

89. 9to5, "Statistical Study of Boston Area Employment," November 1973, box 5, folder 127, 9to5 Records.

90. The report gives $6,200 as the official CSA poverty line. "Office Work in Boston: A Statistical Study," [1978/1979], box 5, folder 127, 9to5 Records.

91. Karen Nussbaum, statement, Women at Work Exposition, October 1979, box 92, folder 31, Women's Action Alliance Records.

92. 9to5, "Claim Against Boston's Insurance Industry: A Study of the Treatment of Women Office Workers in Insurance," September 1974, box 5, folder 127, 9to5 Records.

93. Until 1978 the OFCCP only supervised the various agencies that conducted compliance reviews in each industry. Bernard E. Anderson, "The Ebb and Flow of Enforcing

Executive Order 11246," *American Economic Review* 86, no. 2, Papers and Proceedings of the 108th Annual Meeting of the American Economic Association (May 1996), 299.

94. Janet Selcer, 9to5 Staff, letter to Insurance Committee Members, July 30, 1974; attachment to letter, "Boston Insurance Companies and Affirmative action Requirements," 1974, carton 3, folder 105, 9to5 Additional Records A.

95. For instance, when Everette Friedman, SSA chief compliance officer, was planning to review Prudential in Boston, the company fought to keep its records confidential. Selcer, letter to Insurance Committee Members, July 30, 1974, and attachment to letter, "Boston Insurance Companies and Affirmative action Requirements"; 9to5 chart, Insurance Committee Activity with the Social Security Administration, [1976], carton 3, folder 110, 9to5 Additional Records A.

96. In addition, Frank B. Hall and Marsh & McLennan maintained that they did not have to submit information to the SSA. Both claimed that they did not have more than $50,000 in federal contracts, which was the minimum required for a company to be subject to affirmative action guidelines. Despite delays and disputes, the SSA scheduled reviews at Blue Cross Blue Shield and Travelers Insurance; eventually 9to5 convinced the SSA to review both John Hancock and Liberty Mutual. 9to5 chart, Insurance Committee Activity with the Social Security Administration, [1976]. John Hancock review mentioned in 9to5, *Women's Insurance News*, Summer 1976, carton 3, folder 111, 9to5 Additional Records A. Liberty Mutual mentioned in 9to5, *Women's Insurance News*, Summer 1977, carton 3, folder 111, 9to5 Additional Records A.

97. 9to5 chart, Insurance Committee Activity with the Social Security Administration, [1976].

98. 9to5, "Claim Against Boston's Insurance Industry: A Study of the Treatment of Women Office Workers in Insurance," September 1974, box 5, folder 127, 9to5 Records.

99. 9to5 chart, Insurance Committee Activity with the Social Security Administration, [1976].

100. 9to5, *Marsh & McLennan Newsletter for Women Employees* 1, no. 1 (October 1975), carton 3, folder 111, 9to5 Additional Records A.

101. 9to5, *Marsh & McLennan Newsletter for Women Employees* 1, no. 1.

102. 9to5, *Marsh & McLennan Newsletter for Women Employees* 1, no. 1.

103. 9to5, Committees Three Month Plan, Insurance, 1976, carton 1, folder 7, 9to5 Records.

104. 9to5, Planning Committee, 3 Month Plan, July, August, September 1976, carton 16, folder 1024, 9to5 Additional Records B.

105. "How to Evaluate Your Company," [1976], carton 16, folder 1034, 9to5 Additional Records B.

106. 9to5, *Women's Insurance News* 1, no. 1, [1976].

107. 9to5, *Women's Insurance News* 1, no. 2, [Summer 1976].

108. At Liberty Mutual, however, an employee relations manager refused to speak with 9to5 about job postings; Liberty remained one of the last major Boston companies that refused to alter its posting practices. 9to5, *Women's Insurance News*, [1976/1977], carton 3, folder 111, 9to5 Additional Records A.

109. 9to5, *Women's Insurance News*, [Summer 1977]. For more on campaigns and potential campaigns in specific offices, see 9to5, Minutes of the Women's Insurance Forum Steering Committee, September 15, 1976, carton 3, folder 110, 9to5 Additional Records A.

110. 9to5, Attachment to Demands to SSA, January 27, 1977.

111. The new male hire began earning $700 a month, which was more than the average $400 to $450 per month that most female employees were earning. Only one female officer with twelve years of experience earned $750 a month. Dorothy Sue Cobble, "Willmar, Minnesota, Bank Strike of 1977–1979," in *Labor Conflict in the United States: An Encyclopedia*, ed. Ronald L. Filippelli (New York: Garland, 1990), 572; "8 Women Protest Low Salaries, Begin First Bank Strike in Minn.," *Washington Post*, December 17, 1977. For president's quote, see Bill Peterson, "Women's Strike at Bank: 6-Month Walkout Roils Minnesota Town," *Washington Post*, June 12, 1978.

112. The strike received coverage in major papers such as the *New York Times* (December 17, 1978), *Wall Street Journal* (January 30, 1981), *Washington Post* (December 17, 1977; December 17, 1978; June 12, 1978), and *Los Angeles Times* (March 26, 1981). Female protesters appeared on the *Phil Donahue Show* in early 1979.

113. Cobble, "Willmar, Minnesota, Bank Strike," 571–74.

114. Another professional organization for bankers, the Washington, D.C.–based Bankers Association, also showed the film to its members. Julie Salamon, "Bankers Flock to See Saga of 'Willmar 8' Before Public Does," *Wall Street Journal*, January 30, 1981.

115. Salamon, "Bankers Flock to See Saga"; Kevin Thomas, "'Willmar 8': Women Strike for Rights," *Los Angeles Times*, March 26, 1981.

116. Peterson, "Women's Strike at Bank." This anonymous Minnesota banker continued, "I feel he's like Bert Lance. His bank is giving banking a poor image just like Lance did."

117. Nelson Lichtenstein, *State of the Union: A Century of American Labor* (Princeton, N.J.: Princeton University Press, 2002).

118. Thomas, "'Willmar 8.'"

119. Peterson, "Women's Strike at Bank."

120. Laird, *Pull*, 291–96.

121. *A Report on the Glass Ceiling Initiative*, U.S. Department of Labor, 1991.

122. Renae Broderick and Carolyn Milkovich, "Breaking the Glass Ceiling," Center for Advanced Human Resource Studies, Cornell ILR School (October 1991), 9.

123. *Women in Corporate Management: Results of a Catalyst Survey* (New York: Catalyst, 1990), 28.

124. Ruth Blumrosen, Rutgers law professor, Equal Pay Workshop, Women at Work Exposition, October 1979, box 91, folder 32, Women's Action Alliance Records.

125. 9to5 Organization for Women Office Workers, Boston, *Minority Women Office Workers: A Status Report*, 1976, carton 3, folder 106, 9to5 Records.

126. 9to5, *Hidden Assets*, 5–7. This report also noted that many full-time clericals in the survey qualified for food stamps.

127. Deslippe, *Protesting Affirmative Action*.

5. THE DECLINE OF THE OFFICE WIFE AND THE RISE OF THE "AUTOMATED HAREM"

1. Studs Terkel, introduction to *Working: People Talk About What They Do All Day and How They Feel About What They Do* (New York: Pantheon Books, 1974). The term "automated harem" is from Barbara Garson, *The Electronic Sweatshop: How Computers Are Transforming the Office of the Future Into the Factor of the Past* (New York: Simon & Schuster, 1988), 177.

2. "Sharon Atkins, Receptionist," in Terkel, *Working*, 29, 30–31.

3. See the discussion of the General Motors strike in Lordstown, Ohio, 1972, in Jefferson Cowie, *Stayin' Alive: The 1970s and the Last Days of the Working Class* (New York: New Press, 2010). Also *Hearings on S. 3916, Worker Alienation, 1972, Before the US Senate Subcommittee on Employment, Manpower, and Poverty of the Committee on Labor and Public Welfare*, 92nd Cong., 2nd session, July 25–26, 1972.

4. *Automation of America's Offices, 1985–2000*, U.S. Congress, Office of Technology Assessment (OTA) (Washington, D.C.: U.S. Government Printing Office, OTA-CIT-287, December 1985), 9. Automation of clerical work dated back to the beginning of the twentieth century. See Margery W. Davies, *Woman's Place Is at the Typewriter: Office Work and Office Workers, 1870–1930* (Philadelphia: Temple University Press, 1982); Elyce J. Rotella, *From Home to Office: U.S. Women at Work, 1870–1930* (Ann Arbor: University of Michigan Research Press, 1981); Ileen DeVault, *Sons and Daughters of Labor: Class and Clerical Work in Turn-of-the-Century Pittsburgh* (Ithaca, N.Y.: Cornell University Press, 1990); Sharon Hartman Strom, *Beyond the Typewriter: Gender, Class and the Origins of Modern American Office Work, 1900–1930* (Champaign: University of Illinois Press, 1992); Lisa M. Fine, *The Souls of the Skyscraper: Female Clerical Workers in Chicago, 1870–1930*, Women of Letters Series (Philadelphia: Temple University Press, 1990); Angel Kwolek-Folland, *Engendering Business: Men and Women in the Corporate Office, 1870–1930* (Baltimore: Johns Hopkins University Press, 1994).

5. Walter Kleinschrod, *Critical Issues in Office Automation* (New York: McGraw-Hill, 1986), 10.

6. SRI predicted that by 1990 the number would grow to 17.5 million. Anne-Marie Schiro, "For Secretaries, Now It's Word Processors," *New York Times*, August 16, 1982.

7. National Research Council, *Computer Chips and Paper Clips: Technology and Women's Employment*, vol. 1 (Washington, D.C.: National Academies Press, 1986), 118.

8. S. L. Sauter, L. R. Murphy, and J. J. Hurrell, Jr., "Prevention of Work-Related Psychological Disorders: A National Strategy Proposed by the National Institute for Occupational Safety and Health (NIOSH)," *American Psychologist* 45, no. 10 (1990): 1146–58.

9. See, for instance, Nancy Woloch, *A Class by Herself: Protective Laws for Women Workers, 1890s–1990s* (Princeton, N.J.: Princeton University Press, 2015).

10. William Smith, "Lag Persists for Business Equipment," *New York Times*, October 26, 1971. Georgia Dullea, "Is It a Boon for Secretaries—or Just an Automated Ghetto?," *New York Times*, February 5, 1974.

11. Jennifer Schuessler, "The Muses of Insert, Delete and Execute," *New York Times*, December 26, 2011. The article cites two different word processors, one for $11,500 and another for $12,000. Karlyn Barker, "Automation Revolution Brings Efficiency, Foreboding to Office," *Washington Post*, November 8, 1982.

12. Anne Collier, "Secretaries See New Vistas with Office Automation," *Christian Science Monitor*, March 23, 1983.

13. Joan Sweeney, "Does the Automated Office Dehumanize Jobs?," *Los Angeles Times*, November 16, 1980.

14. Transcript of remarks at clerical work conference, April 24, 1982, MC365, folder 2, Massachusetts History Workshop Records. (Identity of worker withheld for privacy reasons.) Also see Eileen Appelbaum, "The Economics of Technical Progress: Labor Issues Arising from the Spread of Programmable Automation Technologies," paper presented to the Subgroup on Microelectronics and Work Process, Working Group on Reindustrialization, University of Massachusetts, Amherst, July 27, 1982, in *Automation and the Workplace: Selected Labor, Education, and Training Issues*, Office of Technology Assessment (Washington, D.C.: U.S. Government Printing Office, March 1983), 66. Clericals worried that they might not be able to find new positions if the demand for clerical labor were to decrease because of technology. Appelbaum predicted that the clerical growth rate would slow considerably, which happened in the 1980s and 1990s. Also see Roslyn L. Feldberg and Evelyn Nakano Glenn, "Technology and Work Degradation: Effects of Office Automation on Women Clerical Workers," in *Machina Ex Dea: Feminist Perspectives on Technology*, ed. Joan Rothschild, Athene Series (New York: Pergamon Press, 1983), 67. Clerical workers and scholars also wondered how the remaining workers would adapt to automated jobs, and who would train them to use the computers. See *Automation and the Workplace*, 34–43.

15. Vivian Leigh Edwards, "Secretary's Fear of Word Processor Quickly Vanishes," *Los Angeles Times*, April 25, 1983; *Automation of America's Offices*, 52–55.

16. *Automation of America's Offices*, 55; Feldberg and Glenn, "Technology and Work Degradation," 62, 64–65.

17. Garson, *Electronic Sweatshop*, 175–76.

18. Thomas Haigh, "Remembering the Office of the Future: The Origins of Word Processing and Office Automation," *IEEE Annals of the History of Computer* 28, no. 4 (October 2006): 6–31.

19. Mary Murphree, "The Decline of the 'Secretary as Generalist,'" in *Office Automation: Jekyll or Hyde? Highlights of the International Conference on Office Work and New Technology*, ed. Daniel Marschall and Judith Gregory (Cleveland, Ohio: Working Women Education Fund, 1983), 115.

20. Garson, *Electronic Sweatshop*, 192.

21. Dullea, "Is It a Boon for Secretaries?"

22. Haigh, "Remembering the Office of the Future."

23. Garson, *Electronic Sweatshop*, 177, 186.

24. Anne Machung, "Turning Secretaries Into Word Processors," in *Office Automation: Jekyll or Hyde? Highlights of the International Conference on Office Work and New*

Technology, ed. Daniel Marschall and Judith Gregory (Cleveland, Ohio: Working Women Education Fund, 1983), 121.

25. Murphree, "The Decline of the 'Secretary as Generalist,'" 115.

26. Dullea, "Is It a Boon for Secretaries?"

27. Feldberg and Glenn, "Technology and Work Degradation," 60–61; Schiro, "For Secretaries, Now It's Word Processors."

28. Edwards, "Secretary's Fear of Word Processor Quickly Vanishes."

29. Garson, 186, 191, 193.

30. Garson, 188, 191.

31. "Word Processing—Hardware/Software," *Business Automation* 19, no. 9 (1972): 48.

32. Jean Tepperman, *Not Servants, Not Machines: Office Workers Speak Out!* (Boston: Beacon Press, 1976), 46.

33. Smith, "Lag Persists for Business Equipment."

34. R. Natale, "'Selectrifying' the Typing Pool," *Chicago Tribune*, October 31, 1971.

35. Elizabeth Kolbert, "What's New in the Secretarial World," *New York Times*, August 4, 1985.

36. Schiro, "For Secretaries, Now It's Word Processors."

37. Arnold R. Deutsch, "The Employment World," *Detroit Free Press*, June 7, 1981.

38. Schiro, "For Secretaries, Now It's Word Processors."

39. NSA Prototype Secretarial Job Description, *Secretary* (May 1978), 21

40. *Future Secretaries Association News* 16, no. 2, (November 15, 1978), folder 6, folder 31, NSA, Philadelphia Records.

41. Dullea, "Is It a Boon for Secretaries?"

42. "Word Processing: What Is It?," *Philadelphia Tribune*, April 27, 1982.

43. Ann Wead Kimbrough, "Office Automation," *Atlanta Constitution*, April 25, 1984.

44. Sarah Oates and Alexander Barnum, "Secretarial Schools Learn Ropes of Automation," *Washington Post*, September 2, 1985. The survey was conducted in cooperation with Minolta Corporation, with a sample of around 2,000 PSI members and 1,000 executives nationwide.

45. Collier, "Secretaries See New Vistas with Office Automation." Gant believed that the creation of new managerial jobs related to word processing would increase the demand for more executive secretaries.

46. Schiro, "For Secretaries, Now It's Word Processors." With the coming of automation, word processing could become a "high-paying skill," according to one personnel officer who predicted that the job would pay upward of $600 per week.

47. Nancy Crowe, "Help Wanted: Only Secretaries Need Apply," *Vermont Business*, February 1987. Palmer explained that it was "a slow process. It's not moving as fast as I'd like it to." But she said that change was happening.

48. Machung, "Turning Secretaries Into Word Processors," 120.

49. Carol Kleinman, "Level of Work, Not of Boss, Should Set Secretarial Pay," *Chicago Tribune*, April 15, 1997. Fried became interested in clerical compensation when she was working as a secretary to pay for college. Eventually she earned a doctorate from Ohio State University and founded her own consulting firm.

50. N. Elizabeth Fried, "Employers Need to Rethink the Way They Pay Secretaries," *Journal of Compensation and Benefits* 4 (September–October 1988): 95–98.

51. Carol Kleinman, "Secretary Pay No Longer Tied to Boss," *Chicago Tribune*, April 29, 1993; Alan Farnham, "Where Have All the Secretaries Gone?," *Fortune*, May 12, 1997; Tamar Lewin, "As the Boss Goes, So Goes the Secretary: Is It Bias?," *New York Times*, March 17, 1994.

52. Fried, "Employers Need to Rethink the Way They Pay Secretaries," 98.

53. Garson, *Electronic Sweatshop*, 173–74.

54. Murphree, "Decline of the 'Secretary as Generalist,'" 115.

55. Machung, "Turning Secretaries Into Word Processors," 123.

56. Judith Nies, "Secretaries Versus the Automated Office," *Boston Globe*, June 21, 1983.

57. Joan Sweeney, "Does the Automated Office Dehumanize Jobs?, *Los Angeles Times*, November 16, 1980.

58. William Henry Leffingwell, *Office Management: Principles and Practice* (New York: Shaw, 1925). In 1925 he published *Office Management: Principles and Practice*, which sought to standardize the clerical workday so that less time was spent on coordination or communication with others.

59. Harry Braverman, *Labor and Monopoly Capital: The Degradation of Work in the Twentieth Century* (New York: Monthly Review Press, 1974), 319; also 112–21, 304–48. For the early application of scientific management in the office, see Lee Galloway, *Office Management: Its Principles and Practice* (New York, 1918); and William Henry Leffingwell, *Scientific Office Management* (New York, 1917).

60. Braverman, *Labor and Monopoly Capital*, 319–26. Braverman relies on the following management literature: Systems and Procedures Association of America, *A Guide to Office Clerical Time Standards: A Compilation of Standard Data Used by Large American Companies* (Detroit, 1960); Richard J. Morrison, Robert E. Nolan, and James S. Devlin, *Work Measurement in Machine Accounting* (New York, 1963).

61. Daniel B. Cornfield, "Women in the Automated Office: Computers, Work, and Prospects for Unionization," in *Advances in Industrial and Labor Relations*, vol. 4, ed. David Lewin, David B. Lipsky, and Donna Sockell (Greenwich, Conn.: JAI, 1987), 177–98.

62. Jeanne Stellman and Mary Sue Henifin, *Office Work Can Be Dangerous to Your Health: A Handbook of Office Health and Safety Hazards and What You Can Do About Them* (New York: Fawcett Crest, 1983), 79–80.

63. Garson, *Electronic Sweatshop*, 174.

64. 9to5, "Claim Against Boston's Insurance Industry: A Study of the Treatment of Women Office Workers in Insurance," September 1974, box 5, folder 127, 9to5 Records.

65. Sweeney, "Does the Automated Office Dehumanize Jobs?"

66. Stellman and Henifin, *Office Work Can Be Dangerous to Your Health*, 6.

67. Craig Brod, "Managing Technostress: Optimizing the Use of Computer Technology," *Personnel Journal* 61, no. 10 (October 1982): 753–57.

68. Barker, "Automation Revolution Brings Efficiency."

69. Working Women, Race against Time: Analysis of the Trends in Office Automation and the Impact on the Office Workforce, Cleveland, 1980, carton 5, folder 154, 9to5

Additional Records A. Also see *Hearings on the Human Factor in Innovation and Productivity by the Science, Research, and Technology Subcommittee of the House Committee on Science and Technology*, September 18, 1981 (Judith Gregory, testimony for 9to5, National Association of Working Women), carton 5, folder 154, 9to5 Additional Records A.

70. Ellen Cassedy, Karen Nussbaum, and Debbie Schneider, interview by Ann Froines, November 1, 2005, SEIU District 925 Legacy Project.

71. "9to5 President Raps Office Automation, Says it Deskills, Devalues Office Jobs," *Computerworld*, May 3, 1982, carton 5, folder 167, 9to5 Additional Records A.

72. 9to5 Campaign on VDT Risks: Analysis of VDT Operator Questionnaires of VDT Hotline Callers, February 1984, carton 5, folder 164, 9to5 Additional Records A. Also see Kathy Chin, "VDT Users Negatively Eye Study's Finding," *InfoWord*, August 1, 1983, 5.

73. "WARNING: Health Hazards for Office Workers," Working Women Education Fund, April 1981, p. 47, carton 5, folder 165, 9to5 Additional Records A. Page 48 of this report contains a table showing that low pay and lack of promotions were also common sources of stress among banking and insurance workers. Other studies that support these connections are in folder 150. The second 9to5 survey was conducted in 1984 and specifically investigated job stress. See "National Secretary's Day Message for Clerical Workers: Action Best Remedy for Stress, According to National Survey on Women, Work, and Stress," press release, April 25, 1984, carton 3, folder 79, 9to5 Additional Records A.

74. Working Women Education Fund, International Conference on Office Work & New Technology, Tentative Agenda, October 20, 1982, carton 5, folder 163, 9to5 Additional Records A.

75. *Hearings on New Technology in the American Workplace by the Subcommittee on Education and Labor, Committee on Education and Labor, U.S. House of Representatives*, June 23, 1982 (statement by Judith Gregory, research director, testimony for 9to5, National Association of Working Women), carton 5, folder 154, 9to5 Additional Records A.

76. "The National Institute for Occupational Health and Safety (NIOSH)," Centers for Disease Control and Prevention, http://www.cdc.gov/niosh/about.html, accessed May 5, 2011.

77. Kitty Calavita, "The Demise of the Occupational Safety and Health Administration: A Case Study in Symbolic Action," *Social Problems* 30, no. 4 (April 1983): 439–40; David Weil, "If OSHA Is So Bad, Why Is Compliance So Good?" *RAND Journal of Economics* 27, no. 3 (Autumn 1996): 618. Sidney A. Shapiro and Thomas O. McGarity, "Reorienting OSHA: Regulatory Alternatives and Legislative Reform," *Yale Journal on Regulation* 6, no. 1 (1989), suggested that OSHA could benefit from congressional restructuring.

78. *Automation of America's Offices*, 138.

79. Lawrence R. Murphy, "Job Stress Research at NIOSH: 1972–2002," in *Historical and Current Perspectives on Stress and Health*, vol. 2, ed. Pamela L. Perrewé and Daniel C. Ganster (Oxford: Elsevier Science, 2002), 4, 22.

80. Judith Gregory, memo to Karen Nussbaum, re: Recent Research Findings on Productivity, Job Stress and Trends in Office Automation, May 11, 1981, carton 5, folder 150, 9to5 Additional Records A.

81. Murphy, "Job Stress Research at NIOSH," 28.

82. Marvin J. Dainoff and Marilyn Hecht Dainoff, *People & Productivity: A Manager's Guide to Ergonomics in the Electronic Office* (Toronto: Holt, Rinehart and Winston of Canada, 1986), 23, 27, 29.

83. John W. Jones, "A Cost Evaluation for Stress Management," *Medical Benefits* 2, no. 2 (1985): 5–6; John W. Jones, *The Burnout Syndrome: Current Research, Theory, Interventions* (London: London House Press, 1981).

84. *Automation of America's Offices*, 162 and 162n.150; Committee on Science and Technology, Subcommittee on Investigations and Oversight, *Potential Health Effects of VDT Terminals and Radiofrequency Heaters and Sealers*, 97th Cong., 2nd sess. (May 12–13, 1981); Committee on Education and Labor, Subcommittee on Health and Safety, OSHA Oversight, *Video Display Terminals in the Workplace*, 98th Cong., 2nd sess. (1984). For NIOSH recommendations, see statement of J. Donald Millar, M.D., before the Subcommittee on Health and Safety, Committee on Education and Labor, House of Representatives, May 15, 1984, carton 5, folder 155, 9to5 Additional Records A.

85. According to Director Michael McGinnis of the Office for Health Promotion and Disease Prevention. Benjamin C. Amick, III, "Health and Safety in the Automated Office: National Policy, Organizational Initiatives and Individual Choices," *Office: Technology and People* 3 (1988): 355–56.

86. Judith Gregory, "Safety and Health for the Office Worker with an Emphasis on Job Stress," SEIU Women's Conference in Storrs, Connecticut, June 3, 1981, carton 5, folder 154, 9to5 Additional Records A.

87. Hearings on the Human Factor in Innovation and Productivity (Gregory).

88. Hearings on New Technology in the American Workplace (Gregory).

89. Ellen Cassedy, memo to Joan Quinlan, Elaine Taber, Judy Gregory, "re: Coordination of Office Machine Design Project," November 9, 1981, carton 5, folder 160, 9to5 Additional Records A.

90. Diane Berry, chairwoman of 9to5 Health and Safety Committee, letter to Prime Computer, Inc., January 14, 1982, carton 5, folder 160, 9to5 Additional Records A. The following manufacturers received letters from 9to5: Prime Computer, Lanier Business Products, Texas Instruments, Xerox Corporation, Wang Laboratories, Digital Equipment Corporation, Inforex Corporation, Data General Corporation, Raytheon Data Systems, and IBM Corporation. See Diane Berry, chairwoman of 9to5 Health and Safety Committee, letters to various companies, February 3 or 8, 1982, carton 5, folder 160, 9to5 Additional Records A.

91. "Thoughts on recent visits to view office machines," March and April 1982, carton 5, folder 160, 9to5 Additional Records A.

92. Judi, memo to Karen and Nancy S., "re: Trip east to meet with computer company people," December 10, 1982, carton 5, folder 162, 9to5 Additional Records A.

93. "9to5 Releases Buyers Guide to Word Processors," 9to5 press release, August 12, 1982, carton 5, folder 164, 9to5 Additional Records A.

94. "The Human Factor: 9to5's Consumer Guide to Word Processors," 1982, carton 5, folder 164, 9to5 Additional Records A. Using fifteen different criteria, 9to5 rated the most recent models of the manufacturers, noting that many clericals would most likely not be using the models that were rated.

95. *Automation of America's Offices*, 138.

96. Marvin J. Dainoff, "The Illness of the Decade," *Computerworld*, April 13, 1992, 27.

97. Vernon Mogensen, "Glued to the Tube: Labor's Unlikely Victory for Computer Safety in Suffolk County," *Regional Labor Review* 1 (Spring 1999): 19.

98. Kleinschrod, *Critical Issues in Office Automation*, 140–42.

99. Amick, "Health and Safety in the Automated Office," 344.

100. Kleinschrod, *Critical Issues in Office Automation*, 140–42.

101. J. Donald Millar, M.D., statement before the Subcommittee on Health and Safety, Committee on Education and Labor, House of Representatives, May 15, 1984, carton 5, folder 155, 9to5 Additional Records A.

102. Janice C. Blood, "9to5 Discovers Possible New Adverse Pregnancy 'Cluster' at VDT Worksite," press release, February 16, 1984, carton 5, folder 164, 9to5 Additional Records A.

103. While some protective labor laws could benefit women workers by mandating rest breaks, many limited their earning capacity and kept labor markets segregated. Banning women from working overtime or from working jobs requiring heavy lifting often meant hindering them from more lucrative opportunities. Susan Lehrer, *Origins of Protective Labor Legislation for Women, 1905–1925* (Albany: State University of New York Press, 1987).

104. Millar, statement before the Subcommittee on Health and Safety.

105. 9to5 supporters, forty-one letters to Dr. J. Donald Millar, director of NIOSH, 1984, carton 5, folder 155, 9to5 Additional Records A.

106. *Automation of America's Offices*, 20.

107. 9to5 Automation Committee, letter to Representative Elizabeth Metayer, March 13, 1983, carton 5, folder 169, 9to5 Additional Records A.

108. "Fact Sheet: H. 4537," 1984, carton 5, folder 169, 9to5 Additional Records A. The proposed bill provided for enforcement guidelines and an advisory committee to oversee the creation of the protections. Folder 169 also contains a poor-quality photocopy of a version of the Massachusetts bill.

109. Loren Stein, "Coalition Fights VDT Legislation," *InfoWorld*, September 17, 1984, 48.

110. "New Jersey Issues Cautions on VDT Use," *New York Times*, November 30, 1989.

111. 9to5 Summary of Safety Legislation for VDT Operators, September 2, 1984, carton 5, folder 169, 9to5 Additional Records A. In Maine, for instance, the resolution called for data collection using state and other public employees to determine if protective standards were necessary. See Representative Edie Beaulieu, letter to the *Guild Reporter*, June 1, 1983, carton 5, folder 169, 9to5 Additional Records A; Helena F. Rodrigues, "The Ergonomic Impact of Technology on Libraries," Johnson & Wales Universities

Libraries, http://web.simmons.edu/~chen/nit/NIT%2793/93-313-rodri.html, accessed May 5, 2011.

112. Christine Gorman, Elaine Lafferty, and Janice C. Simpson, "All Eyes on the VDT," *Time*, June 27, 1988, http://www.time.com/time/magazine/article/0,9171,967753-1,00.html.

113. While these organizations are mentioned in numerous articles about VDT safety, they are all cited in Cotton Timberlake, "Expectant Mothers Face Hard Choices as VDT Safety Debate Continues," *Houston Chronicle*, April 25, 1986.

114. David Tong, "Committee OKs Watered-Down VDT Measure," *Oakland Tribune*, June 8, 1984, carton 5, folder 169, 9to5 Additional Records A.

115. Beaulieu, letter to the *Guild Reporter*.

116. Stein, "Coalition Fights VDT Legislation," 47–49.

117. Micky Baca, "Revived VDT Bill Sparks Debate Over Office Conditions," *New Hampshire Business Review* 9, no. 35 (January 29, 1988).

118. Donald Coleman, "NAM Urges Employers to Take VDT Actions," *San Diego Union-Tribune*, September 12, 1984.

119. Laurie Flynn, "Computeritis: Who's Responsible When PCs Make Employees Sick?," *InfoWorld*, May 1, 1989, 54.

120. Jane Anderson, "Secretaries Seek New Career Paths," *Christian Science Monitor*, April 27, 1983; Fried, "Employers Need to Rethink the Way They Pay Secretaries."

121. Sweeney, "Does the Automated Office Dehumanize Jobs?"

122. *Processed World* History, http://www.processedworld.com/History/history.html, accessed August 7, 2018. See Hyman, *Temp*, 249–53, on *Processed World*.

123. Garson, *Electronic Sweatshop*, 197–98.

124. *Automation of America's Offices*, 22. The federal government encouraged the offshoring of data entry jobs as a cost-effective option for U.S.-based companies and as a way to promote economic development in Caribbean countries.

125. Carla Freeman, "Designing Women: Corporate Discipline and Barbados's Off-Shore Pink-Collar Sector," *Cultural Anthropology* 8, no. 2 (May 1993): 169–86. Although the pay for these jobs was comparable to factory work, young women in Barbados reported that they enjoyed the prestige and comfort of working in an office for an American company. They emphasized that they liked wearing professional office attire.

126. See Hyman, *Temp*, esp. 245–58.

127. *Forbes* (April 29, 1985, 231) reported that of the nation's 500 largest publicly owned companies, total sales in 1984 rose by 4 percent. Simultaneously, the number of people on payrolls shrank by 4 percent. *Automation of America's Offices*, 34.

128. John Torpey, "Automation Promotes 'Irregular' Work," *Video Views: The VDT Coalition* 2, no. 3 (February/March 1985): 4. See Hyman, *Temp*.

129. Andrew Pollack, "A New Automation to Bring Vast Changes," *New York Times*, March 28, 1982.

130. Barker, "Automation Revolution Brings Efficiency, Foreboding to Office."

131. Janet Abbate, *Recoding Gender: Women's Changing Participation in Computing* (Cambridge, Mass.: MIT Press, 2012); Walter Isaacson, *The Innovators: How a Group of Hackers, Geniuses, and Geeks Created the Digital Revolution* (New York: Simon & Schuster,

2014); Margot Lee Shetterly, *Hidden Figures: The Untold Story of the African American Women Who Helped Win the Space Race* (New York: William Morrow, 2016); Judy Wajcman, "Patriarchy, Technology, and Conceptions of Skill," *Work and Occupations* 18, no. 1 (February 1991): 38.

132.   "Office Work in America," a report by Working Women, April 1982, carton 5, folder 147, 9to5 Additional Records A; Feldberg and Glenn, "Technology and Work Degradation," 59–66; Tepperman, *Not Servants, Not Machines,* 46. In the 1970s women constituted only 15 percent of programmers and analysts but 93 percent of lower-level operators at an average insurance data-processing center.

133.   *Automation of America's Offices,* 24. Young workers and racial minority workers were predicted to be among those most likely to become unemployed. See *Automation of American's Offices,* 77.

134.   Articles from the American Bankers Association and *American Banker* about preventing employee turnover and unionization, 1980–81, carton 4, folder 129, 9to5 Additional Records A.

6. COULD PINK-COLLAR WORKERS "SAVE THE LABOR MOVEMENT"?

1.   "Secretarial School Honors Working Women," *Baltimore Afro-American,* May 2, 1981. The quote in the title for this chapter is from Karen Nussbaum, "Can Women Save the Labor Movement?" (comment), *Los Angeles Herald Examiner,* September 5, 1982, box 14, folder 81, SEIU District 925 Collection.

2.   Carol Krucoff, "Careers: Unions for Secretaries?" *Washington Post,* April 29, 1981.

3.   Krucoff, "Careers: Unions for Secretaries?"

4.   Barbara Brotman, "Katharine Gibbs School: From 'Educated Women' to 'Office Teams,'" *Chicago Tribune,* November 30, 1980.

5.   NSA Reports No. 4, Suggested News Release, November 1979, box 6, folder 32, NSA, Philadelphia Records.

6.   R. C. Deans, "Productivity and the New Work Ethic," in *Editorial Research Reports on the American Work Ethic,* ed. W. B. Dickenson, Jr. (Washington, D.C.: Congressional Quarterly Press, 1972), http://library.cqpress.com/cqresearcher/cqresrre1972041900. Given the relative stagnation of the U.S. economy, presidents and senators devoted resources to investigating the sluggish growth of the gross domestic product (GDP). At an annual average rate of 2.1 percent from 1965 to 1970, the productivity gains of the United States fell behind those of other industrialized countries, such as the United Kingdom (3.6 percent), Canada (3.5 percent), France (6.6 percent), Germany (5.3 percent), and in particular Japan (14.2 percent). From World War II until 1965, the average annual productivity increase for the United States had always been above 3 percent, yet the United States in the 1970s began falling behind in output per labor hour.

7. In *The Transformation of American Industrial Relations* (New York: Basic Books, 1986, 146–77), Thomas Kochan, Harry Katz, and Robert McKersie grouped these reforms into three categories: the workplace, collective bargaining, and business strategy.

8. Herman Gadon, "Making Sense of Quality of Work Life Programs," *Business Horizons* 27, no. 1 (January/February 1984): 43. Gadon describes QWL programs as focused on areas such as personal and professional development, team building, and work scheduling (ideas such as flextime and job sharing).

9. Fred K. Foulkes, *Creating More Meaningful Work* (New York: American Management Association, 1969).

10. Jefferson Cowie, *Stayin' Alive: The 1970s and the Last Days of the Working Class* (New York: New Press, 2010); Nelson Lichtenstein, *State of the Union: A Century of American Labor* (Princeton, N.J.: Princeton University Press, 2002).

11. According to a Quality of Employment Survey funded by the Department of Labor in 1977, most Americans had less confidence in union leaders than they did in government or business leaders. Kochan, Katz, and McKersie, *Transformation of American Industrial Relations*, 216–17.

12. Although public opinion polls showed that respondents believed that unions could improve working conditions and pay, the negative image of unions resulted in declining membership rates. See James L. Medoff, "The Public's Image of Labor and Labor's Response," Harvard University, National Bureau of Economic Research, November 1984, box 3, folder 11, SEIU District 925 Collection.

13. Kochan, Katz, and McKersie, *Transformation of American Industrial Relations*, 216–17.

14. Dorothy Sue Cobble, "'A Spontaneous Loss of Enthusiasm:' Workplace Feminism and the Transformation of Women's Service Jobs in the 1970s," *International Labor and Working-Class History* 56 (Fall 1999): 23–44; Katherine Turk, *Equality on Trial: Gender and Rights in the Modern American Workplace* (Philadelphia: University of Pennsylvania Press, 2016); Lane Windham, *Knocking on Labor's Door: Union Organizing in the 1970s and the Roots of a New Economic Divide* (Chapel Hill: University of North Carolina Press, 2017).

15. Frank Spotnitz, "America's Labor Unions Trying for a Comeback After a Decade That Saw Membership at an All-Time Low," *Fort Lauderdale Sun Sentinel*, September 1, 1985.

16. Yet white-collar unions were successful in the public sector, arguably because employees viewed them more like professional associations that happened to have the power of collective bargaining. Richard Freeman and Jonathan Leonard, "Union Maids: Unions and the Female Workforce," NBER Working Paper No. 1652 (Cambridge, Mass.: National Bureau of Economic Research, June 1985), 4. Also, university clericals unionized, which scholars have explained by pointing to a more progressive culture on college campuses. Richard W. Hurd, "Learning from Clerical Unions: Two Cases of Organizing Success," *Labor Studies Journal* 14, no. 1 (1989): 30–51; Richard W. Hurd, "Organizing and Representing Clerical Workers: The Harvard Model," in *Women and Unions: Forging a Partnership*, ed. Dorothy Sue Cobble (Ithaca, N.Y.: ILR Press, 1993), 316–36.

17. Nussbaum, "Can Women Save the Labor Movement?"

18. "Stop the Music," *Wall Street Journal*, July 26, 1972; "Cry of 'Productivity Crisis' Hit," *Washington Post*, May 21, 1972; Sanford Rose, "The News About Productivity Is Better Than You Think," *Fortune*, February 1972; Sandra Stencel, *America's Changing Work Ethic, Editorial Research Reports*, vol. 2 (Washington, D.C.: CQ Press, 1979), http://library.cqpress.com/cqresearcher/cqresrre1979121400; Edward Rohrbach, "Hits Concern on Productivity," *Chicago Tribune*, April 27, 1972.

19. Richard Nixon, "Address to the Nation on Labor Day," September 6, 1971, American Presidency Project, ed. Gerhard Peters and John T. Woolley, https://www.presidency.ucsb.edu/node/240755. See also Richard Nixon, "President's Address to Nation on Inflation and Economic Policy (transcript), *New York Times*, June 18, 1970. Harry Braverman, *Labor and Monopoly Capital: The Degradation of Work in the Twentieth Century* (New York: Monthly Review Press, 1974), 35.

20. *Hearings on S. 3916, Worker Alienation, 1972, Before the Subcommittee on Employment, Manpower, and Poverty of the Committee on Labor and Public Welfare*, U.S. Senate, 92nd Congress, 2nd session (July 25–26, 1972) (statement of Senator Edward M. Kennedy), 8, 9.

21. Wilfrid C. Rodgers, "Working Less, Producing Less," *Boston Globe*, May 27, 1979; William T. Moye, "Presidential Labor-Management Committees: Productive Failures," *ILR Review* 34, no. 1 (October 1980): 51–66.

22. "Productivity Rise Eased in Quarter," *Wall Street Journal*, April 26, 1972. Also see Moye, "Presidential Labor-Management Committees."

23. W. E. Upjohn Institute for Employment Research, *Work in America: Report of a Special Task Force to the Secretary of Health, Education, and Welfare* (Cambridge, Mass.: MIT Press, 1973), 114, 10–13.

24. *Work in America*, 34, 39–40; Braverman, *Labor and Monopoly Capital*, 32–35; Robert H. Guest, "Quality of Work Life: Prospects for the 80s," *Vital Speeches of the Day* 46, no. 10 (March 1, 1980): 310–14; Doug Rossinow, *The Politics of Authenticity: Liberalism, Christianity, and the New Left in America* (New York: Columbia University Press, 1998).

25. Rossinow, *Politics of Authenticity*. Rossinow suggests that activists of the 1960s sought to live an authentic existence by working with other authentic people to improve society at large. Although his book is a case study of the University of Texas, it makes a powerful point that these activists saw themselves as correcting morals and values that had gone awry, not just as lobbying for issues that were on the left of the political spectrum.

26. Daniel Yankelovich, "The New Psychological Contracts at Work," *Psychology Today*, May 1978, 46, 47, 49.

27. "Wildcat" means it was not planned or sanctioned by the United Auto Workers (UAW) local in Lordstown.

28. Cowie, *Stayin' Alive*, 47–48, 23–74. Also see Lichtenstein, *State of the Union*, 178–211, on the "rights conscious strategy" that arose in the 1960s and 1970s and weakened the organized labor movement in the United States.

29. *Hearings, Worker Alienation*, 10–17 (statement of Gary Brynner, president, UAW Local 1112, Lordstown, Ohio). Brynner also explained that automation was resulting in employees who were disconnected from their work and uninterested in unionization.

30. Stephen H. Fuller, "How Quality-of-Worklife Projects Work for General Motors," *Monthly Labor Review* 103, no. 7 (July 1980): 37. A GM vice president wrote that quality of work life is many things, including "developing among all members of an organization an awareness and understanding of the concerns and needs of others, and a willingness to be more responsive to those concerns and needs."

31. Robert H. Guest, "Quality of Work Life—Learning from Tarrytown," *Harvard Business Review*, July 1979, 76–87.

32. Daniel Zwerdling, *Toward a More Human Way of Working in America: A Report on the First National Conference of the American Quality of Work Life Association*, conferenced convened by the American Center for the Quality of Work Life, May 20–22, 1977 (Washington, D.C.: U.S. Government Printing Office, 1979).

33. M. Elkind, memo to G. Sudbey and R. Wood, "re: Project 2808, Quality of World Life Program Status," February 23, 1976, box I.388, folder 27, Polaroid Corporation Administrative Records, Baker Library Historical Collections, Harvard Business School, Cambridge, Mass. (hereafter cited as Polaroid Corporation Records).

34. *Hearings, Worker Alienation*, 89 (statement of Harold Sheppard, Upjohn Institute).

35. Notes—Polaroid PP 101, Work Life Quality Etc., April 25, 1976, box I.388, folder 27, Polaroid Corporation Records; W. R. Page, memo to Quality of Working Life Group, "re: Notes on Discussion with Page, Duncan, Berlew on the QWL in Polaroid," April 6, April 22, 1976, box I.388, folder 27, Polaroid Corporation Records.

36. "New Industrial Relations," *Business Week*, May 11, 1981, 85.

37. Thomas A. Kochan and Michael J. Piore, "Will the New Industrial Relations Last? Implications for the American Labor Movement," *Annals of the American Academy of Political and Social Science* 473 (May 1984): 177–89; John T. Dunlop, "Have the 1980's Changed U.S. Industrial Relations?," *Monthly Labor Review* 111, no. 5 (May 1988): 33; Kochan, Katz, and McKersie, *Transformation of American Industrial Relations*.

38. Zwerdling, *Toward a More Human Way of Working*, 32.

39. Paul S. Goodman, "Realities of Improving the Quality of Work Life: Quality of Work Life Projects in the 1980s," *Labor Law Journal* 31, no. 8 (August 1980): 487–94.

40. Zwerdling, *Toward a More Human Way of Working*, 35–36.

41. Most QWL projects shared "joint union and management 'ownership,' or joint representation." Zwerdling, *Toward a More Human Way of Working*, 7.

42. *Work in America*, 38.

43. *Work in America*, 315, 325–26.

44. Judith Gregory, "Safety and Health for the Office Worker with an Emphasis on Job Stress," SEIU Women's Conference in Storrs, Connecticut, June 3, 1981. carton 5, folder 154, 9to5 Additional Records A; *Hearings on the Human Factor in Innovation and Productivity by the Science, Research, and Technology Subcommittee of the House Committee on Science and Technology* (September 18, 1981) (Judith Gregory, testimony for 9to5, National Association of Working Women), carton 5, folder 154, 9to5 Additional

Records A. Gregory called on the government to help clericals curtail the adverse health effects—stress, visual, musculoskeletal, and nervous system problems—resulting from automation. According to Gregory, "Action must be taken now before irreparable harm is done to office workers' jobs, health, and quality of working life."

45. Anne Wyman, "Question of the '80s for Labor: What Do Workers Really Want," *Boston Globe*, September 7, 1981; Peter F. Drucker, "Drucker on Management: How to Measure White-Collar Productivity," *Wall Street Journal*, November 26, 1985, 1.

46. "Ergonomics: The Cure for Computer Blues," *Savings Institutions* 105 (January 1984): 97–99; Robert F. Bettendorf, "VDTs: Turning Good Ergonomics Into Good Economics," *Employment Relations Today* 18, no. 1 (Spring 1991): 15.

47. Louise Kapp Howe, *Pink Collar Workers: Inside the World of Women's Work* (New York: Avon Books, 1977), 146–47.

48. While many employers considered pay to be distinct from QWL initiatives, psychology professor Edward E. Lawler III disagreed with this thinking. Much of his research showed that employees' perceptions about pay could influence their motivation. Lawler contended that QWL programs should address more than cosmetic changes. If employees saw the base pay system as inequitable, then other changes (like repainting the cafeteria or repaving the parking lot) mattered little to them. Edward E. Lawler III and R. J. Bullock, "Pay and Organizational Change," *Personnel Administrator* 23, no. 5 (May 1978): 32–35; Philip H. Mirvis and Edward E. Lawler III, "Accounting for the Quality of Work Life," *Journal of Organizational Behavior* 5 (1984): 207.

49. Howe, *Pink Collar Workers*, 155.

50. Zwerdling, *Toward a More Human Way of Working*, 31.

51. Howe, *Pink Collar Workers*, 146–47.

52. Marguerite Michaels, "Can Labor Unions Survive?," *Boston Globe*, September 2, 1984, SMA14.

53. Wyman, "Question of the '80s for Labor," 2.

54. "The Changing Situation of Workers and Their Unions," AFL-CIO Committee on the Evolution of Work, February 1985, box 3, folder 12, SEIU District 925 Collection. In this report, the committee claims that in 1957 the National Labor Relations Board secured reinstatement for 922 workers who had been fired for union activity. By 1980 that number had reached 10,000. In addition, although the labor force, and particularly the service sector, grew rapidly during the 1970s, labor membership numbers remained static in that decade. Most likely gains in service-sector organizing were offset by job loss in traditional industries like manufacturing.

55. Brotman, "Katharine Gibbs School." Nancy DeMars, NSA president, reported in this article that secretaries are an integral part of management.

56. NSA Reports No. 5, December 1979, Fran Riley, NSA public relations counselor, memo to Chapter Presidents and Secretaries Week Chairmen, "Getting a Head Start on 1980 Secretaries Week, April 20–26," box 6, folder 32, NSA, Philadelphia Records. Later in this chapter actress Jane Fonda's association with 9to5 is addressed.

57. Karen Nussbaum, speech, Future of Working Women Movement (at a women's magazines breakfast, no location), October 18, 1988, box 15, folder 30, SEIU District 925 Collection.

58. In addition to clerical unionizing, there was also a rise in female union membership among teachers, librarians, social workers, autoworkers, electricians, and bus drivers. Public-sector unionism was incorporating clericals, too. Roberta Lynch, "Organizing Clericals: Problems and Prospects," *Labor Research Review* 1, no. 8 (1986): 90–101.

59. Quote is the subtitle of Cowie, *Stayin' Alive*. Nussbaum, "Can Women Save the Labor Movement?" Statistic is from 1967 to 1982.

60. Unions of the 1970s had been winning 59 percent of the representation elections where women's issues had been the focal point, as opposed to the 50 percent average win rate for all elections regardless of issue. Nussbaum, "Can Women Save the Labor Movement?"

61. John G. Kilgour, "Office Unions: Keeping the Threat Small," *Administrative Management*, November 1982, 23–24, 58–59, box 6, folder 8, SEIU District 925 Collection.

62. Ellen Cassedy, Karen Nussbaum, and Debbie Schneider, interview by Ann Froines, Washington, D.C., November 1, 2005, SEIU District 925 Legacy Project.

63. Women's Work Project, *Women Organizing the Office* (Washington, D.C.: Women in Distribution, 1978).

64. "Confidential: Report to the International President on Local 925 Organizing Strategy," October 15, 1977, box 3, folder 4, SEIU District 925 Collection. Regarding finances, the budget for Local 925 in 1977 was $1,000 per month for basic expenses plus three organizers' salaries. Furthermore, 9to5 leaders knew that the time was ripe to align more strongly with organized labor. Opportunities for promising clerical drives existed in many different cities, such as Philadelphia, Detroit, Columbus, and Newark, where they had heard that clericals were looking for union affiliation.

65. "Confidential: Proposal to Unionize Clerical Workers," ca. 1979–80, box 5, folder 24, SEIU District 925 Collection.

66. Lorraine Sorrel, "Working Women Organize 925," *Off Our Backs* 11, no. 4 (April 30, 1981): 8. For instance, see Minutes, Minority Task Force, February 11, 1982, carton 5, folder 171, 9to5 Additional Records A. This document discusses low participation by women of color in 9to5's Boston affiliate and explores ways to attract them to the organization. For more on recruiting women of color to 9to5, also see carton 5, folder 172, 9to5 Additional Records A; carton 16, folders 1013 to 1023, 9to5 Additional Records B; carton 3, folder 106 and 116, 9to5 Records.

67. Geri Palast, interview by Stacey Heath, July 14, 2006, SEIU District 925 Legacy Project.

68. Sorrel, "Working Women Organize 925."

69. Karen Nussbaum, notes from meeting with Kim Fellner, September 6, 1977, box 3, folder 4, SEIU District 925 Collection. On Nussbaum's focus on consciousness raising and publicity, see her letter to Elinor Glenn, March 31, 1978, box 3, folder 4, SEIU District 925 Collection. She wrote to Glenn, "Though winning elections and contracts is as painstaking as ever, we are succeeding in our 'consciousness-raising' work of bringing the issues of women office workers out into the public and mobilizing support. In addition to the Wall Street Journal article (of Feb. 24, 1978), we had a nationally syndicated AP story, and I recently appeared on the Phil Donahue Show as a guest. One of our people even appeared on *To Tell the Truth*." Nussbaum is pointing to the influence

of District 925 on the SEIU and labor unions in general, as stated by many of the SEIU
925 Legacy Project oral history subjects.

70. Report to the International President on Local 925 Organizing Strategy, October 15, 1977,
box 3, folder 4, SEIU District 925 Collection.

71. Karen Nussbaum, letter to John Geagan, January 7, 1978, box 3, folder 4, SEIU District
925 Collection.

72. Karen Nussbaum, memo to John Geagan, "re: Local 925 organizing efforts out-of-state,"
December 26, 1977, box 3, folder 4, SEIU District 925 Collection. For more on the unsuc-
cessful drive at the University of Pittsburgh, see Anne Hill, interview by Ann Froines,
December 6, 2005, SEIU District 925 Legacy Project.

73. Karen Nussbaum, letter to John Geagan, February 14, 1978, box 3, folder 4, SEIU District 925 Collection. She also was writing directly to George Hardy to ask for extra
money for Pittsburgh, citing a strong anti-union campaign on the part of the university. See her letter to George Hardy, May 11, 1978, box 3, folder 4, SEIU District 925
Collection.

74. Karen Nussbaum, letter to John Geagan, October 24, 1978, box 3, folder 4, SEIU District 925 Collection. See also Nussbaum to Geagan, September 26, 1978, box 3, folder 4,
SEIU District 925 Collection.

75. Karen Nussbaum to Elinor Glenn, September 7, 1977, box 3, folder 4, SEIU District 925
Collection. See also Nussbaum to Glenn, September 20, 1977; Nussbaum to Rosemary
Trump, September 20, 1977; Nussbaum to Marilyn Alexander, October 16, 1977; and
Nussbaum to Trump, October 21, 1977 (all in box 3, folder 4, SEIU District 925
Collection).

76. Karen Nussbaum, letter to Rosemary Trump of SEIU, September 20, 1977, box 3, folder
4, SEIU District 925 Collection. Also see Nussbaum, notes from meeting with Jackie
Ruff, September 7, 1977, box 3, folder 4, SEIU District 925 Collection.

77. SEIU District 925 Collection, Karen Nussbaum, letter to John Sweeney, April 15, 1980,
box 5, folder 24, SEIU District 925 Collection.

78. George Hardy, SEIU president, memo to all affiliated local unions, "re: Office Worker
Unionization," March 7, 1978, box 3, folder 4, SEIU District 925 Collection. Hardy did
circulate a *Wall Street Journal* article to all SEIU affiliates, which gave Nussbaum credit
for her Local 925 organizing efforts. The memo consisted of the *Wall Street Journal* article on Local 925 success.

79. Karen Nussbaum, letter to Bob Welsh, assistant to President Sweeney, November 25,
1980, box 5, folder 24, SEIU District 925 Collection.

80. "Memorandum of Understanding," February 1, 1981, box 5, folder 24, SEIU District 925
Collection.

81. Ray Abernathy, letter to Bob Welsh, January 19, 1981, box 5, folder 25, SEIU District 925
Collection. The Miami meeting was schedule to take place in the middle of February.

82. Ray Abernathy, letter to Bob Welsh, January 29, 1981, box 5, folder 25, SEIU District 925
Collection.

83. Ray Abernathy, memo to participants in SEIU/WW press conference, "re: Message Control," February 17, 1981, box 5, folder 25, SEIU District 925 Collection.

84.   Abernathy to Welsh, January 19, 1981.

85.   Karen Nussbaum, letter to Bob Welsh, January 5, 1981, box 5, folder 24, SEIU District 925 Collection.

86.   Carrie Baker, *The Women's Movement Against Sexual Harassment* (New York: Cambridge University Press, 2008), 42; Emily E. LB. Twarog, "Before #MeToo: The History of the 9to5 Job Survival Hotline," *Labor: Studies in Working-Class History* 19, no. 1 (March 2022): 96–108.

87.   Some unions, like AFSCME, had committees for sexual harassment. Turk, *Equality on Trial*, chap. 4. Sexual harassment was cited as a key issue for organizing and for union contracts. Baker, *The Women's Movement Against Sexual Harassment*.

88.   Lisa W. Foderaro, "New Focus on Sexual Harassment," *New York Times*, July 23, 1986; JoAnn Lublin, "Sexual Harassment Is Topping Agenda in Many Executive Education Programs," *Wall Street Journal*, December 2, 1991, B1.

89.   Julie Berebitsky, *Sex and the Office: A History of Gender, Power, and Desire* (New Haven, Conn.: Yale University Press, 2012).

90.   Baker, *Women's Movement Against Sexual Harassment*, 15-17; Serena Mayeri, *Reasoning from Race: Feminism, Law, and the Civil Rights Revolution* (Cambridge, Mass.: Harvard University Press, 2011).

91.   Kathy Mackay, ". . . And the Secretaries' Revenge," *Washington Post*, December 16, 1980; Philip Shabecoff, "March of the Nine-to-Five Woman," *New York Times*, March 29, 1981.

92.   Georgia Dullea, "Secretaries See Parallels in 'Nine to Five,'" *New York Times*, January 2, 1981.

93.   Eleanor Ringel, "Trio Works Overtime in 'Nine to Five,'" *Atlanta Constitution*, December 19, 1980.

94.   Carol Stocker, "Getting Into Shape with Famous Figures," *Boston Globe*, November 19, 1982.

95.   Kathy Mackay, "Jane Fonda Takes a Dip in the Typing Pool," *Working Woman* 5, no. 12 (December 1980): 66.

96.   Dullea, "Secretaries See Parallels in 'Nine to Five.'"

97.   Vincent Canby, "Screen: 'Nine to Five,' Office Comedy: Revolt of the Women," *New York Times*, December 19, 1980; Ringel, "Trio Works Overtime in 'Nine to Five'"; Caitlin Manning, "9to5: We're So Pretty . . . Pretty Vacant!" *Processed World* 1 (April 1981), http://www.processedworld.com/Issues/issue01/i01_925.html.

98.   Dullea, "Secretaries See Parallels in 'Nine to Five.'"

99.   Ringel, "Trio Works Overtime in 'Nine to Five.'"

100.   Rosabeth Moss Kanter, *Men and Women of the Corporation* (New York: Basic Books, 1977), 98–99.

101.   Caroline Bird, "Working Your Way Up," *Working Woman* 1, no. 1 (November 1976): 86.

102.   District 925 press release, Washington, D.C., February 24, 1981, box 5, folder 25, SEIU District 925 Collection.

103.   District 925 announcement brochure, 1981, box 5, folder 25, SEIU District 925 Collection.

104.   Abernathy, memo to participants in SEIU/WW press conference, February 17, 1981.

105. *Los Angeles Times,* March 6, 1981; *New York Times,* March 4, 1981; *Cincinnati Post,* March 4, 1981; *Longview, WA News,* March 18, 1981, all in box 5, folder 25, SEIU District 925 Collection. The story also appeared in many other papers, including the *Cincinnati Post, San Francisco Post, Bowling Green, Ohio Sentinel-Tribune, Arizona Business Gazette, St. Paul, Minnesota Pioneer Press, Pomona Progress-Bulletin,* and *Longview Washington News.* Other articles from named newspapers in the previous sentence can also be found in box 5, folder 25, SEIU District 925 Collection.

106. Harry Bernstein, "Film 'Nine to Five' Sparks Interest in Unionization of Office Workers," *Los Angeles Times,* March 6, 1981, box 5, folder 25, SEIU District 925 Collection.

107. District 925 press release, February 24, 1981.

108. John J. Sweeney, memo to all local unions, "re: District 925," March 17, 1981, box 5, folder 25, SEIU District 925 Collection.

109. Cassedy, Nussbaum, and Schneider, interview by Ann Froines. Quote is from Schneider.

110. Denise Mitchell, public relations for District 925, memo to Jackie Ruff, Karen Nussbaum, and Bob Welsh, "re: Public Relations Activities Update," July 13, 1981, box 5, folder 39, SEIU District 925 Collection. By the summer of 1981 District 925 already was contemplating ways to increase its visibility and considering advertising in popular women's magazines.

111. In the 1980s Harvard economist James Medoff wrote about the importance of labor's public image, claiming that the public image of unions determined or at least affected their success as organizations. In the 1970s and '80s, Medoff reported that the public viewed unions more as monopolies than as voices for the people, causing their public approval ratings to drop. He claimed that public opinion polls showed that people thought unions could improve working conditions and pay, thus making the public image factor all the more significant. Karen Nussbaum sent one of his articles from *Business Week* (December 17, 1984) to other leaders of 9to5 in 1985. See Medoff, "The Public's Image of Labor and Labor's Response."

112. Report to the International President on Local 925 Organizing Strategy, October 15, 1977.

113. *Work in America,* 39. Between 1958 and 1968, there had been a 46 percent increase in white-collar unionization; there was also a 34 percent decline in the belief that an employer would do something to address an individual worker's problems during that same period.

114. Alfred Vogel, "Your Clerical Workers Are Ripe for Unionism," *Harvard Business Review,* 1971, 48–51.

115. "Anti-Union Seminar Held," *Charleston, Illinois Times-Courier,* January 20, 1982, box 5, folder 38, SEIU District 925 Collection. The University of Pittsburgh hired a firm that included a former SEIU official. Karen Nussbaum, letter to George Hardy, president of SEIU, May 11, 1978, box 3, folder 4, SEIU District 925 Collection. Former counsel for the NLRB, for instance, began to consult on these issues in Chicago.

116. Cassedy, Nussbaum, and Schneider, interview by Ann Froines.

117. Joann S. Lublin, "Labor Strikes Back at Consultants That Help Firms Keep Unions Out," *Wall Street Journal,* April 2, 1981.

118. "In 1957, the NLRB secured reinstatement for 922 workers who had been fired for union activity. By 1980, that figure had reached 10,000. Professor Paul Weiler of HLS [Harvard Law School] has concluded that in 1980 there were at least 1.5 discriminatory discharges for every representation election conducted." AFL-CIO Committee on the Evolution of Work, "The Changing Situation of Workers and their Unions," February 1985, 10, box 3, folder 12, SEIU District 925 Collection. The 75 percent statistic was according to the AFL-CIO by the early 1980s.

119. Denise Mitchell and Ray Abernathy, interview by Ann Froines, November 5, 2005, SEIU District 925 Legacy Project.

120. Phyllis Payne, "The Consultants Who Coach Violators," *AFL-CIO American Federationist*, September 1977, MC 624, box 21, folder 6, Harvard Union Records.

121. Windham, *Knocking on Labor's Door*, 64.

122. "Anti-Union Seminar Held." Quote is from a labor attorney at the State of Illinois Chamber of Commerce meeting in Chicago during a "how to stay nonunion" seminar attended by many bank representatives.

123. Mitchell and Abernathy, interview by Ann Froines. According to Abernathy, "The workers were easily intimidated" because clericals very much needed the money they were earning.

124. Anne Field, "The Management: Union Busters Target Women," *Working Woman* 5, no. 12 (December 1980).

125. Kilgour, "Office Unions." Ensuring that supervisors felt that they were part of the management team was also recommended.

126. Field, "The Management," 72.

127. Doreen Levasseur, interview by Ann Froines, February 23, 2005, SEIU District 925 Legacy Project. "It was not only as bad as we thought, but worse," according to Levasseur.

128. Ellen Karasik, "Union Organizing Office Workers," *Philadelphia Business Journal*, [1982], box 5, folder 38, SEIU District 925 Collection.

129. Field, "The Management," 70.

130. *Women Organizing the Office*, 50–51. Other tactics included management-sponsored conferences on "preventative labor relations" as well as "captive audience meetings," where a supervisor or employer would mandate that employees attend an arguably one-sided discussion of the negative consequences of union membership.

131. R. C. Longworth and Bill Neikirk, "Dig In to Keep Jobs: Unions Aging but Ready to Fight," *Chicago Tribune*, September 20, 1979, 1.

132. Steve Askin, "Female Rights Spell Trouble for Bosses," *In These Times*, July 27–August 9, 1983, box 5, folder 38, SEIU District 925 Collection.

133. Longworth and Neikirk, "Dig In to Keep Jobs."

134. Phil Donahue, *The Last Word* (transcript), ABC News, January 31, 1983, box 6, folder 8, SEIU District 925 Collection.

135. Robert S. Greenberger, "Quality Circles Grow, Stirring Union Worries," *Wall Street Journal*, September 22, 1981.

136. "Equitable Life Oks Labor Contract," *Los Angeles Times*, November 12, 1984.

137. Karen Mudd, "Work, Race, and Class: Making the Links in Theory and Practice," *Off Our Backs* 15, no. 8 (September 30, 1985): 3.

138. Cathy Trost, "Equitable Life Accord with Service Union Marks Breakthrough," *Wall Street Journal*, November 12, 1984.

139. Walter Kleinschrod, *Critical Issues in Office Automation* (New York: McGraw Hill, 1986), 144.

140. Peter Perl, "Clerical Workers Organized at Major Insurance Firm," *Washington Post*, November 10, 1984.

141. Trost, "Equitable Life Accord with Service Union Marks Breakthrough."

142. Perl, "Clerical Workers Organized at Major Insurance Firm."

143. Trost, "Equitable Life Accord with Service Union Marks Breakthrough."

144. William Serrin, "Upstate Office Workers Gain a Landmark Pact," *New York Times*, November 10, 1984.

145. Perl, "Clerical Workers Organized at Major Insurance Firm."

146. Cobble, "Spontaneous Loss of Enthusiasm," 33. When CWA organized MCI Communications in Detroit, the company announced the closing of the Detroit office, citing financial difficulty. Peter Perl, "The Lifeline for Unions: Recruiting," *Washington Post*, September 13, 1987.

147. "Conference Report: ABA (American Bankers Association)" and "National Conference on Human Resources," *White Collar Report* 56 (Washington D.C.: Bureau of National Affairs, September 26, 1984), 370–73, box 6, folder 8, SEIU District 925 Collection.

148. Tessa Melvin, "Alternative to Unions Suggested," *New York Times*, January 24, 1982.

149. Carol Pucci, "His Business Is Breaking Unions and Keeping Them Out," *Seattle Times*, November 28, 1982, box 5, folder 38, SEIU District 925 Collection. Bank and insurance clericals were described as "ripe for unionization."

150. *Women Organizing the Office*, 50–51. Some union officials agreed with consultants: the best way to keep unions out was to pay workers more and improve working conditions. Longworth and Neikirk, "Dig In to Keep Jobs," 1.

151. Lichtenstein, *State of the Union*, 210. Lichtenstein demonstrates that the rights discourse "has proven increasingly incapable of grappling with the structural crisis, both economic and social, that confronts American society."

152. Melvin, "Alternative to Unions Suggested." According to a labor relations lawyer at the seminar, this workplace strategy had successfully defeated union campaigns, including a District 925 effort, in several New York City banks.

153. "Conference Report: ABA (American Bankers Association)" and "National Conference on Human Resources," *White Collar Report* 56. There was also a session on comparable worth.

154. Berebitsky, *Sex and the Office*, 221.

155. Longworth and Neikirk, "Dig In to Keep Jobs."

156. John Logan, "The Union Avoidance Industry in the United States," *British Journal of Industrial Relations* 44, no. 4 (December 2006): 654; Jack Barbash, "Like Nature, Industrial Relations Abhors a Vacuum," *Relations Industrielles/Industrial Relations* 42, no. 1 (Winter 1987): 168–79.

157. Joseph A. McCartin, *Collision Course: Ronald Reagan, the Air Traffic Controllers, and the Strike That Changed America* (New York: Oxford University Press, 2011).

158. Thomas J. Raleigh, "Adapting to a Union-Free Environment," *Wall Street Journal*, October 22, 1984.

159. Frank Dobbin, *Inventing Equal Opportunity* (Princeton, N.J.: Princeton University Press, 2009); Lauren B. Edelman, *Working Law: Courts, Corporations, and Symbolic Civil Rights* (Chicago: University of Chicago Press, 2016).

160. Barbash, "Like Nature, Industrial Relations Abhors a Vaccum," 170.

161. Kilgour, "Office Unions." Statistic is compared to a 20 percent unionization rate for the total labor force. Public-sector clericals were more likely to unionize than were private-sector clericals.

162. Francis Carling, "AMA Forum: What Happened to the 'Threat' of White-Collar Unionization?," *Management Report* 74, no. 3 (March 1985): 53.

163. "Blue-Collar Boomers: The Most Frustrated of All," *Business Week*, July 2, 1984.

164. Diane Lewis, "Labor's Quiet Crusader Sweeney Sees Wave of Revolt Putting Him at AFL-CIO Helm," *Boston Globe*, September 3, 1995.

165. Herbert R. Northrup, "The AFL-CIO Blue Cross-Blue Shield Campaign: A Study of Organizational Failure," *ILR Review* 43, no. 5 (July 1990): 532.

166. Mitchell and Abernathy, interview by Ann Froines. At most, District 925 had 15,000–20,000 members. In contrast, SEIU public-sector and health-care-sector unions could have 250,000 members.

167. Northrup, "AFL-CIO Blue Cross-Blue Shield Campaign," 536.

168. Karen Nussbaum, memo to department heads of Working Women, "re: AFL-CIO Committee on the Future," January 3, 1985, box 3, folder 11, SEIU District 925 Collection. Attached to the memo: John Hoerr with Michael Pollock, "Labor Prescribes Some Strong Medicine for Itself," *Business Week*, December 17, 1984, 35; Louis Harris and Associates, "A Study on the Outlook for Trade Union Organizing," submitted to the Labor Institute for Public Affairs and the Future Work Committee, 1984. Also in box 3, folder 11, SEIU District 925 Collection: Medoff, "Public's Image of Labor and Labor's Response."

169. Dobbin, *Inventing Equal Opportunity*.

170. Richard Beckhard and Reuben T. Harris, *Organizational Transitions: Managing Complex Change* (Reading, Mass.: Addison-Wesley, 1977); Edgar H. Schein, *Career Dynamics: Matching Individual and Organizational Needs* (Reading, Mass.: Addison-Wesley, 1978); Mary Anne Devanna, Charles Fombrun, and Noel Tichy, "Human Resources Management: A Strategic Perspective," *Organizational Dynamics* 9, no. 3 (Winter 1981): 51–67; Michael Beer, Bert Spector, Paul R. Lawrence, D. Quinn Mills, and Richard E. Walton, *Managing Human Assets* (New York: Free Press, 1984).

171. Schein, *Career Dynamics*, 189, 192.

172. Fred K. Foulkes and Henry M. Morgan, "Organizing and Staffing the Personnel Function," *Harvard Business Review*, May–June 1977, 142.

173. Adrianna Nasch Stadecker, "9to5: Women Office Workers Interpret a Social Movement" (Ph.D. diss., Massachusetts Institute of Technology, Department of Urban Studies and

Planning, 1976), 203–5, carton 2, folder 57, 9to5 Additional Records A. Stadecker rein-
forces the point that employers would calm irritated workers by granting some of their
requests. Granting certain requests could cause 9to5 members to become less interested
in activism or have more difficulty mobilizing workers.

174.   Field, "Management: Union Busters Target Women," 70.
175.   Jackie Ruff, interview by Ann Froines, November 7, 2005, SEIU District 925 Legacy
       Project.
176.   Perl, "Lifeline for Unions."
177.   Benjamin C. Amick, III, "Health and Safety in the Automated Office: National Policy,
       Organizational Initiatives and Individual Choices," *Office: Technology and People* 3
       (1988): 341–60.
178.   Turk, *Equality on Trial*, chap. 4, location 2154.
179.   Richard W. Hurd and Adrienne McElwain, "Organizing Clerical Workers: Determi-
       nants of Success," *ILR Review* 41, no. 3 (April 1988): 361.
180.   Cassedy, Nussbaum, and Schneider, interview by Ann Froines.
181.   Victoria Irwin, "Office Workers' Movement Makes a Bid to Unionize," *Christian Sci-
       ence Monitor*, April 21, 1981.
182.   Shoshana Zuboff, *In the Age of the Smart Machine: The Future of Work and Power* (New
       York: Basic Books, 1988), 122, 235–37. Zuboff relied on Kanter's description in *Men and
       Women of the Corporation* of the secretarial function whereby there were two broad
       groups of secretaries. Some secretaries worked in a pool and therefore performed more
       "acting-on" types of tasks, while others worked for a particular boss and performed
       more "acting with" tasks.
183.   Anne Machung, "Turning Secretaries Into Word Processors," in *Office Automation:
       Jekyll or Hyde? Highlights of the International Conference on Office Work and New Tech-
       nology*, ed. Daniel Marschall and Judith Gregory (Cleveland, Ohio: Working Women
       Education Fund, 1983), 120.
184.   William H. Form, "Auto Workers and Their Machines: A Study of Work, Factory, and
       Job Satisfaction in Four Countries," *Social Forces*, September 1973.
185.   Yankelovich, "New Psychological Contracts at Work," 46.

7. A FEMINIST "BRAND CALLED YOU"

1.   Judge John Nordberg, "Memorandum Opinion and Order," Equal Employment Oppor-
     tunity Commission v. Sears, Roebuck and Co., U.S. District Court, Northern District
     of Illinois, Eastern Division, January 31, 1986. Ruth Milkman, "Women's History and
     the Sears Case," *Feminist Studies* 12, no. 2 (Summer 1986): 375–400.
2.   Rosalind Rosenberg, "From the Witness Stand: Previously Unpublished Testimony in
     the Sex Discrimination Case Against Sears," *Academic Questions*, Winter 1987–88,
     15–35.
3.   Alice Kessler-Harris, "Equal Employment Opportunity Commission v. Sears, Roebuck
     and Company: A Personal Account," *Feminist Review* 25, no. 1 (Spring 1987): 46–69.

4. Rosenberg, "From the Witness Stand," 15.

5. Samuel G. Freedman, "Of History and Politics: Bitter Feminist Debate," *New York Times*, June 6, 1986.

6. Kessler-Harris, "Equal Employment Opportunity Commission v. Sears, Roebuck and Company," 54–55, citing Rosenberg's written testimony. Rosenberg claimed that women had internalized feminine values, which society reinforced through its customs, culture, and laws, such that women retained their commitment to the home and did not seek jobs in male-dominated fields.

7. Alice Kessler-Harris, "American Women and the American Character: A Feminist Perspective," in *American Character and Culture in a Changing World: Some Twentieth-Century Perspectives*, ed. John A. Hague (Westport, Conn.: Greenwood Press, 1979), 240.

8. Katherine Turk, *Equality on Trial: Gender and Rights in the Modern American Workplace* (Philadelphia: University of Pennsylvania Press, 2016), chap. 3.

9. For social science literature on supply side, see Solomon William Polachek, "Occupational Self-Selection: A Human Capital Approach to Sex Differences in Occupational Structure," *Review of Economics and Statistics* 63, no. 1 (February 1981): 60–69; Gary Becker, "Human Capital, Effort, and the Sexual Division of Labor," *Journal of Labor Economics* 3, no. 1 (1985): S33–S58. For social science literature on demand side, see William T. Bielby and James N. Baron, "Men and Women at Work: Sex Segregation and Statistical Discrimination," *American Journal of Sociology* 91, no. 4 (January 1986): 759–99; Barbara Reskin and Patricia Roos, *Job Queues, Gender Queues: Explaining Women's Inroads Into Male Occupations* (Philadelphia: Temple University Press, 1990).

10. Social scientists and management scholars have shown that lower-class individuals tend to be more conformist and interdependent, while upper-class individuals tend to value self-expression and independence. Sean R. Martin and S. Côté, "Social Class Transitioners: Their Cultural Abilities and Organizational Importance," *Academy of Management Review* 44, no. 3 (2019): 618–42.

11. Previous histories have explored the social perceptions of becoming a clerical worker, demonstrating not just the changing nature of the work, but also the changing perceptions of the work. Ileen DeVault, *Sons and Daughters of Labor: Class and Clerical Work in Turn-of-the-Century Pittsburgh* (Ithaca, N.Y.: Cornell University Press, 1990). DeVault shows how perceptions of clerical work varied within the working class itself—and thus the social status of performing clerical work differed throughout early twentieth-century Pittsburgh.

12. See Nancy Fraser, "Feminism, Capitalism, and the Cunning of History," *New Left Review* 56 (March–April 2009): 97–117. On occupational choice, see Peter M. Blau, John W. Gustad, Richard Jessor, Herbert S. Parnes, and Richard C. Wilcock, "Occupational Choice: A Conceptual Framework," *ILR Review* 9, no. 4 (July 1956): 531–43; Ofer Sharone, "Constructing Unemployed Job Seekers as Professional Workers: The Depoliticizing Work-Game of Job Searching," *Qualitative Sociology* 30 (2007): 403–16; Steven Vallas and Andrea Hill, "Reconfiguring Worker Subjectivity: Career Advice Literature and the 'Branding' of the Worker's Self," *Sociological Forum*, 33 (2018): 287–309.

13. Peter Cappelli, "Career Jobs Are Dead," *California Management Review* 42, no. 1 (Fall 1999): 151–53. Reasons cited are pressures to increase shareholder value, shifting firm boundaries, the changing nature of firm competition, new organizational structures, public policy, and more outsourcing of jobs. For another perspective, see Sanford M. Jacoby, "Are Career Jobs Headed for Extinction?" *California Management Review* 42, no 1 (Fall 1999): 123–45.

14. William H. Whyte, *The Organization Man* (New York: Simon & Schuster, 1956).

15. Michael B. Arthur and Denise M. Rousseau, eds., *The Boundaryless Career: A New Employment Principle for a New Organizational Era* (New York: Oxford University Press, 1996).

16. Cappelli, "Career Jobs Are Dead," 147.

17. Jacoby, "Are Career Jobs Headed for Extinction?"

18. Arthur and Rousseau, *Boundaryless Career.*

19. Paul Ingram and Jean Joohyun Oh, "Mapping the Class Ceiling: The Social Class Disadvantage for Attaining Management Positions," *Academy of Management Discoveries*, March 2022. Also see Kathleen L. McGinn and Eunsil Oh, "Gender, Social Class, and Women's Employment," in "Inequality and Social Class," ed. Hazel Markus and Nicole Stephens, special issue, *Current Opinion in Psychology* 18 (December 2017): 84–88; and Lauren A. Rivera, *Pedigree: How Elite Students Get Elite Jobs* (Princeton, N.J.: Princeton University Press, 2015).

20. Siobhan O'Mahony and Beth A. Bechky, "Stretchwork: Managing the Career Progression Paradox in External Labor Markets," *Academy of Management Journal* 49, no. 5 (October 2006): 918–41. Also see Hannah Riley Bowles, Bobbi Thomason, and Julia B. Bear, "Reconceptualizing What and How Women Negotiate for Career Advancement," *Academy of Management Journal* 62, no. 6 (2019): 1645–71. The authors find that women who have ascended into leadership have been more likely to "shape" organizational norms (which, like stretchwork, requires time, effort, and creativity). *Shaping* is defined as "making a proposal for an individual allowance or authorization that would change organizational structures or practices for strategic purposes" (1652).

21. Tom Peters, "The Brand Called You," *Fast Company*, August 31, 1997, 83.

22. Carol Krucoff, "Careers: Take a Memo . . . It's National Secretary's Day," *Washington Post*, April 23, 1980. Management scholar Peter Drucker elaborated, "An unfortunate byproduct of the women's movement has been to make women feel guilty about pursuing traditional roles."

23. Frank Parsons, *Choosing a Vocation* (Boston: Houghton Mifflin, 1909).

24. For a brief overview of career choice theories, see Bill Gothard, "Career Development Theory," in *Careers Guidance in Context*, ed. Bill Gothard, Phil Mignot, Marcus Offer, and Melvyn Ruff (London: SAGE, 2001), 10–37.

25. Anne Roe, "High Hopes," *Vocational Guidance Quarterly* 8, no. 4 (Summer 1960): 196, 197.

26. Robert K. Conyne and Donald J. Cochran, "From Seeker to Seer: The Odyssey of Robert Hoppock," *Personnel and Guidance Journal* 54, no. 5 (January 1976): 273–79 (esp. 278).

27. Kevin McManus, "Making a Career of Careers," *Forbes* 129, no. 6 (March 15, 1982): 144; "Choosing a Career—the Agony and the Ecstasy," *Forbes* 129, no. 6 (March 15, 1982): 138–44.

28. James Yenckel, "Getting Rich on a Manual for the Unemployed," *Boston Globe*, July 7, 1982.

29. Virginia Postrel, "The Book of Jobs," *New York Times*, January 16, 2005.

30. Micki Magee, *Self-Help, Inc.: Makeover Culture in American Life* (New York: Oxford University Press, 2005), 117. Also see Amy Wrzesniewski, Clark McCauley, Paul Rozin, and Barry Schwartz, "Jobs, Careers, and Callings: People's Relations to Their Work," *Journal of Research in Personality* 31, no. 1 (1997): 21–33.

31. Postrel, "Book of Jobs."

32. Richard Sennett and Jonathan Cobb, *The Hidden Injuries of Class* (New York: Vintage Books, 1972), 250.

33. Samuel Bowles and Herbert Gintis, *Schooling in Capitalist America: Educational Reform and the Contradictions of Economic Life* (Routledge, 1976), 102–3; quotation on 105; Samuel Bowles and Herbert Gintis, "Schooling in Capitalist America Revisited," *Sociology of Education* 75 (January 2002): 1–18.

34. Kenneth B. Hoyt, "Career Education: History and Future," National Career Development Association, 2005.

35. Edwin L. Herr, "Kenneth B. Hoyt—Visionary, Statesperson, Leader, Activist," *Career Development Quarterly* 58, no. 2 (December 2009): 108–17.

36. Cappelli, "Career Jobs Are Dead"; Jacoby, "Are Career Jobs Headed for Extinction?"

37. Edgar Schein, "Increasing Organizational Effectiveness Through Better Human Resource Planning and Development," in *The Art of Managing Human Resources*, ed. Edgar Schein (New York: Oxford University Press, 1987), 30–31. Also see Schein's *Career Dynamics: Matching Individual and Organizational Needs* (Reading, Mass.: Addison-Wesley, 1978).

38. James W. Walker, *Human Resource Planning* (New York: McGraw Hill, 1980), 249–50; quotation on 253.

39. Barbara Welter, "The Cult of True Womanhood: 1820–1860," *American Quarterly* 18, no. 2 (1966): 151–74; Nancy F. Cott, *The Bonds of Womanhood: "Woman's Sphere" in New England, 1780–1835* (New Haven, Conn.: Yale University Press, 1997); Linda K. Kerber, "Separate Spheres, Female Worlds, Woman's Place: The Rhetoric of Women's History," *Journal of American History* 75, no. 1 (1988): 9–39.

40. Eileen Ogintz, "Secretarial Field Caught Short-Handed," *Chicago Tribune*, October 14, 1979, Q3.

41. Peter Grier, "Why Jobs Go Begging While Unemployment Grows," *Christian Science Monitor*, September 18, 1980.

42. Kathleen Gerson, *Hard Choices: How Women Decide bout Work, Career and Motherhood*, California Series on Social Choice and Political Economy (University of California Press, 1986), 82, 83. The woman quoted said she found the work "boring" and felt that she was "merely doing somebody else's work."

43. Gerson, 81, 84, 82.

44.   Jane Gaskell, "Course Enrollment in High School: The Perspective of Working-Class Females," *Sociology of Education* 58, no. 1 (January 1985): 51–57.

45.   James E. Rosenbaum, *Making Inequality: The Hidden Curriculum of High School Tracking* (New York: Wiley, 1976).

46.   Ivy Kennelly, "Race, Class, and Gender in Women's Pathways to Occupational Gender Segregation" (Ph.D. diss., University of Georgia, 1999), 80–81. About half of the sample wanted to work in female-dominated occupations and half in more gender-integrated occupations when they grew up.

47.   Bette A. Stead, "The National Secretarial Shortage: A Management Concern," *MSU Business Topics*, Winter 1980, 44.

48.   Kennelly, "Race, Class, and Gender in Women's Pathways," 98, 101, 106, and 109. From her sample, the older, white women, who were almost all members of Professional Secretaries International, reported satisfaction with their jobs, perceiving themselves in a role of caretaker and nurturer to their bosses.

49.   Ogintz, "Secretarial Field Caught Short-Handed," Q3.

50.   John Vacca, "Most Secretaries Prefer Automation, Survey Finds," *Atlanta Constitution*, March 11, 1984.

51.   Grier, "Why Jobs Go Begging While Unemployment Grows."

52.   Ogintz, "Secretarial Field Caught Short-Handed," Q3.

53.   Jane See White, "The Growing Secretarial Shortage," *Los Angeles Times*, December 16, 1981.

54.   White, "Growing Secretarial Shortage."

55.   Ogintz, "Secretarial Field Caught Short-Handed," Q3. Job offers received was according to Gordon Borehardt, president of MacCormac Junior College.

56.   N. Elizabeth Fried, "Employers Need to Rethink the Way They Pay Secretaries," *Journal of Compensation and Benefits* 4 (September–October 1988): 98.

57.   "The Secretarial Shortage: Lessons from the Past," *Personnel Journal* 59 (June 1980): 483.

58.   Anthony Dreyfus, "Responses to Skill Scarcity in a Changing Service Industry and Implications for School-Business Partnerships" (M.A. thesis, Massachusetts Institute of Technology, September 1991), 28.

59.   White, "Growing Secretarial Shortage."

60.   "Suddenly, a New Shortage of Secretaries," *Business Week*, August 8, 1977, 85; Vera Hilliard, "How a Secretarial Training Program Can Increase Company Efficiency," *Personnel Journal* 56, no. 8 (August 1977): 410–13.

61.   Irol W. Balsley, "View from the Top: That Secretarial Shortage," *Management World*, March 1979, 1. According to Balsley, "An executive who has never had the privilege of working with a college-educated secretary simply does not know the level of assistance that can be provided by such a person."

62.   Stead, "National Secretarial Shortage," 44.

63.   "Secretarial Shortage," 483.

64.   NSA Reports No. 3, Fran Riley, NSA public relations counselor, memo to all members through division and chapter presidents, October 1979, Special Memo—*Three's a Crowd* TV program, box 6, folder 32, NSA, Philadelphia Records.

65. Secretaries are Forever!, NSA Reports No. 4, November 1979, box 6, folder 32, NSA, Philadelphia Records.

66. Bryce Covert, "The Slow Death of the Secretary," *New Republic*, May 4, 2015, https://newrepublic.com/article/121712/slow-death-secretary.

67. Mary C. King, "Black Women's Breakthrough Into Clerical Work," *Journal of Economic Issues* 27, no. 4 (December 1993): 1097–1125.

68. Minority Outreach Task Force, Draft Proposal, n.d., carton 16, folders 1014, 9to5 Additional Records B.

69. For sensitivity training, see Jan Gadson of Women, Inc., *First Impressions: Black Womanhood Workshops* and *Employment Seminar: Minority Women—What's Happening in the Workforce?*, 1977 carton 3, folder 106, 9to5 Records.

70. See Minority Outreach/Current Plans and Possibilities, April 8, 1980, carton 16, folder 1014, 9to5 Additional Records B; Three Month Plan, Minority Outreach Task Force, March, April, May 1983, carton 16, folder 1014, 9to5 Additional Records B; Minority Outreach Task Force, Draft Proposal, n.d.

71. Minority Outreach 1984, carton 16, folder 1021, 9to5 Additional Records B.

72. Jodie Berlin Morrow and Myrna Lebov, *Not Just a Secretary: Using the Job to Get Ahead* (New York: Wiley, 1984), ix.

73. Deborah Churchman, "The Role of Secretary: A Career with a New Future," *Christian Science Monitor*, April 24, 1984.

74. Morrow and Lebov, *Not Just a Secretary*, ix.

75. Churchman, "Role of Secretary."

76. Morrow and Lebov, *Not Just a Secretary*, 6–7.

77. Churchman, "Role of Secretary."

78. Morrow and Lebov, *Not Just a Secretary*, 125, 20–21.

79. Churchman, "Role of Secretary."

80. Cappelli, "Career Jobs Are Dead"; Jacoby, "Are Career Jobs Headed for Extinction?"

81. Morrow and Lebov, *Not Just a Secretary*, 157, 140, 60–61, 162–63. The authors also suggest being careful of bosses who treat secretaries like "Daddy's Little Girl."

82. Chris Gardner, " 'Working Girl' Turns 30: On-Set Romances and Secrets of the Staten Island Ferry Revealed in Juicy Oral History," *Hollywood Reporter*, December 3, 2018, https://www.hollywoodreporter.com/movies/movie-features/harrison-ford-melanie-griffith-working-girl-oral-history-1164247/.

83. Kevin Wade, *Working Girl*, directed by Mike Nichols, produced by Douglas Wick, script, Twentieth Century Fox, https://thescriptsavant.com/pdf/Working_Girl.pdf.

84. Susan Faludi, *Backlash: The Undeclared War Against American Women* (New York: Crown, 1991).

85. Betty Lehan Harragan, *Games Mother Never Taught You: Corporate Gamesmanship for Women* (New York: Warner Books, 1978), 38, 40.

86. Edwin McDowell, "Betty Harragan, 77, Advocate of Women's Workplace Rights," *New York Times*, July 14, 1998.

87. Nan Robertson, "For Ambitious Women, A Survival Guide to the Land of Bosses," *New York Times*, June 28, 1977; Rhonda Seegal, "Business School Started by 2 Women Professors," *Nashua Telegraph* (New Hampshire), November 8, 1977.

88. Margaret Hennig and Anne Jardim, *The Managerial Woman* (Garden City, N.Y.: Anchor Press/Doubleday, 1977), 58, 60.

89. Cited in Marylin Bender, "Behavioral Differences Stressed in Women's Management Training," *New York Times*, February 11, 1974.

90. Helen Whitcomb and John Whitcomb, *Strictly for Secretaries*, rev. ed. (New York: Whittlesey House, 1965), 112, 15.

91. "Women's Conference to Hear Kate Lloyd," *Los Angeles Times*, August 17, 1983.

92. Barbara Bradley, "As Women Climb, So Does a Magazine," *Christian Science Monitor*, February 9, 1987.

93. Kate Rand Lloyd, "To Our Readers," *Working Woman* 3, no. 6 (June 1978): 4.

94. Kate Rand Lloyd, "To Our Readers," *Working Woman* 5, no. 11 (November 1980): 8.

95. Morrow and Lebov, *Not Just a Secretary*, 32, 78

96. Judith B. Bremner, "Black Pink Collar Workers: Arduous Journey from Field and Kitchen to Office," *Journal of Sociology & Social Welfare* 19, no. 3 (1992); King, "Black Women's Breakthrough Into Clerical Work"; Jacqueline Jones, *Labor of Love, Labor of Sorrow* (New York: Basic Books, 1985).

97. Because few Black women worked in offices, Black newspapers reported on the occasional woman who had earned an executive secretary position (chapter 1).

98. Field and kitchen to office language from Bremner, "Black Pink Collar Workers," 7–27; King, "Black Women's Breakthrough into Clerical Work."

99. Turk, *Equality on Trial*, 87.

100. Minority Outreach 1984.

101. Marcia McNair and Elaine C. Ray, eds., "You're the Boss: The Essence Guide for Managers and Supervisors," *Essence* 15, no. 11 (March 1985): 75–76.

102. Marcia McNair, "You and Your Boss: Cultivating That Bond," *Essence* 13, no. 1 (May 1982): 32.

103. Harriet Jackson Scarupa, "Second Careers," *Essence* 7, no. 11 (March 1977): 50.

104. Audrey Edwards, "Staying Alive from 9 to 5," *Essence* 16, no. 12 (April 1986): 92.

105. Betty Winston Bayé, "Getting to the Top," *Essence* 22, no. 6 (October 1991): 75.

106. Scarupa, "Second Careers," 50.

107. Scarupa, 46.

108. Scarupa, 49, 50.

109. Scarupa, 85.

110. Beatryce Nivens, "Save Time and Money—Stop Accumulating Dead-End Skills," *Essence* 8, no. 6 (October 1977): 21.

111. Beatryce Nivens, "Quick and Easy Job Changes," *Essence* 19, no. 3 (July 1988): 110.

112. Nivens, "Save Time and Money," 18, 21.

113. Nivens, "Quick and Easy Job Changes," 110.

114. Bayé, "Getting to the Top," 75. Also see Betty Winston Bayé, "Back to School," *Essence* 19, no. 11 (March 1989): 68–114.

115. Bayé, "Getting to the Top," 69.

116. Theresa A. Horton, "Resumes: Tooting Your Own Horn," *Essence* 10, no. 6 (October 1979): 40.

117. Richard Nelson Bolles, *What Color Is Your Parachute?* (self-published, 1970; Berkeley, Calif.: Ten Speed Press, 1972). Numerous articles in *Working Woman* recommend this book to readers, including Jaqueline Mason, "Career Fixers," *Working Woman* 2, no. 9 (September 1977): 80.

118. Karen Levine, "Selling Big," *Working Woman* 2, no. 12 (December 1977): 30. Also see Rochelle Distelheim, "Is There Life After Teaching?" *Working Woman* 5, no. 12 (December 1980): 52–54, 59; Enid Harlow, "Learn, Grow, Prosper," *Working Woman* 3, no. 9 (August 1978): 40–45. Harlow suggested that teachers leave what she claimed was a dead-end field and find work that was better paid. She featured the story of a teacher who becomes a broker at Goldman Sachs.

119. Vicki W. Kramer, "HOTLINE," *Working Woman* 5, no. 11 (November 1980): 114.

120. Letter of September 24, 1981, to Kate Rand Lloyd, *Working Woman* Magazine, Letters to the Editor, 1981–1983, unprocessed, location 58A, acc. 83-60, Sophia Smith Collection.

121. Letter of July 8, 1982, to Kate Rand Lloyd, *Working Woman* Magazine, Letters to the Editor.

122. Letter of August 24, [1981], to Kate Rand Lloyd, *Working Woman* Magazine, Letters to the Editor.

123. Letter of [1982] to *Working Woman* Magazine, Letters to the Editor.

124. Letter of 1982 to Kate Rand Lloyd, *Working Woman* Magazine, Letters to the Editor.

125. Letter of 1983 to Kate Rand Lloyd, *Working Woman* Magazine, Letters to the Editor.

126. Letter of February 16, 1983, to Kate Rand Lloyd, *Working Woman* Magazine, Letters to the Editor.

127. Letter, n.d., *Working Woman* Magazine, Letters to the Editor.

128. Letter of September 22, 1982, to *Working Woman* Magazine, Letters to the Editor.

129. Letter of February 8, 1983, to Kate Rand Lloyd, *Working Woman* Magazine, Letters to the Editor. For "mover and shaker" language, see letter from Kate Rand Lloyd to reader, July 22, 1982, *Working Woman* Magazine, Letters to the Editor.

130. Barbara Rahke, interview by Stacey Heath, May 23, 2006, SEIU District 925 Legacy Project.

131. Kate Rand Lloyd, Women at Work Exposition, October 1979, box 93, folder 7, Women's Action Alliance Records, Sophia Smith Collection.

132. Elizabeth R. Murphy, *The Assistant: New Tasks, New Opportunities* (New York: AMACOM, 1982), 162.

133. Taylor H. Cox and Stacy Blake, "Managing Cultural Diversity: Implications for Organizational Competitiveness," *Executive* 5, no. 3 (August 1991): 45–56.

134. Premilla Nadasen, *Household Workers Unite: The Untold Story of African American Women Who Built a Movement* (Boston: Beacon Press, 2015); Eileen Boris and Jennifer Klein, *Caring for America: Home Health Workers in the Shadow of the Welfare State* (New York: Oxford University Press, 2012).

135. Morrow and Lebov, *Not Just a Secretary*, 55.

136. *The Working Woman Success Book*, Working Woman Magazine (New York: Ace Books, 1981), 43.

137. Sheryl Sandberg, *Lean In: Women, Work, and the Will to Lead* (New York: Alfred A. Knopt, 2013); Janet Maslin, "Lessons from the Stratosphere, and How to Get There: Sheryl Sandberg's 'Lean In' Offers Lessons," *New York Times*, March 6, 2013; Lisa Bonos, "A Year After 'Lean In,' These are Sandberg's Truest Believers," *Washington Post*, March 7, 2014. Of course, professional women still face hurdles when navigating their careers and often are pushed out of the leadership pipeline. See Colleen Ammerman and Boris Groysberg, *Glass Half-Broken: Shattering the Barriers That Still Hold Women back at Work* (Cambridge: Harvard Business Review Press, 2021).

138. Plans for Workshop/Secretaries Week, April 23, 1977, box 5, folder 23, acc. 478, NSA, Philadelphia Records.

139. Dawn Foster, *Lean Out* (London: Repeater Books, 2015), 46.

EPILOGUE

1. Three percent reported that they voted for the independent candidate. "2016 Election Exit Polls," *Washington Post*, November 29, 2016, https://www.washingtonpost.com/graphics/politics/2016-election/exit-polls/.

2. Joan C. Williams, *White Working Class: Overcoming Class Cluelessness in America* (Cambridge, Mass.: Harvard Business Press, 2017).

3. Amy Choznick, "Hillary Clinton and the Return of the (Unbaked) Cookies," *New York Times*, November 5, 2016.

4. Kimberle Crenshaw, "Demarginalizing the Intersection of Race and Sex: A Black Feminist Critique of Antidiscrimination Doctrine, Feminist Theory, and Antiracist Policies," *University of Chicago Legal Forum* 1 [1989]: 139–67.

5. Ariane Hegewisch, Hannah Liepmann, Jeffrey Hayes, and Heidi Hartmann, "Separate and Not Equal? Gender Segregation in the Labor Market and the Gender Wage Gap," Institute for Women's Policy Research, September 2010, https://iwpr.org/wp-content/uploads/2020/08/C377.pdf; Kelly Field, "Why Are Women Still Choosing the Lowest-Paying Jobs?," *Atlantic*, January 25, 2018.

6. Katherine Turk, *Equality on Trial: Gender and Rights in the Modern American Workplace* (Philadelphia: University of Pennsylvania Press, 2016), loc. 163.

7. Using data from 1990 to 2016, an economist finds that occupational segregation in clerical work has been declining. Men have been entering service and clerical occupations due to decreasing opportunities in blue-collar work. Their entrance is crowding out some lower-educated women. Joana Duran-Franch, "Oh, Man! What Happened to Women? The Blurring of Gender-Based Occupational Segregation," working paper (July 2021), https://drive.google.com/file/d/1H2XWd5WPqRPeBrlqbWMQfrO3pryxBZ2H/view.

8. Although management scholars have argued that those in stigmatized occupations can construct a strong, positive identity, the contested boundaries of the clerical occupation and the diverse array of jobs under the clerical umbrella make this sort of identity work difficult. Blake E. Ashforth and Glen E. Kreiner, "'How Do You Do It?' Dirty Work

and the Challenge of Constructing a Positive Identity," *Academy of Management Review* 24, no. 3 (July 1999): 413–34.

9. Karen Nussbaum, written statement, no. 53, 1974–1975, MC366, box 2, folder 13, Tepperman Papers.

10. Katherine Newman, *Falling from Grace: Downward Mobility in the Age of Affluence* (Berkeley: University of California Press, 1999), 79.

11. Ofer Sharone, *Flawed System/Flawed Self: Job Searching and Unemployment Experiences* (Chicago: University of Chicago Press, 2014); Newman, *Falling from Grace*.

12. Micki Magee, *Self Help, Inc.: Makeover Culture in American Life* (New York: Oxford University Press, 2005).

13. Derek Thompson, "Workism Is Making Americans Miserable," *Atlantic*, February 24, 2019.

14. Pamela Walker Laird, *Pull: Networking and Success Since Benjamin Franklin* (Cambridge, Mass.: Harvard University Press, 2007).

15. Olga Khazan, "'Find Your Passion' Is Awful Advice," *Atlantic*, July 12, 2018.

16. Marsha Sinetar, *Do What You Love and the Money Will Follow: Discovering Your Right Livelihood* (New York: Dell, 1989).

17. On passion and inequality, see Erin Cech, *The Trouble with Passion: How Searching for Fulfillment at Work Fosters Inequality* (Berkeley: University of California Press, 2021).

18. Tom Peters, "The Brand Called You," *Fast Company*, August 31, 1997, 83. Many factors explain the unraveling of the employment relationship and weakening of internal labor markets. See Louis Hyman, *Temp: How American Work, American Business, and the American Dream Became Temporary* (New York: Viking, 2018); Gerald F. Davis, *The Vanishing American Corporation: Navigating the Hazards of a New Economy* (New York: Barrett-Kohler, 2016); Arne Kalleberg, *Good Jobs, Bad Jobs: The Rise of Polarized and Precarious Employment Systems in the United States, 1970s to 2000s* (New York: Russell Sage Foundation, 2011); Peter Cappelli, *The New Deal at Work: Managing the Market-Driven Workforce* (Cambridge, Mass.: Harvard Business School Press, 1999); Peter Cappelli, "Career Jobs Are Dead," *California Management Review* 42, no. 1 (Fall 1999): 146–67. There is less attention to the way that employees themselves embraced precarity. Some notable exceptions are Erin Hatton, *The Temp Economy: From Kelly Girls to Permatemps in Postwar America* (Philadelphia: Temple University Press, 2011); Carrie M. Lane, *A Company of One: Insecurity, Independence, and the New World of White-Collar Unemployment* (Ithaca, N.Y.: ILR Press, 2011); Allison J. Pugh, *The Tumbleweed Society: Working and Caring in an Age of Insecurity* (New York: Oxford University Press, 2015).

19. See, for instance, Everett C. Hughes, "Good People and Dirty Work," *Social Problems* 10, no. 1 (Summer 1962): 3–11; Ashforth and Kreiner, "'How Can You Do It?'"

20. Sarah Smarsh, *She Come by It Natural: Dolly Parton and the Women Who Lived Her Songs* (New York: Scribner, 2021), 4, 169, 48.

INDEX

CPSIA information can be obtained
at www.ICGtesting.com
Printed in the USA
LVHW041652130323
741524LV00002B/296

9 780231 180757